S0-BDW-817

EVERYBODY'S
HOCKEY
BOOK

EVERYBODY'S HOCKEY BOOK

Stan & Shirley Fischler

Research Editors:
Dave Gravano
and Vincent Losinno

CHARLES SCRIBNER'S SONS / NEW YORK

Except where noted, all photos are courtesy the Collection of Stan Fischler.

First Charles Scribner's Sons paperback edition published 1985.

Copyright © 1983 Stan Fischler and Shirley Fischler

Library of Congress Cataloging in Publication Data

Fischler, Stan.
  Everybody's hockey book.

  Includes index.
  1. Hockey.   I. Fischler, Shirley.   II. Title.
GV847.F458   1983   796.9622   83-16411
ISBN 0-684-18507-5

Published simultaneously in Canada
by Collier Macmillan Canada, Inc.—
Copyright under the Berne Convention.

1 3 5 7 9 11 13 15 17 19   F/P   20 18 16 14 12 10 8 6 4 2

Printed in the United States of America.

To Bobby Clarke, Mike Milbury, Lanny McDonald, Wayne Gretzky, Dave Lewis, Darcy Rota, John Ferguson, Al Secord, Jim Schoenfeld, Glen Sonmor, Ed Kea, Dick Beddoes, Chico Resch, John Tonelli, John Davidson, Paul Baxter, Ken Houston, Tony McKegney, Greg Millen, Larry Robinson, and Peter Stastny, among others, who have made a great game so much fun to write about and view.

And especially to young Marco Bertolozzi, goalie premier for the Dutchess Hawks, and part of hockey's bright future.

ACKNOWLEDGMENTS

Like the scoring of a goal, the production of a book requires more contributions than meet the eye. Often a goal will simply be the fruit of diligent research, translated to arduous practice and, finally, the ultimate execution on the ice. Similarly, the development of this book was predicated on the cooperation of many unsung heroes who delivered mightily behind the scenes.

Bob Stampleman, editor of *Recreational Ice Skating* magazine, provided invaluable insights into skating technique. Sandy MacDonald, manager of the McCann Ice Arena in Poughkeepsie, N.Y., delivered helpful tips on strategy and other aspects of hockey fundamentals. Rich Liebnow of Corona-Liebnow was the maven we sought for advice on equipment along with Michael Cosby, manager of the Gerry Cosby sporting goods shop in Madison Square Garden.

We were fortunate to have as our editor a woman with a special feel for sports. To Louise Ketz we extend a special thanks as well as to her excellent aide-de-camp Annasue McCleave.

Not to be overlooked is Jeremy Brown, publisher of Brownstone Press in Toronto, who originally planted the seed for this book during a Stanley Cup playoff game.

As always, members of the NHL high command, including President John Ziegler, Vice-President Steve Ryan, Public Relations Director Rodger Gottlieb, as well as others on the league staff—Allyne Price, Dan Leary, and Joel Nixon—were of assistance when necessary.

Others who contributed mightily and for whom we have unbound gratitude include:

Craig Ellenport, Rich Friedman, Sharon Kopitnikoff, Debbie Klein, Michael Berger, Paul Fichtenbaum, George Hall, David Ferry, Kenny Kaplan, Arthur Bulin, Joel Sherman, Phil Davis, Don Frumkin, Phyllis Newbeck, George Edmondson, Bob Colasuonno, Doug Sutherland, Paul Koumourdas, Carol Szel, Dave

Lippman, Sharon Eberson, Andrew D'Angelo, David Hom, Ralph Russo, Steve Ginsberg, Gary Fuchs, Chris Sahner, Joni DiTullio, Phil Czochanski, Andrew Deane, Steve DiTullio, David Zaccarine, Jock Wilson, Bob Friedlander, Steve Glickman, Mike Lyster, Mark Falkner, Donna Spaner, George Dalek, Greg Elliott, Ron Fremont, Mark Weber, Jill Cornfeldt, Kevin Rivard, Kevin Bradley, Stephen Choppy, Diane Gerace, Dave Emmerling, Steve McCall, John Arenberg, Robert Duff, Fred Sommer, Kathy Johnson, and Howard Hook.

A special thanks goes to the lads of the Dutchess (County, New York) Youth Hockey Association Pee Wee Team—the Dutchess Hawks: David Bell, Marco Bertolozzi, Steve and Scott Brown, Chris Chobar, Paul and Peter Galletta, Gardy Murphy, Robbie O'Brien, Kurt Van Bramer, as well as special additions Jock and Keenan MacDonald.

Photo credits for the Skills, Training, and Goalie chapters belong to Stanley S. "Doc" Brown, Tim Hewitt, and Paul Fichtenbaum, while Guy B. Wheeler III and Tom Cooney of Berkey K&L Developers were a big help, too.

CONTENTS

Contents

INTRODUCTION

In December 1937, a five-year-old boy was taken to a hockey game at Madison Square Garden. It was the first time he had ever seen a contest on ice and the lad marveled at the panoply of heavily armored athletes in bright-colored uniforms.

The boy was fascinated by what had been billed as "The Fastest Game On Earth" and asked his father to take him again and again. The request was granted and, in time, the youngster became so infatuated with hockey that he took pen in hand and wrote a letter to the *New York Times* Magazine, commenting on what he believed to be rather shabby treatment of his favorite sport in an article that had appeared on its pages.

"Hockey," the boy pointed out, "has the grace of ballet, the speed of a 100-yard dash, the color of a July Fourth pageant, and the rumble of a battlefield. There is no other sport quite like it because all of this action takes place on an unreal surface—ice."

To the youngster's amazement, the article was printed, and he became an even more fervent hockey zealot. He soon was given a pair of ice skates and then learned firsthand that everything he had written about the sport was true, only now he was viewing it from a different perspective. The day he scored his first goal he vowed that he would make hockey his life's work.

Although he played organized hockey for many years, he never was good enough to earn a living as a professional, so he decided to do the next best thing—write about it, and get paid to boot.

From his vantage point in the press box, the fan-turned-journalist chronicled the evolution of hockey. He marveled at the Russian players the first time he saw them and their scientific approach to the game. He was there when the Montreal Canadiens, perhaps the greatest team of all time, won an unprecedented five consecutive Stanley Cups.

He spent weekends with Gordie Howe and was Bobby Orr's guest in Parry

Sound, Ontario. The great ones gave him insights into hockey that he never could obtain from his own playing experience or as a member of the Fourth Estate.

As hockey grew, he viewed the growing process with concern. Expansion from six to twelve teams in 1967 brought about a profound change in the sport he knew and loved so well. The sudden—and cataclysmic—emergence of the World Hockey Association also brought on further trauma.

While all this was going on, he met, loved, and married a woman whose knowledge of the game was scant but who instantly became enamored of hockey. In time she, too, was translating her affection and knowledge of the game to the printed page and, along with her husband, to the television screen.

Now they would like to share their romance with hockey with you.

SHIRLEY and STAN FISCHLER
New York City,
March 1983

THE HISTORY OF HOCKEY

HURLEY, SHINNY, AND HOQUET

Pinpointing the precise origin of the modern game of ice hockey is no easier than defining the infinite number of moves Wayne Gretzky employs when he confronts a goalkeeper. Even the most knowledgeable hockey historians have found themselves lost in a sea of mythology, quasi-fact, and fancy as they probe the puck chasers' past.

One of the more appealing hoaxes was perpetrated by John H. (Jack) Filman, a jovial gentleman who had been the public address announcer at Madison Square Garden hockey games in the 1930s, as well as publicist for the New York Rangers. It was Filman's job, among other things, to fill the pages of the Garden program with interesting tidbits about the ice game, then still a novelty to many New Yorkers.

In a fit of fancy one day, Filman credited the Indians of the Six Nations with inventing hockey in North America. As Filman put it, explorers penetrating the St. Lawrence Valley in 1740 discovered the Iroquois playing a well-organized game called *baggataway,* or lacrosse. During the course of action braves would frequently be whacked in the shins, Filman noted. When that happened the Indian would grunt "ho-Gee," or as we might put it today, "ouch." Filman insisted that the white men quickly translated "ho-Gee" to "hockey."

Filman added, "The surviving sachems of the Six Nations tell how the game was played on the plains in summer and on ice-covered ponds and rivers in winter."

Plausible as it may have sounded, Filman's flight of fancy subsequently was debunked by his pal Frank Boucher, an all-star center and later general manager of the Rangers.

Other theories on the origin of hockey, all more believable than Filman's story, abound like slapshots at a hockey scrimmage. By filtering through them it is possible to produce some viable assumptions.

Richard F. Vaughan and Holcomb York, former coaches of Princeton and Yale universities, respectively, did considerable research on the subject, concluding that hockey's roots are in the British Isles and France. Field hockey was played in Scotland as *shinny*, in France as *hocquet*, and in Ireland as *hurley* as far back as the sixteenth century.

Clearly, hockey was an infinitely more violent game then than it is now, although some critics of the game might differ on that matter. One line of thinking has it that the earliest forms of hockey were winterized versions of hurley. The Irish employed brass balls and weighty shillelaghs. "More than that," noted Vaughan and York, "the losing players not only tasted defeat, but were often slain."

To this day the type of skate used by the early British players remains a mystery. It has been ascertained that the Dutch developed the first serviceable skate in the middle of the nineteenth century, but hockey already had been played, albeit in a crude form, in the British village of Bury Fen.

Located in the English marshlands, Bury Fen was a natural location in which ice hockey could develop. During late autumn the Fen district was often flooded by heavy rains. The shallow water covering the flat meadows would freeze in winter, enabling the Bury Fen villagers to take to the ice and produce their cold weather version of field hockey.

As befits the innovators, Bury Fen became as dominant in this makeshift version of hockey as the New York Yankees were in baseball in the late 1920s. Teams from Bury Fen simply did not lose to those from the hinterlands. Typical was a match between a team from Willingham and Bury Fen that was played on the Old West River in 1827. The game was called "bandy," not "hockey."

The rubber puck as we know it today had not yet been developed. Instead the English players used a wooden or cork ball, alternately called the "cat" or "kit." In later years a rubberized version was put into play.

Meanwhile the Dutch had developed an efficient metal blade that could be strapped onto a shoe, and this was the first commonly used ice skate. Also, the Bury Fenners had gradually developed a hockey stick, or "bandy," molded from the lower branches of the pollard willow trees that flourished in the vicinity of the village. A man's hockey stick was cherished by the owner and his family, and it was not uncommon for a player to bequeath his stick to his son, who, unless it happened to break, would also pass it down to the next generation of players. Just as a Wayne Gretzky would hang a history-making stick over his mantelpiece, a champion Bury Fenner would save a particularly meaningful bandy as "an object of veneration to all villagers who beheld it."

The Bury Fenners were responsible for one of the first international matches, having accepted an invitation from the Netherlands Football and Athletic Union in 1890 for a series of matches throughout Holland. They crossed the English Channel and opened their tour with a victory against Haarlem, after which they moved on to Amsterdam, where they again routed the opposition in a number of other contests.

The rules of the game were not composed at any one time; rather, they just grew. According to Vaughan and York, the dimensions of the early goal were six by four feet and would have remained that size were it not for an enterprising coach who found an especially corpulent villager and urged him to tend goal. The obese goalie simply reclined across the ice in front of the net, placed one leg over the other, and made it virtually impossible for the foe to find an opening. The ploy was effective at first, but it inspired demands for change, with the result that a new, enlarged net, twelve feet wide and seven feet high, became de rigueur.

It was inevitable that the long period of victories enjoyed by the Bury Fen community would not last into the twentieth century. For one thing, winters had become less severe in Great Britain and artificial ice had yet to be introduced to Bury Fen.

A sizeable number of British troops who had been posted to duty in Canada found that the long, harsh winters left them bored and unhappy. Some had brought their ice skates with them, and a few even brought along hockey sticks. Playing hockey was the ideal antidote to their ennui, and the troops—many of whom were sent to remote outposts in western Canada—soon spread the new game across the Dominion.

There were no precise rules to the soldiers' games. They made them up as they went along, depending upon the number of skaters available and the size and condition of the ice. Exactly where a more formal version of hockey emerged remains a matter of dispute, depending upon whether one believes the spokesmen from Kingston, Ontario; Montreal, Quebec; or Halifax, Nova Scotia.

The most popular explanation is that Kingston was the site of the first truly organized game. In that Ontario city, the Royal Canadian Rifles were stationed at the Tête-du-Pont barracks. In 1867 the militiamen, seeking some diversion on a cold winter morning, shoveled the snow off the ice in Kingston harbor and played a game of hockey. What made this particular contest different from others was its form. The players used sticks, makeshift pucks, and goal posts. It is quite possible that other more formal versions of ice hockey had been played prior to the soldiers' match at Kingston, but if so they went unrecorded. As a result, Kingston was unofficially dubbed the birthplace of hockey and hockey's first Hall of Fame was established there.

Kingston's claim could be supported in a number of ways, and a distinguished Canadian sportsman named James T. (Captain Jim) Sutherland made a very strong case for the Ontario city. An excellent player himself, Sutherland argued Kingston's case in the late nineteenth century by pointing out that the first organized hockey league in North America got its start there in 1885. The league comprised four teams: the Athletics, the Kingstons, Royal Military College, and Queens University. Sutherland played the point position (defense) for the Athletics when Queens University defeated his club, 3–1, for the first Canadian league championship.

The skates used in that first league were, as one might expect, exceptionally crude. The most commonly used skate was not riveted to special boots like contemporary blades. Instead, the players wore their regular boots or shoes and clamped what were called "spring" skates on to them. At game's end, the player simply unclamped the skate. Because of their crude construction, the early "spring" skates presented problems. Captain Sutherland remembered:

> In one game our goalie was using his skates to block the ice-hugging shots. The impact would release the trigger-type fastener of the skate and the skate would fly off the goalie's boot and go sailing across the rink. The referee would have to stop play, the skate would be put back on the goalkeeper's boot, and the game would proceed.

It is quite possible that the development of hockey followed the same pattern at about the same time in other parts of eastern Canada. It is simply a matter of Kingston's producing the most tangible evidence, while also having an articulate and forceful spokesman in Captain Sutherland. But one would be hard pressed to refute claims made by other Canadian centers, especially Montreal and Halifax.

The claim made for Halifax is based on matches played by soldiers at English garrisons beginning in 1870. Although their version may have been a trifle more sophisticated than the games played in Kingston, the Maritime-based players were three years behind their counterparts.

While all this was going on, some Canadian entrepreneurs realized that there was money to be made in the formalized pastime of skating and its tangential offshoots, such as curling and lacrosse on ice. As a result, a number of them contemplated a structure that would retain ice while keeping the snow off the rink. Ultimately this led to the construction of covered skating rinks. One of the most impressive, the Victoria in Montreal, was a haven for pleasure skaters and soon made room for other ice pursuits. For a change it wasn't soldiers but rather scholars who began chasing a puck around the Victoria Skating Rink—students at McGill University in downtown Montreal. In March 1875 they played an eighteen-man game—nine on each side—and, according to several historians, called it "ice hockey" for the first time. Neil Isaacs, a professor of English at the University of Maryland, probed hockey's roots in 1977 and determined that the first codified set of rules was produced at McGill in 1879.

The original McGill rules makers, W. F. Robertson and R. F. Smith, adapted a number of rugby, lacrosse, field hockey, and polo regulations to the game. Oddly enough, one of the cornerstones of the early game was a regulation forbidding the use of bodychecking. Robertson and Smith apparently did well by the McGill student body, for soon there was a bustling league within the university, and two years after the codification of rules, McGill organized its first varsity team.

The long Canadian winters—natural ice often was available as early as October in some areas and remained skateable through early March—gave the Dominion preeminence over England when it came to hockey's early development. Between 1880 and the turn of the century most of the major refinements took place: the ball was replaced by the flat puck; the ice surface was considerably reduced in size; the field hockey stick, which limited use to one side of the blade, was altered so that skaters could stickhandle with both faces of the stick; and the snowbanks that had marked the rink's perimeters were replaced by forty-inch sideboards. New goal-tending regulations enabled a return to the early six-foot by four-foot goal, and then someone got the bright idea of nailing a net to the back of the goal posts, which at the time was regarded as the very height of hockey technology. The game clearly was on the move.

At first the nine-man teams were considered perfectly acceptable as well as practical. No objection was made to eighteen uniformed players—sixteen skaters—on the ice at one time, but a reduction to seven-man teams was inevitable, although the change, interestingly, occurred quite by accident. A pair of teams were scheduled to play a game as part of the 1886 Montreal Winter Carnival. One of the clubs showed up with two players missing. What to do? The opponents very sportingly agreed to lop a pair of skaters off their squad and decided that a seven-man game might be just as much fun. As it happened, they liked it better than the nine-man affair, and soon seven-man hockey became the rule.

Surprisingly, Toronto, now one of North America's major hockey centers, was lagging behind other Canadian cities in terms of interest in the ice game. Oddly enough, it was a Montrealer who proved to be the hockey missionary to Toronto. T. L. Patton, a goalkeeper who happened to be visiting Toronto in 1887, made rapturous descriptions of the new game played on ice and thoroughly captivated his Toronto cronies, who demanded that he improve their lives by importing some hockey equipment to Toronto. Patton obliged by ordering a spate of hockey sticks, skates, and pucks. In no time at all, Toronto was sprinkled with hockey teams, the most prominent being the Toronto Athletic Club, the Granites, and St. George's.

Once the Torontonians mastered the game, it was only natural that they should challenge their rivals from Ottawa. The intensity of the combat, even though the Toronto clubs were relatively new at the sport, is remarkable even by today's standards. Those who lament the boisterousness of the modern game would have been appalled by the behavior of players and fans involved in an 1890 contest between the Ottawa Rebels and a team from Toronto. It wasn't enough that the players exchanged numerous punches, but they so incited members of the audience that several fans sprinted on to the rink to join the brawl.

Despite the many improvements, the essential nature of the new game was crude, primarily because it relied so much on the whims of nature. Ice surfaces often had the texture of a dirt road with ruts and bumps abounding, and in a thaw the ice would melt, placing the game in jeopardy.

Uniforms at first were nonexistent, but the formal clubs soon borrowed from other sports. The first jersey was no more than a uniform team sweater worn over a shirt and tucked into a pair of pants.

Variations on passing and bodychecking evolved as the various teams and organizations saw fit. In time the prohibition against use of the body simply to stop the foe was altered in favor of the more physical game. The basic Canadian frontier spirit encouraged the rougher game, and hockey quickly evolved into a sport that demanded physical hardiness as well as endurance. Stamina was an important ingredient, if for no other reason, than the rule forbidding substitutions. A player was expected to skate every one of the sixty minutes—divided by an intermission—that comprised the game.

Necessity compelled players to find ways and means of protecting themselves from sticks that missed pucks and caromed off shins and from pucks that had an affinity for thumping into delicate parts of the anatomy. In some cases the hockey players borrowed equipment ideas from cricket, and in others from baseball, which, like cricket, was already a popular pastime in Canada. At first players found it useful to stuff department store catalogs around their tender portions for protection. Then someone got a brainstorm that a baseball catcher's chest protector could do the job better, and the first goalie chest guard was introduced.

The catalogs, usually from Canada's distinguished Eaton's store, also protected the shins and were held in place by strips of rubber, obtained from old farm or household equipment, tied around the pants. It seems that hockey, being so relatively young, borrowed from everywhere. (The term "rink" derives from the Scottish game of curling: rink, meaning course, was the place where curlers played.) Hockey's burgeoning popularity brought on the business of equipping the teams. McGill students no longer had to appropriate field hockey sticks (or, if they couldn't afford them, a branch from an elm tree), since by the early 1880s a Montreal company was manufacturing sticks expressly for ice hockey.

No longer a pastime limited to the precincts of Bury Fen or the British army garrisons in Kingston or Halifax, ice hockey was on the move. Inevitably, the next step in its growth and development would be the organization of governing bodies that would control the teams and players as well as codify the rules to a point where the game would enter the twentieth century in a manner truly sophisticated—relative to other sports of the times.

CANADA

The early lead Great Britain enjoyed as an originator of ice hockey was lost once and for all when the English soldiers exported their primitive version of the game to Canada. Both English-speaking and French-speaking Canadians, as well as a number of North American Indians, took an instant liking to the speed and robust play that so ideally fits their rugged climate. Whereas play in England was at best sporadic, Canadians in every center, from the Maritimes to the Rockies, embraced the game with a zeal unmatched even for their "national" game, lacrosse. Concurrently a number of personalities contributed significantly to the refinements of the game. Arthur Farrell, a member of Montreal's Shamrock Hockey Club and a pioneer among hockey writers, wrote up a compendium of hockey rules before the turn of the century that tended to make more official what heretofore had been generally accepted regulations.

Farrell noted that there shall be seven men to a team, that the goal shall be 6 feet wide by 4 feet high, dimensions that have remained up to the contemporary game, and the playing rink should measure no less than 112 feet long by 58 feet wide. Today the ice surfaces, with few exceptions, are 200 feet by 85 feet. The players, by position, were goalkeeper, point, cover point, rover, right wing, center, and left wing. Speaking for himself and indubitably thousands of other Canadians, Farrell described Canada's new craze in these terms:

> [It is] a game for men, essentially, it is a game for the youth. It needs strong, full-blooded men. Weaklings cannot survive in it, the puny cannot play it, and the timid have no place in it. It is, perhaps, the greatest game that man can play unaided. It possesses all the spice of polo without the necessity for calling upon the animal kingdom.

Fortunately, there were also a number of more genteel souls throughout Canada who found other virtues in hockey. One of them was Arthur Stanley, the son of Canada's governor-general, Sir Frederick Arthur Stanley, Baron Stanley of Preston. A likeable British nobleman, Lord Stanley was terribly fond of sports and glowed with pride when his sons Arthur and Algernon became devotees of the ice game.

Lord Stanley's residence, Government House in Ottawa (also known as Rideau Hall), became a hotbed of hockey. Servants would flood an outdoor rink for Lord Stanley's sons, and Arthur and Algie soon found teammates among the Coldstream Guards, a military unit posted at Government House. Algie and Arthur instantly became members of the team, which was called the Rideau Rebels. They didn't know it at the time, but the Stanley brothers, simply by whacking the puck about the Government House rink for a few years, would have a profound influence on hockey for almost a century.

Most important was the fact that the two boys loved the game and passed along their enthusiasm to their dad. Second, there was the matter of their team, which proved to be more than run-of-the-mill. The Rebels, who booked games on foreign ice as well as in Ottawa, played the best opposition available. One of their finest moments took place during a game against the mighty Ottawa City Club, whom they challenged for the championship of Canada. That they ultimately lost was irrelevant; the point was that they were there.

Significantly, the victors had little spoils. They were the champions, to be sure, but they had no tangible pennant or trophy to show for it. This point did not elude Lord Stanley, who apparently mulled over the matter for some time. When he was about to return to Great Britain, he finally did something about it, while awaiting the appointment of his successor. Sitting down at his great desk, Lord Stanley took pen in hand and wrote a letter to his aide, Lord Kilcoursie, suggesting that a challenge cup for hockey be struck.

Lord Kilcoursie was the ideal man to send such a letter to. If hockey had an unpaid public relations man in the late nineteenth century, it was Lord K., who not only loved to watch the matches but was an active member of the same team on which Arthur and Algie Stanley played. Some Canadian hockey historians, among them broadcaster-author Brian McFarlane, believe that it was Lord Kilcoursie who planted the idea of a Stanley Cup with his boss:

> One can reconstruct the scene in Rideau Hall on the eve of Lord Stanley's departure. . . . The servants are busy packing the luggage and Lord Stanley is having a farewell Scotch and soda with his aide, who proposes the trophy. "Yes, sir, a cup," says Lord Stanley. "The Ottawas will win it, of course. And when they do, they shall remember me with warm regard—they shall remember me as a loyal fan and a devoted friend."

In any event, Lord Stanley's letter reached Lord Kilcoursie in time for a dinner honoring the Ottawa Hockey Club on March 18, 1892. The governor-general's idea was toasted with enthusiasm by all hands, and Lord Kilcoursie reported the good news to his superior. With that, Lord Stanley commissioned a British silversmith to strike a special trophy for the Canadian stick handlers.

When it was completed, Lord Stanley paid ten guineas (or $48.67 in Canadian cash) for the silver bowl with an interior gold finish. It rested comfortably on an ebony base and was christened the Stanley Cup. The Right Honourable Sir Frederick Arthur Stanley, Baron Stanley of Preston in the County of Lancaster, in the Peerage of Great Britain, Knight Grand Cross of the Most Honourable Order of the Bath, had done right by hockey.

Lord Stanley rooted passionately for the Ottawa Hockey Club and, as he had no doubt informed Kilcoursie, expected that he would have the pleasure of presenting—by proxy, if necessary—the first Stanley Cup to his favorites from Ottawa. But since he was happily residing on the other side of the ocean, Lord Stanley deputized two Canadians to oversee the cup and to ensure that it was honorably captured by the growing number of challengers.

As is often the case in the history of Canadian hockey, a journalist became intimately involved with the affairs of the cup. P. D. Ross, who eventually became publisher of the *Ottawa Journal*, was one of the original cup trustees. The other was John Sweetland, then sheriff of Ottawa. "They knew and enjoyed the game of hockey," wrote Brian McFarlane. "They took their duties as cup trustees very seriously; they were men of enormous integrity and of forceful personality."

Such attributes would prove essential once cup play began. The Amateur Hockey Association (later known as the Canadian Amateur Hockey Association) had been organized and would contribute contenders for the cup.

Only three years earlier the Ontario Hockey Association—also an amateur group—had been founded and began holding regular championships of its own. That is precisely where the trouble began. Lord Stanley's favorite hockey club, the Ottawa team, had become a part of the Ontario Association and in 1893 won the league title. Employing a rather perverse brand of logic, the Ottawa skaters—assuming they had the backing of Lord Stanley—demanded the Stanley Cup. Their theory was simple enough; since they *believed* they had the best team in Canada, they *were* the best team and, therefore, they deserved the cup. The logic eluded the new trustees, who ordered the Ottawa team to meet a challenger for the cup. Ross and Sweetland designated the Osgoode Hall team of Toronto as a worthy opponent for Ottawa and further specified that the game be played in Canada's Queen City, Toronto, not in the nation's capital.

Instead of welcoming the decision like sportsmen, the Ottawa players rejected the trustees' decision. Ross and Sweetland were adamant. They treated the Ottawa club as if it had been suspended and then scanned the records of the just-completed season. Ottawa had lost twice, to the inferior Montreal Victorias Club in the first game of the season and then to the Montreal Athletic Association. Ross and Sweetland huddled over the matter and decided that the Montreal Athletic Association was Canada's foremost hockey club and dispatched the cup to Montreal without further ado. The Montreal Athletic Association had won the first Stanley Cup without having engaged in a single playoff game!

A year later there were more bizarre happenings. Four out of the five teams in the Amateur Hockey Association tied for first place following completion of the eight-game schedule. This provided the ideal opportunity for an exciting playoff to determine the champion, but, alas, the off-ice feuding began anew. The Quebec delegation walked out in a huff, leaving the Montreal Athletic Association, holder of the cup, the Montreal Victorias, and Ottawa to battle it out. The two Montreal teams were chosen to launch the series, and Ottawa was given a "bye." Suddenly the Stanley Cup challenge took on greater significance than anyone had believed possible, and when the two Montreal clubs skated out onto the Victoria rink on March 17, 1894, the stands were filled with more than five thousand spectators. The Montreal Athletic Association prevailed, 3–2, and now it was Ottawa's turn to take aim at the silver mug.

The favorites a year earlier, before they had begun pouting, the Ottawa troupe was bolsered in 1894 by the addition of Harvey Pulford, a hockey wizard of his time. Pulford or no Pulford, the Montrealers won, 3–1.

Another inexplicable decision by the trustees caused an uproar in 1895. The Montreal Victorias had won the league championship, but the trustees had designated the Montreal Athletic Association, as previous cup winners, to play a team from Queen's University who were challenging for the cup. It was an absurd decision because the Victorias, if any team was to challenge, were the logical opponents.

The Montreal Athletic Association defeated the collegians and, naturally, expected to be rewarded with the cup, but that was not to be. The trustees presented the Stanley Cup to none other than the Montreal Victorias on the strength of their first-place finish during the regular season.

Although the upstart Winnipeg Victorias showed up on February 14, 1896, to defeat the Montreal Victorias 2–0, the defending Stanley Cup champions, Montreal was producing more classy teams than any city in the Dominion. The Montreal Victorias rebounded in December 1896 to regain the cup and repeated the feat in 1897 and 1898. Montreal could now lay claim to being the hockey capital of North America, and, as if to underscore this fact, a handsome new arena was opened on the corner of St. Catherine and Wood streets in downtown Montreal on December 31, 1898. As NHL historian, Charles L. Coleman wrote:

> This was considered to be the last word in accommodation for hockey fans with a seating capacity of 4,300. A refreshment buffet and smoking rooms were provided and announcement was made that rugs would be available for rental, which no doubt would be appreciated by those who feared draughts.

The new rink was built just in time. Montreal boasted two excellent hockey clubs, the champion Victorias and the powerful Shamrocks led by high-scoring Harry Trihey. On February 4, 1899, Trihey scored ten goals as the Shamrocks routed Quebec, 13–4. Not to be outdone by their crosstown rivals, the Victorias shellacked Ottawa, 16–0, a week later. (The only NHL club to come close to matching that mark was the Detroit Red Wings, who defeated the New York Rangers, 15–0, on January 23, 1944.)

The 1899 season featured a marvelous home stretch run by the Shamrocks and Victorias, who were tied for first in the final week of the season. Nearly eight thousand fans jammed the new rink for the showdown between the two clubs and, as one might expect, betting was heavy, ticket scalping was rife, and emotions were keen at face-off time.

The usually dependable Victorias lacked the mustard they had applied in previous big games, whereas Harry Trihey was at his best. He scored the lone goal of the game, enabling the Shamrocks to finish first. They went on to win the Stanley Cup.

With the turn of the century a number of significant improvements were made in the rules of the game. One of the most meaningful was the introduction of the face-off by referee Fred Waghorne. The face-off came about as a result of many "exasperating and often painful experiences for referees," as Waghorne once put it.

One night Waghorne refereed a game near Brantford, Ontario. It was an especially acrimonious game during which the referee took a battering about the legs every time he arranged a face-off. The well-bruised, thoroughly frustrated Waghorne finally decided to revise the rules to suit his anatomy.

"I told the centermen they were to place their blades on the ice about a foot or foot-and-a-half apart, and I'd stand back and toss the puck between the sticks. After the rubber hit the ice, they could do as they darned well pleased."

Waghorne's innovation pleased all parties, especially the referee. A year later he was asked to handle a playoff game at Almonte, Ontario, between teams from Arnprior and Renfrew. Prior to the match he suggested to both coaches that they allow him to use his new face-off system, and they went along with the proposal. Several other officials witnessed the game and were suitably impressed with the Waghorne face-off. Word of the bruiseless face-off spread throughout eastern Canada, and soon Waghorne's innovation was accepted throughout the hockey world.

A referee for more than fifty years, Waghorne handled more than 2,400 hockey games, spanning the nineteenth and twentieth centuries. He personally encouraged referees to switch from the use of a whistle to a bell and back again to the whistle.

The early rinks were unheated to prevent the thawing of the natural ice. Illumination was provided by coal-oil lamps or acetylene gas. It was a frigid scene that was not conducive to the easy blowing of whistles. Often, when a referee attempted to penalize a player he would blow on a frozen whistle and take the skin off his lips. Waghorne got a brainstorm en route to a hockey game near Kingston and introduced the bell as a substitute for the whistle.

The bell proved an excellent replacement for the frozen whistle as long as the arenas were unheated, but with the advent of the modern, well-heated hockey rink, the lighter whistle made its return, and the bell was returned to the dining room.

One feature of the first Stanley Cup playoff game of the twentieth century, between the Shamrocks and Winnipeg, was a new, lighter stick used by the western skaters. The stick used by the Winnipeggers had the upper edge of the blade tapered and, in many ways, resembled the stick blade in general use later in the century. Despite the innovative sticks, Winnipeg lost the series two games to one. The Halifax Crescents immediately issued a cup challenge. It was accepted, and the Shamrocks defeated them 10–2 and 11–0, thereby eliminating any doubts about who deserved the cup.

Those who would ultimately play for the champion teams had none of the benefits of contemporary youngsters who are often presented with a pair of $75 professional model skates before they are six years old. At the turn of the century a young hockey player had to make do with whatever primitive equipment was available, and skates were a major problem.

Now that the Stanley Cup playoffs had become firmly established in the Canadian psyche the Dominion's youth turned away from the once-favored lacrosse, and hockey became known—if not officially—as Canada's national pastime. No longer was it confined to a few military outposts; wherever there was ice, kids were out playing.

There were intercollegiate leagues, manufacturers leagues—everything, it seemed, but the full-blown professional variety that, ironically, made its North American debut in the United States rather than Canada.

A latecomer to Canadian hockey competition, Toronto was not represented in Stanley Cup competition until 1902, when the cup trustees accepted a challenge from the Toronto Wellingtons. The Wellingtons journeyed to Winnipeg for their two-game challenge round against a powerful Victoria team from Manitoba. The home club demonstrated that a good big hockey club will beat a good little hockey club nine times out of ten. Doughty and artistic, the Wellingtons nevertheless could not cope with the bigger Winnipeg skaters. Toronto lost the first and second games, 5–3.

Interest in the Wellingtons and their fortune in Winnipeg indicated that Toronto had become a major hockey center. Fans from what then was known as "Hog-town" circled the offices of the *Globe* newspaper in downtown Toronto to obtain word over the telegraph wire from Winnipeg. An arrangement was made whereby Toronto's trolley car motormen would signal the outcome of the championship game via their warning whistles. If the Toronto contingent won, they would deliver two blasts; three if the Wellingtons were defeated.

With the ever-growing hockey fervor came an increasing number of outstanding players, but the game still awaited the arrival of its first genuine superstar. That was Fred (Cyclone) Taylor, who in the minds of some hockey analysts was the greatest player of all time. "There will never be his equal," said Hall of Famer Lester Patrick, whose own career as a player and manager covered almost half a century.

Taylor honed his talents to sharpness on the outdoor rinks of Ontario late in the nineteenth century and soon moved up to the Listowel Junior Club. During the winter of 1904 he played his first game in Toronto for Listowel against the Kingston Frontenacs. Those were the days when hockey games were divided into halves. Listowel fell behind 4–1 in the first half before Taylor took over.

Captain James T. Sutherland, who was a timekeeper at the game, recalled the sight of Taylor: "He skated down the ice like a veritable streak of lightning."

Curiously, Taylor's debut in Toronto also marked the day when officials realized that time clocks, overhanging the rinks, were necessary rather than relying on timekeepers sitting somewhere in the stands. This came about during the first half of the match between Listowel and Kingston. Taylor scored three consecutive goals to tie the score 4–4, but two of the goals were scored after the first half had officially ended. Captain Sutherland's dilemma was that he had been seated in a section crowded with other fans, and it was impossible for him to get out of his seat, make his way past the throng of spectators, and reach the referee in time to inform him that time had run out on the game.

Sutherland said, "Hard as it is to believe, each time Taylor scored, the crowd became more boisterous and more impossible for me to surmount in order to get to the referee."

Taylor had scored his third goal just seconds before Sutherland reached ice level. Referee Pink Lillie was so consumed with the action that he failed to notice Sutherland at the sideline. Sutherland finally leaped over the boards, getting referee Lillie's attention. Informed of the matter of the extra time, the referee huddled with John Ross Roach, president of the Ontario Hockey Association. They ruled that all of Taylor's goals should count even though two of them had been scored after regulation time had elapsed. "Since the referee had never ordered play to be stopped," said Sutherland, "the goals were considered legal."

Justice triumphed in the second half when Kingston rallied to take the contest 9–5. There was, however, a twofold significance to the match; it inspired the general use of more formal, sophisticated timekeeping devices, and it brought Cyclone Taylor to the public's attention. The lad from Tara, Ontario, ripened much in the manner of Wayne Gretzky in the early 1980s.

Taylor played so well in Manitoba that he caught the eye of those people—Americans, of all people—organizing the continent's first professional league in northern Michigan. He played superbly for the Houghton team until he was lured to his nation's capital to play for the Ottawa Senators.

Taylor's arrival in Ottawa marked another milestone in the growth and development of Canadian hockey. The big business era had arrived, and for the first time a select few players were receiving what, for the time, was regarded as extraordinarily high salaries. (Taylor was paid more than $5,000 a season before he arrived in Ottawa.) The game had become such a major source of income to promoters that bigger and bigger rinks were opening every year. Late in 1907 the citizens of Ottawa hailed the city's new Laurier Arena, which was to Taylor what Yankee Stadium would be to Babe Ruth in a later era.

On opening night, Taylor's Senators faced off against the Stanley Cup champion Montreal Wanderers. A league record crowd of 7,100 jammed the building, providing a field day for scalpers. Reserved seats were selling for $1.25 apiece, but scalpers were receiving up to $7.00 per ducat. Taylor gave the home crowd its money's worth.

Malcolm Bryce of the *Ottawa Free Press* declared: "Starting today, based on his performance last night, I am rechristening him 'Cyclone' Taylor." Taylor, himself, later observed: "Cyclone fit best."

Frank Patrick, a man who would soon make an indelible impression on hockey, both as promoter and innovator, was among the spectators on hand for Taylor's Ottawa premiere. Like so many others, Patrick found it an arresting performance. "I had never seen such an explosive hockey player, nor one with such skills. I was literally mesmerized by the man. I knew right away that he was something special."

Another milestone in Canadian hockey took place on January 2, 1908, when the first league all-star game was held. As was the case with many all-star contests in the future, this one came about as a result of tragedy. Hod Stuart, who had been a marvelous hockey player with the Montreal Wanderers, was killed in a diving accident during the summer of 1907. A Hod Stuart Memorial Match was arranged to commemorate the late Wanderers star. The all-stars were drawn from other teams in the Eastern Canada Hockey League and they faced the Wanderers. Following a major build-up, to which the press contributed mightily, the game was a sellout, drawing more than four thousand fans. The Wanderers won, 10–7, and earned two thousand dollars, which was handed over to Stuart's widow.

As hockey interest soared—it now was played with equal frequency in British Columbia on the west coast—so too did the intensity with which the game was played, especially on the professional level. At times the artists were overwhelmed by the brutes, and very early in hockey's history it earned a negative image for its seemingly wanton violence. A number of incidents led to this development.

A match between the Montreal Wanderers and their Ottawa rivals early in the twentieth century erupted in a near massacre during a game played at Montreal. A *Montreal Star* report of the match included the following: "They [the players] should get six months in jail is the opinion as to Saturday's hockey brutality. . . . Old players say it was the worst exhibition of butchery they ever saw. . . . Recorder Weir states that if he had been present he would have ordered arrests."

One hockey center, among many, became notorious for its hockey bloodshed: the factory town of Cornwall, Ontario, which had a franchise in the Federal League. The Cornwall rink held upward of three thousand people, most of whom turned into raving fanatics once the puck was dropped.

One of the most vicious matches pitted Cornwall against the Ottawa Victorias at Cornwall on March 6, 1907 in what was billed in advance as a bitter contest. Ironically, Frank Patrick had been asked to officiate this one but had respectfully—and sensibly—declined.

As expected, the teams went at it hammer and tongs, which meant that a number of grudges were ignited. Bud McCourt of Cornwall clashed with Art Throop of Ottawa. McCourt's troubles weren't over. He soon was clobbered fatally on the head, allegedly with a stick carried by Charles Masson of Ottawa. Charged with murder, Masson was acquitted when the judge was unable to determine whether it was, in fact, another foe's stick that struck McCourt. Several witnesses at the trial testified that other Ottawa players had apparently clouted McCourt earlier in the fracas, and the testimony clouded the case against Masson.

14

Play in the Eastern Canada League was no more temperate than in the Federal League. Even the showcase, the challenge for the Stanley Cup, had its merciless moments when the Cornwall and Ottawa players were at each others' throats—and heads. It mattered not whether the teams were loaded with gifted skaters or not; they played for blood. Consider the Ottawa Silver Seven, winners of the Stanley Cup in 1903, 1904, and 1905. The Ottawas were loaded with such superlative skaters as Harvey Pulford, Harry Westwick, Frank McGee, and Alf Smith; yet they were murderous on the ice.

Somehow, the game survived and even thrived in spite of the bloodshed. But in the early days of the turn of the century, there was a missing element that would be unheard of today—the participation of large numbers of French-Canadians on the highest levels of the game. This omission would soon be rectified by Le Club de Hockey Canadien, more popularly known today as the Montreal Canadiens.

The birth of the Canadiens, hockey's most popular team, would signal yet another giant step forward for hockey in Canada and continent-wide acceptance. As it happened, hockey's best-known organization was born in the midst of a fierce battle between arena owners in Montreal. The year was 1909 and the dispute centered about a desire by the Eastern Canada Hockey Association owners to force the Montreal Wanderers out of the league. (The Wanderers had wanted to play in the Jubilee Rink, but the ECHA wanted them to play at Westmount Arena.) The ECHA moguls came up with a clever ploy; they dissolved the league and then instantly created a "new" one, dubbed the Canadian Hockey Association (CHA). It welcomed—at a cost of thirty dollars apiece—franchises from Ottawa, Montreal Shamrocks, Quebec, the Nationals, and All-Montreal. When the Wanderers applied for membership, the door was slammed in their face, as was the bid by J. Ambrose O'Brien on behalf of the Renfrew (Ontario) Millionaires.

Both the Wanderers and the Millionaires might have accepted their respective defeats without protest were it not for a chance meeting between O'Brien and Wanderers boss Jimmy Gardner. After commiserating with each other, the pair suddenly realized that the obvious vehicle for revenge would be a rival professional league. To start they had the Wanderers and Millionaires. O'Brien owned teams in Cobalt and Haileybury, Ontario, and another pal owned a team in Renfrew. That was fine, but the hockey lords agreed that, to be a success, the new league—to be called the National Hockey Association of Canada (NHA)—required another club in Montreal.

With rare insight, Gardner perceived that the huge French-Canadian population of Montreal was aching to support a team of its own. The Wanderers were dominated by English-speaking players and provided no inspiration to the French-speaking habitants. "Let's start a French team," Gardner suggested. "If we can get Jack Laviolette, we'll have the perfect manager."

Laviolette, a popular French-speaking athlete, was immediately recruited, and the NHA was formally organized on December 2, 1909. Laviolette, a restaurateur in downtown Montreal, swung into action and signed Edouard (Newsy) Lalonde, one of the most accomplished—French or English—players in Canada. That done, he huddled with Didier Pitre, a fleet right wing. Untroubled over the fact that Pitre had just signed an $1,100 contract to play for the Nationals of the CHA, Laviolette placed $1,700 on the table before the startled player.

When news of Pitre's acceptance of the Canadiens' offer circulated through Montreal, the Nationals' attorney, Harry Trihey, declared that Pitre would be fined two thousand dollars and sent to jail if he put on a Canadiens uniform.

Pitre was suitably concerned, but his fears were somewhat assuaged when Laviolette promised him that he could keep the $1,700 whether he played for the Canadiens or not. Meanwhile, all of Montreal was wondering which way the right wing would turn, and the attendant publicity served to bring the new club the attention it needed. On opening night, January 5, 1910, the question of Pitre's allegiance still was unresolved—at least as far as the public was concerned. A capacity crowd showed up for the match between the Canadiens and the visiting Cobalt team at the Jubilee Rink.

The Canadiens were betting on Pitre's loyalty to the French-Canadian cause, and they were rewarded when, as originally promised, he skated out on the ice as five thousand fans roared their approval. Les Canadiens, soon to be known as The Flying Frenchmen, Les Habitants, the Tricolor, and Les Glorieux, lived up to their advance billing. Heroic from the very beginning, they rebounded from 3–0 and 6–4 deficits to tie the game in regulation time and win the contest in sudden-death overtime.

Landing Pitre was an enormous coup for Les Canadiens. "At times," recalled Hall of Famer Frank Boucher, "Pitre was inclined to be rather fat, but he could put on an extraordinary burst and stop on a dime. Once, when I was with Ottawa and playing against him, my coach, Pete Green, sent me out to check him. Pitre went past me so fast that Green almost broke a blood vessel screaming for me to come off the ice before more damage was done."

The Canadiens' debut turned out to be another landmark in Canadian hockey because the new club helped give the budding NHA the element of class that it needed right at the start.

As good as the ECHA had been—and nobody was denying its quality—the NHA promised yet another dimension: French participation. Add to that what one observer described as the "speed, even balance, furious rushes, tension, skill, and combination play," and it was clear that O'Brien and friends had produced a winner.

The ECHA was dealt still another blow when its anti-Pitre sanctions were ignored by both the player, the Canadiens, and the courts. A French-Canadian hockey hero was now on center stage—the first of a long line of Quebeçois to grace the ice lanes.

Remarkably, although Canada had become the foremost hockey-playing nation in the world, not a single artificial ice skating rink existed in the entire Dominion.

There was one in New York City (St. Nicholas Arena), as well as in Pittsburgh, Detroit, Cleveland, and Boston, a fact that Frank Patrick was painfully aware of. The son of a Canadian lumber tycoon, Frank and his brother Lester were superb hockey players who had already made a name for themselves in both eastern and western Canada by the time they had decided to settle in British Columbia in 1911. Innovative to a fault, the Patricks were responsible for more of hockey's revolutionary developments than any other personality involved with the game.

Lester was the first defenseman to regularly lead counterattacks into enemy territory and do considerable puck carrying. Until 1903 the defenseman was simply expected to defend; when he stopped the foe, he was expected to hoist the puck to the other end of the arena. Not Lester Patrick. Playing for a team in Brandon, Manitoba, he intercepted the puck and then dashed down the ice.

The move was so unorthodox that the club directors ordered a meeting at halftime to discuss Patrick's thrust. They called him in, bawled him out, and insisted that he play defense with proper restraint. "But," snapped Lester, "I've done pretty well by rushing. Why not keep on? It's new. Maybe the public will like it."

After thinking it over for a moment, the directors consented and Patrick went out, rushed like a demon, and scored a goal. "Defense players," said Montreal columnist Elmer Ferguson, "were rushing ever since."

Encouraging defensemen to carry the puck was the least of the Patricks' progressive moves. Certainly one of their most formidable accomplishments was the creation of a major hockey league in the west. The idea germinated in 1911 when Lester was twenty-seven and Frank twenty-five. It was a courageous move in many ways, not the least of which was the fact that British Columbia lacked the natural ice advantages of other parts of Canada, was not a hockey center, and lacked even a single artificial ice plant.

The Patricks would change that. After considerable research on the subject, they decided to build their own arenas in Vancouver and Victoria, replete with ice-making equipment. They would also have a team in New Westminster, British Columbia, near Vancouver, and possibly add teams from Edmonton and Calgary. "They were laying it on the line," commented Eric Whitehead, "in what surely would be the most daring, ambitious, and imaginative scheme of its kind in the history of sport."

Working according to an exceptionally tight schedule, the Patricks broke ground for their new buildings in April 1911. The Vancouver structure would be palatial by hockey standards of the day—10,500 seats in a building of Promethean proportions. It would cost more than $210,000. The proposed 4,000-seat Victoria rink was estimated at a price of $110,000. New Westminster's building would come later.

Meanwhile, the Patricks had gone about the business of raiding eastern teams of top-flight personnel with whom to staff their clubs. They succeeded in every way, and on January 3, 1912, the Pacific Coast Hockey Association (PCHA) launched

17

its first season, with the Victoria Senators, operated by Lester, facing off against the New Westminster Royals. The game, captured 8–3 by New Westminster, only half filled the Victoria rink. Now the question was how would Vancouver greet its new team in the mammoth new arena, the largest of its kind in the world? Once again the Patricks were disappointed; the crowd of just over four thousand didn't fill half of the building's seats.

The PCHA's first season was a struggle, but the Patricks got a break when their old pal Art Ross, an excellent player (later the power behind the Boston Bruins franchise), collected a formidable group of eastern stars and brought them west at the end of the season for a three-game exhibition series in British Columbia. Although he had been injured in the east, Cyclone Taylor accompanied the all-stars. He was limited to a few minutes' ice time in the first two games, won by the Patricks' stars, but played regularly in the third game and, according to Eric Whitehead, an authority on the subject, "all but blew the West All-Stars off the ice with his blinding speed and hell-for-leather aggressiveness."

The three East–West All-Star exhibition games drew well enough to encourage the Patricks that better days were ahead. They resumed their raids on the eastern teams and came away with a number of stars, not the least of whom was the plum of plums, Cyclone Taylor. Frank Patrick signed him for the Vancouver Million-aires at a salary of $1,800, supposedly the highest in hockey. Displaying the gumption that was—and still is—inimitable among hockey players, Taylor turned out for the opening game of the second season in Vancouver although he had suffered an attack of appendicitis two days earlier. More than seven thousand fans turned out and Cyclone responded to their cheers with a goal as Vancouver routed New Westminster, 7–2. That hockey was here to stay in the west was evident a few nights later when the Millionaires hosted Lester Patrick's Victoria team. Every seat in the huge Vancouver arena was occupied.

Not that the PCHA was without headaches. New Westminster proved too small a town to support a franchise, so eventually it forfeited its league membership in 1914 and the team was transferred to Portland, Oregon. This, too, was historic, for the establishment of the team in the American city marked the first time a United States–based team played in a predominantly Canadian league.

Meanwhile, interest in official East–West match-ups for the Stanley Cup championship was stirred by more exhibition series between the two parts of Canada. In March 1913, the Stanley Cup champion Quebec squad played a three-game playoff with Victoria, and the Patrick men came out on top, two games to one. A year later Victoria took the train east and engaged the cup-winning Toronto club in a three-game set, but this time the westerners lost all three matches.

The persistence of the Patricks finally paid off in 1915 when the Stanley Cup trustees grudgingly agreed that, for the first time, the Stanley Cup playoffs could be played on the west coast. Ottawa, which had defeated the Montreal Wanderers in a two-game, total-goal test, would represent the east against Frank Patrick's Vancouver Millionaires. A victory for the west would eliminate any doubts about the credibility of the PCHA as a force in professional hockey. Although the Ottawa outfit was fortified with a number of expert players, including goalie Clint Benedict and left wing Eddie Gerard, the Millionaires skated at them with a vengeance, showing no mercy in the three-game playoff. Frank Patrick's pride and joy ripped the visitors, 6–2, in the opener. Ottawa came back and held a 2–0 lead over Vancouver after the first period of the second game, but when the dust had cleared the Millionaires had triumphed 8–2. In the finale, Ottawa again was competitive for one period, hanging on for a 2–2 tie, but the Millionaires humbled them from that point on and ended the playoff with a 12–3 decision. Charles L. Coleman, the NHL historian, observed: "It was the opinion of many members of the press that the calibre of hockey in the PCHA was so far ahead of the NHA it would remain there for some time."

Thanks to the Patricks, the westerners were way ahead of their eastern rivals in other departments. They introduced the penalty shot into hockey after watching its use in a soccer game. They were the first to have numerals placed on the jerseys, a decision soon adopted by all sports. Until the PCHA came along referees could dole out unlimited penalties until there were only two men left on the ice besides the goalie. The Patricks perceived the foolishness in this and worked out the delayed penalty rule.

Under the Patrick plan there could not be less than four men—including the goalkeeper—on the ice at any time. The Patricks were the first to adopt forward passing and legalize puck kicking in certain areas as a means of keeping play in motion. By the outbreak of World War I the Patricks' fertile minds were directed toward the improvement of their league and the game of hockey in general. It was a fortuitous coincidence.

"Many of their new rules were already in use," said Eric Whitehead, "with others on the way. True, as they were the owners of their own league they had virtually their own proving ground. When it came to proposing a new rules change, Frank or Lester merely had to make the suggestion and the change was instituted, or at least tested. It was a classic case of a benevolent dictatorship in action."

At Lester's urging, the rule forbidding goaltenders from leaving the vertical position to make a save was altered. "Why," reasoned Lester, "shouldn't a goaltender be allowed to fall to the ice to block the puck? Or do anything he wants with his body if it will help him make a save?"

Who could argue with Lester's logic? His idea was accepted, and an entire new dimension was added to the art of goalkeeping. "The Patricks," commented Elmer Ferguson, one of the game's most perceptive critics, "gave the goalie a break, allowing him to assume any position he wished, and today hockey is packed with thrills on close plays around the nets, with the goalie leaping and spread-eagling while the attacking forwards pile up on top of him."

Another significant Patrick innovation, which drastically altered the attacking patterns of the game, was their decision to speed up the movement by dividing the ice into three distinct sections—two defensive zones and a neutral area in between. To do so they devised blue lines and wrote new rules to go with them. Previously, players would frequently race ahead of the pack to capture the puck and were whistled down for being offsides. This produced a dreary succession of whistles during a 1913 playoff and set the brothers thinking. Under their blue lines rule, passing *was* permitted in the neutral area. It was a marvelous rule, which later was embellished to allow passing within all zones and, as Whitehead noted, "blew the game of hockey wide open."

Interestingly, a moneymaking ploy used by sports entrepreneurs over the years and still vigorously debated today by both journalists and fans was the brainchild of the Patricks. That is the playoff system, whereby teams that are not necessarily the leaders in their respective divisions are allowed to compete for the championship in a postseason tourney. Previously the playoffs had been limited to the top clubs in each sector, but in 1918 Frank Patrick became disturbed over a runaway race in the PCHA and believed that some sort of incentive should be provided for the lower teams and their fans. His solution was the system whereby a second-place team would take on the first-place club in a playoff after the regular schedule had been completed, with the winner then qualifying to meet the champions of the east. Patrick broached the subject with his pal Cyclone Taylor, who readily assured him that it wouldn't work and that the fans wouldn't stand for such a frivolous scheme. Frank insisted that it would, and since it was his league—or at least half of it was— the playoff system was tested and, ultimately, approved by everyone.

It is noteworthy that one seemingly progressive move that the Patricks opposed was the change from the seven-man game—a goalie, two defensemen, three forwards, and a rover—to the six-man style without the rover. Oddly enough, the six-man game developed quite by accident. The perpetrator was a forward named Charlie McClurg, who played for the Sault Ste. Marie (Ontario) team in the International League, hockey's first pro circuit.

This was in December 1904, a time when teams did not carry substitutes; a man skated for the entire sixty minutes or not at all. A team from Pittsburgh had arrived in Sault Ste. Marie for a two-game test with the home club when it was discovered that McClurg, who had previously been injured, was hors de combat for the upcoming games. What to do? It appeared that the hosts would have to face their foe short a man throughout the contest. According to Fraser MacDougall of the *Canadian Press*, the problem was solved when "an unnamed Pittsburgh player quickly made things even by disappearing on a post-Christmas spree."

Now each team sported only six players, so they sat down and made a deal; they would forget about the rover and, thus, the first six-man professional game was played. The episode did not go without criticism. Toronto journalists were appalled by the unorthodox tactics employed by the International League and said so in print, but the *Sault Ste. Marie Weekly* produced a prophetic riposte, suggesting that eventually all leagues would perceive the value of having six-man rather than seven-man teams.

The Patricks' preference for the seven-man game may have been rooted in their knowledge that they possessed one of the largest rink surfaces in the world in Vancouver, with ice dimensions of 90 by 220 feet. (Compare that with the NHL rink standards today, 85 by 200 feet, on which the six-man game is played.) On the expansive Vancouver rink, a seven-man game still did not make for a crowded ice surface.

As persuasive as Lester and Frank had been in luring superior players to the west, they failed to retain the services of one gifted athlete who might have assured the permanent success of their organization. The player in question was Edouard (Newsy) Lalonde, who emerged as one of the most meaningful characters in hockey's early development in Canada.

A native of Cornwall, Ontario, Lalonde was nicknamed Newsy during a brief stint in a newsprint plant. In the view of Canadian author Bill Roche, Lalonde was "the greatest French-Canadian athlete of all time and one of the best who ever laced on a skate or fondled a lacrosse stick."

Lalonde was also influential in demonstrating that, right or wrong, toughness was the essential ingredient for success. He not only intimidated the enemy with his skill, but was also quick with his stick and his fists. Playing for the Canadiens against the Montreal Wanderers in December 1912, Lalonde provided a vivid demonstration of what hard-nosed hockey was all about.

Midway in the game Lalonde dispatched Odie Cleghorn of the Wanderers into the boards with such force that Odie's brother, Sprague, charged across the rink and smashed Newsy across the forehead with his stick. The blow barely missed Lalonde's eye, and he required twelve stitches to close the gaping wound. After the game a constable served a summons on Cleghorn, and he was fined $50 in court in addition to the $50 fine imposed by the league.

The penalties served as no deterrent at all to Lalonde. During a game against Quebec a year later, Newsy bashed Joe Hall across the head with his stick, opening an eight-stitch wound. His memory sharp, Hall returned the favor in a subsequent game, crashing Lalonde into the boards so vigorously that Newsy needed ten stitches to close his wound.

Mostly, though, Lalonde was a terrific gate attraction who helped develop the Canadiens mystique—one that would be embellished over the next few decades— and fill rinks in the east. "Newsy not only had class," noted Montreal columnist Elmer Ferguson, "but he had color. Once he scored nine goals in a game his team won with an eleven-goal performance. He was born about 50 years too soon."

Fortunately for the good of hockey, a number of talented players survived the brutality of Lalonde's ilk and still performed on the highest possible level. The man who epitomized the clean-but-effective mode of play and who did much to save the game in its still primitive state was Frank Nighbor, who had a profound influence on many others who would follow him. Nighbor believed implicitly that hockey should be played according to the rule book and refused to lower himself to the level of Lalonde and other ruffians.

In the beginning, amateur hockey was the one and only brand of the sport in Canada. The transformation from an amateur to a professional sport was slow and relentless, spanning several decades, but the most significant developments occurred after the turn of the century. In 1906 the Canadian Amateur Hockey League was dissolved and, simultaneously, the Eastern Canada Hockey League was born. With each year—although amateurs and professionals were allowed on the same teams—more players were being paid. By 1907 charges and countercharges were being leveled against clubs such as the Montreal Wanderers and the Rat Portage (now Kenora), Ontario, teams for packing their rosters with imports from other teams.

The turning point in the battle between the amateurs and the professionals came in 1908 when the Toronto Maple Leafs, champions of the Ontario Professional Hockey League, challenged for the Stanley Cup. They were beaten by the Wanderers, but it was clear that the pros were here to stay, as demonstrated a year later when Edmonton challenged the Wanderers.

Never before had a team so blatantly revealed how far it would go in its attempts to land Lord Stanley's mug. The Edmontonians iced one team during the regular schedule, but when it came time for its cup test against the Wanderers, only one player who had skated for Edmonton during the regular season remained with the team for the playoff round.

"The blatantly-loaded Edmonton club," wrote Brian McFarlane, "confronted the public with a situation that could be hidden no longer. Amateurism was on the way out. Professionalism, outright or thinly disguised, had come to stay."

Much as they wanted to ice the best possible teams, the early professional entrepreneurs, as a rule, were extraordinarily tight with their purse strings. A majority of club owners in the 1912–1914 period attempted to limit player's salaries to six hundred dollars a season, although exceptions were made in some cases. The first known attempt to organize players into a union was conducted by Art Ross, whose revolutionary move forced owners to pay an average salary of one thousand dollars a season.

The Patrick brothers were not the only innovators. Others produced such changes as the red line extending from goal post to goal post so that goals could be more clearly defined. Officiating became more sophisticated, with a distinction made between minor and major penalties, and for the first time teams were allowed to provide substitutes for players who left the ice. The substitution rule would have both amusing and distressing ramifications in the early days, primarily because most players preferred participating in an entire sixty-minute contest without relief. Most of the time the poor ignored substitute would vegetate and do little to serve his team.

The outbreak of World War I wreaked havoc with both amateur and professional hockey clubs in Canada. Players enlisted in the Canadian armed forces and rosters were decimated, yet there was no thought of dissolving any of the more important leagues. Quite the contrary: the federal government realized the importance of hockey for home front morale and encouraged the leagues to stay in business. When Frank Patrick attempted to organize a Sportsmen's Battalion to fight overseas, he was informed by the government that his hockey games were just as vital to Canada. He was ordered to stay put.

Toronto's Stanley Cup–winning team of 1914 suffered a grievous blow when its crack right wing, Alan (Scotty) Davidson, enlisted in the Canadian army. He was killed fighting with the Allied forces in Belgium.

In Toronto a number of prominent athletic figures organized the 228th Sportsmen's Battalion. The unit boasted so many top-flight hockey players that the 228th entered a team in the NHA for the 1916–1917 season. Since the battalion members were members of the armed forces and therefore not salaried, they represented one of the last amateur teams to compete actively with the professionals. But one member of the 228th didn't fancy that situation, so Gordon (Duke) Keats, a center from Montreal, decided to play for the Toronto Arenas. When his army buddies discovered what he was up to, they quickly got even. "Keats," said Babe Donnelly, a former NHL defenseman, "did more latrine duty than any other soldier in the Canadian army!"

Keats's extracurricular adventures with the pros were halted for the duration when the 228th Battalion received orders to go overseas on February 10, 1917. Duke, naturally, went with them. Despite the loss of innumerable players, the leagues managed to stagger through the war years and provide the ever-growing numbers of fans with the hockey they desired. What nobody realized at the time was that the dawn of a new era was about to break and with it would come the first golden period of professional hockey in North America.

THE UNITED STATES

Although one would not think so today, the United States followed close behind Canada as a prime developer of ice hockey talent in the nineteenth century, and interest in the sport multiplied in direct proportion to its growth in Canada, except on a more modest scale.

Since many Canadian hockey devotees made trips to the United States on both business and professional ventures, it was inevitable that they would discuss the new pastime with their American friends and relatives, demonstrate how it was played, and ultimately spread the ice gospel. As energetic as their compatriots north of the border, Uncle Sam's athletes took to hockey with their accustomed vigor. Before the turn of the century, it was being played in such areas as northern Michigan and many major centers. In 1898 J. A. Tuthill reported in his *Ice Hockey and Polo Guide* that Chicago, Detroit, and Minneapolis were among the first large cities with keen hockey interest, but that in 1898 Baltimore was "the most enthusiastic ice hockey city in the country." Tuthill further emphasized that the hockey interest was not a passing fancy, but "wherever ice could be found, East and West, ice hockey was being played."

Not surprisingly, New York and Boston soon joined the hockey bandwagon, although loosely organized games had been played there well before 1900. In addition, there was considerable movement on the college level, especially when American colleges exchanged visits with their Canadian counterparts.

It is known that in 1894 a group of American college players toured Canada and, although they were outclassed, they learned much about the game and were determined to improve. In the winter of 1896–97, another major step forward was taken in New York City, where the American Amateur Hockey League was organized.

Harvard University iced a team, and in 1906 the Crimson partook in the first intercollegiate hockey game; Harvard versus McGill at Cambridge. The Canadian visitors won handily.

Hockey interest continued to grow in Boston and other parts of New England, but it was positively a major hit in the copper-mining area of Michigan's Upper Peninsula. It was there, in 1904, that professional hockey in North America was born. The father of the continent's first pro circuit was Dr. J. L. Gibson, a dentist in Houghton, Michigan.

There had been an occasional barnstorming tour by profit-sharing professional players in Canada at the turn of the century, but the pro game was never fully organized until the International Pro Hockey League was formed in Houghton, a community of fewer than four thousand citizens. Dr. Gibson, himself a former Canadian player, launched the league by assembling a paid team of Canadian stars and called the club the Portage Lakes. A native of Berlin (now Kitchener), Ontario, Dr. Gibson played defense and captained the Portage Lakes squad. Houghton's squad proved so strong, and such an embarrassement to teams representing other communities in the area, that the other towns decided to recruit professionals of their own. Thus, the International League made its debut late in 1904. It lasted through 1907, folding because the tiny rinks in the various towns simply could not hold enough fans to make it pay. Nevertheless, Doc Gibson's Houghton club had earned an honorable reputation wherever hockey was played. Not only did it dominate its own league, but the Portage Lakers put to rout such teams as the Pittsburgh Bankers, St. Paul Victorias, Montreal Wanderers, Pittsburgh Keystones, and Pittsburgh Victorias. Considering the Portage Lakes' lineup, the admirable record is not that surprising. Future Hall of Famers Cyclone Taylor, Riley

Hern, and Hod Stuart graced the lineup along with the very tough (Bad) Joe Hall. Six of the Houghton players went on to Stanley Cup triumphs.

Cyclone Taylor, who played such an important role in the Portage Lakes success story, would soon become an intrinsic part of hockey's development in another part of the United States—New York City.

A major indoor ice facility, the St. Nicholas Arena, had been built in Manhattan, and its owners were anxious to try professional hockey as a gate attraciton. In the spring of 1908, the New York promoters lured the Stanley Cup champion Montreal Wanderers and Ottawa Senators to St. Nick's for a two-game exhibition series. New Yorkers responded to this landmark event by filling the arena and were rewarded with a game that offered a remarkably high level of skill. Taylor, clearly, was the outstanding player and captured the imagination of the man from the *New York Times*, who called him "the Ty Cobb of Hockey." Taylor responded by orchestrating the two victories for Ottawa over their Montreal foe.

Ever quick to lionize a superstar, the New York fans likened Taylor to James Jeffries, one of their boxing heroes, and soon everyone in the arena was cheering for "Little Jeff." Eric Whitehead reported that hucksters were circulating among the crowd of seven thousand hawking "Little Jeff" lapel buttons. Almost overnight New Yorkers had taken Cyclone Taylor—and professional hockey—to their hearts.

The Wanderers and Senators returned to St. Nick's the following spring and again were hailed for their efforts. However, it was obvious to all the onlookers that one player above all magnetized the audience—Taylor. With that in mind, the New York promoters insisted that no matter which Canadian contingents visited New York in future seasons, Cyclone Taylor had to be among them. Sure enough, in 1910 the Renfrew club was invited to play a mixture of players from the Wanderers and the Senators, and Taylor was with them.

A prize of $1,500 would go to the winner of the three-game series and, once again, the building was filled to capacity. The visitors from the little known creamery town of Renfrew defeated their more celebrated foe.

In all, Taylor made five appearances in New York City—he also was lured to Boston, where he was equally well received—and no doubt would have continued to pay his annual hockey visits were it not for the outbreak of World War I, with its concomitant restrictions on travel and the playing of hockey. But the seed had been sown, and now it was only a matter of time before professional hockey would flower not only in New York and Boston, but in several metropolises throughout the United States.

The first American super hockey hero—the United States' equivalent of Canada's Cyclone Taylor—was Hobey Baker, whose play was so sensational when he wore the colors of Princeton University prior to World War I that he filled rinks wherever he played. It was suggested on innumerable occasions that Baker would surely have been a professional star had he chosen that route, but the intrepid

Princetonian elected to join the flying corps and ultimately went overseas to fight the Germans.

Baker survived the air battles and was scheduled to return to America. One morning he decided to test fly a faulty plane that had just undergone repairs. Against his mates' wishes, Baker took the craft aloft, but its engine failed and the fighter crashed, carrying a magnificent athlete and warrior to his death.

Interestingly, it was Baker's Canadian counterpart, Cyclone Taylor, who helped further propagate hockey in New England as well as the New York area. Taylor was the featured attraction in 1909 when the first professional match was played in Boston in 1911, between Ottawa and the Wanderers. The Beantown fans were delighted with what they saw, and the press concurred. "The first professional hockey game here was a great success," reported the *Boston Globe*. "One would have to conclude from the enthusiastic response of the fans that the city will demand to see much more of the Canadian game."

Already there were rumors that a professional league, including a team from Brooklyn and three from Manhattan, was in the works, but it turned out to be a pipe dream, for the moment at least. The real action, in terms of American participation in pro hockey, was on the west coast, for which the Patricks could be thanked. Having failed to inspire New Westminster, B.C., interests to build a hockey rink in the suburb of Vancouver, the Patricks decided to move the franchise out of Canada altogether and relocate it in Portland, Oregon. In 1914 the New Westminster Royals became the Portland Rosebuds. America's first pro team in a Canadian league performed adequately, producing a 9–9 record behind the coaching of Pete Muldoon.

The Americanization of Canadian pro hockey took another giant step forward late in 1915, when the Patricks elected to place a franchise in Seattle. Contract offers were made to almost all members of the Toronto team, with the result that the new Seattle Metropolitans iced a creditable team in its first season. It finished with a 9–9 record, tied with Vancouver for second place. Portland became the first American team to finish atop a Canadian-based organization. The Rosebuds had a 13–5 record fortified with excellent defensive work. Goalie Tom Murray delivered a league-leading 2.8 goals-against average. Although Seattle's Bernie Morris led the league in scoring, Portland's Charlie Tobin was only two points behind.

More important, in terms of its effect on hockey's development in the United States, was the fact that Portland became the first U.S. representative in the Stanley Cup finals. The Rosebuds finished their regular PCHA season with a 5–2 victory over Seattle at home on February 25, 1916, and then entrained for Montreal, where they would meet the Canadiens in a best-of-five playoff for the cup.

The series was scheduled to begin on March 20, but the Rosebuds didn't arrive in Montreal until March 19. No matter. The PCHA upstarts betrayed no effects of their transcontinental hegira. They outskated their hosts in the opening match and produced a 2–0 victory. The Canadiens rebounded for a 2–1 win in game two and seemed to have the series well in hand with a 6–3 triumph in the third contest, but Portland's fortitude would not be denied, and they surprised everyone with an impressive 6–5 decision to tie the series at two wins apiece.

An Oscar-winning dramatist couldn't have scripted a better scenario than the pulsating match produced by the two teams in the finale. Tommy Dunderdale scored for Portland and Skene Ronan for the Canadiens. "There was little to choose between the teams," reported one observer. Both Tommy Murray of Portland and Georges Vezina of Les Canadiens played airtight goal as the teams clawed for the tie breaker. The unlikely hero turned out to be a Canadiens sub, Goldie Prodgers, who scored the third and final goal of the game. Montreal won 2–1 and gained the Stanley Cup.

Portland's defeat did nothing to dampen hockey enthusiasm in Oregon, or any other part of the United States, for that matter. The PCHA, once perceived as an all-Canadian league, dropped its Victoria franchise and moved it to Spokane, Washington. The team, known in Canada as the Aristocrats, now were dubbed the Canaries. Now the PCHA had three American teams, with only Vancouver representing the Dominion.

As befitting a hockey team called the Canaries, the Spokane team finished last in the standings and last at the gate. They played every game of the season but the last match, a home game against Vancouver that was canceled. It marked Spokane's first and last experience with major league hockey, although the eastern Washington city would have a long and colorful history of minor league hockey. By contrast, Seattle was doing very well. The Metropolitans had a marvelous scorer named Bernie Morris, who had led the PCHA the previous season and finished first with a 16–8 record. Harry (Hap) Holmes, the Seattle goalie, produced the best net-minding average—3.3 over 24 games.

Having led the PCHA, the Metropolitans qualified for the Stanley Cup championship, and, this time, the defending titlists, Les Canadiens, journeyed to Seattle for the showdown. Although Bernie Morris scored three goals for the Metropolitans, Montreal's attack overwhelmed the hosts, and the visitors skated off with an emphatic 8–4 victory.

In the second game Morris scored twice, but his teammate Frank Foyston had three as Seattle strafed Georges Vezina for six goals in a 6–1 win. The Canadiens still could not stop Morris, who came through with another three-goal effort in game three. Foyston added the other goal, but the Canadiens could put but one puck past Hap Holmes. Never before were the chances better for an American team to win the Stanley Cup. The Metropolitans needed but one win in the next two games to achieve this historic milestone. Meanwhile, the Canadiens' braintrust went about the business of producing a defense against Morris. Without it they would never survive for a fifth game.

Aware of the challenge before him, Morris simply redoubled his efforts, and the results showed on the scoreboard. Seattle's crack center shot six goals, his buddy

Foyston got two, and Jack Walker of the Metropolitans annexed the cup with a 9–1 triumph. Lord Stanley's trophy, which originally was never meant to cross the border, was now proudly held by the skaters from Seattle. Under normal conditions Seattle would have been the PCHA's representative in the 1918 Stanley Cup round. The Metropolitans finished first with an 11–7 mark, and runner-up Vancouver could do no better than 9–9, but 1918 was the year that the Patricks introduced the playoff system. In order to qualify for the cup finals, Seattle had to defeat Vancouver in a two-game, total-goals series.

The Millionaires did what the Canadiens couldn't do the previous year—stop Morris. He scored one goal in the opening game at Vancouver, a 2–2 tie, but was blanked in the second game, which the Millionaires won, 1–0.

A year later the tables were turned. Vancouver finished first and Seattle second, but the Metropolitans were able to squeeze out a total-goals victory in the two-game playoff by crushing Vancouver 6–1 in the opener at Seattle and then surviving the Millionaires 4–1 win in the second game.

Once again the Metropolitans and the Canadiens would go head to head in the cup finals at Seattle. The collision attracted considerable attention and no doubt would have been one of the outstanding playoffs were it not for a black cloud that hovered not only over the cup round but all of North America as well. The continent was in the grip of a devastating influenza epidemic, and there was talk of canceling the series rather than permitting a large group of people to convene at Seattle's arena for the matches. The chance of the disease spreading among the audience, not to mention the players, was regarded as too great a possibility to ignore. But the stage credo "the show must go on" was invoked and the championships were begun on March 19, 1919.

The series opener was all Seattle, from goalie Hap Holmes who registered a shutout, to Frank Foyston, who scored a three-goal hat trick. The final score was 7–0, and one wondered whether the Canadiens belonged on the same ice with the American challengers. But, as so often happens in cup competition, turnarounds come easily. Newsy Lalonde scored all four Montreal goals in a 4–2 surprise over Seattle.

Now the experts were in a tizzy trying to dope out the series, and they were further confused when the Metropolitans rebounded in the third game with a 7–2 decision. The irrepressible Foyston scored four goals and Lalonde was blanked.

By now the series had developed a pulsating crescendo, each game being more dramatic than the previous encounter. Game four, in the estimation of NHL historian Charles L. Coleman and others, was the greatest match ever played on the Pacific coast. Goalies Vezina and Holmes shut out their foes during regulation time and, though each team had its chances, nobody could score in sudden death. After an hour and forty minutes of overtime was played, the game was a 0–0 draw.

Seattle had a splendid opportunity to win the cup in the fifth game. The Metropolitans raced to a 3–0 lead, but the Canadiens, led by Lalonde, counterattacked and tied the score with only four minutes remaining. Odie Cleghorn scored the winner (4–3) for Montreal at 15:57 of overtime.

Despite the win, there were ominous overtones for the Montrealers. Joe Hall, who in earlier games had battled so intensely with Seattle's equally tough Cully Wilson, seemed to lose his mustard and unexpectedly skated off the ice and headed for the dressing room with the issue still in doubt. Hall collapsed en route to the Canadiens' locker area and was immediately taken to the hospital. Other players on both teams were reported under the weather, but the sixth game was scheduled for April 1, and was even sold out. This was, after all, one of the finest Stanley Cup championships on record.

Amazingly, those who jammed Seattle Arena appeared unmindful of the epidemic's potential. In addition to Joe Hall, Newsy Lalonde, Didier Pitre, Jack McDonald, and manager George Kennedy of the Canadiens were hospitalized. The decision as to whether a sixth game would be played rested with PCHA president Frank Patrick. If money was his only object, the game would have been played, and Seattle, his league's entry, no doubt would have won, since the Metropolitans were not as badly stricken as the Canadiens. Patrick visited Kennedy in the hospital to discuss his plans to cancel the game. When Kennedy was told by Patrick that the sixth game was a guaranteed sellout, Kennedy urged the PCHA boss to let it be played. Patrick refused the request, although the Seattle owners were equally determined to have the game played.

"I ordered the ticket money refunded," said Patrick. "I discovered later that at least half of the Seattle team were suffering from the flu."

On April 5, 1919, Joe Hall died in a Seattle hospital. His was the only fatality, but Kennedy's case was severe enough to permanently impair his health. He died in less than three years.

The Metropolitans rebounded admirably from the disastrous playoff and continued to show the American colors to advantage the following season. With Foyston leading the PCHA in scoring, Seattle finished on top and then engaged Vancouver in another two-game total-goals playoff. Although the series opened in Seattle, the Metropolitans were stung with a 3–1 defeat and appeared incapable of reaching the cup finals, especially with the second game to be played in Vancouver.

But Hap Holmes closed the door on Vancouver's shooters, and Frank Foyston regained his scoring touch with three goals. Three other Seattle players scored, giving the Metropolitans a 6–0 decision and the right to meet Ottawa for the championship.

The hometown Senators won the first two games, but Seattle rallied for the next pair of wins. That was the best the Metropolitans could do; Ottawa shellacked them, 6–1, in the rubber game. Although no one knew it at the time, the defeat marked Seattle's last major bid for the Stanley Cup, although the Metropolitans did ice respectable teams in several ensuing years. However, the American entry fell victim to the general malaise afflicting the PCHA: too few teams to sustain interest.

For the most part the Patrick circuit comprised only three clubs and in 1924 Seattle finally went under.

The PCHA was soon replaced by a new pro league, an all-Canadian Western Canada Hockey League (WCHL), but once again an American city had to bail it out in time of need. Regina, one of the WCHL entries, sank in a sea of red ink. The franchise was shifted to Portland, and the Western Canada Hockey League suddenly became the Western League, thanks to the American entry. The new Rosebuds lasted only a year, finishing fourth in a six-team league. When they finally folded after the 1925–26 season, the opening era of American professional hockey had drawn to a close. Gone and long forgotten, the Seattle and Portland teams nevertheless proved to be vital forces in propagating major league hockey in the United States, and the proof was in the developments that followed in the eastern part of the country, where pro hockey had, for the most part, been unknown and uncultivated.

If nothing else, the Seattle and Portland experiences demonstrated that professional hockey, under the proper conditions, could attract a following in the United States. The problems afflicting the teams in the Northwest were twofold: they were basically out of the hockey mainstream and they lacked the population base to fill rinks, which centers such as New York, Boston, and Chicago had. Thus it was inevitable that the puck pendulum in America would swing from the Northwest to the Northeast, but only after considerable groundwork had been laid in the New York and New England areas, not to mention Pittsburgh. Of the three hockey centers, Boston proved the most meaningful in terms of the game's continued maturation.

With construction of the handsome (for its time) Boston Arena, citizens of Boston now had a rink with artificial ice that would be the center of hockey activity for years to come. According to the best available information, the first organized team to call Boston Arena home was the Brae Burn Hockey Club, which began working out at the new building early in 1912. A season later a full-scale hockey program was in progress with three teams competing—the Irish-Americans, the Boston Athletic Association (BAA), and the Intercolonials. Each team drew its talent from specific sources; the Intercolonials from Canada, the BAA from Dartmouth and Harvard graduates, and the Irish-Americans from outdoor rinks and ponds in the Greater Boston area. Competition was keen enough in the 1912–13 season for the Intercolonials and the BAA to schedule a postseason City Series for what amounted to the Hub championship.

The team played a best-of-five series and, reported Boston hockey historian Howie McHugh, it was a thudding affair. "It produced some really brutal body-checking," said McHugh. "Ralph Winsor hung one on Rollie Molyneau, a Sherbrooke, Quebec, citizen, that knocked Molyneau out of hockey for life. Winsor went on from there to become one of America's foremost hockey coaches at Harvard."

1-1 *Herb Gallagher of Northeastern University was one of the earlier U.S. hockey heroes.*

Hitching their wagon to the hockey star, the Boston Arena owners decided to organize their own hockey team, creatively naming it the "Arenas." Well sprinkled with "ringers" from Canada, the Arenas launched an ambitious schedule, booking games with New York's respected St. Nicholas Club as well as with the Brooklyn Crescents. In time the Arenas would issue challenges to clubs from such distant centers as St. Paul and Pittsburgh.

The Boston Arena wasn't the only gathering place for Hub hockey fans. The St. Botolph Street Rink featured teams from Canada, including the Quebec City Sons of Ireland, Toronto Aura Leas, and the Sherbrooke Red Raiders.

Collegiate hockey also was whetting the appetites of Boston puck fans. Harvard's matches with the Hobey Baker–led Princeton teams became prime sources of sports talk. Because of Baker's command of the rink, Princeton generally prevailed, but on one occasion the teams played for more than thirty-five minutes of overtime before a previously undistinguished Harvard skater pumped home the winning goal. The hero of the night was Leverett Saltonstall, who eventually became the governor of Massachusetts. Among other top collegians was Herb Gallagher of Northeastern University.

Mushrooming hockey interest in the post–World War I era led to the creation of still more teams and new powers. In addition to the BAA, the Pere Marquettes and the Westminsters dominated Boston hockey, and the top three players comprised a line of Tubber Cronin, Duke Garen, and Hago Harrington. Harrington's roots were deep. He eventually became coach and manager of the Boston Olympics, the Bruins' excellent farm team in the Eastern Amateur Hockey League.

In the early 1920s, when amateur hockey still reigned in Boston, the professional game was the dominant factor in Canadian hockey. Many of the more proficient Boston-based players had become well aware of the play-for-pay boys north of the border, and the move to bring pro hockey to Boston had quietly begun.

"In those days," noted McHugh, "it was an open joke that the 'simon pures' were gathering in the back office each weekend to get their envelopes out of a now famous cigar box. Threats and counterthreats flew back and forth. And when one of the players brought the issue out into the open, the amateur game suffered a black eye which took years to live down. The professional game moved in during the lull and a new saga of hockey was about to be written."

One disenchanted Boston hockey fan would play a very prominent part in the ascendency of the professional game in the Hub. Charles F. Adams, a New England grocery magnate, had been an amateur hockey afficionado and the sponsor of a team. But Adams grew disgusted with the growing practice of under-the-table payoffs to amateurs and the insistence of some clubs to import Canadian talent. If the so-called amateurs were going to be paid, figured Adams, why not bring in out-and-out professionals and get it over with? For Adams, the pivotal move was a trip to Montreal in 1924 when he had the good fortune to watch the colorful Canadiens win the Stanley Cup.

"That did it," recalled his son Weston Adams. "When he returned home he told us this was the greatest hockey he had ever seen. He wouldn't be happy until he had a franchise. It was the Canadiens that got us started."

The Canadiens, yes, but also a shrewd promoter by the name of Tom Duggan. He had been outbid in an attempt to purchase the Montreal Canadiens a few years earlier, but he had his hand well into the sports jar. He owned two Montreal race tracks, Mount Royal and King's Park, was a partner with Bill Dwyer in another track in Cincinnati, and owned a piece of Coney Island in Brooklyn.

"The role of Tom Duggan," observed Montreal sports writer Andy O'Brien, "was an odd one, but a tremendous contribution nonetheless, to the expansion of hockey into the United States."

Duggan was among the first to appreciate the money-making possibilities of professional hockey in the United States and, to that end, went to the NHL owners and made an interesting bid. He would pay them a certain amount of cash for the rights to three potential franchises in the United States. Since the NHL still was a cocoonlike four-team league, the idea of additional clubs appealed to the owners. Even more appealing was the possibility of being paid $7,000 each for the three so-far phantom franchises. So for $21,000 Duggan owned the rights to three unnamed

American professional hockey clubs. Coincidentally, Adams was suddenly enamored of the NHL brand of hockey, so it was no problem at all for Duggan to sell the grocery baron the first legitimate American major league hockey franchise. Thus, the Boston Bruins were born in time for the 1924–25 season along with a new Montreal entry, the Maroons.

To run his team, Adams selected a crusty, dour Scot, Art Ross, who had played hockey both for and against Frank and Lester Patrick. Ross had honed his promotional skills on the streets of the Westmount section of Montreal, and maintained a keen hockey mind as both a player and referee. However, Ross was given precious little time to collect enough competent players for Boston's first NHL squad. He scraped up some PCHA retreads, such as Bernie Morris, Fred Harris, Lloyd Cook, and Bobby Rowe, as well as a sprinkling of promising amateurs.

Ross, among others, was amazed when his Bruins opened at Boston Arena on December 1, 1924, with a 2–1 win over the Maroons, but his club would enjoy few victories after that. He had only one player, Jimmy (Sailor) Herberts, among the top twenty-seven scorers and employed three goaltenders, one worse than the other. "We had three teams that year," Adams recalled, "one coming, one going, and one playing."

It mattered not, for what really counted was the enthusiasm of Bostonians for professional hockey. They loved watching the likes of Howie Morenz, Babe Dye, Aurel Joliat, Georges Vezina, and Clint Benedict. With a losing season behind him, Ross went about the business of icing a winning hockey club. He sought help from his old chum, Frank Patrick, but the PCHA boss put him on hold, knowing full well that he, Patrick, had big plans that ultimately would involve helping not only the Bruins but other potential American franchises. And now, in the summer of 1925, it appeared that a brave new world of hockey in the United States was about to unfold. The Adams experiment in Boston was an unqualified success, proving that Tom Duggan was a wise man if not an outright genius. Duggan's second franchise was sold to Pittsburgh, where Odie Cleghorn would manage the team, but the NHL directors understood that in order to make it big—*really* big—they would have to conquer New York. Thanks to Duggan and a bootlegger named William (Big Bill) Dwyer, that day would soon come.

BIRTH OF THE NATIONAL HOCKEY LEAGUE

The National Hockey Association, (NHA), which unknowingly was the predecessor of the National Hockey League, (NHL), barely survived World War I. A pincer movement combined to put extreme pressure on the then six-team league that comprised, in 1917, the Montreal Wanderers, Montreal Canadiens, Ottawa Senators, Toronto, the 228th Sportsmen's Battalion (from Toronto), and the Quebec Bulldogs. On the one side was the Pacific Coast Hockey Association led by Frank Patrick, which was endlessly raiding the NHA of talent and thereby limiting its attractiveness. On the other side were the Canadian recruitment centers luring patriotic NHA players into the armed forces.

Before the 1916–17 season even got under way, a number of classy players had traded in their jerseys for the khaki. Among them were Amos Arbour, George McNamara, Goldie Prodgers, Howard McNamara, Harry Meeking, Percy Lesueur, Nick Bawlf, Frank McGee, Gordon Meeking, Alan Davidson, and Jack Brown. Davidson and McGee were killed in action.

The situation was so desperate in Ottawa that one club official favored folding the club for the duration of the war, but arrangements were made to maintain the Senators. In keeping with the patriotic spirit in the land, Sam Lichtenheim announced that his Montreal Wanderers would sign only married men and munitions workers. And in the midst of all the confusion some players looked into the possibility of unionizing—they were that displeased with management.

The players' union demands were intensified by the handling of Cy Denneny, one of the better Toronto players, who had obtained a job in Ottawa. Needless to say, Denneny was hoping to be traded to the Senators so that he could maintain full-time residence in the capital, and the Ottawa club obliged by offering to trade goalie Clint Benedict for Denneny. Toronto owner Eddie Livingstone nixed the deal and instead demanded Frank Nighbor, one of the very best Ottawa skaters. As an alternate proposal, Livingston said he would accept $1,800 for Denneny. None of the offers was acceptable, and Denneny refused to play for Toronto once the season was under way.

Denneny's colleagues both on the Senators and other teams felt that he was getting a raw deal. They wanted the player regulations altered so that a player would be allowed to switch from one team to another for a fixed transfer fee in the event of—as in Denneny's case—a legitimate change of residence. "It was contended," wrote NHL historian Charles L. Coleman, "that Denneny, living in Ottawa, could not possibly support his family on the $600 offered to him by Toronto."

The brouhaha finally was resolved in January when Denneny was transferred to Ottawa in a package deal involving cash and another player.

The first half of the season—that year the schedule had been divided in half—ended on February 10, 1917, with ominous predictions about the future. For one thing, there always had been the threat that at any moment the player-soldiers of the 228th Battalion would be transferred overseas.

This would be doubly damaging since the battalion was one of the NHA's top drawing cards, and it would also force a complete revamping of the schedule. The 228th skaters managed to squeeze in ten games, of which they won six and lost four to place third in the league for the first half. But prior to a game scheduled for

February 10 at Quebec, the battalion was officially notified that it was going overseas.

What to do? There were several suggestions, one of which was that one of the two Montreal clubs be switched to Toronto and that those games that had already been played in the second half be cancelled. The Senators, who had won three consecutive games in the second half, rejected that idea.

Toronto owner Eddie Livingstone, a nettle in the hands of the other hockey barons, favored a five-club double schedule to round out the season. The Livingstone plan was rejected, and all hell broke loose in the smoke-filled room. The acrimony among the NHA directors was as bloodthirsty as many of the games on the ice. Charges and countercharges were hurled across the table until, finally, Toronto withdrew from the league for the remainder of the 1916–17 campaign, leaving the NHA with only Ottawa, Quebec, and the two Montreal representatives. The Toronto players were divided among the existing teams, and Livingstone screamed that his second season plan had been misinterpreted by his fellow owners. The only satisfaction Livingstone received was an assurance that his now dispersed players would return to Toronto in time for the 1917–18 season.

As if the NHA didn't have enough troubles, there was scandalous talk that Eddie Oatman, who had been skating with the 228th Battalion, might not be a soldier after all. Oatman had played the previous season in the PCHA and was released to the NHA on the assumption that he had joined the army and would remain with the 228th when it went overseas.

Oatman did stay with the 228th until it reached St. John, Newfoundland, where he was discharged for special circumstances. The PCHA's Frank Patrick screamed foul, demanding that Oatman be expelled. Still another fuss erupted when Gordon Meeking was discharged from the 228th at St. John. Meeking claimed he had been promised a commission to play hockey and now was wearing a private's stripes. All in all the NHA's face was well splattered with egg by the time the second half of the schedule ended on March 3. Quebec beat Ottawa, 16–1, and the Canadiens defeated the Wanderers, 6–3, but the NHA would never see another season.

The NHA's last playoff pitted the Canadiens against the Senators in a two-game total-goals series, opening in Montreal. The Flying Frenchmen prevailed, 5–2, in a vicious contest during which Newsy Lalonde of the Canadiens butt-ended Frank Nighbor over the eye, forcing the Ottawa ace to the infirmary for several stitches. Although Lalonde was suspended from the second match, the Senators outscored Montreal by a count of only 4–2, which meant that the Canadiens took the series, 7–6. As the NHA's final entry in Stanley Cup competition, Les Canadiens were beaten, three games to one, by Seattle for the professional hockey championship of North America.

If nothing else, the NHA could justifiably compliment itself on completing the turbulent 1916–17 season. Where it would go from there remained a moot point that would for the moment be decided at the league meeting in Montreal on

November 3, 1917. One of the most pressing dilemmas involved the ill feeling generated by the club owners toward their disputatious fraternity member Eddie Livingstone. If that could not be resolved, a furious—and perhaps fatal—season would ensue.

The November 3 meeting solved nothing other than to exacerbate the ill feelings toward Livingstone and, in the end, that may have proven to be the solution. In any event there suddenly were rumblings of a coup d'etat that, if successful, would remove Livingstone from the NHA picture. How this ploy could be developed remained a mystery except, of course, to the plotters who had the scenario all worked out. The proof, as often happens in machinations of these kinds, was in the denials. NHA President Frank Robinson insisted that the NHA had no plans to dissolve, nor would it change its name or pull off any other unmentionable surprises.

Another meeting was held a week later at which time the secret began leaking out; the NHA owners would declare their league null and void for the sole purpose of ridding themselves, once and for all, of Livingstone. It has been said that more Machiavellian tricks were explored in the ensuing days than were tried in all the foreign ministries of Europe.

When all was said and done, the winner in the long run was the North American hockey fan, and the loser was Eddie Livingstone. Wending their way through a legal labyrinth, the NHA leaders conducted a series of maneuvers that achieved their purpose, which was the expulsion, however possible, of their bête noir.

A number of official and unofficial meetings were held, culminating with a conference on November 26 at the Windsor Hotel in Montreal. By this time Robinson had made it clear he no longer wished to be president of the NHA nor any new league if one was to be formed.

While outfeinting Livingstone, the NHA leaders had always been aware that their foe's team played on the league's only artificial ice surface, and there would have to be some way of ensuring that it would remain usable—without Livingstone, of course. Himself a lawyer, Livingstone should have been more keenly aware of the potential pitfalls ahead of him, but his abrasive personality had taken him beyond the point of no return. On November 26, 1917, the door was once and for all slammed on Livingstone.

At the Windsor Hotel meeting, the NHA board dissolved the old league and created a new one, the National Hockey League. The new NHL looked remarkably like its sire. It carried the same constitution and was represented at the meeting by the Canadiens, Wanderers, Senators, Quebec, and even Toronto. The major differences were twofold: Frank Calder, who had been secretary of the NHA, was named president and secretary of the NHL—and Eddie Livingstone was out.

"We didn't throw Livingstone out," Sam Lichtenhein sardonically remarked. "He's still got his franchise in the old National Hockey Association. He has his team, and we wish him well. The only problem is he's playing in a one-team league."

Another participant, Tommy Gorman, described the proceedings as a "great day for hockey." That, of course, remained to be seen. Quebec dropped out of the NHL for the moment at least, but the Senators, Canadiens, Wanderers, and a Toronto representative were welcomed to the "new" circuit. A sportsman named Charles Querrie, after much haggling, was awarded the Toronto entry. Querrie emerged with full power to hire and fire players.

With the war still on in Europe and no sign of peace in sight, there still remained an element of doubt about player availability for the NHL's maiden season, which was to begin December 19, 1917. Yet despite all the threats to its existence, the NHL began operation as promised. The Canadiens defeated Ottawa, 7–4, at Montreal, and the Wanderers edged Toronto, 10–9, also at Montreal. But tragedy was just around the new year. Lichtenhein, still desperate for players, threatened to pull his team out of the NHL unless he received some help from the other teams. But before he could make good on his threat the Montreal Arena was leveled by a fire on January 2, 1918.

Although Lichtenhein had the option of transferring his club to Hamilton, he decided to withdraw the Wanderers from competition, on January 4, 1918. He estimated his hockey losses at thirty thousand dollars. His players were released as free agents, and the NHL moved along toward completion of its first season, but this was far from a simple matter, the manpower shortage being what it was. There were times, in fact, when teams could not be certain of icing a complete team. On January 16, 1918, the Senators arrived in Toronto without a single substitute. Graciously the host Arenas agreed to play without substitution as well. Perhaps it was appropriate that Toronto triumphed, 5–4.

Fortunately, the league remained blessed with enough gifted players to keep the turnstiles whirring. By far the most productive was Joe Malone, one of the best all-around scorers in hockey history. "He might have been the most prolific scorer of all time if they had played more games in those days," said Frank J. Selke, Sr., the former Canadiens' managing director, who remembered Malone as a young professional. "It was amazing the way Joe used to get himself into position to score. In that respect his style was similar to Gordie Howe's. Joe was no Howie Morenz as far as speed was concerned. But he was a clean player like Dave Keon and Frank Boucher. On the other hand, though, Joe never took a backward step from anybody." At the completion of the NHL's first season, Malone had scored forty-four goals in twenty-two games. As he recalled:

> Quite often I played fifty or fifty-five minutes a game. They didn't bother too much about changing lines, only individuals. There were only about nine players on each team. I used to stickhandle in close and beat the goalie with a wrist shot. There was no forward passing allowed in the offensive zone and not as much scrambling as there was to be in the hockey playing in the 1940s and 1950s. We wore shoulder and elbow pads, but the equipment wasn't too heavy, and this was a good thing considering the number of minutes we had

to play each game. The goalkeepers stood up a lot more. Georges Vezina was a wonderful stand-up goalie who used to stop most shots with his stick. There were no slapshots, but much more passing and stick handling than today.

On the night of January 31, 1920, Malone set a record, scoring seven goals against Toronto for Quebec. "There was no great fuss made about the seven goals at the time," said Malone. "It was only a night's work as far as I was concerned. The only thing I remember about it is that it was very cold outside." (The temperature hovered around 25 below zero that night.)

The 1917–18 season has remained significant to this day because of Malone's extraordinary scoring prowess. He scored in each of fourteen consecutive games and three times scored five goals in one game. Nobody has been able to match his percentage of more than two goals per game, yet one would never know it by his contract. "My salary," Malone remembered, "was about one thousand dollars with the Canadiens, and maybe a few dollars more by endorsing hockey equipment. But there were no trophies or additional money for being leading scorer."

Malone's Canadiens faced off against the Toronto sextet in the NHL's first playoff, a two-game, total-goals test beginning March 11, 1918, in Toronto. Malone was stymied without a goal, and the home club took the match, 7–3, before more than four thousand fans. The Canadiens outscored Toronto, 4–3, in the second game, but Toronto took the tourney, 10–7.

The victory enabled Toronto to advance to the Stanley Cup finals against Vancouver. The best-of-five series went the limit. It was a classic confrontation, the more artistic westerners against the rugged eastern club. Vancouver led 1–0 in the final game on Toronto ice, March 30, 1918, on a goal by the inimitable Cyclone Taylor. But Toronto rallied on a score by Alf Skinner and won the game, 2–1, when Corbett Denneny beat goalie Hugh Lehman in the Vancouver net. The Toronto Arenas had presented the NHL a Stanley Cup in its first season, a matter that caused no end of consternation to Eddie Livingstone.

Still seething over the manner in which he was ousted from the NHL, Livingstone explored a number of legal avenues to get back into the game and the league. The lawyer's relentless crusade began with an attempt to revive the NHA and ended with a bid to launch a Canadian hockey association with two teams based in Toronto, one in Hamilton, and another in Cleveland. Livingstone failed on all counts, which was a blessing to the NHL. But equally fortuitous to the league was the end of World War I on November 11, 1918, more than a month before the 1918–19 season was to begin. That was the good news; the bad news was that the NHL had barely enough teams to legitimately call itself a big league.

When the NHL convened on October 20, 1918, it was a league still under siege. Ever present was a threat from Livingstone. The NHL fortified the battlements by working out a deal stipulating that only its teams could play in the coveted Toronto Arena, but the fledgling league still had to face the fact that it was entering its second competitive season with only three franchises—the Canadiens, Senators, and Toronto. Should any of them fold it would strip the league of whatever credibility it had.

Even with a full complement of three teams, there remained a question of credibility. Crowds were unimpressive and those who did show up often were more cantankerous than the most violent players, who were many in number. "The old Jubilee rink in Montreal had to run a netting along the end of the rink to catch the empty gin bottles hurled by the steamed-up fans," said *Toronto Sun* columnist Trent Frayne.

In many cases the spectators were merely responding to the NHL's brand of brutality on the ice. Although there were protests against the excessive rough play, it continued unabated. Even a team like the Canadiens, loaded with the most gifted players—such as Georges Vezina, renowned for his sportsmanship—still betrayed a frightening mean streak. The *Toronto Mail* reported on this negative aspect of the NHL following a game between the Canadiens and the Toronto Arenas:

> For the entire first period, the Canadiens hammered and battered these game youngsters. They put Ken Randall out of the game for keeps, cut Jack Adams's head to ribbons, battered Rusty Crawford from heat to foot, sent Harry Mummery hobbling off halfway through the period with one leg limp from a sweeping slash, broke the teeth of goalkeeper Harry Holmes, knocked out Harry Meeking and Alf Skipper.

Somehow the Arenas survived the onslaught, but it certainly was not the last, for the frontier spirit of professional hockey would continue to be a part of the NHL's fabric for several more years.

Gore notwithstanding, the NHL slogged through the 1918–19 season with the Senators and Canadiens meeting in a best-of-five playoff for the right to play the PCHA winner in the Stanley Cup finals. Montreal won the series three games to one and then journeyed west for the ill-fated series that ultimately was cancelled because of the influenza epidemic that claimed the life of the Canadiens' Joe Hall.

The Toronto Arenas survived the flu epidemic, but another disease afflicted the club—fan apathy. When Querrie examined his books in the spring of 1919 he was anything but a jolly Charlie. Toronto's pro crowds were depressingly small, and it was decided that the time had come to abandon ship. The club was put up for sale to the highest bidder; the directors were not particularly choosy.

At last a group of Toronto sportsmen put up two thousand dollars for the team, whereupon the Arenas' directors nearly fell all over each other in an attempt to get the money and approve the sale. They gave the new owners rights to the club name and good will and generously added sticks, ice privileges, sweaters, and a dozen athletic supporters. An additional five thousand dollars was delivered to the NHL for the franchise, which, hereafter, would be known as the St. Patricks. This was a major plus for the NHL, as was the communiqué from Quebec that the Bulldogs' franchise would be reactivated for the 1919–20 campaign. Faced with the possibility of having but two franchises in the spring of 1919, the NHL now was accommodating four teams and looked to the new season with a modicum of hope, if not outright optimism.

Certainly, NHL President Frank Calder could boast that there was some light at the end of the league's tunnel. The Toronto St. Pats, unlike their predecessors, displayed a healthy magnetism, and on February 21, 1920, pulled in a record crowd of 8,500 for a game with the Senators.

With the good news there invariably came the other kind. With a neat sheet of artificial ice, the Toronto Arena could be counted on for first-class hockey through the advent of spring. But this, unfortunately, was not the case with the teams still playing in rinks that relied on natural ice. The Senators, for example, hosted the Seattle Metropolitans in the 1920 Stanley Cup finals, but the natural ice at Ottawa's arena had become so mushy by the time the second match began that the players often suspected they were skating in mud. After the third game—during which conditions were even worse—the playoffs were transferred to Toronto's Mutual Arena.

The primitive quality of ice conditions in some rinks was matched by the antedeluvian equipment. Skates, quite often, were similar to those used decades earlier, and even such necessities as the nets were poorly manufactured.

The NHL was not so well put together itself, particularly in Quebec, where the Bulldogs permanently closed shop in the spring of 1920, reducing the circuit to three teams until the good citizens of Hamilton, Ontario, came forth with both an arena and cash. In the autumn of 1920 the Quebec Bulldogs were reincarnated as the Hamilton Tigers, and the NHL got down to business for 1920–21 with four teams once more. The Toronto franchise was solid, and Ottawa, which would win the 1921 Stanley Cup, had no serious problems. But there were questions about the ability of Hamilton to maintain a big-league franchise as well as doubts about the ownership of Les Canadiens.

Sure enough, in October 1921 the widow of Canadiens' owner George Kennedy put his club on the auction block. A healthy Montreal team was essential to the long-term vigor of the NHL, which is why there was considerable interest in the wheeling and dealing that accompanied the sale. Among those in the running were Tom Duggan, representing the Mount Royal Arena Company and an Ottawa group, curiously enough, being handled by NHL President Frank Calder. A third party, known to intimates as the Three Musketeers, comprised sportsmen Leo Dandurand, Joe Cattarinich, and Louis Letourneau, who were partners in a Cleveland race track. The Musketeers were out of town when the final auction of the Canadiens took place, but they asked their friend Cecil Hart, later coach and manager of the Montreal team, to sit in for them. It was a fortuitous move. When Duggan startled the audience by placing ten $1,000 bills on the table in his bid for the team, it appeared that no one would come close to matching the offer. But Hart requested a brief respite and phoned Dandurand in Cleveland. "Raise it to eleven thousand," snapped Dandurand.

At first Duggan and Calder thought it was a joke, but when they realized that Hart meant business, they refused to bid higher and the Three Musketeers, via Hart, carried the day. It would be one of the most significant turning points in NHL history. Under the Dandurand baton the Canadiens flowered into pro hockey's premier drawing card and one that helped lure American investors into the NHL.

The Musketeers' investment paid off immediately, because Les Canadiens collected a twenty-thousand-dollar profit the first year they owned it, although the club finished third in the four-team league. "Dandurand was quick to see that the team was disintegrating," said Elmer Ferguson, who was covering the Canadiens at the time, "and he quickly set about rebuilding. The accent in hockey in those days was largely on weight and power, though a few lighter-weight players had risen to stardom. Dandurand was thoroughly convinced that speed and skill were the real essentials."

Using his knowledge of hockey, which he had acquired as a player, Dandurand discovered Pit Lepine in Montreal's own Mount Royal League and plucked from the amateur ranks such future aces as Albert (Battleship) Leduc, Armand Mondou, Wildor Larochelle, and Billy Boucher. In a daring move, Dandurand dealt the heroic Newsy Lalonde for youthful Aurel Joliat and replaced Lalonde on the front line with truculent Sprague Cleghorn.

A native of Montreal, Cleghorn earned a special niche in league annals as perhaps the single most terrifying player the game has ever known.

King Clancy, who would enjoy a lengthy NHL career as a defenseman for the Senators and then the Toronto Maple Leafs, once took a long run at Cleghorn. Leafs' manager Conn Smythe remembered it well. "When Clancy dropped off," said Smythe, "he dropped unconscious. We had another guy named Bill Brydge, who was going to give us muscle, and he tried to give it to Cleghorn one night when Sprague came down the ice. Brydge did give it to him; the knee, the elbow, the stick. But Cleghorn paid no attention; he just waited. Then the time came and he did straighten out Brydge. He just made a mess of him. Fifty stitches."

The Canadiens would have to wait for their renaissance under Dandurand. In 1922 the NHL's heroes were the Toronto St. Pats, who defeated Vancouver three games to two for the Stanley Cup. But it was the last hurrah for the St. Pats as champions. The next time they won the cup the club was known as the Toronto Maple Leafs.

Ottawa replaced Toronto as the class of the NHL, regaining the cup the following year. The Senators went west in 1923 to play the PCHA's Vancouver Maroons, whom they beat three games to one. Ottawa finished first in 1924 and the Canadiens second, but with Georges Vezina sparkling in the nets, Montreal ousted the Senators from the playoffs in two games, thus qualifying to meet a representative from one of the two western professional leagues, the PCHA or the relatively new Western Canada Hockey League.

As a result of a squabble between the two western groups, two teams came east to challenge Les Canadiens for the Stanley Cup—Calgary from the WCHL and Vancouver from the PCHA. It was decided that Montreal would first play the Maroons, and that set produced a genuine sports oddity. Frank Boucher skated for Vancouver, and his brothers, Billy and Bobby, were with the Canadiens. Montreal won the opener, 3–2, and the second match, and thus the series, 2–1. In the second match, the Boucher family scored all the goals.

"I'll never forget walking downtown in Montreal after the game," said Frank Boucher, "and seeing an illuminated sign on which the game result was posted: Billy Boucher 2, Frank Boucher 1."

The Canadiens then beat Calgary in two straight games for the cup. With the victory another star emerged on the NHL's horizon, goalie Georges Vezina, after whom the Vezina Trophy is named.

"When I think of Vezina," Hall of Famer Frank Boucher once recalled, "the first thing that pops into my mind is that he always wore a *toque,* a small knitted hat with no brim in Montreal colors—bleu (blue), blanc (white), et rouge (red). I also remember him as the coolest man I ever saw, absolutely imperturbable. He stood upright in the net and scarcely ever left his feet; he simply played all his shots in a standing position. He'd pick off more shots with his stick than he did with his glove."

Vezina was one of a growing number of stars reaching the NHL in the post–World War I years, attractions who could ultimately compel the attention of American cities craving hockey's action. New, vibrant personalities were now appearing in abundance on each of the teams, and many of them had the brand of charisma that sold tickets. In the case of Ottawa there was King Clancy, who despite a 5'7", 127-pound frame, played defense with the biggest and best of them. Few who were there will ever forget Clancy's effort on March 31, 1923, when he almost singlehandedly won the Stanley Cup for Ottawa by playing all six positions. It happened this way: Defenseman Eddie Gerard suffered a shoulder separation and Clancy took his place. Then the other defenseman, George (Buck) Boucher, needed a rest, so Clancy moved into his spot and another player moved into Clancy's position. In the second period Ottawa center Frank Nighbor was exhausted and needed relief, so Clancy replaced him. When Nighbor returned, both left wing Cy Denneny and right wing Punch Broadbent needed rests, and Clancy successively took their positions. By then he had played every position but goal.

Later in the game, Senators goalie Clint Benedict was penalized for slashing. This was during an era when goaltenders were required to sit out their own penalties and were replaced in the nets by one of their teammates. Needless to say, Clancy got the call again. En route to the penalty box Benedict gave Clancy his big goalie's stick and chirped: "Here, kid, take care of the store 'til I get back!"

Ottawa was leading 1–0 when Clancy took over the goaltending chores. He held the fort—Clancy claimed he experienced no fear because he didn't know better—and blanked Edmonton until Benedict returned. The Senators won the game 1–0.

What Clancy meant to the Senators, Cecil (Babe) Dye was to the Toronto St. Pats. A right wing with limitless potential, Dye could orchestrate the crowd to a frenzy with his baton, the hockey stick. "Babe," said Canadian hockey critic Ron McAllister, "could shoot the puck from any length or from any spot on the rink. He could score with his back turned, or from any side at all. He had a shot like a thunderclap and an astounding accuracy. He could snap a two-inch plank with one of his drives."

Dye fulfilled his potential in the 1922 Stanley Cup finals against Vancouver. After the Millionaires had taken the opening game, Dye won the second match for Toronto in sudden death. Vancouver won the third game, but Dye came back with a pair of goals in game four to tie the series at two games apiece. The final game, played at Toronto's Mutual Street Arena on March 28, 1922, was a gem. Toronto nursed a 2–1 lead into the third period, when the fabulous Dye scored what became known as the "mystery goal" of Stanley Cup hockey.

Corbett Denneny took the puck from the face-off and slid a short pass to Dye. Dye released his shot with such alacrity that nobody among the spectators saw it take off. Nor did the Millionaires' highly rated goalie Hugh Lehman. "Fooled by its blinding speed," said Ron McAllister, "Lehman still waited, crouched in goal. A hurried search for the puck began, while Dye, the only man who knew where it lay, skated back to his own defense. The crowd finally roared and pointed to the Vancouver net. There was the puck! Then the light was flashed on and the goal registered." From that point on the St. Pats roared over the Millionaires and won the game 5–1—and the cup.

However magnificent Dye, Clancy, and Vezina may have been—and they *were* superb—there remained one and only one player who can legitimately be credited with lifting the NHL from the obscurity of eastern Canadian rinks to prominence as a major league attraction on both sides of the border. Howie Morenz was the Maurice Richard–Gordie Howe–Bobby Orr–Wayne Gretzky of his time, which began in the early 1920s with Les Canadiens. The son of a railroad man, Morenz was born in Mitchell, Ontario, a hamlet about thirteen miles from Stratford, in 1903. He was discovered by Leo Dandurand and Cecil Hart for the 1923–24 season and immediately was dubbed Lightning Legs. Just a rookie, he caught the attention of all who played with or against the lad. "He was the picture player," said Nels Stewart, who later would join Morenz in the Hockey Hall of Fame. "Howie had the grace and speed to finish off plays like no one else could."

As quickly as Morenz could skate, word zipped around the NHL of his prowess and speed. He gathered almost as many nicknames—"the Stratford Streak" and "the Mitchell Meteor" among them—as he had moves, and he became a legend before his first tour of the circuit.

"Weeks before I ever played against him," Clancy remembered, "I had read story after story about this kid and I couldn't believe any boy that age could be *that* good. The stories also said he was making a lot of the veteran defensemen look like

1-2 *Howie Morenz of the Montreal Canadiens was the first NHL superstar to capture the imagination of American fans.*

fools. I made up my mind that Clancy wasn't going to be one of them."

When they finally did meet, Clancy thought Morenz would be a pushover, especially since the Canadiens' ace was not particularly big. When they arrived on the ice at the same time, Clancy eyed Morenz carefully as the Montreal skater headed toward his zone. Morenz was a left-handed shot and figured to cut to his left when he reached poke-checking distance. Clancy had it all figured out: "I remember telling myself, 'get nicely set on your feet, watch a quick reverse and you got him.'"

Morenz barreled right in on Clancy and neither zigged nor zagged. He released a snapshot, skated right into Clancy, and bowled him on his behind. Morenz didn't score on the play, but as he returned to center ice he heard Clancy warn him: "One more run like that and I'll knock your block off."

The rookie was so impressed that he shot back that he would try the same play as soon as he received the puck again. "Believe it or not," said Clancy, "he did *exactly* what he said he'd do."

In Morenz's second season he finished runner-up to Babe Dye in scoring and was executing plays that astonished even those who had become inured to greatness.

44

Conn Smythe, who would become manager of the Toronto Maple Leafs, credited Morenz with performing "the most amazing impossible play" he had ever seen in hockey up until that time.

The play began when Morenz split the defense. He was immediately intercepted by a third foe, but not before releasing his shot. It went wide of the net and was captured by the enemy, which launched a quick counterattack. "I was watching Howie all the time," said Smythe, "and I saw him follow up his shot with a long leap in preparation to circling the net. To this day I can't figure out how he managed to stay on his skates as he rounded the cage."

Meanwhile, the enemy puck carrier was well on his way to the Montreal goal when Morenz put his head down in pursuit. "Morenz," said Smythe, "flashed from the net to the blue line faster than I can say 'blue line.'"

Morenz did, in fact, catch the puck carrier, cut directly *in front* of him, released the puck from the player's blade, and immediately changed direction for another play on goal. "I was absolutely dumbfounded," said Smythe. "Morenz had done what he was to do for years to come—he took my breath away."

Although not a French-Canadian—his parents were of Swiss origin—Howie portrayed the role of the Flying Frenchman better than any other player who wore Montreal's tricolor.

Peter Gzowski, one of Canada's foremost radio-television commentators and authors, once wrote of Morenz: "While most fans remember Morenz mainly for his blistering speed and his headlong rushes on goal, he also provided one of the most remarkable examples of the passionate dedication to the game—to winning—that has been another characteristic of Canadien teams."

Of all Morenz's accomplishments, none was more important than his ability to sell the Canadiens, the NHL, and the game of hockey first in Canada and then to the other side of the border. "The electric excitement sparked by Morenz," said Canadian critic Andy O'Brien, "did more than any other single factor to establish the NHL in the United States, True, hockey had made some inroads into the United States before Morenz, but none had led to the Big Time."

In spring 1924 a number of divergent events jelled to bring about the most dramatic—if not traumatic—change in the complexion of professional hockey on the continent.

New arenas, replete with artificial ice and high-intensity lighting, were sprouting up over the continent, and Montreal boasted one of the best with the addition of its Forum. Owned by the Canadian Arena Company, The Forum opened in 1924 as the home of Les Canadiens. But the Arena owners, quick to detect the growing interest in hockey, realized that a second Montreal team, one loaded with English-speaking skaters rather than the French-Canadians who dominated the Habitants, would be a natural.

The Canadian Arena Company directors approached Leo Dandurand in the hopes of obtaining half of the Canadiens' territorial rights in the Montreal area for their proposed new club, the Maroons. Dandurand agreed, provided that the Canadian Arena Company pay him fifteen thousand dollars, none of which would be divided among the existing teams—Toronto St. Pats, Ottawa Senators, and Hamilton Tigers.

When the other clubs learned of the payoff, they demanded a piece of the pie, but Dandurand refused.

> Their demands didn't suit me because it had been privately agreed that the cash was to go to the Canadiens. The rub was that there was no written record of any such agreement, nothing in the minutes of the league. However, the Canadiens did, eventually, receive the full $15,000 to which they were entitled. Meanwhile, I had learned a lesson, and when the next NHL meeting was held, I insisted that there be a stenographer on the job to make a verbatim report of all proceedings.
>
> In 1926, several groups in Chicago and Detroit applied for NHL franchises. In order to clarify the situation and to establish the worth and responsibility of the applicants, I made a motion that in the future the price of a franchise be $50,000. That's what Chicago and Detroit paid to get in.

The Maroons had a mediocre season in 1924–25, when they made their debut along with the Boston Bruins, but they came on strong the following year, bolstered by the acquisition of Nels (Ole Poison) Stewart. After finishing second to the Ottawa Senators, they relentlessly rolled over the opposition, ultimately defeating the Victoria Cougars for the Stanley Cup.

Victoria's loss marked the final battle in the decade-old war between east and west for supremacy—both artistic and financial—in professional hockey. With the end of the 1925–26 campaign, the westerners (then known as the Western Hockey League) disbanded and the NHL reigned alone, king of the ice mountain. From this point on, only NHL teams would qualify to compete for the Stanley Cup and, with still more franchises on the way, the best was yet to come.

THE AMERICAN CONQUEST OF THE NHL

The Boston Bruins proved to be an important addition to the National Hockey League but, in the prestige sense, Boston was small potatoes compared to New York City. If the NHL planned to assume truly major league trappings, it would have to locate a franchise in the Big Apple. Montreal promoter Tom Duggan was acutely aware of this fact when he cornered the market on three franchises, the first of which was established in Boston. Once the Bruins were in business under the

Adams dynasty, Duggan went about the business of planting the NHL flag in New York.

On the surface, at least, this seemed a simple enough matter. A new arena was under construction on the corner of Eighth Avenue and 49th Street in Manhattan, which, when opened in autumn 1925, would be the new Madison Square Garden. Surely, it would welcome a professional hockey team. The reality, however, was something different. The Garden's main man, George H. (Tex) Rickard, came fron an area of the United States where the only ice available was found in mint juleps. The man from Texas neither knew nor cared about ice hockey. "Nobody," wrote hockey historian Andy O'Brien, "in the United States was less interested in 'that Canadian game' than Tex." But Rickard did have a long-standing affection for money, and he was advised that the Bostonians were minting cash at the Bruins' turnstiles. Rickard began to have second thoughts about the Madison Square Garden blueprints, which, at the time, did not include ice-making machinery.

Enter Tom Duggan. He zeroed in on Rickard with a mixture of facts, figures, and blarney. Tex listened but remained unconvinced. Frustrated, Duggan persisted, but Rickard would not be convinced.

Said Andy O'Brien: "Duggan used to wander back, dejected and despairing to the A & E Club in New York, where he'd sit with a group of other Canadian-borns awaiting the latest news. The moans would eventually turn into roars against Rickard. On one occasion an ex-Canadian sports editor, Bill MacBeth, then writing racing for the *New York Tribune*, had to be restrained from leaving 'to sock Tex in the nose.' "

Duggan realized that he had one trump card left—a hockey game. If he could lure Rickard to a Canadiens match in Montreal, the way Charles Adams had been, he was convinced the results would be eminently positive. "How about coming with me to Montreal to have a look at the Canadiens and Howie Morenz?" Duggan proposed.

Rickard's confidantes insist that he relented for two good reasons: to once and for all halt Duggan's badgering, and to escape, for the moment, Prohibition-locked New York. In Montreal, Tex could drink to his heart's content. "Okay," snapped Rickard, "let's go!"

The results were identical to those experienced by Adams. As soon as Tex returned to New York he ordered an immediate alteration in the new Garden's blueprints. Ice machinery would be installed and a hockey team would represent the new building—as long as Rickard didn't have to pay for it. That's where Duggan, Rickard—and New York—got lucky.

One does not normally happen upon a first-rate hockey franchise without having to pay handsomely for it. Adams made that discovery in 1924 when his rag-tag Bruins finished a dreadful last in the NHL. So why should it be different for Duggan, Rickard, *et al.?* Precisely because strange things were happening in Hamilton, Ontario, home of the Tigers.

An NHL member since 1921, Hamilton's sextet had neatly ripened into the classiest of the league. It finished the 1924–25 season in first place and boasted such attractive scorers as Billy Burch, and the brothers Redvers and Wilfred Green. The Tigers were favored to win the first Stanley Cup in the city's history when, as luck would have it, a rather unlikely event—a players' strike—intervened.

Before the playoffs were to begin, Red Green posted a list of grievances to Tigers' owners Percy Thompson. The Tigers noted that the NHL season had been lengthened from twenty-four to thirty games, yet they had received no boost in their salaries. They requested that they be paid two-hundred dollars extra per player—or else! Thompson, backed by NHL President Frank Calder, opted for the "or else." The Tigers were suspended and fined, the playoffs went on without them, and Thompson, disgusted by the entire state of affairs, put the Tigers on the block. Duggan couldn't have been luckier. Thompson, who had paid only five-thousand dollars for the franchise when he had obtained it from Quebec, was tickled to receive seventy-five thousand dollars from anyone, and the "anyone" in question happened to be Duggan and Bill MacBeth's pal, Big Bill Dwyer, bootlegger extraordinaire.

A native New Yorker, the corpulent Dwyer had grown up in Hell's Kitchen, the notorious neighborhood just a shout from the new Garden. Dwyer had walked the Dead End Kid route with a brief stopover at Sing Sing Penitentiary, and like others of his ilk he had seemed destined for obscurity until Prohibition arrived. In no time at all Dwyer became the foremost bootlegger in New York, then branched out into night clubs, race tracks, warehouses, and even a fleet of ships and trucks.

Dwyer had not been especially enamored of hockey, although he enjoyed sports and was anxious to embellish his image as a first-class citizen. MacBeth persuaded him that ownership of a big-league hockey team would be the ideal trapping. The seventy-five thousand dollar sale price was well worth such a significant image change, so everybody—Thompson, Duggan, MacBeth, and Dwyer—was happy.

The idea of a bootlegger entering the world of hockey didn't seem to disturb the NHL moguls one whit.

Technically, there remained one obstacle in the transfer of the Tigers to the Big Apple. Red Green and his cohorts had been fined and suspended by the NHL. Furthermore, they displayed no signs of penitence. No matter, the league realized that it now had a bonanza on its money-seeking hands. With the Tigers (redubbed the New York Americans), Pittsburgh, and Maroons in the fold, the NHL had suddenly blossomed into a seven-team international organization. Always the pragmatist, NHL President Calder conveniently forgot about the fines and suspensions. The sale of the franchise was approved in April 1925, and the Tigers were now the Americans.

"Tex Rickard," noted Andy O'Brien, "now had a rink, an ice plant, and an established team for which he hadn't paid a cent."

Of course, there was no guarantee that major league hockey would be a hit on Broadway, but Dwyer and his cohorts made a point of seeing that it couldn't miss. For starters, Rickard began lobbying with Calder to have the Canadiens, "those Flying Frenchmen from Montreal with Morenz," open the New York hockey season at his new Garden. Calder, who saw a good thing in the New York entry, was delighted to oblige. The Canadiens would meet the Americans on December 15, 1925, at the Garden.

As for the striking Tigers-Americans, they became overnight capitalists. Dwyer presented his new manager, Tommy Gorman, with a well-fortified checkbook, and Gorman, in turn, paid handsomely. During an era when most players were happy to receive a five-thousand-dollar contract, Americans players, such as Jakie Forbes and Billy Burch, among the strikers, received twenty thousand dollars for three-year contracts.

With all the players in the fold, the Americans now awaited their New York premiere. They were, in a sense, like a glamorous debutante preparing for her society debut. In fact, high society would play a major part in the grand opening of Madison Square Garden's hockey season. Rickard had ordained that it would be a black-tie affair in every way. "By donating a percentage of the proceeds to charity," O'Brien recalled, "Rickard had the social elite of New York working as ticket salesmen for the game."

The Governor General's Footguard's band, along with the marching band from the Military Academy of West Point, supplied the music. Mayor Jimmy (Beau James) Walker pumped the hands of everyone in sight, and even Great Britain's Prince of Wales donated a trophy to commemorate the occasion. The fact that the Canadiens defeated the Americans didn't seem to bother anyone. Why should it— Big Bill Dwyer invited as many as he could to a postgame champagne party to hail his—and New York's—latest toy.

In the broader sense, the Americans' arrival created a positive chain reaction in the NHL and in the hockey world in general. The new club did so well at the gate—artistically they were good, but not great—that word of hockey's popularity now spread across the forty-eight states, not to mention the Dominion of Canada. Suddenly, there was a clamoring for major league hockey. Chicago wanted it. Detroit wanted it. Philadelphia wanted it. Even Tex Rickard wanted a second team—his own, not just Dwyer's—for the Garden. Now this was a delightful state of affairs for Frank Calder and cohorts, but there was a matter of finding hockey players. This was precisely what Frank Patrick had been anticipating as he presided over the slow death of pro hockey in western Canada.

CANADA'S LOSS IS AMERICA'S GAIN

According to the blueprints of far-seeing hockey men, the overnight success of the Bruins in Boston and the Americans in New York guaranteed the eventual establishment of NHL outposts in Chicago, Detroit, Philadelphia, possibly even St. Louis and other large cities. Frank Patrick, the PCHA boss, was one such insightful entrepreneur.

Eric Whitehead, who chronicled the adventures of Frank and Lester Patrick, noted that the brothers understood, as the Roaring Twenties got under way, that they could not match the big money that now was being made available to hockey players in the east. "The power merchants were in," said Whitehead, "and the Patricks and their ilk were out, and nobody knew this better than the family that had a dollar or two at stake in this dilemma. Frank was already working on a salvage plan even as the patchwork Western Canada Hockey League embarked on its final season."

Although it once had supported a team with the best of cities, Seattle began losing interest in its club. In 1924 it was decided to build a garage on the site of the Seattle Arena, so the Metropolitans had no choice but to exit the PCHA. Now left with just the Victoria and Vancouver franchises, the Patricks merged with the Western Canada Hockey League, which comprised Regina, Calgary, Saskatoon, and Edmonton. "The Patricks," Whitehead noted, "were already plotting survival with honor, plus a few dollars cash."

Before they would make a move, the Patricks first had to survey the WCHL scene. From the viewpoint of personnel the circuit was impressive, but in terms of future growth the league betrayed no promise whatsoever.

Each of the WCHL rosters were sprinkled with players who ultimately would make their way to the Hockey Hall of Fame. Eddie Shore was an up-and-coming defenseman for Regina. Saskatoon boasted an excellent right wing named Bill Cook, and his future linemate, Frank Boucher, skated for Vancouver. Nothing said it better for the WCHL's power than the 1925 Stanley Cup playoffs. Lester Patrick's Victoria Cougars defeated the vaunted Montreal Canadiens three games to one. Nobody knew it at the time, but the WCHL was in the twilight of its brief existence.

Shortly before the 1925–26 season began, the WCHL approved the transfer of the ailing Regina franchise to Portland, Oregon, and once again the Rosebuds were alive, if not well. Unfortunately for Portland fans, the Rosebuds did not inherit Eddie Shore and Art Gagne, who certainly would have helped the gate; they were transferred to Edmonton.

Meanwhile, Patrick did everything possible to keep the league afloat, even to the point of publicly denying that the NHL players actually were receiving the substantial salaries being reported in the east. Somehow Patrick managed to obtain a confirmation from reporter Andy Lytle, who insisted that nobody was receiving a salary in excess of three-thousand dollars.

It was all academic. "It was becoming apparent," said Frank Boucher, then playing for Vancouver, "that the Canadian West couldn't—or wouldn't—support six professional teams."

All six WHL teams managed to push their way through the regular season. Victoria won the league playoff and then headed east to meet the Montreal Maroons for the westerners' last shot at the Stanley Cup. The westerners managed one win, but that was all, as the mighty Montrealers took the series in four games.

Much as he hoped his WHL skaters would emerge with one last championship, Frank Patrick had more important matters on his mind, namely, disposition of the WHL. Despite all the bluster about eastern salaries being no higher than those in the west, Frank knew different. He had resigned himself to the inevitable burgeoning of the NHL and the fact that his league would be raided bare (which he had once done to the NHA) or, at best, be in a position to sell many players to the easterners. Patrick concluded that, in either case, the WHL would irreparably be stripped of talent. His plan was to disband the entire circuit by selling all—or nearly all—players to the NHL teams, especially the new ones.

In his chronicle of the Patrick family, Eric Whitehead noted that Frank had no question as to which route to take.

> It was going to be sell all or none. I told this to the other owners, and before going East I got five of the six clubs to entrust their players to me, to do with what I thought best. As Saskatoon had already given an option on its players to the Maroons, they were not part of the arrangement. My plan was to merge the remaining five rosters into three strong teams and then sell the teams intact for $100,000 each.

To accomplish this, Patrick planned to merge the players on the Edmonton, Calgary, and Vancouver clubs as one package, while offering the Rosebuds and Victoria Cougars as separate entities. His eastern sources already had given him valuable intelligence that convinced him that he was on the right track. The Americans had done so well that another team would be invited to play at Madison Square Garden. Then there were teams bidding to move into the Chicago territory, as well as Detroit. Besides, Patrick's Montreal crony reiterated several times that he would be delighted to make a deal for any of Frank's WHL players if and when such a time came that they were on the block.

That time was not long in coming. Colonel John Hammond, who had been the first president of the New York Americans, resigned the post after the 1925–26 season and was deputized by Madison Square Garden boss Tex Rickard to visit Montreal and obtain another NHL franchise for New York. In Chicago, businessman Tack Hardwick and Major Frederic McLaughlin were actively pursuing a franchise for the Windy City and seemed oblivious to the cost, even if it exceeded $100,000. Not far away in Detroit a syndicate including tycoon James Norris and Charles Hughes was dickering for a team. Frank Patrick couldn't have been more pleased. When all the wheeling and dealing was over, Canadian hockey had suffered an irreparable loss of talent, teams, and prestige, and American business-men began their relentless takeover of the NHL.

With considerable help from Art Ross and Bruins' owner Charles Adams, the Hardwick–McLaughlin combine was persuaded to purchase the Portland players, and the Detroit contingent did likewise with the remains of the Victoria team. Both of the new clubs had some significant additions from the other WHL teams. Ross, who had been the very first to bid for WHL players, was not forgotten. The Bruins would receive a handsome group of stick handlers from Vancouver as well as the other teams, including Eddie Shore, who would, almost singlehandedly, put Boston on the hockey map. The sum total, which Patrick received on behalf of the now defunct WHL, was $317,000, not counting the $60,000 that had been delivered independently to the Saskatoon team.

The WHL quietly folded its tent, but not without protest from Canadian interests who, with the chauvinism typical of the time, realized that their national game was moving south with a vengeance. One such critic was D'Alton Coleman, vice-president of the Canadian Pacific Railway and, as such, one of the most powerful figures in the Dominion. When Coleman heard rumblings about the WHL's immediate interment, he rushed forward with a lend-lease plan that would, for the time being, keep it in Canada. But Patrick's negotiations had advanced beyond the point of no return, and big-league hockey would vacate western Canada until 1970, when the Vancouver Canucks were admitted to the expanding NHL.

Significantly, only one of the new American teams refused to do business with Frank Patrick. As it happened, that stonewalling turned into a bonus for brother Lester. The Rangers, then unnamed, happened to be that club. Frank Patrick thought he could land it, but Colonel Hammond, now boss of the fledgling club, had other ideas.

Colonel Hammond believed that Patrick's $100,000 asking price for one of the WHL packages was far too steep. Instead, he hired an aggressive young Toronto hockey promoter named Conn Smythe to recruit players for Tex Rickard's new team. "I knew every hockey player in the world right then," said Smythe.

One by one, Smythe visited players who, he believed, would blossom into big-leaguers. He signed goalie Lorne Chabot from Port Arthur, Ontario, and headed for Minnesota where two solid defensemen, Taffy Abel and Ching Johnson, had earned headlines for their reputable play. The difficulty Smythe had in signing Johnson is indicative of the labors he put in for the Rangers when the other American clubs were content to settle for groups of players at a large sticker price.

"I must have reached agreement with Ching Johnson forty times," Smythe remembered. "Each time, when I gave him my pen to sign, he'd say, 'I just want to

1-3 *The early Boston Bruins teams were bolstered by the stout play of George Owen. Photo courtesy of the U.S. Hockey Hall of Fame.*

phone my wife.' Then there'd be a hitch and he wouldn't sign. In my final meeting with him I said before we started, 'Ching, I want you to promise that if we make a deal you will sign, and *then* you'll phone your wife.' He promised. We made a deal. He said, 'I've got to phone my wife.' I said, 'You promised!' He said, 'Okay, Connie,' and signed."

Signing Abel was no simpler. The big defenseman refused Smythe's terms over and over. In desperation, the Rangers' representative invited Abel to his Pullman compartment and made another offer. Abel nixed that as well, just as the train began rolling slowly out of the station. Smythe leaped from his seat and locked the Pullman door before the flabbergasted Abel could run for it.

"Taffy," demanded Smythe, "the money's good, you won't do better, and the next stop is two hundred and fifty miles away. If you don't sign, you won't be getting off this train until then."

Abel put his pen on the dotted line, shook hands with Smythe, Smythe unbolted the door, and Taffy leaped off the train. This was the only known player Smythe signed behind a locked Pullman door, but he used the railways to advantage on other occasions.

A few months before the 1926–27 season was to begin, Smythe learned that the Montreal Maroons were anxious to sign the brothers Bill and Bun Cook, who had starred for Saskatoon in the WHL. Someone tipped off Smythe that the Cooks were coming east by train to huddle with James Strachan, the boss of the Maroons. "I intercepted them in Winnipeg," said Smythe, "and signed them for bonuses totaling $5,000!"

One by one Smythe amassed a team he thought would put Tex Rickard's Rangers on a competitive par with the other new NHL entries, not to mention some of the established clubs. And all he had spent was $32,000, compared with the $100,000 price tag his competitors had approved for their packages. One reason for the bargain-basement price was Smythe's tough bargaining position coupled with the fact that many of the players were relatively unknown minor leaguers. Smythe implicitly believed they would pay off for New York—his faith later was justified—but others had gained Colonel Hammond's ear. They told him that Smythe was wasting Tex Rickard's money on amateurs who would not be able to cut the ice in the NHL.

"I wasn't worried," said Smythe. "I knew the caliber of our team, but Colonel Hammond didn't."

The last straw, in Hammond's estimation, was Smythe's refusal to sign Babe Dye, who had starred for the Toronto St. Pats and now was being offered to the new New York club. When Smythe passed on Dye, Chicago's new Black Hawks immediately contracted him, and more of Colonel Hammond's advisors began bad-mouthing Smythe. "I guess," Smythe recalled, "Colonel Hammond thought he'd better replace me with someone more likely to do what he was told."

Actually, it was Rickard who decided to can Smythe—he didn't think Smythe had enough class for the socialites who were frequenting New York hockey games—and replace him with Lester Patrick, who was signed for eighteen thousand dollars a year. It developed into an extraordinarily fortuitous move for Rickard, his Rangers, and the NHL in general.

Frank Boucher recalled, "I've often wondered about the kind of hockey club the Rangers would have become had Lester Patrick not replaced Conn Smythe. Certainly, in our first decade at least, we'd have been a vastly different one. Through that whole period there was a great comradeship and a maturity that could not have been possible under Smythe the martinet. Smythe ruled by the sword; Lester had discipline but he was one of us, too. Smythe could never have been."

Only one hockey figure was disenchanted with the arrival of the Rangers, and that was Big Bill Dwyer. When Duggan originally peddled the NHL franchise to the notorious bootlegger, Dwyer never thought about reading the fine print in the contract, which turned out to be an egregious mistake. The unread clause would, ultimately, lead to the death of the New York Americans.

Somewhere in the clutter of verbiage was a proviso that another NHL franchise would be permitted in New York if the league received an acceptable offer. When

Colonel Hammond informed Dwyer that the Rangers would be accepted into the fold, the bootlegger was suitably livid. "If that's the case," he snapped at his former employee, "my contract isn't worth the paper it is written on."

This was to be the start of a magnificent rivalry between the two New York clubs, one that would last for sixteen years. Dwyer's protestations notwithstanding, the Rangers opened amid suitable pomp and circumstance at the Garden one year after the New York Americans had laid the groundwork for professional hockey in the Big Apple.

Once again, hockey was a four-star hit. In his autobiography, *When the Rangers Were Young*, Frank Boucher described the feeling he had on opening night at the Garden. "When I stood at the blueline lofting warmup shots at our goaltender Hal Winkler, I was edgy and nervous. The crowd was still coming in. Down close to the boxes, women were wearing furs and evening dress; their men were natty in tuxedos. High up in the balcony above the mezzanine the smoke was already building a haze."

The Rangers opened against the Stanley Cup champion Maroons and, that day, one of the local dailies headlined the attraction in less than ecstatic terms for the home team: "World's Best Meets World's Worst Tonight in Garden."

Comely Lois Moran, a film starlet, walked to center ice as seventeen thousand fans watched her drop the puck between Boucher and his center-ice foe, Nels Stewart. The following day Ed Sullivan, writing in his "Talk of the Town" column in the *Daily News*, noted that the slim, blond Miss Moran was not the only beauty in attendance. "Miss Moran," wrote Sullivan, "was in the elegant company of Mayor Jimmy Walker and his beauteous companion of the evening, actress Betty Compton."

The Walker–Compton–Moran party was delighted as the Rangers carved out a pulsating 1–0 victory over the champions. "As we plodded toward the dressing room," Boucher recalled, "the crowd was standing in the Garden's three tiers pounding their hands together, noisy, grinning, happy."

Both Smythe and Lester Patrick had reason to grin. The former had, indeed, molded a splendid hockey club out of a number of heretofore anonymous skaters, whereas the latter had orchestrated a marvelous hockey symphony on Broadway. The Rangers, to the great good fortune of the NHL, were first-rate from the opening face-off to the final game. Bill Cook, one of Smythe's top choices, emerged as the league's leading scorer.

More important, in terms of the future images of the two teams, the Rangers were clearly superior to Bill Dwyer's Americans. The Patrickmen finished first in the American Division with twenty-five wins, thirteen losses, and six ties, whereas the Americans wound up fourth in the Canadian Division, producing but seventeen wins, twenty-five losses, and two ties.

From that point on the Rangers developed an aura of aristocracy, and their colorful Garden cousins, the Americans, took on the trappings of the clown princes of hockey. It would be that way until the Americans finally made their last exit

1-4
Lester Patrick smiles as he studies the photos of his three Stanley Cup champion hockey teams, the Rangers of 1927–28, 1932–33, and 1939–40. Patrick was one of the most significant innovators in the game.

1-5 *During the early days in the NHL, it was not uncommon for the goalie to wear a hat. Here Andy Aitkenhead of the New York Rangers makes a save against the Detroit Red Wings.*

from the NHL in 1942, victims of World War II and shabby treatment from their Garden landlords who owned the Rangers.

Although the New York fans adored professional hockey—two NHL teams were now being supported with grand crowds—the same could not be said for the media. To many American-born members of the press, weaned on baseball, football, and basketball, the icemen from Canada were baffling, to say the least. Others were not quite sure what to make of it and remained skeptical to the end. Such a critic was Paul Gallico, the influential columnist of the *Daily News*. Gallico allowed that hockey was harder and tougher than football, but he could not get himself to admit that he had become a fan of the imported game.

Fortunately for the NHL, for every Gallico there was a supporter of the sport among the press. John Kieran, the influential columnist of the *New York Times*, was one of hockey's foremost boosters.

They were taking hockey with no less enthusiasm in Chicago and Detroit, where mammoth new arenas soon would replace the older buildings used to showcase the game. A report in the *Chicago Herald and Examiner* waxed lyrical about the Black Hawks and the game they played.

> The fastest game Chicago has seen since the ember-laden winds of '71 raced with the fire department was witnessed last night at the Coliseum. Pro ice hockey is faster than horse racing, dog racing and pugilistic punch telegraphy. Lightning itself with an Ederle coat of grease has to be stepped up to compete with Eskimo Polo as demonstrated last evening.

As for the net minder, the Chicago hockey critic was less enthusiastic: "The goaler has the laziest job next to the foreman of an ice-cutting gang on the Panama Canal. He's padded worse than some political payrolls. All he has to do is spread himself and he can stop the puck—but it is a contest between puck and luck."

Hockey's missionaries were doing their job in the United States. Between the Cooks, Boucher, and the zany Americans, hockey was set in New York. Eddie Shore guaranteed Boston's love affair with the Bruins. George Hay turned on the Detroit fans, and Dick Irvin, before suffering a crippling injury, wooed the Chicago rooters. Only Pittsburgh limped along without true fan fervor and, eventually, dropped out of the league.

Big-league hockey was in the United States to stay. In 1926–27 the NHL had ten teams, and only four of them were from Canada.

THE NHL'S FIRST GOLDEN ERA

Except for a few minor aberrations, the National Hockey League's expansion into the United States illuminated the first truly golden era of the professional game. The ice game was so successful in Chicago that a mammoth arena—the largest in the league at the time—was erected on West Madison Street, called the Chicago Stadium. An equally impressive structure was built at the corner of Grand River and McGraw in Detroit—Olympia Stadium.

The Boston Bruins, Uncle Sam's first NHL entry, played four years in the undersized Boston Arena until the clamor for tickets was such that a new building had to be built to accommodate them. Curiously, the new Hub hockey palace was originally named Boston Madison Square Garden. It opened on November 20, 1928, in riotous fashion.

The "Gahden," as they called it in Boston, had a seating capacity of 13,900 for its world premiere, yet somehow a larger number managed to filter through the turnstiles. Writing in the *Boston Herald*, columnist Stanley Woodward described the maniacal tableau. "It was a riot, a mob scene, reenaction of the assault on the Bastille. It is estimated that 17,500 persons, 3,000 in excess of the supposed capacity of the Garden, saw the game."

Oddly enough, Toronto, one of the best hockey cities on the continent, was one of the last NHL cities to be graced with a full-sized rink. Conn Smythe, who returned to Toronto after being bounced out of the New York Rangers job, eventually assumed control of the St. Pats and had the name changed to the Maple Leafs. He then went about the business of building a formidable rink, but appeared thwarted on all sides because the Great Depression persuaded most businessmen to sidestep such frivolous projects as sports arenas.

Undaunted, Smythe plunged forward in 1930, determined to have Maple Leaf Gardens erected and ready for customers for the 1931–32 season. There were, of course, many setbacks. "As the Depression deepened," Smythe remembered, "some people who had committed themselves couldn't come up with the money."

But Smythe kept finding others who would, and work on the building began five months before the 1931–32 season was to begin. Experts in the construction business could not imagine the arena would be ready for play, but on November 12, 1931, the Chicago Black Hawks and Toronto Maple Leafs lined up at center ice, just as Smythe had promised.

Smythe: "When the Black Hawks came to town a day before the grand opening, there were still some finishing touches being done. But on the night of November 12, 1931, when the bands of the 48th Highlanders and the Royal Grenadiers marched out on the ice and played 'Happy Days Are Here Again,' the scene was pretty much as I had imagined it in my rosiest dreams."

Artistically, the dreams were getting better all the time. Superstars were sprouting in every corner of the league. Boston had Eddie Shore, "the Edmonton Express." The Rangers proudly displayed the fabulous line of the Cook brothers and Frank Boucher. Toronto countered with its dazzling "Kid Line," with Joe Primeau, Busher Jackson, and Charlie Conacher. The Americans produced a minuscule goalie, appropriately dubbed "Shrimp" Worters, and the Maroons traumatized goaltenders with Nels (Ole Poison) Stewart. They all sold hockey as never before, but one among them proved the most galvanic of stick handlers, the metaphor for hockey as it embarked on its first golden era, and that was Howie Morenz.

A typical Morenz performance was delivered in 1930 when the Canadiens were playing the Senators in Ottawa. Howie had been sidelined with a painful ankle injury, but nevertheless asked coach Cecil Hart if he could dress and sit on the bench. The request was granted, and Morenz watched as his club fell behind 4–2 with only six minutes remaining. "Let me get into the game," Morenz implored Hart.

The coach was dubious about the possibility of his star's aggravating his injury, but Morenz forced the issue, and before Hart could stop him, Howie was on the ice. On his first shift he blasted through the Ottawa defense and set up linemate Aurel Joliat for Montreal's third goal. Now there were five minutes remaining. Baz O'Meara, sports editor of the *Montreal Star*, recalled:

> Canadiens swarmed to the attack, and the puck spun loose as Alex Smith of Ottawa batted it to the blue line and raced after it fully twenty feet ahead of the nearest Canadien, who was Morenz. Flashing on his skates, his bad ankle forgotten, Howie cut down the twenty feet to ten as Smith hit the defence zone. Then fairly hurling himself forward on his skates Howie reached ahead to top Smith's stick just as the latter shot.
>
> The puck went wide, behind the net. Howie kept his momentum and circled the net in a blurring flash, passing Smith before the amazed Ottawa star had a chance to set himself for the return rush. Morenz was now a meteor—the full length of the ice, through the disorganized Ottawa defence alignment which was now watching Joliat, in on goal, and finishing with a blasting shot that could have torn the head off a sphinx.
>
> The game went into overtime. Morenz was all over the ice. You could sense what was coming—and it did. Morenz broke up the game with the 5–4 goal. The hostile crowd broke into a storm of cheers—for years Ottawa talked about that game Morenz had played.

Morenz didn't guarantee sellouts everywhere, but he ensured headlines for hockey wherever he played. The roots planted when the NHL began its grand expansion in the mid-1920s took firm hold in the 1930s, with a few exceptions. New York with its two teams, Boston, Detroit, and Chicago had become hotbeds of the sport. The same was true of Toronto and Montreal, the latter of which also

1-6 *United States–born Bill Stewart, who doubled as a National League baseball umpire, led the Chicago Black Hawks to a Stanley Cup in 1938. Photo courtesy of the U.S. Hockey Hall of Fame.*

boasted two teams. Through the Great Depression hockey thrived in these key cities. "The brand of electricity generated by Morenz shocked the new rinks of the United States," said Canadian author Andy O'Brien. "American fans now had a tingling awareness of a pulsating 'imported' sport."

Morenz and Company could not guarantee success for every NHL franchise, either in the United States or Canada. Pittsburgh, St. Louis, Philadelphia, and Ottawa had brief flirtations with the NHL and failed. The Maroons, once the proudest name in hockey, couldn't survive the 1930s, leaving Montreal with only the Canadiens.

Precisely when the golden era ended is a moot point. Many respected critics believe that the curtain fell in the mid-1930s. Morenz began slowing down and was dealt to the Black Hawks in 1934. The Cooks and Boucher also were skating in three-quarter time, and the Maple Leafs' Kid Line weren't kids anymore. The Black Hawks surprised the NHL in 1938, winning the Stanley Cup while coached by baseball umpire Bill Stewart.

The decade of the 1930s ended with the NHL still rather robust. Although the league had trimmed down to seven teams—Rangers, Americans, Maple Leafs, Canadiens, Bruins, Black Hawks, and Red Wings—an influx of new, vibrant players promised another ten years of excitement and good box office. A dynamic Bruins club won the Stanley Cup in April 1939, powered by the Kraut Line of Milt Schmidt, Bobby Bauer, and Woody Dumart with an American, Frankie (Mister Zero) Brimsek, starring in goal. But between April and September, when the NHL next convened, World War II had erupted, and pro hockey, for the next decade at least, would not be the same.

THE NHL GOES TO WAR

On September 1, 1939, the Nazi army crossed the Polish border, igniting World War II. Just nineteen days later the NHL governors convened to consider the effects the conflict would have on their operations. "It was resolved," commented the NHL history, "that for the time being operations should be carried on in a manner as close as possible to normal, with due regard to economy and matters of expenditure."

While the rest of the world watched anxiously to determine just how widespread and intense the European conflict would be, the NHL proceeded with business as usual. The Bruins finished first, but the Rangers dispatched them from the playoffs and marched on to their third Stanley Cup. Ironically, Colonel John Hammond, the man who helped steer them into the league, died in mid-season before his Blueshirts could deliver the silverware to Broadway.

When the NHL governors huddled again in September 1940, the war, still not fully heated up, seemed a tangential item not to be taken too seriously. Expansion was again on the owners' mind and, this time, they looked to Buffalo as a potential site, awaiting conclusion of a study on the possibility of adding an eighth team. Once again the Bruins topped the league, but this time they powered their way to the Stanley Cup, winning four straight over Detroit in the finals.

Bootlegger Big Bill Dwyer had long since passed from the scene, leaving the New York Americans with a painful string of debts. The club had been annexed by former defense star Red Dutton, the son of a wealthy construction magnate. Dutton kept the Americans in business through the 1941–42 season, after it had become apparent that the Madison Square Garden Corporation no longer welcomed the "Amerks," as they had come to be called. Undaunted, Dutton produced a number of promising young players and renamed his club the Brooklyn Americans, although it still was based in Madison Square Garden. "I had hoped," said Dutton, "that some businessmen would follow through on their plans to build a competing arena in Brooklyn."

But all bets were off on December 7, 1941, when the Japanese bombed Pearl Harbor. World War II became a global conflict, and the NHL's life was on the line. On January 18 the first tremors were felt when Woody Dumart of the Bruins and Don Metz of the Maple Leafs received their calls from the Canadian Army. Muzz and Lynn Patrick of the Rangers enlisted in the U.S. Army, and one by one the teams were stripped of their stars. The Rangers, who finished the 1941–42 season in first place, were hardest hit of all, losing Neil and Mac Colville, Alex Shibicky, and Dudley (Red) Garrett to the armed forces. Garrett, a promising youngster, was killed in action. The Black Hawks soon lost their fine young goalie Sam LoPresti when he enlisted in the U.S. Naval Armed Guard.

The one pleasing distraction was the 1942 Stanley Cup finals, during which the Maple Leafs, trailing the Red Wings three games to none, became the first team in history to rebound by winning four consecutive matches and, of course, the cup.

Long before the 1943–44 season got under way there was considerable sentiment to have the NHL suspend operations for the duration of the war. The New York Americans, hard hit by the draft, were forced to suspend operations, although Dutton was assured that the Amerks could relocate in the proposed Brooklyn rink at war's end. At a league meeting in September 1942 NHL President Frank Calder rejected suggestions by others that the league padlock its doors.

So, carry on it did—just barely. The Rangers, who had been the class of the league, plummeted headlong into the basement. Lester Patrick's once-proud Blueshirts were demolished during the war years by such outrageous scores as 15–0 (this one with Lester Patrick himself behind the bench), 12–2, and 10–1. The Stanley Cup champion Maple Leafs also were crippled by the draft and were forced to insert an ulcer-riddled rookie named Frank McCool in the nets. Draft rejects and NHL retreads joined fuzzy-cheeked kids as teams desperately attempted to remain competitive while their stars fought the Axis powers.

As if the NHL didn't have enough troubles, it found itself without a president in January 1943 when Frank Calder died. Red Dutton was named his replacement until the war ended.

The Red Wings finished first in 1942–43 and swept to the Stanley Cup. Despite the low caliber of play, fans filled the rinks throughout the league. They appeared to enjoy the new corps of characters and didn't mind a bit when an oldtimer like Frank Boucher came out of retirement at forty-two or an eccentric like Ulcers McCool allowed a goal. "Every game was a life-and-death struggle for McCool," Maple Leafs publicist Ed Fitkin remembered. "He sipped milk in the dressing room between periods to calm his fluttering stomach. There were times when he

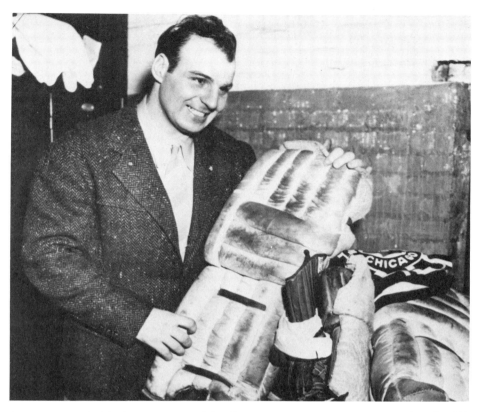

1-7   Sam LoPresti holds the NHL record for the most saves in a game by a goaltender. He starred for the Chicago Black Hawks and later was a hero in World War II. Photo courtesy of the U.S. Hockey Hall of Fame.

took sick during a game—but one thing about him, he'd never quit." He also was voted rookie of the year in 1944–45.

Two significant changes in the conduct of hockey games took place during the war years—sudden-death overtime was abolished, except for playoff games, and the center red line was introduced.

During the war thousands upon thousands of trains had to be diverted to haul servicemen and war-related goods, and as a result hockey teams could not travel with the ease they had enjoyed in peacetime. It had become increasingly difficult for teams to catch trains after particularly lengthy matches, and overtime simply aggravated the situation. It was agreed to dispense with the extra session—at least until hostilities had ceased. (Once the war ended, the league decided against reinstituting overtime, primarily on the grounds that the fans were receiving their money's worth from three periods of hockey. Demands for resumption of regular season overtime were made in each decade after World War II, but the NHL continually rejected them until 1983 when a proposal to renew the extra period for five minutes was accepted.

Introduction of the center red line came about as part of a general reassessment of all league rules. Until then the NHL book of regulations was a shabby affair that one official described as being close to incomprehensible. "The book had no index," he said, "there were repetitions and contradictions, and there were even different penalties for the same rule infraction." President Red Dutton named Frank Boucher to the position of rules revisionist and, after much painstaking work, a new, revised rule book was accepted by the league. By far its most significant addition was the addition of the center red line, which was a product of hockey's rapidly changing style.

Prior to the start of World War II, defensemen traditionally positioned themselves about halfway between the goalie and the blue line, where they would attempt to thwart the enemy with bodychecks or stickchecks. Now a new trend was developing in defensive play whereby the backliners were becoming more daringly mobile and began moving ahead of the blue line to intercept the foe.

During the 1942 Stanley Cup finals between the Maple Leafs and the Red Wings, the first major alteration in offensive strategy—to counteract the new defensive formations—was made. Coached by wily Jack Adams, the Red Wings began to shoot the puck into the corners of the rink *behind* the Toronto defenders and then chase in to retrieve it while the partially immobilized Leafs attempted to regroup. "For a time," said Boucher, "only the three forwards moved in, but then their own defensemen began to follow, realizing that once they got the puck into the end zone it was just about impossible for the defending team to get it out."

Employing that technique, the Red Wings came close to upsetting the stronger Maple Leafs, and all the hockey world took note. (At the time, it should be noted, forward passing from one zone to the next was still illegal.) As a result of the new strategy, lengthy jamming sessions took place in front of the net, and the end-to-end rushes, which had so captivated the fans, became less apparent. Officials became concerned about the possible loss of spectator appeal and ordered a rethinking on the matter.

Boucher proposed a revolutionary change that would permit forward passing from zone to zone, even allowing a defending team to pass the puck all the way to the enemy blue line. Critics insisted that that was going too far. "If one blue line's too near," explained Boucher, "and the other's too far, what about halfway between? We can put a line at center ice and we'll paint it red to avoid confusion."

The red line rule, adopted in September 1943, for all intents and purposes heralded the first modern era in professional hockey. The immediate result was an increase in the number of breakaways as defensemen who had been playing too far up the ice were now trapped by long passes. Then defensemen made adjustments and the former ebb and flow of the play returned, although goal scoring was evidently on the rise.

By war's end all teams had acclimated themselves to the red line, and many players adapted to it by devising new offensive tricks that would, over the next decade, further change the face of the game.

But in 1945, at least, all eyes were on Europe and the Pacific where the war finally was reaching its climax. Germany and Japan surrendered to the Allies and the former NHL stars began returning to their respective teams in the hopes of recapturing past glory. One of them was Lynn Patrick, who had enlisted as a first lieutenant in the U.S. Army military police. Lynn showed up at his dad's Madison Square Garden office one day and snapped, "Well, Lester, here I am. I need work."

Like so many other NHL manager, Patrick hoped that his returning veterans had not lost their skills. The Rangers, in particular, had a major investment in those who were being mustered out. The Patrick brothers, Lynn and Muzz, the Colvilles, Neil and Mac, Alex Shibicky, Alf Pike, Bryan Hextall, and Bill Juzda all rejoined the Broadway Blueshirts. For the most part it was a case of you can't go home again. Only Neil Colville and Juzda displayed a semblance of big-league luster; the others had irrevocably lost it during the war. One surprise was American-born Bill Moe from Danvers, Massachusetts.

The same scenario was being enacted in the other five NHL cities, where players such as Frank Brimsek, Bobby Bauer, and Johnny Mariucci discovered that their skills had rusted beyond redemption. It was time for a new order, and the one team best prepared for the postwar era was the Maple Leafs. The foresight of manager Conn Smythe would result in the league's first true dynasty, the Toronto sextet from 1947 through 1951.

AMERICAN HOCKEY AND WORLD WAR II

The quality of hockey played in the United States was reaching new heights when Uncle Sam went to war in 1941. Frankie Brimsek from Eveleth, Minnesota, had emerged as the best goaltender in the NHL, and fellow Minnesotan Johnny Mariucci had become the bedrock of the Chicago Black Hawks' defense. A few years earlier the Black Hawks had won the Stanley Cup with a number of American-born skaters playing predominant roles. A New York–born referee, Bill Chadwick, had launched a big-league career that would ultimately win him a niche in the Hall of Fame, and the game was extending its roots throughout the country, not simply in the Northeast and Minnesota.

"In Hollywood," said Richard Vaughan, "while bathing beauties basked on the sand, the University of Southern California played a city rival in a championship game, with some 5,000 jammed into the rink and another 5,000 turned away for

1-8 A native of Danvers, Massachusetts, defenseman Bill Moe was a master of the hip check. Photo courtesy of the U.S. Hockey Hall of Fame.

lack of room. In Texas ice is no longer a curiosity, and cowboys with their ten-gallon sombreros lean back and get excited about the newest game in the Southwest, ice hockey."

New York City offered hockey on the public and parochial high school levels in addition to the fast Metropolitan League, featuring the Sands Point Tigers, Jamaica Hawks, New York Exchange Brokers, and Manhattan Arrows. Sunday afternoon amateur games at Madison Square Garden averaged more than three hundred thousand cash customers a season.

Likewise, minor professional hockey was thriving throughout Minnesota and other parts of the Midwest and Northeast. American-born players helped keep these leagues in business.

When President Franklin Delano Roosevelt asked Congress to declare war, many of these players were called up by their draft boards, and the fabric of hockey in the United States was torn asunder. One by one the American-born players in the various leagues put aside hockey uniforms and picked up guns. Surprisingly, the minor leagues did not fold up with the advent of war but, rather, adjusted. The Eastern League operated throughout the war with the New York Rovers, Boston Olympics, Philadelphia Falcons, and Washington Lions as the nucleus of its roster. Teenaged Canadians, still too young to be drafted, staffed many of the teams and proved to be popular attractions.

But by far the most intriguing American hockey team to flourish during the war years was one bearing the insignia of the United States Coast Guard. American hockey has never known another team like them and, no doubt, never will.

The Coast Guard team came from Eveleth, Winnipeg, Sault Ste. Marie, and New York City. They included a goalie called Mister Zero, a menacing Italian-Jewish defense combination, the captain of the last New York Rangers Stanley Cup–winners, a National Hockey League referee, and a graduate of the Long Island City YMCA Roller Hockey League.

They comprised the best blend of amateur and professional hockey players ever to represent Uncle Sam—with a couple of Canadians thrown in—and they had a pair of championships to prove it. Of all things, they were called the U.S. Coast Guard Cutters out of Curtis Bay, Maryland.

The brainstorm of a former Michigan hockey player turned sailor, the Cutters were organized after the Japanese attacked Pearl Harbor. They played through the 1942–43 and 1943–44 seasons in the minor but mighty good Eastern Amateur Hockey League. They also played a number of exhibition games, and at Carlin's Iceland in Baltimore, their home rink, the Cutters went head-on against the Stanley Cup champion Detroit Red Wings.

Although they were involved in only two full campaigns, the Cutters detonated more fights, filled more seats, and generally raised more hell than the Eastern League had ever known. "There was nothing like them, before or since," says Hartford Whalers boss Emile Francis, who was strafed by the Cutters while goaltending for the Philadelphia Falcons.

Ironically, the Cutters' most intense competition was among themselves. "Our intrasquad games," says former Coast Guard star Bob Gilray, "were like bloody massacres."

A special ambiance surrounded the Cutters wherever they played. They wore unusual red-white-and-blue, star-spangled jerseys with crossed anchors emblazoned on the front and, unlike any other hockey club, they were accompanied by a thirty-piece marching band providing razzmatazz at every game. "Whenever we scored," says Mike Nardello, a onetime roller hockey ace, "they'd strike up *Semper Paratus,* the Coast Guard marching song."

Nardello was in select company. Hall of Famer Frank (Mister Zero) Brimsek,

1-9
Dubbed Mister Zero, Frankie Brimsek went from Eveleth, Minnesota, to the Boston Bruins, where he established himself as one of the greatest goalies of all time. Photo courtesy of the U.S. Hockey Hall of Fame.

1-10   *Although he originally made his mark as a football star at the University of Minnesota, Johnny Mariucci became an ace on the Chicago Black Hawks defense. Photo courtesy of the U.S. Hockey Hall of Fame.*

1-11
Enshrined in the U.S. Hockey Hall of Fame, Hubert (Hub) Nelson was a member of the Coast Guard Cutters championship team in 1943 and 1944. Photo courtesy of the U.S. Hockey Hall of Fame.

1-12
United States–born ace Eddie Olson starred for the Cleveland Barons after World War II. During the war, he was a member of the famed Coast Guard Cutters hockey team. Photo courtesy of the U.S. Hockey Hall of Fame.

who orchestrated the Boston Bruins to a 1941 Stanley Cup title, was one of three superb goalies on the Cutters, along with Muzz Murray and Hub Nelson.

The Coast Guard defense bristled with ex-Rangers Captain Art Coulter and Alex Motter of the Red Wings, as well as the terrifying tandem of Chicago Black Hawks bruiser Johnny Mariucci and Manny Cotlow, a Jewish defenseman who would just as soon eat railroad spikes as T-bone steaks.

"Manny," says his former teammate Bob Gilray, "was responsible for one of the biggest riots in hockey history."

The eruption occurred at the Philadelphia Arena after Cotlow and Marty Madore of the Falcons clashed on the ice and, again, in the penalty box. A posse of Philadelphia fans ambushed Cotlow, thereby inspiring a counterattack by Cotlow and Bob Dill. Another battle started on the ice with the officials soon on their knees in hand-to-hand combat with players of both teams. A police riot squad was required to subdue the battlers.

Much as they reveled in rough play, the Cutters didn't have to fight to win. The line of Gilray, Joe Kucler, and Eddie Olson delivered a formidable offense and provided endless joy for Lieutenant Commander C. R. MacLean, a former player from Sault Ste. Marie, who fathered the team in 1942.

Personnel officer at the Curtis Bay Coast Guard Yard, MacLean encouraged American-born hockey players to join his unit. The Canadian-born Coulter was an exception. He had always wanted to obtain American citizenship and seized the opportunity when war broke out. The Ranger stalwart enlisted in "Hooligan's Navy," joined the Cutters, and became a naturalized American citizen.

In time MacLean had so many stick handlers that he divided the Cutters into two teams—the Clippers and Cutters—who competed against each other when they weren't involved in Eastern League action. They once played a brutal four-game series, which Cotlow describes as "the most physical games of my life." George Taylor, writing in the *Baltimore News-Post*, observed: "The rubber tilt was more exciting than the Stanley Cup playoffs."

When the Clippers and Cutters united against the common ice foe they were virtually unbeatable, winning the U.S. National Senior Open championship of the Amateur Hockey Association in 1943 and 1944. Former NHL referee Mel Harwood coached the Coast Guard skaters on both occasions.

For diversion the Cutters would play exhibition games against strong Canadian service teams liberally sprinkled with pros and invariably beat them. In a contest against the powerful Ottawa Commandos, led by ex-Rangers stars Neil Colville and Alex Shibicky, as well as Joe Cooper of the Black Hawks, the Cutters triumphed, 5–2.

The only downer was a game against the 1943 Stanley Cup champion Red Wings on January 6, 1944, before a capacity crowd in Baltimore. With Brimsek in goal the Cutters hung tough until well into the third period—they trailed 4–3—but were ultimately shellacked, 8–3. "They didn't intimidate us," assures Cotlow, sixty-eight, now retired in Crystal, Minnesota, "but they were a little smarter."

Despite the Cutters' popularity in Boston and New York, where they regularly drew crowds of more than twelve thousand, they were criticized in some quarters and finally were disbanded in 1944. "A lot of parents of servicemen couldn't understand why their sons were overseas fighting while we were still playing hockey," says Kucler. "The Coast Guard was under a lot of pressure to break us up."

The end was in sight one afternoon when an announcement blared over the Madison Square Garden public address system while the Cutters were playing the New York Rovers. Kucler, the club's leading scorer, was ordered to report for action after the match. Olsen, later an off-ice official at NHL games in St. Louis, recalled the end of the Cutters. "They said that Joe was playing his last game for us and then would be shipping out. As soon as Joe left they began getting rid of the other guys, and by then we knew the honeymoon was over."

After the war Coulter retired, but Mariucci and Brimsek returned to play several years in the NHL, and others, such as Nardello, played minor league hockey. "I kept wearing my jersey," says Nardello, "because it always gave me the feeling that those great guys—Cotlow, Kucler and the rest—were somehow around for another chorus of *Semper Paratus*."

THE ROCKET IGNITES THE POSTWAR ERA

At a time when Joe DiMaggio and Ted Williams were activating baseball fans in the years immediately following World War II, professional hockey received a similar jolt from a pair of extraordinarily gifted and singularly different forwards. Maurice (the Rocket) Richard of the Montreal Canadiens and Gordie Howe of the Detroit Red Wings, both right wings, were to the NHL in the late 1940s and early 1950s what Howie Morenz had been to an earlier era.

Richard came first, joining the Canadiens during World War II. Like Morenz before him, the Rocket—almost all the fans in Canada and the United States came to know him by his nickname—arrested attention the moment he stepped on the ice. But he had dimensions to his game that Morenz never possessed. In addition to his relentless speed, Richard had a leonine quality to match his enormous strength. Conn Smythe, one of the most insightful appraisers of hockey talent, perceived the greatness in Richard the very first night he laid eyes upon him. Smythe recalled the episode in his memoirs:

> It was a 1–1 tie and Rocket got the Montreal goal. He went in from the blue line with a big defenseman draped all over him on one side and Johnny Gottselig draped all over him on the other. Still the Rocket walked in, pulled the goalkeeper, and put the puck in the net.

Although the smallish Morenz was more apt to absorb physical abuse without retaliation, Richard was more apt to respond with a left and a right and ask questions later. One night the Rocket was challenged by New York Rangers defenseman Bob (Killer) Dill, a notorious slugger. The Rocket dismissed Dill with a rapid right to the jaw. When Dill was scraped off the ice and led to the penalty box, he challenged Richard to a rematch—on the spot. Before awaiting a reply, Dill swung hard but couldn't dislodge the Rocket from his pins. Dan Daniel, who covered the game for the *New York World-Telegram*, summed up the scene: "Here Maurice the Mauler once again measured his man. Roberto suffered a cut left eye and other bruises and contusions."

Apart from his fire and brimstone, Richard's foremost weapons were his shots, both forehand and backhand. A left-handed shot who nevertheless patrolled right wing, Richard owned the most devastating backhand in hockey. During the

1944–45 season he made modern hockey history by scoring fifty goals in fifty games, and this despite defenders who assaulted him in every conceivable manner.

"No player in hockey history has been so illegally shackled and interfered with by a host of personal checkers and shadows as Richard," said Canadian hockey critic Bill Roche. "Small wonder that he occasionally blows his top. Maurice should know a lot about the sour science of wrestling, for he has had nearly all the headlocks, arm scissors, and other grips and grabs applied to him in ice action."

The Rocket brushed his attackers aside and entered the postwar era with all guns blazing. Those who thought he might have been a wartime phenomenon, who would fizzle when the prewar aces returned, were sadly mistaken. He beat the best of them, including Hall of Famer Frankie (Mister Zero) Brimsek, who was playing goal for the Boston Bruins at the time.

"The Rocket," said Brimsek, "can shoot from *any* angle. You play him for a shot to the upper corner and he wheels around and fires a backhander into the near, lower part of the net."

Brimsek's teammate defenseman Murray Henderson said it was virtually impossible to predict one of the Rocket's moves. "When he breaks on one defenseman, there's no telling what he'll do. If he gets his body between you and the puck, you just can't get at it. He cradles the puck on the blade of his stick, steers it with one hand, and wards off his check with the other. Strong? That guy is like an ox, but he sure doesn't look it."

More than anything, Richard filled seats throughout the then six-team NHL. "The Rocket," explained *Detroit Times* columnist Bob Murphy, "is made to watch and write about." Montreal writers Elmer Ferguson, Baz O'Meara, and Dink Carroll ran out of adjectives trying to keep up with Richardian feats. As Dink Carroll wrote, "There was a playoff game against Toronto when he had only Jim Thomson between him and the goal. Thomson may have been an All-Star defenseman, but they all looked alike to the Rocket in those circumstances. He went around Thomson like a hoop around a barrel, pulled goalie Al Rollins out, and fired the puck into the empty net." Richard had an unerring sense of the dramatic and, more than anyone, produced the triumphant sudden-death goals in Stanley Cup competition.

When Richard was suspended for striking linesman Cliff Thompson by NHL President Clarence Campbell at the end of the 1954–55 season and for the duration of the playoffs, the city of Montreal erupted in riots. Fans surrounded the Forum on the night of a Canadiens–Red Wings game, torched trolley cars, demolished stores along Ste. Catherine Street West, and nearly killed Campbell. No other player, not even a Morenz, could stir the constituency to such utter fury.

Ironically, Richard emerged from the furor a much more restrained but no less efficient athlete, partly because of the trauma the riots inflicted on his psyche and partly because his younger brother Henri (Pocket Rocket) Richard joined the Canadiens for the 1955–56 season and would remain with the team for more than a decade.

With the creative Henri at center and dynamic Dickie Moore on left wing, the Rocket seemed to take on new life in what should have been his twilight years. The fact that former linemate Hector (Toe) Blake—finely tuned to Richard's idiosyncrasies—was now coaching the team also helped. The ingredients combined to produce a halcyon half-decade for Richard during which he captained the Canadiens to an unprecedented five consecutive Stanley Cup championships. He retired after the spring of 1960 and, not surprisingly, Montreal's cup string was snapped the following year.

By this time Richard could retire secure in the knowledge that he, more than anyone, had helped the NHL bridge the gap between the uncertain war years and the NHL's postwar regeneration. At the time Richard hung up his skates, the league was enjoying an unparalleled boom in every city. Even the Bruins and Rangers, who had slipped in the standings, were playing to capacity crowds almost every night they opened their doors. This prosperity, which ultimately would lead to expansion from a six-team to a twenty-one-team circuit, was also due to the contributions of the game's other blue-chip superstar, Gordie Howe.

As different from Richard as a trombone is from a bass drum, Howe was the ultimate stylist. His repertoire of maneuvers were often so subtle that only a particularly attentive professional was able to detect them—if he was lucky. He was an infinitely better stick handler than Richard and was the only player in his era—one of the few ever—to shoot ambidextrously. "There should be two pucks in each game," a member of the Maple Leafs once opined, "one for Howe and another for the rest of the players."

To those who witnessed Howe's escape from death on the ice in 1950 it was truly miraculous that he endured an NHL career that began in the mid-1940s and lasted until the start of the 1980s. During the opening game of the then always bitter playoff between Howe's Red Wings and the Maple Leafs, Toronto captain Ted Kennedy collided with Howe near the boards. Gordie plunged headlong into the wooden barrier and suffered so severe a head injury that doctors doubted his ability to survive. When he did weather the operations, they doubted that he would play hockey again, yet Gordie returned the following season and led the NHL in scoring. Those who watched the slope-shouldered youth in action realized that his array of weaponry—both offensive and defensive—virtually guaranteed long-term stardom.

"Rocket Richard broke my old scoring record," said Nels (Ole Poison) Stewart, "but Gordie Howe is going to pass both Richard and me one of these days. Only a career-ending injury can stop him."

The last line is particularly relevant in terms of Howe's style and ultimate durability. Following the Kennedy episode, Gordie became infinitely more aggressive than he ever had been. Unlike Rocket Richard, who tended to *react* to abuse, Howe more often than not was the instigator.

Howe was as deft with an elbow in the face or a butt end of his stick in the enemy's stomach as he was stickhandling the puck. Referees such as Vern Buffey often were astonished at Howe's ability to commit an offense and escape with impunity. "You're working a game," said Buffey, "and you see a player is down. You know that Howe did it. But how can you prove it? Howe is so strong and tricky. He's got a dozen little moves he can make with his stick and elbow."

By the early 1950s the rivalry between Howe and Richard—both right wings— was the most intense among any two players in the history of hockey. Analysts would spend endless hours debating the merits of each and could come to a few valid conclusions. First, Richard was militantly more exciting to the average fan. Second, Howe was the more totally skillful. And, finally, the two were the most dominating personalities of the 1950s.

Some players were downright frightened by Howe's presence. A member of the Rangers once confided to a reporter that Howe was, by far, the dirtiest player in the game. When the newsman quoted the player by name the next day, the player expressed outrage. "If Gordie reads that," the Ranger worried, "he's liable to kill me."

Defensemen found it difficult to thwart Howe on the attack, not simply because of his puckhandling ability but also his strength *and* the possibility of Howe's attacking him. "The only way to stop him," Toronto defenseman Kent Douglas once explained, "is to crowd him, throw him off stride. But nobody wants to get near Gordie Howe."

By the time Richard retired in 1960, Howe was far and away the most dominant player in the NHL, both on and off the ice. Unlike the French-Canadian Richard, who had difficulty with English during the early part of his career, Howe was articulate—he had a passion for crossword puzzles—and droll. He became a hit with the media, fans, and even referees. Once, after being penalized by referee Frank Udvari, Howe skated up to the official and declared, "Frank, you're the second-best referee in the NHL."

Curious, Udvari inquired as to who topped Howe's list. "Everybody else," snapped Howe. "They're tied for number one."

Howe was the centerpiece on a number of lines, the most expert of which was the Production Line I, featuring Ted Lindsay on left wing and Sid Abel at center. Both linemates were equally as rough as Howe. "You could be sure," said former teammate Larry Zeidel, "that you didn't get away with anything against them. And I mean anything. They'd use the stick on you as easily as they'd breathe."

When Abel became player-coach of the Chicago Black Hawks, he was replaced on Production Line II by Alex Delvecchio, a less violent performer but as adroit as Abel. Lindsay eventually retired, but Howe kept rolling along, later with Norm Ullman as his pivot. Remarkably, at the age of forty-one, Howe enjoyed his most productive campaign, totaling 103 points.

Although Richard played on championship teams with aces such as goalie Jacques Plante as he wound down his glorious career, Howe suffered an ignoble ending with a dissension-riddled Detroit club. Poorly managed and badly coached,

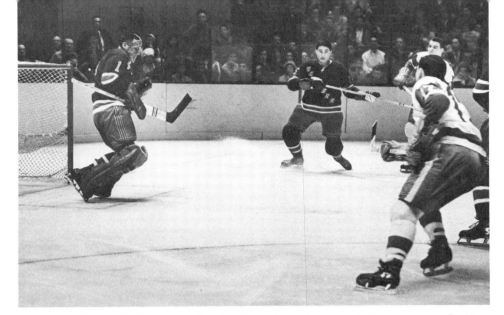

1-13   *Jacques Plante (left) was the first NHL goaltender to regularly wear a mask. Here, as a member of the New York Rangers, he stops a shot by the Detroit Red Wings.*

1-14   *Jacques Plante stops a shot by the Toronto Maple Leafs.*

the Red Wings no longer were contenders in the late 1960s and early 1970s. Although many hockey people believed that Gordie was good enough to continue, he retired in 1971 after a quarter-century in the NHL. He had played 1,687 games and scored 1,809 points. He had earned the sobriquet Mister Hockey.

After a four-year retirement, Howe stunned the hockey world by returning as a full-time right wing with the Houston Aeros of the World Hockey Association. His sons, Mark and Marty, skated alongside him. Gordie was forty-five at the time and continued playing—later with the Hartford Whalers—even after the WHA was absorbed by the NHL.

Between them, Howe and Richard steered the NHL through an unprecedented period of success. The six-team league was envied by promoters in baseball, football, and basketball for its ability to fill buildings even in cities with the worst teams. (The Bruins, NHL doormats during the early 1960s, would continually outdraw the champion Celtics of the National Basketball Association at Boston Garden.) There was only one problem: professional hockey's world extended from Boston to Chicago on an east–west basis and from New York to Montreal on a north–south axis. It still was a regional sport and one that would have to expand if it hoped to gain the brand of national attention bestowed upon its rivals for the sports dollar.

The pressures on the NHL to admit new franchises finally became irresistible in the mid-1960s until the antiexpansionists finally capitulated, and the NHL entered another perilous but terribly exciting era.

THE GROWING PAINS OF EXPANSION

Since 1946 every National Hockey League game at Maple Leaf Gardens in Toronto had been a sellout. Soon after, the same delightful (for the promoters) situation was true for the Forum in Montreal and, to a lesser degree, Detroit's Olympia Arena and the Boston Garden. Even Madison Square Garden, notorious for its side balcony with thousands of obstructed-view seats, began having regular sellouts by the 1960s.

The Chicago Black Hawks had been a problem for a time in the postwar era. Inefficient management had hurt what was potentially an excellent franchise until the Norris and Wirtz families committed millions of dollars toward the rejuvenation of Windy City hockey. Other NHL teams, particularly the Montreal Canadiens, helped out by selling quality players to Chicago until general manager Tommy Ivan could develop a respectable farm system. That done, the Black Hawks were a team to behold.

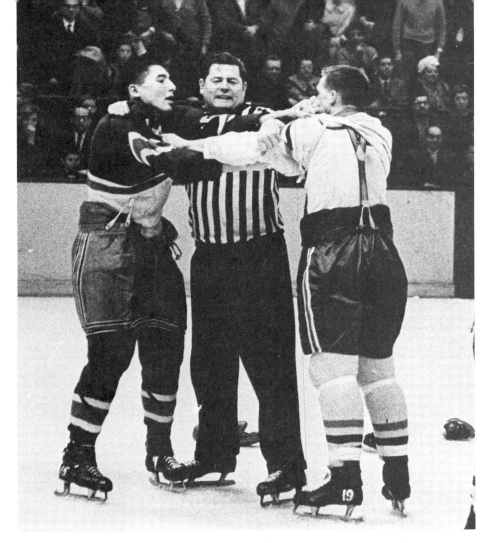

1-15   *It has been said that hockey players rarely suffer serious injuries in a fight when they vent their anger. It seems to be the case here as Jim Neilson of the New York Rangers (left) and Terry Harper of the Montreal Canadiens are separated by linesman George Hayes.*

From their player nursery in St. Catherines, Ontario, the Black Hawks groomed a cornucopia of magnificent talent. Stan Mikita, Bobby Hull, Elmer (Moose) Vasko, and Pierre Pilote were among the aces who thrived with the Black Hawks. By 1961, when Chicago won its first Stanley Cup since before World War II, hockey became number one in that city, and once the Black Hawks had been resurrected the NHL became a veritable gold mine for its owners. Some fans came to the games to see the occasional fights that the owners allowed as "safety valves."

Delighted with their wealth and even happier that the players had not yet unionized, the NHL governors could fret about only one thing—they didn't have enough seats to accommodate those who wanted a look at Howe, Hull, and Richard. They realized that there was still more money to be made, and it would come, if properly mined, from the mother lode of television.

Long before the television set became as commonplace as the refrigerator, some NHL teams were earning big money from network radio. The Toronto Maple Leafs in particular were earning a pretty penny from the "Hockey Night in Canada" radio broadcasts heard nationwide on the Canadian Broadcasting Company's network. With the advent of television in the 1950s, the CBC television network began carrying the Maple Leafs games. In the late 1950s the powerful Montreal Canadiens were added to the trans-Canada shows. "This became a stirring weekly radio and television show alternating out of Toronto and Montreal," said Frank J. Selke, the Canadiens' manager who helped put together the radio-television package.

When the Maple Leafs and Canadiens met in the 1959 Stanley Cup finals, the thrilling tournament set an all-time high among television ratings in the Dominion. The four American NHL teams also were making gains, albeit smaller ones, in the new world of sports television. The problem in the United States was basic: hockey was shown only on local television. Neither the National Broadcasting Company, Columbia Broadcasting System, nor the American Broadcasting Company were interested in televising a game that had only Chicago, Detroit, Boston, and New York among its members in the United States. "We knew," said one NHL official, "that if we *really* wanted a network contract with any of the Big Three we had to go west."

More easily said than done. For one thing, the essentially conservative NHL owners were quite comfortable in their six-team cocoon, and the Canadian teams, in particular, were sharing a gold mine from their "Hockey Night in Canada" shows. Furthermore, NHL President Clarence Campbell—himself more conservative than his employers, the owners—dismissed any expansion talk whenever the question was raised in the first five years of the 1960s.

But forces emerged that compelled even the most conservative of the hockey lords to reconsider their seemingly adamant stance against expansion. For one thing, there was a grass roots movement among the public that had taken to hockey as never before. Even sports fans in such non–big-league cities as St. Louis, Philadelphia, Minneapolis, and Los Angeles couldn't help but hear—and read—about the exploits of Bobby Hull, the Golden Jet of Chicago, or his clever sidekick Stan Mikita; Gordie Howe's name was known from Seattle to Bangor; and nearly everyone had heard about the regal Montreal Canadiens dynasty led by Jean Beliveau, Boom Boom Geoffrion, and Jacques Plante.

One who sensed the bonanza that lay ahead for an expanded professional hockey network was a gentle Seattle native named Al Leader. For several years Leader had been president of the Pacific Coast Hockey League, which later became known as the Western Hockey League. With teams in such significant locales as Los Angeles, Seattle, Vancouver, and San Francisco, the Western League was ready to go big league.

Unlike some of the more belligerent and abrasive sports commissioners, Leader was not one to negotiate by threat. He tried to use his friendly powers of persuasion to convince the NHL moguls that it would be in everyone's best interest if a marriage of the original six NHL teams and the big WHL franchises was arranged. The NHL made it clear that it was not interested. After a number of rebuffs, the WHL began at least *thinking* about shaping its own future as a rival league.

In the meantime a young Turk emerged among the NHL governors who would change the entire texture of hockey for decades to come. His name was William (Bill) Jennings, a New York lawyer with a shallow hockey background who quite accidentally backed into the presidency of the New York Rangers. Jennings, more than any of his NHL brethren, understood that the old six-team league not only could exploit the broadening U.S. television market but also could charge an exorbitant fee (for the time) to anyone who wanted to buy a new NHL franchise. In this way the six established teams would fatten their coffers and, while they were at it, also defuse any attempt by the WHL—or anyone else, for that matter—to plant teams in such rich cities as Los Angeles and Philadelphia.

At first Jennings was dismissed as a radical maverick by his Canadian brethren and a few Americans as well. But as the 1960s progressed, the possibility of a rival league grew, and so did the revenues generated by professional baseball and football from network television. In time, the other NHL owners began listening more attentively to Jennings.

What he said began to make more and more sense to them, especially when it was pointed out that the Internal Revenue Service was now making it even more attractive for the wealthy to own hockey teams. The new owner could depreciate the investment over five years and deduct that depreciation from the profits of his other businesses. If, for example, his share of the team was worth a million dollars, he could deduct $200,000 a year for five years from profits of other businesses. The idea that a man could at once "depreciate" his hockey team while it was increasing in value appealed to many potential investors. By 1965 a horde of potential club owners was pounding at the NHL portal, hoping to get in on this wonderful deal.

NHL President Campbell, who had been so vocally antiexpansion in the early 1960s, suddenly did a pirouette in 1965 when the league announced that it was, in fact, considering the addition of at least two entries and maybe more. "We will need a new box office," said Campbell. "Only expansion will give it to us. No TV sponsor is too interested in financing on a national basis a program of big-league hockey that ignores two-thirds of the country [the United States] as far as member cities are concerned."

Next came an almost subtle sales pitch to Madison Avenue. Attractive players such as Rod Gilbert of the Rangers helped sell the game. The league invited a blue ribbon group of New York advertising and television executives to a reception at the Plaza Hotel on May 27, 1965. They were shown a color videotape of a Canadiens–Maple Leafs match, whereupon Campbell insisted that the NHL was not making a sales pitch but rather merely wanted "to demonstrate what is available in the field of hockey—the nature and quality of the product we have to offer."

The sales pitch would come later, and when it did the NHL put a $2 million price tag on each of six new franchises that would be welcomed to the expanded

1-16   *Rod Gilbert, a New York Rangers right wing, was one of the most deadly users of the slapshot in the 1960s and early 1970s.*

circuit. The new teams, whoever they might be, would begin operation at the start of the 1967–68 season.

As expected, there was a long line at the door, and the idea of landing a team in the NHL became a singular matter of prestige for those involved. There was no question that Los Angeles and San Francisco would be admitted for the same reason, that they were in big-league baseball. The NHL was convinced that it needed two California outposts, and since there were brand-new buildings in Los Angeles (Inglewood) and San Francisco (Oakland), it was merely a matter of who would represent the west coast entries. But after that, what? Vancouver also wanted in, but the NHL was disinclined to accept another Canadian entry because it had nothing to gain—televisionwise—since "Hockey Night in Canada" was fully booked with games. Buffalo also wanted in, but it was considered at the time too small a city, too close to Toronto, and with too small an arena. If that wasn't enough reason, Chicago Black Hawks owner James Norris added, "I don't want a town named Buffalo playing in my building."

The league finally rounded out its new division with Philadelphia, Minnesota (Minneapolis–St. Paul), Pittsburgh, and St. Louis. All six were lumped together in an expansion division, and then Campbell and the governors held their collective breaths to see if a twelve-team NHL would sell. Some critics were certain that it would not, especially in Philadelphia and St. Louis, both of which had failed in earlier NHL experiments.

Minnesota was considered the best bet for two reasons: hockey was indigenous to the area, and the new Met Center in Bloomington was a magnificent arena for hockey. The other three were debatable. Pittsburgh had a long and rich hockey heritage, but mostly as a minor league franchise. As for the two California clubs, there was more optimism at the start than pessimism. In Los Angeles the new Kings had a Barnumesque owner in Jack Kent Cooke, a transplanted Canadian who had erected a truly magnificent new arena—the "Fabulous" Forum—in nearby Inglewood. "It must be seen to be believed," commented Eric Hutton in *Maclean's* magazine of Canada, "and maybe not even then. It is the gaudiest sports palace this side of the heyday of the Colosseum of ancient Rome, of which the Forum is, in fact, a modernized copy."

The Oakland Seals, who were supposed to be the Kings' natural rivals on the coast, was run by a group of owners none of whom was as financially stable as the NHL had hoped, or thought. Equally troublesome was the fact that the Seals' home rink, the Alameda County Arena, was far enough from San Francisco to ensure that a sizeable number of potential customers from across the bay would not turn out for a Seals game. This was a problem that never was solved and ultimately led to the demise of the Bay Area franchise.

Once the 1967–68 season got under way it became apparent that fans were not jamming the new buildings in the same exuberant manner as they did for the established teams. But by the same token there was a budding enthusiasm that would, in some cities, turn into a veritable groundswell of hysteria, particularly in Philadelphia and St. Louis, of all places. Some of the Flyers games, especially with the Blues and Bruins, were especially bloody.

The Philadelphia Flyers finished first in the new division with the Los Angeles Kings just one point behind. (Cooke was named executive of the year by the *Hockey News.*) A stirring seven-game playoff between the Flyers and the St. Louis Blues kindled a bonfire of interest in both cities, while both the Minnesota North Stars and the Pittsburgh Penguins did well enough at the gate the first time around to offer hope for the future. Los Angeles gave the Kings a reasonably warm reception, but the Seals remained a dubious quantity in Oakland. If nothing else, all six teams finished the season, in itself commendable.

The quality of hockey was another story, albeit sad. "The price for television was expansion," said Toronto author John MacFarlane, "and expansion did more damage to the game than anything else."

Because the established teams had given their new cousins only the dregs from their various rosters, with an occasional retread or potential star thrown in, all six expansion teams were hardly in the same competitive class with the Big Six. The talent had become diluted, and "dilution" became the dirtiest word in the NHL. Even Campbell was hard pressed to conceal his displeasure with the product now being dispensed by his once-proud league. "You can't take half a bottle of whiskey," Campbell allowed, "and fill it with water and still have the same drink."

The NHL was severely criticized in the cities with established teams for the manner in which it appropriated talent to the new teams. Fans who had become accustomed to high-quality hockey in Montreal and Toronto in particular were appalled by the sight of teams such as the Seals and Penguins.

"Maybe," said John MacFarlane, "we could have developed a tolerance for whiskey with water if it had been watered down with care, but the NHL was sloppy. The only way to keep the fans interested is to ensure that on any given day any team is liable to beat any other."

This was not true in the NHL. When the champions of the expansion division, St. Louis, collided with the winner of the established section in the Stanley Cup finals of 1968, it was a travesty. The Canadiens toyed with the Blues as if they were playing an exhibition game with an American League club. They easily won the series in four straight games and did so the following season. The Blues reached the finals once more in 1970 and, this time, played the Boston Bruins. Again, the established team won in a four-game rout.

But if the fans in Montreal, Detroit, Toronto, Chicago, Boston, and New York were turned off by the watered-down expansion game they still, grudgingly, turned out. In the meantime, the new teams—with the exception of Oakland—began to solidify their fan base. St. Louis, Phildelphia, and Minnesota became downright frenzied over their respective hockey teams. Los Angeles was enthusiastic, but not nearly as much as owner Cooke. Pittsburgh, as much because of disappointing

*1-17 The menacing use of sticks has always been part of the dark side of hockey. Here Ed-
die Shack of the Boston Bruins (left) and Larry Zeidel of the Philadelphia Flyers
trade blows during a bloody match in 1968.*

teams as anything, sputtered, and Oakland's aches multiplied both on and off the
ice. In the meantime, television, the reason for the expansion, was becoming more
apparent as an asset to the NHL. The Columbia Broadcasting System began
showing a regular NHL Game of the Week on Sunday afternoons, and by the
1971–72 season had been encouraged by the response. The twelve NHL owners had
been equally pleased with the overall demand for still more franchises. They upped
the ante to $6 million per team and were delighted when previously snubbed
Vancouver and Buffalo produced the necessary checks.

Now the NHL was a fourteen-team league and feeling very good about its
Canadian network television package and the upbeat attitude of CBS. The progressive element in the high command, led by Jennings, began to think in terms of a de-
cade-long program of continued expansion, culminating in 1980 when the league
would embrace a total of twenty-four cities, including Seattle and others who
previously had been snubbed. To prove that they meant business the governors
added two additional franchises for the 1972–73 season, the New York Islanders,
who would be based in suburban Nassau County, and the Atlanta Flames. The

Islanders not only were compelled to shell out $6 million as the entry fee but also had to pay the Rangers an additional $4 million as indemnification for interloping on their formerly exclusive turf.

By all counts, the expansion era was the most revolutionary and traumatic the game has known. On the negative side was the obvious decline in the extraordinarily high quality that prevailed during the six-team era. On the positive side was the spread of the ice gospel to centers such as Atlanta, Los Angeles, and St. Louis, and the entrance of hockey into the same class as baseball and football in terms of its geographic spread. Additionally, there was what became known as "the Orr Effect."

Simultaneous with the NHL's growth from six to twelve teams was the debut of Robert Gordon (Bobby) Orr as a defenseman with the Boston Bruins. Almost inadvertently Orr brought about the creation of the NHL's players' union, helped raise salaries to unheard of levels, and forever altered the playing style of the game. This was all the more remarkable considering that the youngster from Parry Sound, Ontario, was essentially a bashful, simple kid whose only desire in life was to play hockey.

It was Orr's good fortune—and the NHL's misfortune—that he had Toronto attorney Al Eagleson as a friend. Eagleson disabused Orr and his parents of any naïve thoughts they might have harbored about hockey's being just a game and not a business. He persuaded them that a hard line was necessary in negotiations with the Boston Bruins, which had the rights to the teenage prodigy, and that it was imperative that a hard-nosed negotiator like himself go head-to-head with Bruins general manager Leighton (Hap) Emms.

The Eagleson (Orr)–Emms confrontation would mark a major turning point in the fiscal history of the NHL. Previously, hockey players had been conspicuously underpaid compared with other professional athletes. In the mid-1950s a group of stars led by Ted Lindsay of the Red Wings and Jim Thomson of the Maple Leafs attempted to organize a union and better conditions for the players. The owners swiftly retaliated by trading the rebels to low-grade teams, and the union idea died before it had any significant impact. But that was when the NHL was a six-team league and it was an owners' market. With the advent of expansion it now was a players' market, and Orr, by dint of his extraordinary ability and charisma, was *the* player among superstars. If Orr could force a break through the owners' ramparts, the other players would seize the opening and follow his lead.

In a sense, Orr and Eagleson were lucky. The Bruins had plumbed the NHL depths for years and were desperate for a dynamic, young ace. Furthermore, they had been touting his skills for more than a year to still the demands of frustrated Boston fans. There was no way that Bruins owner Weston Adams, Jr., or Emms could fail to deliver the coveted Orr, and nobody was more aware of that fact than Eagleson. Confident to the point of being cocky, he put his demands on the table.

Emms, figuring he was being a big spender, was willing to offer a ten-thousand dollar-a-year contract, which at the time was high for a newcomer to the NHL.

1-18
Bobby Orr, a defenseman with the Boston Bruins, revolutionized the role of defenseman with his dashing offensive thrusts in the late 1960s and through the 1970s.

Eagleson laughed at the bid and demanded more than four times the amount. Stunned to the core, Emms withdrew from negotiations until he realized that it was Orr or nothing. In the end Eagleson negotiated a forty-thousand-dollar-a-year deal for two years prior to the 1966–67 season.

It was the shot heard around the hockey world. Other players were impressed by Eagleson's irreverence before the mighty NHL leaders and his cool under negotiating fire. Others came to him for advice, and suddenly he had an entire stable of players under his wing. The capper, however, was his leadership in organizing the NHL Players' Association. Suddenly, the owners were on the defensive. Their ripostes at Eagleson had a pop-gun quality, and soon the governors realized that they had better sit down and bargain with Eagleson as an equal or there simply would not be any players on their roster.

Ultimately the owners shaped up and reached an agreement with Eagleson, but they paid dearly. Salaries began an upward spiral that would continue to climb through the 1970s. The union became stronger each year, and Eagleson's power was such that he single-handedly put together the superb 1972 Team Canada–Soviet series and has been the driving force behind the NHL's participation in international hockey ever since.

At first Eagleson seemed to have a monopoly on the hockey agenting market, but his success spawned a number of other eager attorneys who suddenly became player representatives, and these men, unlike Eagleson, who had since befriended the owners, became adversaries of the teams with whom they dealt.

The bottom line, of course, was that hockey players were enjoying a prosperity unheard of in the sport. For that they could thank the Orr Effect, via Eagleson's bargaining. "Eagleson," said Bobby Hull of the Black Hawks, "did more for hockey in two years than anybody else did in twenty."

On the ice the Orr Effect was even more obvious and, in the view of the league's goaltenders, frightening. Utilizing his enormous speed and stickhandling ability, the kid from Parry Sound undermined all previous shibboleths of defense. True, an occasional defenseman from the past—Lester Patrick, Eddie Shore, and Red Kelly among them—would rush the puck, but none of them made an absolute fetish out of the practice. Although he was listed as a defenseman and lined up at the defensive position at the start of a game, Orr by technical standards was no more a defenseman than center Phil Esposito.

Orr's essential forte was leading a rush into enemy territory where he would either shoot on goal or make a play for a teammate. If the riposte failed, his great speed often enabled him to double back to his defensive position before any damage was done. The result was an unprecedented (for a defenseman) assault on scoring records. Orr, the backliner, actually led the NHL in scoring in 1970 and 1975 and was near the top of the list during the other years. Equally meaningful was the impression he made on other defensemen, particularly the new breed just coming out of junior hockey. "The feeling among the kids," said one veteran NHL scout, "was that playing *real* defense was no longer important. What mattered was going on the attack, like Orr, and getting the points. It wasn't just one or two who were thinking this way, nearly *everyone* who was listed as a defenseman wanted to do it the Orr way."

It was as if a new strain of gene had been developed among hockey players. The Norris Trophy, supposedly awarded to the best defenseman, now was virtually Orr's to keep. He won it consecutively between 1968 and 1975. In the process he made a lot of money and convinced his colleagues that the more points a defenseman accumulated, the better his chance for the Norris Trophy and, tangentially, big money. Those who succeeded Orr—among them Denis Potvin of the Islanders and more recently Doug Wilson of the Black Hawks—made their reputations as puck-carrying defensemen in the Orr mold.

1-19
Renowned for his offensive exploits as a splendid defenseman, Bobby Orr (light jersey) protects his goalie from Marc Tardif of the Montreal Canadiens.

Many purists have charged that the Orr Effect has had a deleterious effect on the quality of the game; that the essential beauty of crisp defensive play has been lost to hockey a-go-go. But this did not seem to bother fans in the new expansion cities. When Orr was in town, it was virtually guaranteed that the rink would be filled, and the young defenseman, as much as anyone, was responsible for the successes of expansion in the early 1970s.

Orr played on two Stanley Cup–winning teams, and each time his contribution had a ripple effect, not merely on hockey in Boston but on the image of the game in North America. In May 1970, Orr clinched the Bruins' cup-winning game against the St. Louis Blues, by literally firing the puck past goalie Glenn Hall while flying through the air. The image of Orr in mid-flight, beating Hall, was captured on film and still photos and, more than anything, conveyed the spectacular quality of the player—and the sport. Two years later, the Bruins were pitted against the powerful New York Rangers. It was a brilliant, well-contested series that ended before a capacity crowd at Madison Square Garden where Orr orchestrated the decisive plays that produced Boston's cup victory. Again, international attention was focused on Orr, who generated more positive publicity for major league hockey—perhaps too much.

Like spies studying the enemy territory from a secluded observation post, a group of ambitious young promoters had been analyzing the NHL's progress through the late 1960s and the start of the next decade. (The Broad Street Bullies,

1-20   The "goon era" in the NHL was fostered in the 1970s by the Philadelphia Flyers, alias the Broad Street Bullies. The Flyers' archvillain was Dave Schultz, shown here engaging in the main event with Bobby Schmautz of the Vancouver Canucks.

or Flyers, of Philadelphia made a particularly lasting impression). These promoters marveled at the manner in which the NHL thwarted the Western Hockey League by placing franchises in Los Angeles and San Francisco and the ease with which some of the new NHL franchises as well as the six established teams were filling their buildings. They deduced that there still was plenty of money to be made from big-league hockey—not with the NHL's cooperation, but in competition with the fifty-year-old league.

It was with that premise in mind that the World Hockey Association was formed. By NHL standards the effect the WHA had on it was about as devastating as the eruption of Mount St. Helens on the state of Washington.

THE BIRTH—AND DEATH—
OF THE WORLD HOCKEY ASSOCIATION

Because the National Hockey League had so effectively dealt with prospective challengers in the past, nobody believed that a rebel group could be capable of slicing a piece of the ever-growing pro hockey pie. In fact, few thought that anyone would dare take on a league that now had extended its tentacles to Buffalo and Vancouver, with two more to grow in Atlanta and Long Island. There didn't appear to be enough markets left for anyone to be foolhardy enough to create a rival league.

There was, however, a dissenting voice in southern California where a young attorney named Gary Davidson chose to take on the NHL. Davidson's brainstorm was revolutionary: he would operate a hockey league without a reserve clause or an option clause in its player contracts. "I believe if a major league is to be truly successful, it has to be a league that holds the interests of the owners and the interests of the players in the same esteem," Davidson explained.

At first the NHL paid him no mind. After all, Davidson was from nonhockey country and had no background in the sport and hardly the personal finances to be taken seriously. But Davidson was a voracious promoter and began lining up businessmen willing to invest in the new league. One of them was fellow Californian Dennis Murphy, who had been instrumental in the birth of the American Basketball Association. Between the glib Murphy and the smooth Davidson, a battle plan was formulated; they would attack the NHL at its strongest outposts— New York, Chicago, and Boston, among others—while establishing big-league beachheads in previously untapped locations such as Quebec City, Winnipeg, and Ottawa.

On July 10, 1971, articles of incorporation for the WHA were filed in Delaware and by-laws were drawn with Davidson, Murphy, and Donald J. Regan, a law partner of Davidson's, as officers. Still the NHL was unimpressed, as were the media. One Chiacago journalist observed that the WHA "lacks three things: players, arenas, and television."

Davidson was not unaware of these problems and, in time, would act upon them. For the moment, at least, the WHA decided to make its first bold thrust and did so when it was revealed that Phil Esposito of the Bruins would be offered a $250,000 contract to jump to the proposed league. To fortify their position, Davidson and Murphy contracted with two New York sports representatives, Steve Arnold and Marty Blackman, to lure players away from the NHL.

Each month, through the summer of 1971, the WHA picked up a little credibility. At first it didn't seem like much, but it began adding up, especially when investors continued to pour in. By November 1971 the WHA was sufficiently fortified with backers to hold a widely ballyhooed meeting in New York where the franchise holders and their aides formally laid their cards on the table.

"The WHA meeting attracted a remarkably large turnout," commented Gerald Eskenazi of the *New York Times*, "and there were more than newsmen there. Many people—businessmen, small-time coaches, fringe players—were interested in how well a new major league could do. They wanted to be part of it. Optimism was rampant. The backers of the various teams appeared to be substantial people."

Still the NHL pretended to be unconcerned—although spies for the established league were seen at the WHA conference. NHL President Clarence Campbell maintained a posture of militant indifference whenever questioned about the potential WHA threat.

"We wish them well," snapped Campbell. "I'm pleased that hockey is so successful that other people want to get into the business. But if they encroach upon us by trying to steal our players, then we'll fight them from the ramparts."

The fighting began early in 1972 when WHA emissaries, led by Blackman and Arnold, began serious negotiations with NHL players. Other agents got busy contacting the new WHA teams. A number of NHL aces were targeted for signing, among them Ted Green, Derek Sanderson, and Gerry Cheevers of the Stanley Cup champion Bruins, Jim Dorey of the Toronto Maple Leafs, and J. C. Tremblay of the Montreal Canadiens. But, more than anything, the WHA needed an unequivocal superstar. The man in question was Bobby Hull of the Chicago Black Hawks.

Known as the Golden Jet, Hull was a left wing of prodigious talent. With muscles to match his speed, he had led the NHL in goal-scoring seven times, and three times was overall point-scoring champion. Unlike Orr, who always was wary of the public and the press, Hull was the most gregarious good-will ambassador the NHL ever had in its ranks, never failing to deliver an autograph or take time out for still another interview. Was it possible that the Black Hawks would allow their premier attraction to defect?

The answer was negative as negotiations between Hull and his agent and the Black Hawks' high command dragged on late into the 1971–72 season. But as the campaign came to an end, a sense of frustration was evident in the Hull camp, whereas petulance was the feeling of the day among the Wirtz family that owned the Chicago club. At the age of thirty-four, Hull wanted security—a substantial increase in his contract—and the Black Hawks' offer did not please him. It was then that the WHA made its big move.

"We realized that we would never have credibility unless we signed a player of Hull's stature," said Howard Baldwin, an original WHA governor and now governor of the NHL's Hartford Whalers. "That's why we did everything possible to get him on our side."

While the Wirtzes fiddled, Ben Hatskin, owner of the new Winnipeg Jets, burned the telephone wires between his office and that of Hull's agent. Finally, Hatskin, with the help of his WHA partners, produced an offer that arrested the attention of

1-21   The World Hockey Association made its debut in 1972 led by President Gary Davidson.

even Clarence Campbell. The Jets would give Hull a $1 million cash bonus for signing *and* a ten-year $2,750,000 contract to be player-coach of the Winnipeg entry. The Black Hawks refused to call the bluff and maintained what Hull considered a very frugal position.

But the WHA was not bluffing. The league and the Jets produced sufficient fiscal proof that they could deliver to persuade Hull once and for all that he should bolt to the new league—and he did. "If I said the contract being as big as it was had nothing to do with my signing with Winnipeg," said Hull, "I'd be lying. It made the future secure for my family. That was the most important thing. Then there were some things that disenchanted me in the NHL and the way the Hawks handled their attempts to sign me. They just didn't think I'd consider jumping."

The first significant result of Hull's transfer to the WHA was that it acted as a catalyst for other NHL stars who had been waiting for a truly meaningful personality to make the move. With Hull in the driver's seat, the bandwagon was in motion and many were ready to jump on it before the 1972–73 season got under way.

The champion Bruins lost Gerry Cheevers to the Cleveland Crusaders, Ted Green to the New England Whalers, and Derek Sanderson to the Philadelphia Blazers. J. C. Tremblay jumped from the Montreal Canadiens to the Quebec

1-22   *Two of hockey's greatest stars, Gordie Howe (left) and Bobby Hull, enjoy a light moment with a model.*

Nordiques, and Jim Dorey, who had just been transferred from the Toronto Maple Leafs to the New York Rangers, upped and signed with the Whalers. There were many, many more defections, but still the NHL bosses doubted that the WHA could survive even a season. "That league," said Clarence Campbell with an air of finality, "won't even get off the ground."

Some NHL bosses, particularly Bill Jennings in New York and Ed Snider in Philadelphia, weren't so sure that Campbell was right. Meanwhile, the WHA opened for business in the fall of 1972 with teams in Edmonton, Winnipeg, Chicago, Cleveland, Houston, Los Angeles, St. Paul, Boston, New York, Ottawa, Philadelphia, and Quebec.

In some cities, such as Cleveland, Houston, and Philadelphia, the league was forced to play in ancient bandbox arenas, but in places like St. Paul, Los Angeles, and New York the rinks were of NHL size. The New York Raiders, the WHA's Manhattan entry, shared Madison Square Garden with the Rangers. Municipalities with WHA teams often tried to fortify their new clubs with promises of new buildings. Houston began construction of an 18,000-seat rink to be ready by 1974. Likewise, Cleveland's new sextet would soon be housed in a mammoth arena under construction on a suburban plain.

And, despite the skeptics, the WHA was able to negotiate several television deals, although none were on a major scale. Nevertheless, the league launched its first year with players, arenas, and television. Now the question was—would the public buy it?

The answer was yes—and no. In direct confrontations with the NHL—New York, Philadelphia, Boston, and Chicago, among others—the brash intruders established a beachhead but could not penetrate much farther. At Madison Square Garden, for example, the Raiders attracted a significant following led by scoring ace Ron Ward, but the club was beset by ownership problems almost from the beginning and those never were remedied. Similarly, the New England Whalers, playing out of the Boston Garden, siphoned off some fans from the Bruins but hardly enough to persuade ownership that there was room for two major league hockey teams in Beantown. The Whalers conducted an orderly retreat from Boston to Springfield, Massachusetts, and eventually to Hartford, before the second season was over.

On outward appearances alone, the Philadelphia Blazers persuaded objective critics that they might give the neighboring Flyers a run for their money. With considerable drumbeating, the Blazers signed flamboyant Derek Sanderson as well as the Flyers' former goaltending darling Bernie Parent. Along with a few other NHL names, they looked as if they might be as talented as they were said to be. Instead of sharing the same building as the NHL club, the Blazers rented the refurbished Convention Hall, and a healthy turnout for opening night suggested that big things were in store for this WHA club. But alas, everything went wrong from that moment on. "We couldn't play our first game," said Sanderson, "because they didn't know how to make ice. It cracked wherever we skated so the game had to be called off."

The Blazers lasted as long as a tenement in a three-alarm fire and soon were carted off to Vancouver, where they suffered similar ignominies.

In its desperate bid to lure any available television commitment, the WHA would alter its schedule to suit. As a result, the Los Angeles Sharks once played a game at 11 A.M. on Sunday morning simply because of a TV deal arranged for prime Sunday afternoon time in the east.

When the New York Raiders' ownership failed after the opening year, a new group bought in and changed the name to the Golden Blades. The Blades may have been golden, but the ink remained red. "At the time that I joined the Golden Blades," recalled forward Andre Lacroix, "the league owed me $20,000. For some reason the check was sent to the team instead of me, and before I could get it from them the owners of the Golden Blades spent the money on a team song. As for the song, I never had a chance to hear it; we were gone out of New York before it came out."

The hockey bedouins moved to Cherry Hill, New Jersey, where the erstwhile Raiders and Golden Blades became the Jersey Knights. Playing out of the Cherry

1-23   The WHA developed its own brand of superstars, one of whom was Ron Ward of the New York Raiders.

Hill Arena, the Knights were reduced to abject minor league surroundings. There were no showers in the visiting team's dressing room, so the opposition was compelled to put on their uniforms at a motel two miles away. Reyn Davis, who covered the WHA for the *Winnipeg Free Press*, was appalled at conditions in Cherry Hill:

> Most arenas have a long players' bench for each team, but in Cherry Hill the players' section consisted of three rows of five seats. The teams looked like choirs. There was little room for a coach in Cherry Hill, so one night Winnipeg coach Nick Mickoski sat in the first row of the stands. But every time he stood up to make a line change or give instructions to a player, the fans would complain so loudly that he would have to shout his orders sitting down!

94

From a players' viewpoint the most depressing aspect of the Cherry Hill Arena was the ice. "It was the only arena I've ever been to," said Bobby Hull, "where the visiting team had to skate uphill for two periods of every game. There was also a huge dip in the ice."

According to Davis, the Cherry Hill ice was so uneven that Knights forward Ted Scharf suffered a freak injury while awaiting a pass. "The puck hit the dip," Davis explained, "shot straight up and struck Scharf between the eyes."

Because of such embarrassments it was freely predicted in NHL circles that the WHA's final game was only a week away. But NHL moguls didn't bargain for the resiliency of Davidson and Murphy, not to mention the legion of investors still interested in putting their money behind a stick and puck. Furthermore, there were some WHA entries that were doing moderately well. Les Nordiques in Quebec City was the only major league team in a hockey-mad metropolis. The French-Canadian press there afforded the team extensive coverage, as did radio and television. The Nordiques were here to stay. The Alberta (Edmonton) Oilers were equally strong, especially with the promise of a new sixteen-thousand-seat arena up the road. Bobby Hull, alone, ensured the success of Winnipeg's Jets but, here again, was a case of a major league team with no competition in pure hockey country.

Both the Ottawa Nationals and Cleveland Crusaders came very close to making a long-term go of it but eventually failed for different reasons. The Nationals, after a very troublesome start, seemed to have solved their innumerable problems, when suddenly a better deal emerged in Toronto, so the team was moved slightly westward and became the Toronto Toros.

The Crusaders, owned by galvanic sports entrepreneur Nick Mileti, iced an imposing team in a city steeped in hockey tradition. Mileti made one ironic mistake. He staked the future of the team on construction of a huge new arena in Richfield, Ohio. The assumption was that the rink, although a long drive from central Cleveland, would nevertheless draw not only fans who frequented the old arena in downtown Cleveland but those from Akron as well. In fact, the Crusaders, once they moved, drew few fans from either community and were en route to a disaster. Had Mileti remodeled the old Cleveland Arena, which was a distinct possibility at the time, the Crusaders could have thrived.

Conversely, the Houston Aeros, who were not given much of a chance of succeeding, did so for several years because they, like the Winnipeg Jets, exploited the NHL's inability to take good care of its own superstars. In this case the star in question was Gordie Howe. Insulted by the manner in which he was treated by the Detroit Red Wings, Howe made a startling comeback at forty-five with the Aeros, skating alongside his sons, Mark and Marty. Now the WHA had two of the biggest names in hockey history, Hull and Howe, and millions of dollars of publicity to go with it. The three Howes led Houston to the WHA championship in 1974, and the baby league, instead of expiring, continued to grow.

It did so because, among other things, it simply would not take a back seat to the NHL in any aspect of the game. If the NHL could play an eight-game series with the Soviet all-stars, the WHA high command figured that is could, too, and darned if it didn't, in 1974. There were the venerable Gordie Howe, Bobby Hull, Gerry Cheevers, and other onetime NHL aces taking on the Soviets, only this time wearing the WHA colors. The Russians won, to be sure, but the WHAers comported themselves well and, once again, obtained a good share of press coverage.

Meanwhile, the NHL was beginning to hurt. Losing Howe and Hull meant a loss of prestige, but there was also a chronic pain brought on by the WHA's endless raids against the NHL rosters. Salaries by now had ballooned to all-time highs, and it was nothing for a mediocre skater to command a salary in excess of $100,000 a year.

1-24   *Although he retired as a Detroit Red Wing, Gordie Howe resumed his career in the World Hockey Association with the Houston Aeros.*

When asked about the NHL, Davidson would take an independent stance. "We're not seeking a merger with them," he would say. "We just want the right to compete in the major league marketplace. The courts have already told us we have that right."

Actually, Davidson did want a merger. He understood that there was room for but one big-league team in Los Angeles, Vancouver, New York, Boston, Chicago, Toronto, and wherever the WHA was engaging the NHL in battle. But he also realized that his league had a couple of extremely valuable markets that could do well if they converted to NHL colors. So, interestingly enough, did a few NHL mavericks.

Once again the ultraprogressive Bill Jennings of the Rangers saw the light, as did Ed Snider of the Flyers. Seeing how the NHL was being bled white by the warfare, they chose the path of rapprochement with the upstart rivals. Jennings sought to arrange a peace pact with the WHA whereby the NHL would absorb a certain number of franchises and peace would reign on the ice front once more. But hotter heads prevailed within the NHL inner sanctum, and Jennings was overruled. The battle, which was met in 1972, roared on without solution through the decade.

To NHL viewers, the WHA was like a snake shedding its skin. Every time another WHA team folded, a new one would reappear just as quickly. Down went the Los Angeles Sharks, up popped the Phoenix Roadrunners. Down went the Michigan Stags, up popped the San Diego Mariners. Then there were the Baltimore Blades, Denver Spurs, Cincinnati Stingers, Calgary Cowboys, and Birmingham Bulls.

As the WHA entered its seventh season—the 1978–79 campaign—new and more sincere peace feelers were bruited about. This time there was substance to them, and for a very good reason: Clarence Campbell, who had been steadfastly opposed to negotiating with the new league, had retired as NHL president. His successor, an American attorney named John Zeigler, grasped the moment and decided that the time had come to extend the olive branch. There would be, he hoped, peace with honor. Likewise, the WHA elected a new president, Howard Baldwin, an enterprising young man who had done his apprenticeship in the Philadelphia Flyers organization. Zeigler and Baldwin could talk turkey, and they did, throughout the 1978–79 season.

In the end they hammered out a peace treaty and brought about a merger of the two leagues. Edmonton, Winnipeg, and Quebec—three of the original WHA cities—were admitted to the NHL. In addition Hartford (formerly the New England Whalers playing out of Boston) was the fourth and final WHA club to be admitted to the NHL fold.

The final WHA game was played on May 20, 1979, when the Jets defeated the Oilers to win the Avco World Cup. Both Gary Davidson and Dennis Murphy, who had started the unlikely enterprise, had long since departed for other less romantic ventures, but Bobby Hull still was starring for the Jets, and Gordie Howe was still around, although now sporting the green and white jersey of the Whalers.

Perhaps the most telling irony of the entire WHA saga involved Bobby Orr, whose histrionics helped galvanize hockey interest in the early 1970s and brought about the WHA in the first place. Bedeviled by gimpy knees, Orr was dropped by the Boston Bruins, played briefly for the Chicago Black Hawks, and by the time the WHA hoisted its white flag was gone from the ice wars, forced to retire, although chronologically he still was in the prime of his career.

A year after the WHA folded, Howe had just as casually moved back to the NHL as right wing for the Whalers. Another WHA product, from the Edmonton Oilers, also was making a transition into the established league. His name was Wayne Gretzky. His detractors, who numbered many in the NHL, said he would never cut the ice in the NHL.

Within a year Gretzky, like Orr before him, had done much to rearrange pro hockey's values. While doing so, the youngster never failed to credit the late, lamented WHA for giving him his first break as a professional.

BLACKS IN PROFESSIONAL HOCKEY

Unlike baseball, football, and basketball, pro hockey has seen very few black players enter its ranks. Willie O'Ree was the first black to break the color barrier, with the Boston Bruins in 1960–61 after a two-game trial in 1957–58. There are those who believe that with a break or two O'Ree could have lasted longer than one season.

"I never got a chance in my first tryout in Boston," said O'Ree, who played six years with San Diego of the Western League. "The second time around I had nobody to blame but myself. I had plenty of chances but I was uptight, rushed things, and didn't get the goals I might have if I wasn't so overanxious."

Another who made it temporarily was Alton White, with the WHA. Like O'Ree, White wasn't naïve enough to believe his color was ignored by those who played against him or watched him on the ice.

"Over the years," said O'Ree, "a fan here, a player there slurred me, but there wasn't much of it. In the NHL they rode me, but just like they would any other player. Sure, I've heard things. I've been booed a lot, but I like to think it's because I was one of the stars of a rival team, not because of my color."

By contrast, White insists he had a few problems because of his color. "Once in a while," Alton said, "I heard some wisecracks from people in the stands. But at least they knew I was out there working. I was well accepted in Providence and had no problems whatsoever. I got along with all the people; the fans treated me exceptionally well."

1-25

One of the most promising players ever to enter the National Hockey League was Mike Marson of the Washington Capitals, but he never realized his potential.

Quite a fuss was made when the Washington Capitals of the NHL signed a black, Mike Marson, to a 1974–75 contract. Since then there have been several black players in the majors—Bill Riley, Tony McKegney, and Val James.

Another ripple of excitement was caused in 1981 when the Edmonton Oilers signed Grant Fuhr and he became the first black goalie in NHL history. Fuhr's lot was considerably easier than that confronting black players in the 1930s and 1940s, when blacks in hockey were considered a breed apart, just as they were in professional baseball. Nevertheless, a trio of black stick handlers made a very favorable impression in professional hockey just after the outbreak of World War II. This all-black forward line not only thrived but starred for several years during the 1940s in two of the fastest hockey circuits in North America, the Provincial Hockey League (Quebec) and the Quebec Senior Hockey League.

The black unit was made up of the brothers Herbie and Ossie Carnegie from Toronto, playing center and right wing, and Manny McIntyre of Fredericton, New Brunswick, on left wing. "They would have been good enough to star in the National Hockey League today," claims Larry Zeidel, a former NHL defenseman who played against them in the Quebec League. "But in those days the NHL was a six-team league paying awfully low salaries. Ossie and Herbie were making terrific money in the Quebec League and had side jobs which gave them more security. There was no reason to try for the NHL."

At one time or another, the Toronto Maple Leafs and New York Rangers expressed interest in Herbie Carnegie, the best of the three, but hockey did not have an owner with the courage and foresight of Branch Rickey, who brought Jackie Robinson into major league baseball. So the Carnegies and McIntyre did their thing in the cities throughout Quebec Province, and when the Quebec Senior League went international during the 1946–47 season, the line terrorized teams in New York and Boston with their dipsy-doodle brand of passing and skating.

Those who remember the Carnegies in their halcyon years believe they reached their peak during the 1945–46 season, when they were playing for Sherbrooke Rand in the Provincial League.

Teams played in compact arenas—average capacity 3,500—of prewar vintage, frequently without heating. Spectators generally wore their overcoats throughout the game and visited the refreshment areas for warmth between periods. Few records remain from the long-defunct league, but one man vividly recalls the exploits of the Carnegie-McIntyre line. He is Herbie Carnegie, who was the 1977 Canadian Seniors Golf Champion. In an interview, I conducted with Carnegie for *Hockey* magazine Herbie looked back at the glories—and the disappointments—of the ice games only all-black line.

> HERB CARNEGIE: I was born in Toronto. My brother Ossie, who is three years older than I am, loved hockey and was a great stick handler. Before he even had skates, he could really stick handle, because all we had for about a mile and a half from us were ponds.
>
> FISCHLER: How many kids were in the family?
>
> CARNEGIE: There were seven of us, three girls and four boys. Ossie and I were the only ones who really took to hockey. It was my love, and Ossie's love, that gave us the desire and the drive to play in the National Hockey League.
>
> FISCHLER: Do you remember your first pair of skates?
>
> CARNEGIE: Yes, as a matter of fact. My first pair happened to be my older brother's, which were so large I used my street shoes inside his skates. They fit beautifully.
>
> FISCHLER: Did Ossie influence you?
>
> CARNEGIE: I think I learned a great deal from Ossie. He was a great believer in keeping two hands on his stick. You *had* to have two hands on your stick. And also, I will always remember him saying that your hockey stick was your third leg—if you can picture sort of a tripod. That's where he really taught me to keep my weight on that stick from the shoulders to the waist on down. Then when someone comes to lift your stick, they have to lift a hundred and some-odd pounds. It's not like a toothpick.
>
> FISCHLER: When you were with the Toronto Junior Young Rangers, in the late thirties, where was Ossie?

CARNEGIE: At that point Ossie was playing what we call "mercantile hockey," which would be senior level, in more of a commercial type of operation. Ossie was considered to be the best right winger in the league. Now, that's a pretty broad statement to make. Yet at the same time, he was overlooked by professional teams. He never got an invitation to training camp, which he dearly wanted.

FISCHLER: Normally, would he have got an invitation from the NHL's Toronto Maple Leafs?

CARNEGIE: Well, you would certainly think so, when he's under the noses of all the Toronto scouts, playing right under the nose of Conn Smythe, who owned the Leafs.

FISCHLER: Why didn't he get an invitation?

CARNEGIE: I could only think out-and-out discrimination. I can't say anything else.

FISCHLER: In your case, were you overlooked or bypassed at the junior level, before you got to the Young Rangers?

CARNEGIE: No, I was at Northern Secondary School at that particular time, which is classed as junior B. When you were playing B for a school at that time, there was a regulation that you could not play A. I wanted to play A, so I quit school to go into A before my junior years were over. So I had the one year of junior A. From there I went on into Senior A hockey with my brother, and we won the championship in the Northern Ontario Intermediate League with Timmins. We were the rave of the North, because things started happening. This was the first time Ossie and I played together.

FISCHLER: How did you fit in with your brother?

CARNEGIE: We developed a passing technique that I have never seen any other combination use. To this day I haven't seen it. Just to explain it briefly, it's called a double pass. Ossie, my right winger, would be carrying the puck down to the defenseman. About five to ten feet in front of him, he'd give me the puck, which would bring the defenseman just a little my way. I'd give it immediately back to him. Just click-click. I didn't hesitate at all. I'd give it right back to Ossie. Now, sometimes an opposing player might get used to what you were going to do. So, to keep him off balance, instead of giving it right back, I might push it behind him. Ossie would still be on the fly, and he'd go straight in without breaking at all. It was a beautiful way to beat a pair of defensemen, because I didn't have to go in. The play was really with the wingers.

One of the other things that was great about playing with Ossie was that he was a great positional player. You knew where he was; you knew that he was going to be in the middle or on the left side. This helped tremendously. When he went into the corner with someone, you knew one of two things was going to happen: number one, he was going to come out to get the puck; or number two, his man was not going to come out with the puck. He had the ability to pin his man and maybe we'd get at least a face-off in the corner. This was a tremendous help. And he'd never go into the corner and pass without looking.

If any player could just master those two fundamentals of hockey, it would help him from making errors. Never give the puck away, and look before you pass. Doug Harvey of the Montreal Canadiens was just beautiful at this. He would pull you in, fake you away, but he wouldn't give it away. You'd think the puck was glued onto his stick. Then when he sent it out there—*boom!* A nice, snappy pass, and you're gone. What a treat it would be to play with him, because he waited until you were in position, pulling the men to him, and then, "Okay, now you take it."

FISCHLER: You did well in the second year?

CARNEGIE: Yes. We had several excellent write-ups. We were close to the scoring championship in the four years that we were in Timmins. We won the Northern Ontario championship two years in a row, 1940–41 and 1941–42. In the second season, Manny McIntyre joined our line. This was the first time in Canadian history that a colored forward line had played together in hockey as a unit.

FISCHLER: What attracted McIntyre to Timmins?

CARNEGIE: Manny knew that we were in northern Ontario, and he wrote a letter to our team manager and suggested that he join Ossie and me. The manager could visualize the gate-attraction value of having Manny with us. At first, we were not aware of his hockey ability; we said, "Let's have a try and see how things go." And it worked out beautifully. Great. Manny was a top-notch gentleman. He was always dependable. You knew that he was going to be there. He would do his job and do it well. I think that having Manny on our club gave us a lot of spirit. He had a terrific personality, and was one of the guys who would tell jokes in the dressing room to keep everyone from being too serious. A very likeable fellow.

FISCHLER: What was his playing style like?

CARNEGIE: He was rugged, made good plays, was a fast skater, and would back up from no one. In fact, I think that he and Ossie, at times, tried to take care of me too well. I was one of the untouchables. But we had a great combination. Manny was quite fast and a real good back-checker.

FISCHLER: How did the opposition treat you?

CARNEGIE: They treated us with respect because our ability was equal or superior to a lot of teams we played. We produced, easily, forty to fifty percent of our team's goals. Opponents tried to put a defensive blanket on us, and sometimes they were successful. But most of the time, they were not. If we had a good night, it was a case of coming out of the night with three or five points. And those nights were many.

FISCHLER: Did you think about making it to the NHL?

CARNEGIE: When we saw other players invited to training camps, and we were left behind, it was very depressing. However, we kept trying and saying, "Well, just maybe, someday, it will happen." We never backed down and we always gave our best and never put our tails between our legs because we were overlooked. When I was in northern Ontario, I wrote a letter to the New York Rangers asking for a tryout. I got a letter back from the Rangers' manager, Frank Boucher, saying that their scouts would see that I'd get an invitation if I was good enough. At that point, I was twenty-four or five and just in my heyday. We talked as a group and said, "Wouldn't it be great if we were playing as a line in the NHL?" I don't think it was necessary to imagine ourselves going into the American Hockey League. With all due respect to the AHL, the caliber of hockey that we were playing was as good as the AHL—or better.

FISCHLER: Where did your line go next?

CARNEGIE: We went to Shawinigan Falls and then Sherbrooke. While we were on Sherbrooke, they had a trophy for the most valuable player on the Sherbrooke club. In successive years, 1947, '48, '49, I was voted the most valuable player on the team.

FISCHLER: Did you ever get a shot at the NHL?

CARNEGIE: In 1949 I had a good fortune of going to Lake Placid, to the Rangers' training camp. I was twenty-nine at the time. At the age of twenty-nine, in 1949, as far as hockey was concerned, you might have one year left, maybe two, in the NHL. However, on the third day of training camp, Muzz Patrick came to me and wanted me to go with the Rangers' farm system to Tacoma, Washington, of which Muzz was the coach. I suggested to him that my hockey ability was better than going to Tacoma. He said, "Fine," and nothing more was said.

But on the following day, Lynn Patrick, who had the Rangers' farm team, came to me, and I told him the same thing. And on the third day Phil Watson, who had New Haven in the American League, came to me, and I told *him* the same thing. So that ended the first week of camp. Boucher wanted me to stay in camp until the big stars—Don Raleigh, Edgar Laprade, Sugar Jim Henry, and Jack Evans—came in. On the third day after the big team came in, I was called into Boucher's office. He told me what a great hockey player I was. He said, "You want to be sure that you can play in the NHL, don't you?" And I said, "Mr. Boucher, I *am* sure," and I named some players and I said, "Is my ability less than any one of those?"

So he took the play right away from me and said, "I want to be sure." He wanted to send me to New Haven, of which I didn't want any part. At that stage in my life, I thought I had proven my ability and that was it.

After I left camp, Buddy O'Connor and Edgar Laprade were in an automobile accident, and neither of them played for at least three months because they were hurt pretty severely. Yet I never heard a word from Boucher, and that was the end of my wonderful training-camp experience with New York. I had the highest respect for all of those fellows there, and to me they were perfect gentlemen. We went out, we played golf, we laughed together, we joked together, and we had fun together. When I was leaving, they said to me, "Where are you going?" And that was the end of it.

FISCHLER: You played later for the Quebec Aces with Jean Beliveau, didn't you?

CARNEGIE: Yes, I was in Quebec from 1949 through 1953. I played with Beliveau for two years before he went to the Montreal Canadiens. Punch Imlach (now general manager of the Buffalo Sabres) was our coach.

FISCHLER: How good was Beliveau at the beginning of his pro career?

CARNEGIE: In the initial stages, Beliveau was not living up to expectations. One night I happened to be having dinner with one of Jean's close friends. We were talking about Jean and how come he wasn't producing the way we thought he would. The answer came to me this way: Someone said to me, "Jean feels that there are four favorites of the fans on a team." I was one of them, he said. So I said, "What difference does that make?" He said, "Jean doesn't want to take any play away from the four of you." I said, "You've got to be kidding." And he said, "No, Herb, this is what he told me." So I said, "Would you tell Beliveau to get going before the crowd gets down on him?"

At that point, after six weeks, Beliveau only had seven goals. From that game on, he had better than a point a game, and he went on to win the scoring championship. I've never known an athlete to shy away from doing a job because of other people. But Jean was just a fantastic individual.

In Jean's last year with our club, he was two points ahead of Andre Corriveau. So between myself and the rest of the team, we kept him off the score sheet, Beliveau won the championship, and then he was on his way to Montreal. After the game, Beliveau came over to me, shook my hand, put his arm around me with tears coming down his face, and said, "Thank you." Next thing I knew, I had tears coming down *my* face.

Neither the Carnegies nor Manny McIntyre ever made it to the NHL, but they were big leaguers in the class department. Dick Wilson of the *Sherbrooke Daily Record* is one journalist who saw them in their prime. Wilson believes the Carnegies and McIntyre would have been NHL stars at *any* time, and other critics have supported Wilson's point.

THE ALL-STAR GAMES

The buoyancy, glitter, and fanfare that are part of the contemporary all-star game are in marked contrast to the very first all-star contests played in the 1930s.

By contrast, the earlier tilts—which were unofficial in their nature—were enshrouded in gloom and sentimentality. The very first all-star game, played on February 12, 1934, at Maple Leaf Gardens in Toronto, came about only because a Maple Leaf forward, Ace Bailey, had nearly been killed in an earlier match after a collision with Eddie Shore of the Boston Bruins.

Bailey, who was carried from the ice at Boston Garden, hovered between life and death for several days before he finally emerged from the crisis. Unfortunately, the Toronto ace could never play hockey again and, because of that, an Ace Bailey Benefit Game was held.

The idea was for an all-star team to be chosen from all of the NHL teams with the exception of the Maple Leafs. The Toronto sextet would then go up against the stars.

Maple Leaf Gardens was packed to the roof for three very good reasons: everyone wanted to raise money for the popular Bailey; an NHL all-star game was a revolutionary idea; and reports circulated that Eddie Shore would meet Bailey face to face at center ice.

Shore was there. Frank Selke, Sr., who was then a Maple Leafs executive, recalls: "One of the most dramatic moments was the moment before the opening face-off, when Bailey was able to meet Shore at center ice to shake hands with him."

Bailey, who was in civilian clothes, walked onto the ice with head bared. When Ace clasped hands with Shore, the building rocked with applause. Shore, who had expected to be booed by the Toronto crowd, was astonished each time he moved the puck. "He was applauded warmly," noted one newspaper report, "in a sporting gesture that moved even flinthearted sportswriters."

On paper, at least, that very first all-star game appeared to be tilted in favor of the dream team. Such future Hall of Famers as Howie Morenz, Ching Johnson, Chuck Gardiner, Aurel Joliat, Bill Cook, Lionel Conacher, and Nels Stewart graced the stars lineup. But the well-disciplined Leafs hammered out a 7–3 victory.

More than twenty-three thousand dollars was raised for Bailey, so to that extent the all-star game was a success. However, no further plans were made for a repeat of such a game.

Ironically, Chuck Gardiner, who guarded the goal for the all-stars, was playing his last season. He died the following June after leading his Chicago Black Hawks to a Stanley Cup triumph.

Tragedy again was a catalyst for the second unofficial NHL all-star game, this time on November 2, 1937, following the death of the Montreal Canadiens' superhero Howie (the Stratford Flash) Morenz.

Montreal's Forum was the site of the Morenz benefit. Instead of using players from the Montreal Canadiens, a combined club, comprising members of the Canadiens as well as the Montreal Maroons, united to face the all-stars. The Montrealers lost 6–5, but some twenty-five thousand dollars was raised for the Morenz family.

Babe Siebert, one of the giants of the pre–World War II NHL, was the unfortunate reason for having a third all-star match. After an illustrious career with both Montreal teams as well as with the New York Rangers and Boston Bruins, Siebert was appointed coach of the Canadiens early in the summer of 1939. But Babe never made it behind the Montreal bench; he drowned later that summer in Lake Huron.

The all-star game to benefit Siebert's widow and children pitted the Canadiens, the last team for which Babe played, against the dream team. The all-stars beat the Habitants, 5–2. More than fifteen thousand dollars was raised for the Siebert family.

Such grim surroundings that were a part of the prewar all-star contests disappeared once the games became official following World War II. The original concept, beginning with the 1947 contest, had the Stanley Cup champions skating against the all-stars. The all-stars triumphed, 4–3, over the cup champion Maple Leafs. A year later (November 3) the venue was switched to the Chicago Stadium, but again the Leafs were cup champs and again the all-stars won, this time by a score of 3–1.

Lo and behold, Toronto won an unprecedented third straight Stanley Cup in 1949, so the Leafs tried their luck against the all-stars a third time on October 10, 1949, at Maple Leaf Gardens. Coach Hap Day's skaters obviously had not learned a lesson. They lost again, 3–1.

For the first time, Montreal's hallowed Forum was the site of an official all-star game in 1953, and this time there was plenty of excitement before the opening face-off. Most of it centered around much-publicized rookie Jean Beliveau, whom the Canadiens had been futilely pursuing for several years. The big question prior to the game, on October 3, 1953, was whether or not big Beliveau would be wearing the bleu, blanc, *et* rouge (blue, white, and red) of Les Canadiens that night.

Sure enough, Canadiens general manager Frank Selke, Sr., got Beliveau's signature on a contract that very afternoon and Le Gros Bill skated for the Habs against the stars. He didn't help, though, as the stars skated off with a 3–1 win.

What made the 1962 all-star game so unusual was a pregame event that stole the headlines from the classic itself. Maple Leafs left wing Frank Mahovlich inadvertently proved to be the headline grabber following a closed-door meeting of league governors.

Out of the meeting came the news that Black Hawks owner Jim Norris had offered the Leafs a certified check for $1 million to obtain the gifted Mahovlich. At first it appeared that the committee that then operated the Leafs would accept, but at the eleventh hour the deal was cancelled and Mahovlich remained a Leaf. The game, in which Toronto defeated the all-stars 4–1, was almost an afterthought in view of "l'affaire Mahovlich."

Appropriately, it was the same Mahovlich who grabbed the ink a year later, only this time on the ice. Frank scored two goals for the Leafs and assisted on a third as the Maple Leafs tied the all-stars 3–3. Stan Mikita, the Black Hawks' crack center, was supposed to start for the selects but missed the game because he had failed to sign his contract by face-off time.

Maurice Richard had long since retired by the time the 1965 all-star game was played, but his name remained on the lips of hockey fans partly because the Rocket had held the record (eight) for goals scored in all-star games. That mark finally was shattered on October 20, 1965, when Gordie Howe scored a pair for the dream team as it defeated Montreal 5–2, giving Howe a total of nine goals in all-star play.

The Rocket was in the stands for the January 18, 1967, all-star game at the Montreal Forum. Maurice's kid brother, Henri, kept the Richard colors flying by scoring a goal as the Canadiens defeated the all-stars 3–0. John Ferguson also scored a pair for Montreal.

The contest in Montreal was significant in yet another respect, for it marked the first time that the annual all-star game was played in mid-season. It proved to be the beginning of a tradition that held true until the 1981 match, which was held for the first time in Los Angeles.

Many observers still regard the first *official* game as the best.

If ever a club was destined to instill fear in the hearts of its foe it was the official NHL all-star team assembled for the first time in what was to become an annual event featuring la creme de la creme of professional hockey.

The format for what was dubbed Hockey's Greatest Show at Maple Leaf Gardens on October 13, 1947, called for the Stanley Cup Champion Toronto Maple Leafs to face off against the best of the rest.

Before the first puck was dropped, there was high drama and seething tempers. By sheer coincidence the 1947 cup-winning Leafs had failed to place a single player on either the first or second all-star teams, a fact that infuriated Toronto boss Conn Smythe and his coach Hap Day. The Leafs players themselves weren't too happy about it either.

"I offer my condolences in advance to the Leafs," snapped Bruins general manager Art Ross. "They are going to get a whipping."

Other hockey critics supported Ross. Jim Coleman, then columnist for the *Toronto Globe and Mail*, labeled the 1947 all-star team "the best aggregation of players ever assembled on one ice surface."

There could be little argument with that statement. All-star coach Dick Irvin of the Montreal Canadiens had four-time Vezina Trophy–winner Bill Durnan of the Canadiens in goal with Frankie (Mister Zero) Brimsek of the Bruins as backup. (Brimsek, appropriately, wore a zero on his sweater.) Irwin iced only four defensemen—Montreal's Emile (Butch) Bouchard and Ken Reardon, along with the Detroit Red Wings aces (Black) Jack Stewart and Bill Quackenbush.

Irwin used eleven forwards, nine representing complete lines with their own teams.

Boston offered "the Kraut Line" of Milt Schmidt, Woody Dumart, and Bobby Bauer. The Chicago Black Hawks delivered their "Pony Line" of Max and Doug Bentley and Bill Mosienko. From the Rangers came a complete unit—Edgar Laprade, Tony Leswick, and Grant (Knobby) Warwick.

The only mixed line consisted of Maurice (the Rocket) Richard of the Canadiens, Detroit's Ted Lindsay, and Milt Schmidt of Boston.

Long before the game began, a verbal contest heated up between Conn Smythe and Art Ross. Smythe was miffed after reading a headline in the *Globe and Mail* that proclaimed: " 'Sorry for Smythe' Says Ross. All-Star Team Unbeatable."

To that, Smythe replied: "That Ross had better bring a supply of aspirins with him. Every time he opens his mouth he puts his foot in it. This time we'll shove the whole Leaf team down his throat."

"Our boys are ready, and if the all-stars are in shape it should be quite a game, yes, quite a game. Why that Ross . . . !"

For the inaugural game the all-stars were decked out in special uniforms featuring scarlet and red jerseys, stars across the breast, and white stripes on the arms and shoulders with the letters NHL on a crest in the center.

Referee King Clancy and linesman Jim Primeau and Eddie Mepham wore midnight blue uniforms, the design and color of which was selected by NHL President Clarence Campbell. "I'm a little tired of the same old white sweaters and suggested the dark shirt and slacks as an alternative," said Campbell.

The bizarre officials' attire drew a derisive comment from Jim Coleman. "The chaps," noted Coleman, "looked like hangmen or mortuary attendants."

With all the advanced build-up the game had to be good to avoid the inevitable letdown—and it *was* good.

As predicted, the Maple Leafs' teamwork gave them an advantage over the all-stars—at the beginning, at least. Toronto's top line of Syl Apps, Bill Ezinicki, and Harry Watson dominated play in the first period, with Watson finally breaking the ice with a goal at 12:29 on a pass from Ezinicki.

It was obvious from the opening face-off that players from both sides were putting their pride on the line. "The clash," observed Jim Vipond of the *Globe and Mail*, "was exhibition in name only, as the opposing players ripped into each other with Stanley Cup gusto."

The 14,318 fans jamming Maple Leaf Gardens cheered again when Ezinicki converted Apps's pass at 1:03 of the second period. At this point the all-stars looked as if they were out of it, but Max Bentley aroused his mates by beating Leafs goalie Turk Broda at 4:38 on a pass from Ken Reardon.

Toronto's captain Apps gave the Leafs another two-goal advantage with an assist from Watson at 5:01 of the second period, but the goal only served to inspire the all-stars. Taking a pass from the old smoothie Edgar Laprade, Grant Warwick outwitted Broda at 17:35 of the second period, narrowing the Leafs' margin to one.

"It took the selects the better part of two periods to get acquainted," commented Jim Vipond.

By the start of the third period the dream team looked as if it had been practicing together for weeks. Rocket Richard tied the score at twenty-eight seconds of the third period, bouncing a shot off defenseman Gus Mortson's skate. Then, with Mortson in the penalty box for tripping, Doug Bentley scored on assists from Milt Schmidt and Richard, giving the all-stars a 4–3 lead.

Bentley had been moved off the Pony Line after the game's only serious accident occurred early in the second period. Bill Mosienko attempted to outflank Leafs' defenseman Jim Thomson, but Thomson caught the Chicago forward with a perfectly timed—and clean—bodycheck. Mosienko, who was traveling at high speed, crashed to the ice with a fractured left ankle.

Bristling rough play kept fans on the edge of their seats throughout the match. Butch Bouchard and Ken Reardon dueled several times with (Wild) Bill Ezinicki.

Other victims included Bob Goldham, who suffered a gash on the side of the head, courtesy of Reardon; and Vic Lynn, who suffered a deep gash over the left eye when he crashed into the boards.

The all-stars preserved their slim lead and skated off with a well-earned 4–3 decision.

The game was a success on several counts. "It was an exciting contest," wrote Jim Vipond. Others commended the players for their vigorous effort. NHL President Campbell, who helped launch the Players' Pension Fund, was delighted with the fact that the game drew a gross gate of $25,842, of which $17,228 was paid into the pension fund.

Most important was the fact that the league was able to launch a precedent: an annual all-star game. It was also heartening that the all-stars fulfilled their notices.

Nobody summed up the prevailing opinion better than Jim Coleman, who commented after viewing the all-stars, "Watta team!"

THE NHL'S ONLY "AMERICAN" TEAM

When Herb Brooks led the United States Olympic team to a gold medal triumph at Lake Placid in 1980, the event signaled a high-water mark for American hockey. And when Olympians such as Ken Morrow, Mike Ramsey, Steve Christoff, and Mark Johnson instantly leaped into the NHL, the Americanization of big league hockey was said to have finally taken place,

It made pleasant reading, but the Americanization claim was a mistake. Actually, NHL hockey had taken on a distinctive star-spangled hue forty-four years earlier.

The man responsible for it was the eccentric Major Frederic McLaughlin. The major realized that American athletes were as good as those ranging from Cambodia to Canada. If an American could skate, why couldn't he play major league hockey?

McLaughlin, a multimillionaire who owned the Chicago Black Hawks, decided that he would populate his club with Americans and eventually win the Stanley Cup.

In the 1935–36 season, the major began to plant the seeds for his all-American NFL team. He traded Lorne Chabot to the Maroons and decided to go with Mike Karakas, a ruddy-faced goaltender from Eveleth, Minnesota. The Hawks finished third, six points out of first place. Then they lost to the New York Americans in the semifinal round.

Instead of improving, the Hawks deteriorated as the 1936–37 season progressed. As his team plumbed new depths of ineptitude, the major became more and more determined to fill his lineup with Americans. One of his leading forwards, Johnny Gottselig, expressed the sentiment of the team when he observed, "We thought it [the all-American plan] was pretty ridiculous."

McLaughlin's scouts eventually extracted Albert Suomi, Curly Brink, Bun LaPrarie, Butch Schaefer, and Earnest "Ike" Klingbeil from the Minnesota–Michigan hockey belt and imported them to Chicago under cover. The major wasn't quite ready to spring the surprise on the unwitting public, nor did he want to risk a flop. His first project was to condition the athletes, so he sent them to none other than former coach Emil Iverson, who now bore the title of physical director of the Black Hawks.

"His idea of workouts," said Gottselig, "was to have them stand straight with hands on hips. The tips of the toes were to touch. From that position he'd put the guys through bending and stretching exercises."

Borrowing a leaf from the Godfrey Matheson book, the major ordered his American players to conduct private workouts on the Chicago Stadium ice. It was like having a second platoon completely divorced in strategy and philosophy from the first.

When the Americans finally faced their Canadian teammates, the more experienced veterans treated the newcomers with utter contempt. They refused to sit next to the Americans and ignored them as if they weren't there. When the two teams scrimmaged, the Canadians really laid on the lumber.

"It was awfully rough," said Klingbeil in an interview. "They came at us with the works—high sticks and everything."

To prevent a bloodbath the major agreed to sprinkle the Canadian lineup with Americans and vice versa. In this way Klingbeil and Schaefer played defense with a Canadian forward line. The integration proved a tonic all around. Suddenly, the team's spirits were buoyed and they began climbing in the standings.

Somehow this integrated lineup didn't appeal to the spectators, though. Despite the Americans, they weren't flocking to Chicago Stadium. The reason, the major believed, was that all five Americans weren't on the ice at the same time. Yet he was stymied. The Black Hawks were right in the midst of a play-off race, and to put the Americans out all at once would bring almost certain defeat. His only hope, strangely enough, was for the team to be eliminated from contention. Then he could safely experiment with the American line.

It wasn't until the last weekend of the season that the Black Hawks cooperated and finally bowed out of the race. McLaughlin announced that the Yanks would be present in force for the last home game, against the Boston Bruins. As luck would have it, the publicity did a boomerang turn on the major. Hockey's most beloved star, Howie Morenz of the Montreal Canadiens, was dying in a hospital at the time, and the Black Hawks, though wrongfully, had been blamed because Morenz had broken his leg tripping over a Chicago player.

When McLaughlin's scheme was made public, the Canadian managers and coaches throughout the league were infuriated. They denounced the major and demanded his expulsion from the NHL. Nevertheless, McLaughlin persisted with his plan, and when the Black Hawks met the Bruins they faced a Boston team determined to bludgeon them into the ice. Fortunately, Klingbeil and friends retaliated, but even though they held the Bruins to a draw in the department of fisticuffs, they lost the game 6–2.

In their next challenge the Yanks performed better, however. They invaded Maple Leaf Gardens in Toronto and emerged with only a 3–2 loss. In a way, they won a victory, because they fought the Leafs on even terms and gave every indication of improving. In their third game Klingbeil's pals finally came out on top by edging Lester Patrick's New York Rangers, 4–3. It was a stirring triumph, because earlier Patrick had derided the Americans as "amateurs."

Although the Hawks were eventually whipped by both the New York Americans and the Bruins, the idea of American-born skaters seemed good enough to be continued as far as the major was concerned. When the following season began, more than half of his lineup consisted of United States–born skaters. In addition, he hired an American coach, baseball umpire Bill Stewart.

McLaughlin hired Stewart while he was umpiring a ball game in Philadelphia. The major sent a wire inviting the Massachusetts-born umpire to both manage and coach the Black Hawks. McLaughlin knew Stewart not only for his superb baseball work but also for his hockey refereeing, which had elevated him to chief arbiter in the NHL. "The major proposed a one-year contract," said Stewart, "but I was having none of that. When he finally agreed to a two-year contract, I also insisted on an ironclad agreement that I was to be the absolute boss."

Stewart was well aware of the major's penchant for interfering with the club. And when McLaughlin wasn't around, there always was the threat of Bill Tobin's putting in his two cents' worth. If he could handle the club his way, Stewart believed there would be no problem winning hockey games. "This was the happiest club I ever saw in professional sports," Stewart has said. "And we had some pretty good talent, too. Players like Gottselig, 'Mush' March, Paul Thompson, Art Wiebe, and Doc Romnes. Lionel Conacher once told me he regarded Romnes as one of the finest centers he ever played with. The biggest reason we won, though, was that we had Earl Seibert on our defense. The big guy played about fifty-five minutes of every game."

Stewart's contract may have been "ironclad," but he found the major as omnipresent as ever, and the strong-willed pair feuded and feuded. Usually, Stewart won.

Most of the time, they argued about the relative merits of certain players. Right off the bat there was a clash when a choice had to be made between Oscar Hanson and Cully Dahlstrom, two younger players acquired by the Black Hawks. The major made no bones about his preference for Hanson. McLaughlin was swayed by Hanson's minor league record, but Stewart unequivocally pointed at Dahlstrom as his man. The major won a small concession: Stewart would use Hanson for at least ten games.

Stewart went along with that end of the bargain, but then he dropped Hanson. Dahlstrom thoroughly underlined his coach's faith in him by winning the Calder Trophy as the NHL's rookie of the year. Later, when Stewart obtained Carl Voss from the Montreal Maroons, McLaughlin was absolutely convinced that his coach had goofed. After watching Voss in one game, the major insisted that he be cut from the squad as an obvious loser. This time Stewart was adamant. Voss would stay. Voss not only stayed, but he later played an important part in Chicago's most stirring hockey triumph since the birth of the Black Hawks.

Meanwhile, the Americanized Black Hawks managed to plod along through the schedule at a slightly quicker pace than the Red Wings. The result was that Chicago finished third in the American Division, just two points ahead of its Detroit pursuers but a good thirty points behind division-leading Boston. Their chances for winning the Stanley Cup were considered no better than 100 to 1.

To begin with, the Hawks were the only one of the six qualifying teams to have less than a .500 record (14–25–9), and their first-round opponents were the Montreal Canadiens, who had a considerably more respectable 18–17–13 mark. Further complicating matters for Chicago was the fact that two of the three games would be played in the Montreal Forum.

Predictably, the Canadiens won the First match, 6–4. But when the series shifted to Chicago, goalie Karakas shut out the Montrealers, 4–0. Suddenly the Black Hawks were coming on strong. The final game was tied, 2–2, after regulation time. It was decided in Chicago's favor when Lou Trudel's long shot bounced off Paul Thompson and into the Montreal cage, although some observers insist that the puck was shot home by "Mush" March.

Now the Black Hawks were to face an equally aroused New York American sextet that had just routed its archrivals in Manhattan, the Rangers, in three games. Once again the Hawks would have the benefit of only one home game in the best of three series. The Americans opened with a 3–1 victory at Madison Square Garden. But when the series shifted to Chicago, Karakas took over again, and the teams battled to the end of regulation time without a score.

The game was settled in sudden-death overtime by none other than Cully Dahlstrom, the man McLaughlin had once lobbied against so vigorously. Chicago clinched the series with a third-period goal by Doc Romnes in the third game. The final score was 3–2, and the Black Hawks advanced into the Stanley Cup finals against the Toronto Maple Leafs.

By now the betting odds had dropped considerably in Chicago's favor. But they soared again when it was learned that Karakas had suffered a broken toe in the final game with the Americans. Karakas didn't realize the extent of the damage until he attempted to lace on his skates for the game with Toronto. He just couldn't make it, and the Hawks suddenly became desperate for a goaltender.

The Leafs were not in the least sympathetic to the Black Hawks' problem and summarily rejected requests for goaltending assistance. So the Chicago brass finally unearthed Alfie Moore, a minor league, free-agent goalie, who purportedly was quaffing liquid refreshment in a Toronto pub when he was drafted to play goal for the Chicagoans. Moore answered the call and went into the Chicago nets on April 5, 1938, defeating Toronto, 3–1, in the opening game of the series at Maple Leaf Gardens.

For the second game the Hawks decided to try their luck with Paul Goodman, another minor league goaltender. But this time Toronto rebounded with a strong 5–1 decision.

It was obvious that if the Hawks were to win they urgently required the services of Karakas. This was accomplished when he was outfitted with a special shoe to protect his broken toe. Chicago won the game before a record crowd of 18,496 at the stadium on goals by Romnes and Carl Voss, whom McLaughlin had wanted to discard. The score was 2–1.

By now the Leafs were reeling, and Chicago applied the coup de grâce with relative ease in the fourth game, routing Toronto, 4–1, on goals by Dahlstrom, Voss, Shill, and March. After the game, when the ecstatic Chicago players sought out the Stanley Cup, they finally realized what an upset they had engineered.

"NHL President Calder had earlier caused the trophy to be shipped to Toronto," wrote Edward Burns in the *Chicago Tribune*, "reportedly on the assurance that a hockey team which harbored eight American-born hockey players as did the Hawks couldn't possibly win the Stanley Cup."

The victory was especially gratifying to Stewart, for it vindicated his judgment about several players, especially Voss and Dahlstrom. It appeared that he would be with the Black Hawks for many years, except that with Major McLaughlin, one never knew for sure.

By the 1938–39 season, Stewart was running a fairly solid ship with a record of nineteen points in twenty-one games. Then the Black Hawks played the Canadiens. The coach has recalled the game well because it catapulted him right out a job. "We were leading, 1–0 at Chicago with a minute to go," Stewart has said. "They tied it up on a long shot and 'Toe' Blake beat us in overtime. Funny thing about it is that our club was in third place when the major fired me. I had a two-year contract and they had to pay me every nickel [for the remaining year]. I took off for Florida to spend the major's money and drowned my sorrow in sunshine."

With Stewart gone, the Hawks plummeted to the bottom of the league and finished in seventh place in the newly reorganized seven-team, one-division circuit, Somehow, they rallied for a fourth-place comeback the following year but were quickly vanquished by Toronto in two games of the play-off semifinal.

HOCKEY IN THE 1980s

Throughout the late 1970s, as the World Hockey Association fought for its life, the maverick league hoped that it would ultimately force the National Hockey League to accept a merger in which most of the WHA clubs would be incorporated into a mammoth NHL designed along the grandiose lines of the National Football League.

Although many of the old-guard NHL owners bitterly resented any accommodation with the WHA, two governors from the established league—William Jennings of New York and Ed Snider of Philadelphia—attempted to arrange a truce with the WHA people. The old guard kept believing that, eventually, the WHA would fold and the NHL's problems would be solved, but somehow the new league found ways and means of surviving. When Howard Baldwin took over the WHA presidency, the bitterness that previously existed between the leagues subsided. Baldwin and Snider had been good friends ever since the former worked for the Philadelphia Flyers in 1968. More important, the NHL picked a new president, John Ziegler, to replace the retiring patriarch Clarence Campbell. Campbell had been an archfoe of the WHA, but the younger Ziegler was more inclined to compromise.

Once Ziegler took office, behind-the-scenes negotiations between the NHL and WHA were launched. Since both leagues had been suffering acutely from the lengthy war, it no longer was a question of whether there would be peace but rather how many WHA teams would be included in the merged league when the treaty was signed.

When the smoke finally cleared from the meeting room four WHA franchises—Quebec Nordiques, Winnipeg Jets, Edmonton Oilers, and Hartford Whalers—were welcomed to the NHL. The three Canadian teams were given excellent chances of becoming instant successes, financially if not artistically, but doubt was raised over the acceptance of the Hartford entry. Critics suggested that a relatively small city such as Hartford could not survive in a high-priced major league, but Baldwin, who moved from the WHA helm to the directorship of the Whalers, argued that his club could be just as successful in the NHL as the Green Bay Packers have been in the NFL.

The cessation of hostilities was truly a blessing to the NHL, which was having difficulty dealing with inflated salaries and a few marginal franchises. The Kansas City Scouts had folded and transferred to Denver where they became the Colorado Rockies. The Cleveland Barons could not draw enough people to the Richfield (Ohio) Coliseum and were bought by the Minnesota North Stars. The North Stars placed the best of the Barons in their lineup and became one of the most competitive teams in the NHL

Amid new surroundings, the Scouts-Rockies still had difficulty luring customers. After a tumultuous eight seasons in Colorado the franchise abandoned Denver in

1982 and moved to East Rutherford, New Jersey, where they became the New Jersey Devils, playing out of the Byrne-Meadowlands Arena.

The upheavals off the ice seemed to have affected the play in the rinks. As the NHL entered the 1980s the professional game took on a new face. The success of teenager Wayne Gretzky inspired teams to sign younger players, and the youngsters in turn put the accent on offense instead of defense—with astonishing results.

During the 1980–81 season the league's twenty-one clubs averaged 7.7 goals, the highest since the NHL had introduced the center red line in 1943. Even first-rate goalies such as Tony Esposito of the Chicago Black Hawks were victimized. A year later the average climbed again, this time to a staggering 8.03. "It used to be you'd get three or four goals and you were a cinch to win," said the late Penguins' general manager Baz Bastien. "Now you can score five, and there's a good chance you'll lose."

Typical of the trend was the scores on one night: Boston 10, Quebec 1; Toronto 9, Los Angeles 4; Pittsburgh 7, Philadelphia 2. "Today," said Black Hawk goalie Tony Esposito, "you can go through a whole season without a shutout."

The trend continued through the 1982–83 campaign. On one night in which five games were played, 55 goals were scored. A night later there were five more games and 55 more goals scored. One hundred and ten goals in two nights!

There were several explanations for the new trend. Increased use of the slapshot had enabled even average players to propel the puck at speeds of up to 120 miles per hour, faster than ever. Teams have employed back-up (less competent) goaltenders more often than at any time in the past. Many teams have theorized that high-scoring hockey, by its very nature, is more appealing. "Fans like to see 6–5 games more than 1–0 games," said Wayne Gretzky. "I know we prefer them, too."

Others have suggested that the art of defense, quite simply, has been lost on the younger players. "No one knows how to play defense when it's three-on-three in your own end," said scout Claude Ruel of the Montreal Canadiens. "That's why so many loose puck goals are scored—because somebody isn't covering his area, and the puck comes out to some guy who's all alone. You can't let people stand around alone in the middle."

Some experts predicted that the trend toward inflationary scoring would be halted by the mid-1980s and that there would be a return to more defensive-oriented, lower-scoring games. "The trend has been to eliminate the older, experienced players and get the younger, quicker, offensively aggressive players, and, as a result, the scores went up," said Glen Sather, general manager of the Edmonton Oilers. "The younger players were so good offensively that, after a few years, the area in which they'll improve is defense."

A number of other significant trends occurred at the start of the 1980s, all of them positive. The triumph of the American Olympic team at Lake Placid in 1980 focused attention on collegiate hockey and, particularly, the possibilities of more American skaters playing in the NHL.

Soon after the Olympic games had been concluded, a number of Uncle Sam's

1-26   One of the most durable NHL goaltenders, Tony Esposito, broke in with the Montreal Canadiens but played his best hockey with the Chicago Black Hawks.

skaters signed with NHL teams. In 1981 former Olympic coach Herb Brooks signed a contract with the New York Rangers. A year later Bob Johnson, a successful coach at the University of Wisconsin, was signed by the Calgary Flames of the NHL. It marked the first time that a Canadian major league club had signed an American collegiate coach.

Even more significantly, in terms of the major strides being taken by American players, was the fact that the Washington Capitals signed eighteen-year-old Bobby Carpenter of Peabody, Massachusetts, to an NHL contract in 1981. Carpenter became the first American to leap from high school to the NHL, yet veterans such as Bobby Clarke still proved valuable. This sequence of events had great meaning to serious hockey critics who chart the winds of change in the sport. It signified a major upheaval in the balance of power, on a par with the steady rise in the number of Europeans playing in North America. Americans were making their biggest inroads into the NHL.

Toronto Star hockey analyst Rex MacLeod frankly conceded that Americans might dominate the sport by 1990. "Like it or not," said MacLeod, "there is evidence that Americans will be in the majority in the NHL in a few years."

1-27   Unquestionably the most persevering player of the 1970s and early 1980s, Bobby Clarke of the Philadelphia Flyers has prevailed despite the fact that he is a diabetic.

Some of the best evidence was produced by the 1980 Olympians. Defenseman Ken Morrow moved directly from Lake Placid to Uniondale, New York, where he became an instant regular on the New York Islanders. "Kenny," said Islanders coach Al Arbour, "was one of the main reasons why we won four straight Stanley Cups."

Likewise, Steve Christoff graduated from the Olympians to the Minnesota North Stars, Dave Christian emerged as a star with the Winnipeg Jets, and Mark Johnson signed with the Pittsburgh Penguins.

The roots of the Olympic triumph could be found in several American universities, where hockey has become a prestige sport on a level with football. The training an American stick handler receives is on a par with anything Canada can offer. "Already," says Buffalo Sabres assistant coach Red Berenson, "we're seeing U.S. college players who can do a lot of things, like passing, better than Canadians can."

Perhaps most persuasive in the case for Americanization of hockey is the numbers. There was a time, not very long ago, when an American in the NHL was no less a rarity than Bedouin tribesmen in Lapland. Tommy Williams, a mediocre performer who played for the Boston Bruins from 1961 to 1969, was regarded as something close to a saint only because he was the only American in the NHL at the time. In the years directly after his retirement, there was a great influx of Americans into the NHL ranks.

"At the rate Americans are coming in," said Canadian author Rick Boulton, "there won't be any Canadians left in the NHL by 1999!"

Boulton is exaggerating to make a point, but the point is that Americans have brought a new dimension to the game that was invented on frozen Canadian ponds late in the nineteenth century. One who has effectively orchestrated America's hockey tune is Herb Brooks, architect of the Rangers' renaissance.

Although twenty out of the twenty-one major league clubs managed to thumb their noses at the chessboard passing and endless accent on motion that character- izes the Soviet style, Brooks immediately adopted it to NHL play—and made it work.

"A lot of Canadian hockey coaches were rooting against Brooks *because* he is an American," said an NHL executive, "but he was so good in his rookie season (1981–82) that he just about shut them up."

More than that, Brooks paved the way for Bob Johnson to go from the University of Wisconsin campus to the Stampede Corral, where he began coaching the previously uncoachable Flames. That a Canadian team should look to the United States for a hockey coach was considered roughly equivalent to a Brazilian's journeying to Kenya for coffee. "We hired Johnson, not because of—or in spite of—the fact that he's an American, but because he was the best available," said Flames general manager Cliff Fletcher.

If Johnson's arrival in the pro league shocked a few souls, the Washington Capitals' decision to sign a New England teenager to a three-year contract for $600,000 was right out of Ripley's Believe It Or Not. Yet there was Bobby Carpenter bridging the gap between St. John's Prep in Danvers, Massachusetts, and the Capital Centre in Landover, Maryland.

Carpenter played all eighty games for Washington in 1981–82, scoring an impressive thirty-two goals and thirty-five assists for sixty-seven points. "It was my challenge to be the first American kid to make it from right out of high school to the top pros," said Carpenter. "Now that I'm here, I'm not going to blow it."

Just who is the best American skating in the NHL in the early 1980s is a matter of debate. Winnipeg Jets general manager John Ferguson believed it was his twenty-three-year-old forward Dave Christian from Warroad, Minnesota. "You can count on one hand the number of guys in the NHL who are as complete hockey players as Dave is," said Ferguson. "He was a boy I wanted to build my team around." With Christian leading the way, Winnipeg made the playoffs for the first time last season. But in 1983 Christian was dealt to Washington.

Although hockey is now played in almost every state in the union, professional scouts focus on New England and Minnesota more than the other areas. In the early 1950s the twin cities of St. Paul-Minneapolis had only 3 hockey rinks, whereas now there are 40, not to mention 140 indoor rinks throughout Minnesota.

Thus, eyebrows were not raised in June 1982 when the Buffalo Sabres plucked St. Paul high school star Phil Housley as their first pick in the annual draft. Sabres general manager Scotty Bowman described the Minnesotan as "the closest thing I've seen to Bobby Orr." Higher praise is simply not available.

The pros will double their concentration on American high schools, but Uncle Sam's universities will remain the mother lode of future NHL talent. "These days," said University of Minnesota coach Brad Buetow, "there are at least a half-a-dozen scouts at every one of our games. It's obvious that our American players are being taken seriously."

So seriously, in fact, that Canadian players are feeling increasingly more insecure about their ability to dominate the professional game, and well they might. "There was a time," said Providence College coach Lou Lamorello, "when the American player was overlooked, but the Olympic win in 1980 changed all that. Now all NHL scouts go to high school games."

The NHL believes that one main reason for its increase from six to twenty-one teams over the past fifteen years has been the development of hockey at the college level in the United States. In 1982–83, no fewer than 62 of the 506 players to have appeared in NHL games had obtained their training at an American institution of higher education. Included in that group are numerous Canadian natives who moved to the college ranks in search of strong academic and athletic training.

The oldest NHL player is Chicago Black Hawks' goaltender Tony Esposito (forty), who hails from Sault Ste. Marie, Ontario. The three-time Vezina Trophy winner began his illustrious career in 1968–69 after having played with Michigan Tech. Esposito was one of only eight players that season who had moved to the NHL ranks through the American college system.

The biggest yearly increase occurred during the 1972–73 season when twenty-six U.S. college graduates appeared in at least one NHL game. That was an increase of more than 50 percent over the previous season. Red Berenson was joined by players such as forward Cliff Koroll (University of Denver) with the Black Hawks and goaltender Wayne Thomas (University of Wisconsin) with the Montreal Canadiens. Both retired from playing duty and went on to serve as assistant coaches with Chicago and the New York Rangers, respectively.

The numbers continued to increase each year, and the 1974–75 season featured forty-two American college graduates, including former University of Denver star Peter McNab, who played with Buffalo and then the Boston Bruins. The Vancouver, B.C., native ranks as the highest scorer among active U.S. college alumni. During his first nine seasons in the NHL, McNab scored 276 goals and added 318 assists for 594 points.

In 1979–80, the figures showed another substantial increase, for nearly 12 percent of NHL players had pre-NHL training in U.S. college ranks. Such stars as Dave Taylor of the Los Angeles Kings and team captains Russ Anderson of the

Hartford Whalers (University of Minnesota), Rod Langway of the Washington Capitals (University of New Hampshire), and Dave Christian of the Winnipeg Jets (University of North Dakota) were included in the group.

During the 1981–82 season 13.2 percent of the league's players had attended American colleges. In 1967–68, the figure was 1.6 percent. The University of Minnesota had sixteen former players appear in the NHL followed by the University of North Dakota with eight and the University of New Hampshire with seven. There was a total of twenty-six American universities and colleges represented in the NHL in 1983.

Just as there has been a sharp rise in the number of former U.S. collegiate players to make it to the NHL, so too has there been a dramatic increase in the number of American-born players to make the NHL during the past fifteen years.

In 1982–83 nearly 10 percent of those who played a game were American born, whereas in 1967–68 there were a total of six Americans, or 1.9 percent.

When Rangers' veteran Robbie Ftorek (Needham, Massachusetts) broke into the NHL with the Detroit Red Wings in 1972–73, he was one of only twenty American-born players to appear that season. Current Rangers' general manager Craig Patrick (Detroit) scored twenty goals with California that season, and Hartford's assistant manager Larry Pleau (Lynn, Massachusetts) joined New England of the World Hockey Association after spending three seasons with Montreal.

By the 1976–77 season the number had increased to thirty-four American-born players. That season saw Lee Fogolin, a native of Chicago, help lead the Sabres to a 48-24-8 record. Fogolin, who appeared in his 250th consecutive game with the Edmonton Oilers on October 26, 1982, was one of four American-born players serving as captain of an NHL team in that season, joining Anderson, Langway, and Christian.

The greatest single-season increase came in 1979–80 when sixty-six American-born players appeared in the NHL—twenty-four more than the previous year. During that season, no fewer than eight members of the U.S. Olympic gold medal winning team joined the NHL, including defenseman Ken Morrow, who was a key ingredient in leading the New York Islanders to their first of four Stanley Cups.

Interestingly, the Islanders' four-cup parlay marked the first time that an American-based team had ever accomplished such a feat—both the Toronto Maple Leafs and Montreal Canadiens each had won three or more cups in a row twice—and marked the Long Island club as the closest to achieving a dynasty in the 1980s. Leafs and Montreal Canadiens each had won three or more cups in a row twice—and marked the Long Island club as the closest to achieving a dynasty in the 1980s.

However, the fleet, young Edmonton Oilers defeated the Islanders four games to one in the 1984 Stanley Cup finals. Paced by the incomparable Wayne Gretzky, the Oilers successfully defended the championship and routed the Philadelphia Flyers in five games to retain the cup in 1985.

2

THE STRUCTURE
OF HOCKEY

North America is the world center of professional hockey. There are more professional teams in the United States and Canada than anywhere else in the world, although the play-for-pay game has grown considerably in Europe since World War II.

Nevertheless, the National Hockey League, which has been in existence since 1917, remains the foremost professional league in the world. With twenty-one teams, ranging from New York to Los Angeles in the United States and from Montreal to Vancouver in Canada, the NHL employs more than four hundred players, many of whom are European citizens.

Each National Hockey League team maintains a network of farm clubs on the minor (professional) league level. The most significant farm clubs are in the American Hockey League, which for nearly a half century has been the premier minor hockey league world.

The roots of the American League can be traced back to three leagues—the Canadian Professional League, the International League, and the Canadian-American League. The Canadian Professional and the Can-Am had their beginnings in the 1926–1927 season, but the Canadian Professional gave way to the International after three years of operation, whereas the Canadian-American remained a going concern until the 1936–37 season, when the International-American took over. The International-American then came to be known as the American League.

From the original members of the Canadian-American Hockey League and the Canadian Professional League, which had five teams in each circuit, only one survives today, New Haven.

As the name implies, the Canadian Professional League was composed entirely of clubs located in Dominion cities: Stratford, London, Hamilton, Windsor, and Niagara Falls, all in Ontario. The Canadian-American League got its name because of the inclusion of Quebec City with the original four United States cities: New Haven, Springfield, Boston, and Providence.

Although the Canadian Professional League started with five clubs, it soon grew to an eight-club league with the addition of Detroit, Kitchener, and Toronto. However, the lineup lasted only one season because Stratford, winner of two championships, dropped out and its place was taken by Buffalo for the 1928–29 season. The inclusion of three United States teams in 1929–30 brought about a change of name and the circuit became known as the International League. Cleveland replaced Kitchener and finished in first place. It marked the beginning of a long era of dominance of minor league hockey by the Ohio franchise. Three withdrawals in 1930–31 brought more changes. Toronto, Niagara Falls, and Hamilton dropped out, and Pittsburgh, which already had an unpleasant flirtation with the NHL, entered the league, along with Syracuse, to form a seven-club league through the 1931–32 season. But Pittsburgh soon withdrew, reducing the league to six clubs, and for the following three seasons London, Ontario; Windsor, Ontario; Buffalo; Cleveland; and Syracuse rounded out the league.

Despite the economic hardships of the Great Depression the league expanded in 1935–36 and became an eight-team unit with four clubs comprising an eastern division and four in a western group. Syracuse, Buffalo, London, and Rochester were in the eastern grouping, and Pittsburgh, Detroit, Cleveland, and Windsor were in the western portion. The Canadian Professional and International hockey leagues operated with a combination of thirteen clubs in a ten-year period.

The original Can-Am League comprised New Haven, Springfield, Quebec, Boston, and Providence. Philadelphia was added in 1927–28, but the next year Quebec dropped out and Newark, New Jersey, entered for a single season. When Newark dropped out in 1929–30 the league was reduced to five clubs. In 1931–32 a team from the Bronx, New York, joined the league for one season, folding—along with Springfield—after just a year.

For the 1932–33 campaign Quebec rejoined the league and retained membership for three seasons. Quebec exited in 1935–36 and Springfield returned. Sweeping changes took place with the organization of the International-American League, which soon abandoned the International designation and became known simply as the American Hockey League. Buffalo, Cleveland, Pittsburgh, and Syracuse comprised the western group, and Philadelphia, Springfield, New Haven, and Providence formed the eastern division.

The American League flourished until the outbreak of World War II, when Springfield and Philadelphia dropped out. New Haven survived the first half of the 1942–43 season but then was forced to disband. Despite manpower shortages the AHL survived the war years. It was then that it emerged as a major supplier of talent to the NHL. The Rangers' farm team was located in New Haven; Toronto had Pittsburgh; Detroit had Indianapolis, and so on.

In addition to the American League a number of other minor leagues operated with varying degrees of success. Along the Atlantic seaboard the Eastern League with its major bases in New York (the Rovers) and Boston (the Olympics) often drew crowds that were the envy of the NHL. At least one Sunday afternoon Rovers game at Madison Square Garden drew a larger audience than a Rangers match played that same evening.

Other minor leagues sprouted across the United States from coast to coast. The Pacific Coast Hockey League, which had franchises in San Francisco, Los Angeles, Fresno, Oakland, Hollywood, Seattle, and Portland, among other cities, was one of the most durable even after its name was changed to the Western Hockey League. Because the NHL was then a six-team league essentially located in the east, the PCHL sent fewer players to the majors, although the quality of its hockey was often on a par with the AHL.

Midwestern cities such as Omaha, Tulsa, Kansas City, and St. Paul graced the United States Hockey League, which was a cut below the American League in terms of overall quality. Nevertheless, a number of USHL players eventually made their way to the NHL, some directly, others via the AHL.

Minor professional hockey in Canada never reached the level of quality it attained in the United States. Vancouver, Edmonton, Winnipeg, Calgary, and Saskatoon were represented in either the PCHL or WHL at one time or another, although the leagues were centered in the United States.

In each case the professional league employed players ranging in age from twenty through forty. Occasionally, an especially adept skater in his upper forties was able to linger in the minors but, for the most part, forty was the upper limit in terms of longevity.

Below the professional level, amateur hockey enjoyed a renaissance following World War II. In the United States it was the Amateur Hockey Association of the United States, headed by Tom Lockhart of New York City, that orchestrated its growth and development. The AHAUS regulated leagues from the very youngest to senior leagues for adults as old as fifty and even sixty.

Its Canadian counterpart, the Canadian Amateur Hockey Association (CAHA) handled an even more formidable array of leagues and teams. On the highest level were teams in the Junior A grouping, which for several years were directly linked with NHL clubs. Thus, during the early 1950s the Guelph Biltmore Madhatters of the Ontario Hockey Association Junior A division were directly sponsored by the New York Rangers. Players such as Andy Bathgate, Dean Prentice, Aldo Guidolin, Lou Fontinato, and Harry Howell moved from the Biltmores—sometimes with a minor league stopover—to the NHL club. The introduction of the draft system whereby big-league clubs could directly pluck players from the Junior teams spelled the end of direct sponsorship of the amateur teams.

The "Kid" hockey system in both Canada and the United States has several divisions. With certain local variations, the following categories pertain: the youngest players (boys only) are the "Mites," ages seven and eight. Next comes "Squirt" (the youngest category for girls) for ages nine and ten for boys and eight through twelve for girls, followed by "Peewee" for boys eleven and twelve (girls thirteen through fifteen), and then "Bantam" for boys thirteen and fourteen (there is no Bantam category for girls). After Bantam comes "Midget" for boys fifteen and sixteen (young women sixteen through nineteen), "Junior" for boys seventeen through nineteen, (there is no Junior for women), and finally Senior for men and women (in separate leagues) twenty and over.

Significantly, it is at Bantam level that many promising youngsters are initially scouted, and it is at the Junior level that most talented players are actually being prepared for the NHL—and there are neither Bantam nor Junior categories for girls and women. Although the professional leagues are no longer allowed to actually sponsor youth hockey teams as they did earlier, it is readily apparent that the money spent on youth hockey is still geared toward grooming a child for possible NHL entrance—and money is not going to be wasted where there is no potential for producing professionals.

Until the arrival of the World Hockey Association in 1972 youngsters were forbidden to play in the NHL until they had reached age twenty. But, in its thirst for talent, the WHA began signing "underage" Juniors as young as seventeen and eighteen. Faced with this dilemma the NHL eventually capitulated, and by 1980 it had become commonplace for an NHL club to draft an eighteen-year-old and give him an audition with the big club.

By the start of the 1980s the focus of major league hockey scouts had become redirected toward the top-ranked Junior teams. The foremost of these groups were the Ontario Hockey League, the Western Hockey League, and the Quebec Hockey League, each of which boasted a number of alumni such as Wayne Gretzky, Mike Bossy, and Ron Duguay in the NHL.

Those Junior players unable to make the jump directly from their amateur leagues to the NHL often found their way to any number of lower-level minor leagues. Apart from the American League—which now embraced teams from such diverse centers as Halifax, Nova Scotia, and Binghamton, New York—Junior players graduated to the Central League, the International League, and the Atlantic Coast League.

The Central League, an offshoot of the United States League, included franchises in Tulsa, Wichita, Salt Lake City, Birmingham, Colorado, Indianapolis, and Denver. The International League included Toledo, Fort Wayne, Saginaw, Flint, Milwaukee, Kalamazoo, Peoria, and Muskegon. On a lower rung the Atlantic Coast League featured Mohawk Valley, Carolina, Virginia, Hampton, Erie, and Nashville.

Still another branch of the hockey family tree belongs to collegiate hockey, both in the United States and Canada. By the early 1960s college hockey had become so popular—and so polished—that it became incumbent on professional scouts to recommend top players to the pros. Red Berenson, who ultimately starred for the

St. Louis Blues, was a graduate of the University of Michigan and one of the first to prove that a collegian could excel in the majors. Now it is perfectly normal for universities such as Wisconsin and others in the Western Collegiate Hockey Association to produce future pros.

Each league has its own championship series, the most prestigious (among minor leagues) being the Calder Cup, the American League answer to the Stanley Cup. In the Central League the Adams Cup is given to the playoff winner.

The structure of hockey in Europe is somewhat different, because of the political complexities that resulted from World War II. In Communist countries hockey players, even on the highest levels, never were acknowledged to be professionals, although they received special privileges and were treated much in the manner of the North American pros. Those who played for the Soviet Union, for example, were regarded as "amateurs." Their professions would be listed as army officer or engineer, yet they devoted virtually no time to those jobs since most of their attention was given to the hockey team—either the local club or the national team, depending on the ability of the player in question.

The sham of amateurism became so widely acknowledged among hockey people that attempts were made to compel Soviet officials to admit that their national players were as professional as the National Leaguers. Only in recent years, when the Soviets began playing exhibition games with NHL teams, has there been tacit acknowledgment that the top Russian players are as professional as Wayne Gretzky.

The same situation, with slight variations, has held in Czechoslovakia, another Communist country with a rich hockey tradition. Hockey players there, though euphemistically called amateurs, enjoy the amenities of professionals much as they do in the Soviet Union.

In each case the players and teams ultimately come under the umbrella of their country's national ice hockey federation. Thus, the Czechoslovak Ice Hockey Federation—after a trickle of players such as Vaclav Nedomansky began defecting to Canada in the late 1970s—decided to hammer out an agreement with the National Hockey League permitting some veteran Czech players to sign with NHL clubs. Because of such an arrangement the Vancouver Canucks were able to fortify their lineup with the addition of Ivan Hlinka and Jiri Bubla, two former Czech national stars.

Likewise, the Soviet Ice Hockey Federation bolstered its ties with the NHL as a result of the Team Canada tournaments of the 1970s as well as a series of matches played during the 1982–83 season between a touring Soviet team and several NHL clubs.

Both the Soviets and Czechs resisted the emigration of their players to Canada and, ultimately, the pro teams for both political and competitive reasons: For one thing, it simply did not look good for so many players to leave, and for another it diminished the strength of the respective national teams.

Like the Czechs and Russians, other European teams—as well as the few in Asia—are ruled by the International Ice Hockey Federation, which sanctions the annual world tournament, establishes rules of play, and generally monitors the state of hockey on the continent. In addition to the Soviets and Czechs, all other European hockey powers, large and small, are governed by the IIHF.

The IIHF maintains close ties with the CAHA and the AHAUS, coordinating tournaments and settling disputes whenever they occur between member nations. However, the IIHG generally leaves internal problems to be settled by the member nation in question. When, for example, a large number of top-flight Swedish players began emigrating to North America to play in the NHL and WHA, it was up to the Swedish Ice Hockey Federation to negotiate with the North American professionals on compensation and other related matters.

Until recently the IIHF has lacked the clout of international governing bodies in other sports, such as soccer, primarily because the NHL had long been recognized as the dominant hockey organization in the world. However, the rise of the Soviets, Czechs, and Swedes concomitantly lifted the prestige of the IIHF. What remains to be seen is whether the assorted hockey groups ultimately can unite to organize a genuine World Cup, in which the European titlest enters a playoff against the Stanley Cup champion for the universal championship of ice hockey. The general belief among respected hockey leaders on both sides of the Atlantic is that such a tournament will take place some time in the late 1980s.

3

HOCKEY ON AN INTERNATIONAL LEVEL

THE SOVIET UNION AS A HOCKEY POWER

Nowhere in the world has a nation progressed more rapidly with its development of a major team sport than the Soviet Union with hockey. Blessed with long, severe winters providing ample natural ice and a huge population from which to draw prospective players, the Soviets became interested in hockey shortly after World War II and became a major power in the sport on an international level in less than two decades.

Prior to World War II most of the elements already were in place for the encouragement of hockey play; all that was needed was motivation. The Russians had been aware of hockey because it had long been played on the continent, but the Soviets had been content to play local variations on the sport. But once hostilities had ended, sports authorities in the Soviet Union began taking a more serious view of organized hockey, which led to the organization of the Soviet Ice Hockey Federation. Soon the Russians joined the International Ice Hockey Federation and in 1954—less than ten years after the war's end—at Stockholm, the Soviets won the IIHF world championship. They had watched the Canadian masters and learned.

Many observers were stunned by the Soviet triumph, but those familiar with the Russian system were not surprised. One who probed the methods in the USSR was Frank Effinger, an amateur hockey coach from New York who studied at the National Institute of Sports and Physical Culture in Moscow. "It's no accident that they've made amazing progress since 1946," said Effinger. "They train their players at a very early age, and everything is taken care of for the players by professional coaches. The Russians know exactly what they're doing when it comes to hockey."

The Soviets gleaned as much knowledge from the Czechoslovaks as they did from the Canadians. Hockey had been a major sport in Czechoslovakia before World War II. When the war ended, the Czechs picked up where they had left off and were operating a high-grade hockey system by the late 1940s. This intrigued the Russians and, in no time at all, Anatoli Tarasov, the dean of Soviet hockey coaches, as well as other Russian hockey officials, began analyzing the Czech game.

At first most North American hockey pundits treated the early Soviet ice triumphs as aberrations. The National Hockey League was the predominant professional league in the world and, most critics agreed, there was nothing comparable to its quality level in the late 1940s and early 1950s. But a precious few insightful hockey professionals began to perceive the Russians as a potential threat. One who came to appreciate the Soviet system was Brian Conacher, a member of Canada's national team who also played for the 1967 Stanley Cup champion Toronto Maple Leafs:

> If there was one area of national life that Canadians could be relaxed about during the first half of the twentieth century, it must surely have been their confidence of supremacy in international hockey. When the Russian National Team won the World Hockey Championship for the first time, the feeling in Canada was that something must have gone wrong! The Canadians were beaten at their own game.

Ironically, the Canadians more than anyone else were responsible for the swift advances in hockey technology made by the eager Russians. As Conacher noted, the Soviets analyzed the North American stickhandling style the way a team of Russian scientists would have pored over American plans for a nuclear submarine—with great care. As Conacher describes it,

> Every time a Canadian team toured Europe, the Russians studied and analyzed our every move. They didn't simply adapt and imitate the game they saw the Canadian teams playing; they studied our teams intensively and from then on they synthesized their own approach to the game. They realized that hockey is basically a game of skill combined with strength, not to be confused with just muscle.

Although the Russians admittedly copied from the Canadians, they wasted little time before creating their own playbooks and library. In Conacher's words,

> They wrote their own textbooks on hockey emphasizing excellence through the pursuit of mastering the fundamentals. They felt that because hockey is a game of skill, a small man could compete equally against the big man. However, by deemphasizing the muscular part of hockey, they removed offensive bodychecking and tried to replace it with the perfection of the skills of skating, forechecking, and puck handling, with a limited amount of body work.

Starting from scratch the Soviets devised an elaborate system of player development emphasizing youth hockey programs. They chose to weed out the better players when they reached the age of eleven. Tryouts were scheduled for teams in the Soviet Major League, the USSR counterpart to the NHL, and large numbers of young stick handlers began trying out for the respective teams.

Bob Glauber, a New York–based hockey writer who studied the maturation of the Soviet system, elaborated on the process:

> The best young players (eleven-year-olds) who attend the tryouts were examined by coaches from the major teams, and the children then were sent to boarding school where they were trained intensively in both hockey and studies. Very few made it to the Major League and those that were not deemed fit to play advanced hockey were sent home from the schools. For the handful of adolescents who showed the greatest potential, they were trained further by the elite group of coaches.

As the Soviets began winning, they commanded more and more attention from North American types. "I like their skating," said former NHL forward Ron Stewart. "I wish some of their system would rub off on us. Under their system, if you're not moving you don't get the puck. You never see them giving the puck to a man who is standing still."

Skating came easy to the Russians, whose strategy was rooted in their national game: soccer. In soccer, bodychecking is forbidden; as a result the Soviets were slow to learn to use their bodies on their foes.

The many purists who eyed the Soviet style in its early years maturation noticed that it featured a heavy accent on finesse and a minimal amount of body work. This philosophy of play often put the Russians at a disadvantage when they encountered the rougher North American teams as well as the heavier-checking Czechoslovaks. In time the Russians, orchestrated by Tarasov, perceived that they would have to develop a more rugged brand of hockey if they were to succeed on an international level. Tarasov said, "Since no agreement about clean hockey could be reached, we had to force the opponent to stop playing rough, to force him to respect us."

But once the high command ordained that more rugged play would become part of the Soviet system, the Russian skaters had little difficulty adapting to the North American mode of play. By the 1960s the Soviet Hockey Federation had blueprinted what amounted to a youth hockey production line.

"The coaches had it down to a science," Effinger explained. "Before they took a kid into their schools, they made a complete physiological study of how big they would grow, how big their parents were, how well their hearts worked; everything one could think of. The coaches accepted that they would make a few mistakes and send away players who could have made it, but they realized that they would get enough good players from what they had."

That the system worked was proved by the remarkable string of successes enjoyed by the Russians in IIHF play in the late 1960s. Beginning with their first-

3-1 *After World War II, international hockey games became more intense. Here is a 1961 match between a Soviet team (light jerseys) and a Canadian club from Trail, British Columbia.*

place finish in 1963 at Stockholm, the Soviet sextet won every IIHF championship through the 1970 event, also at Stockholm.

Much as the triumphs were providing balm for the Russian hockey leaders, they were troubled by the fact that their competition still was less than the best. Although matches with the Swedes, Czechs, and Finns featured the finest talent available in those countries, Canada was restricted to sending strictly amateur players. Thus the Russians—who classified all full-time hockey players as amateurs although they were professionals by North American standards—had yet to challenge the NHL stars.

The grass roots sentiment in Canada indicated that citizens of the Dominion were tired of seeing second-rate hockey players represent them in world-class play while the Europeans trotted out their best skaters. "Most Canadians felt that it was better not to compete against the Russians and the Swedes and the Czechs than to play against them and get routed," said Ken Dryden, the scholar-goalie of the Montreal Canadiens. "We had run the gamut from college teams to senior amateur teams to the National Team. We could no longer stomach losing and losing."

It had become apparent that Canadian ice hockey officials as well as the lords of the NHL were eager to find a solution. Furthermore, they knew that it entailed the exclusive use of major league professionals against the Soviet all-stars. At this point, the Russians were becoming bored with competition from the European teams and the weak Canadian representatives. They ached to take on the NHL stars, and the feeling in NHL quarters was mutual.

The catalyst for the North American professionals was Alan Eagleson, head of the NHL Players' Association, who was increasingly becoming the spokesman for the league. An ardent Canadian chauvinist, Eagleson believed that the time had come for the NHL to accept the Soviet challenge. In time the more conservative NHL types—particularly the club owners who had nothing to gain and everything to lose—acknowledged that once and for all some sort of series had to be played. After considerable negotiations it was agreed that eight games would be played by the NHL all-stars and the select Soviet hockey club, with the first four held in Canada and the remaining matches in Russia.

The opening game was scheduled for September 2, 1972, at the Forum in Montreal. Never in the history of hockey has more attention been riveted on one game and one series. In Canada more than twelve million people focused on their television sets when the puck was dropped for the opening face-off.

When Phil Esposito of Team Canada scored after only thirty seconds of play the capacity crowd fully expected a rout. A goal by Paul Henderson six minutes later merely confirmed their suspicions. But the Soviets rallied to tie the score, 2–2, before the period had ended. The Russians scored twice in the second period and three times in the third, but Team Canada could manage only one more goal. The final score was 7–3 for the Soviets, and all of Canada was in shock. "Two marks to the Soviets," shouted an editorial in the *Toronto Sun*.

The Dominion collectively breathed a sigh of relief after game two, played at Maple Leaf Gardens in Toronto. With the score 2–1 for Team Canada in the third period and the Russians threatening, the NHL stars broke the game open and won it, 4–1.

Game three, played at Winnipeg, ended in a 4–4 tie, but several meaningful insights were percolating among the experts. Most significant was the fact that the Russians were, at the very least, a match for the NHL skaters. Furthermore, the Soviets were in better condition and were not likely to be routed in any given game of the series. The hopes for an unequivocal rout administered by the NHL team were now completely dashed. "The only thing I don't like about this series," said Eagleson, "are the games!"

Game four, played at Vancouver, was an utter humiliation for the Canadians. The final score was 5–3 for the Russians, but their mastery of several aspects of the game distressed the players even more than the score. "The Soviets shoot quicker than NHL players," said goalie Ken Dryden. "They start moving around a defenseman and while an NHL player would do the job and then shoot, the Soviets seem to release their shots while they're moving around the defensemen."

The Russians demonstrated beyond a shadow of a doubt that they could defend as well as score and, furthermore, the goaltending of Vladislav Tretiak was impeccable. Even worse for Team Canada, the audience at the Pacific Coliseum turned against them. Harry Sinden, the Canadian coach, would have to huddle with his brain trust to devise new strategies for the four-game set coming up in the Soviet Union. "I knew the Canadian pride was hurt," said Sinden. "Hockey was our game and now someone was trying to take it away from us."

Game five was played at Moscow and, from all appearances, Team Canada seemed en route to victory. The Canadians scored the first three goals of the game and led, 4–1, with only eleven minutes remaining, when suddenly the Russians struck back with four straight goals. The final score was 5–4 for the hosts. "The Russians," said Sinden, "play this game as though there were no scoreboard, no ups and downs. No team in the NHL would have played the way they did in the last ten minutes, down 4–1 and still skating and shooting and passing the puck the same way they did in the first period."

A desperate Canadian team showed up for game six at Moscow and proved its mettle. Trailing 1–0, the Canadians counterattacked for three consecutive goals and held on for a 3–2 victory. The seventh game was another one right out of a Hollywood script. With the score tied, 3–3, late in the third period Paul Henderson pushed the puck through the legs of a Russian defender. "I got a bit of a break," said Henderson. "The puck hit his skate, deflected it to his right, and that gave me the chance I needed. While he was looking for it I moved around him. I had pretty good balance and let the shot go." The shot beat Soviet goalie Vladislav Tretiak at 17:54, and the Canadians skated off the ice with a 4–3 triumph. The series was tied at three games apiece with one tie.

The eighth and final game was played on September 28, 1972, at Moscow. In the opinion of many experts it was one of the greatest games ever played. Certainly, millions of Canadians felt that way—after it was over. Obviously, it was important to the Soviets as well, since they allegedly resorted to a number of ploys to keep the Canadians on edge.

"The Soviets did everything they could to intimidate us," said Phil Esposito, Team Canada's crack center. "They tried to aggravate us off the ice but the fact that we could intimidate them on the ice won it for us."

For two periods the Russians seemed to have the Canadians intimidated. The Soviets nursed a 5–3 lead into the third period when Team Canada fought back. They tied the score with fewer than eight minutes remaining. They won it when Paul Henderson shot the puck at Tretiak and then pounced on the rebound. This time he shot the rubber under Tretiak and into the net. "It was," said Frank Orr of the *Toronto Star*, "the most famous goal in the history of hockey."

When the final score (6–5) was posted, all of Canada was delirious with joy. In some ways the reverberations are still being felt to this day. Certainly, Henderson has never gotten over it. "It's amazing," he said, "but ten years later I still couldn't

3-2　*Paul Henderson (upraised stick) scored the decisive goal against the Soviet National squad during the tumultuous 1972 Canadian–Soviet series.*

3-3　*Henderson became an instant national hero and was hoisted on the shoulders of goalie Tony Esposito and NHL union boss Alan Eagleson.*

walk down the street anywhere in Canada without having someone come to me and mention *the* goal. Many of them just say 'thanks' and it's still a big thrill."

The next day headlines in the newspapers across the continent reflected the ecstasy being felt from Halifax to Vancouver. "Phil Esposito for Pope" declared one headline. "Esposito for Prime Minister" was another editorial suggestion. "Paul Henderson could be mayor of Toronto," noted a politician in Ontario.

Although technically an exhibition tournament, the 1972 Team Canada–Soviet match-up was interpreted as *the* definitive hockey world series. Never before, and not since, has a hockey event had such a profound impact on the public at large, particularly since the Soviets came close to snatching victory from the Canadians.

Overlooked in the fallout of cheering and critical acclaim for the Canadian victory was one very significant element: the closeness of the series. The Soviets, judging by all the pretournament stories, were distinct underdogs. Some observers doubted that they would win a single game, let alone three, yet they came very close to winning the series.

"I'll never forget as long as I live," said Team Canada's assistant coach John Ferguson, "that when the score was tied, 5–5, late in the eighth game, a Soviet hockey official came to our bench and told Harry Sinden and me that if the game ended in a tie, they were claiming the victory on total points. Luckily, Paul Henderson scored that goal or the argument would have been going on for ten years."

What disturbed some followers of North American professional hockey was the abject refusal of many NHL types to either observe, study, or learn from the Soviets.

Many of the Canadian players remained resentful of several aspects of the tournament. A decade after it was over, Phil Esposito was asked for his primary thought in recalling the series. Esposito snapped:

> That I wouldn't want to do it again, at least not under the conditions that we endured in 1972. When we got back to Canada, it turned into a big political hassle about which politicians would be front and center in welcoming us. We spent ten minutes on the plane in Montreal while an argument went on about which door we should go out. I got fed up and didn't leave the plane. Then, in Toronto, the place was full of politicians all trying to be front and center. It never should have happened.

Nevertheless, the NHL, under its progressive president John Ziegler, continued to press for closer relations with the Soviet hockey authorities. One result was the return, during the 1985–86 season, of Russian club teams which played a series of exhibition games with NHL clubs.

THE EUROPEAN REVOLUTION TAKES HOLD

The 1972 Team Canada–Soviet series whetted the appetites of Russian hockey officials. Although the Russians lost the tournament by one game, they gained great insights into the North American game, and, when all was said and done, were delighted with the general results if not the final score of the eighth game.

By contrast, the NHL was less interested in a renewal of hostilities, particularly since it now was involved in a full-scale war with the World Hockey Association. Some NHL owners were openly disturbed by the power of the Soviets and believed that nothing could be gained from a rematch.

Conversely, the WHA, battling to remain alive, had much to gain from a Soviet challenge. If the new league's all-stars played the Russians, it would be tantamount to instant credibility and would result in an infinite amount of publicity. WHA negotiators went to work to arrange a series with the Russians and, to their delight, were given the green light. The series began in September 1974.

"A win for the WHA in the series," said Dick Beddoes of the *Toronto Globe and Mail*, "will help fill the WHA rinks. It's not really a question of being better than the Team 1972 but a question of proving that the WHA is indeed as good as the NHL."

The WHA had a sprinkling of former NHL superstars, although they were up in years. Gordie Howe, Gerry Cheevers, J. C. Tremblay, Bobby Hull, and Pat Stapleton were among the better players on the squad coached by Billy Harris.

When the series opened, the feeling among many critics was that the fleet Russians would skate the older Canadians right into the ice, but such was not the case in the opening game. It ended in a 3–3 tie, and it was Bobby Hull who had the energy to pump home the tying goal at 14:18 of the third period. In fact, Frank Mahovlich of Team Canada came perilously close to scoring the winning goal in the dying moments of the game.

Mahovlich's miss was more than compensated for by his teammates in game two. The Canadians scored the first goal and the last goal of a game they dominated. The final score was 4–1. Dreams of an even greater triumph than 1972 were at least temporarily nurtured by the WHA skaters, but the dream was shattered in game three. The Soviets spotted Team Canada the first goal, then came on strong to produce an 8–5 decision.

In game four, despite a first-period hat trick by Bobby Hull giving the Canadians a 5–2 lead going into the second period, the Russians stormed back. They out-worked the Canadians over the final two periods to gain a 5–5 tie. The series then moved on to Moscow with the teams tied 1–1.

Despite Gerry Cheevers' outstanding goaltending in the fifth game, the Canadians were totally outplayed, losing 3–2.

In losing game six, 5–2, Team Canada also lost prestige. The game began with Bruce MacGregor getting a five-minute major penalty for fighting with Valery Vasiljev. The Russian was clearly the aggressor, argued Team Canada coach Billy Harris: "According to my international rule book the player who starts a fight should get a ten-minute penalty." The Soviet referee lost control of the game from that point to the finish. The game ended with Team Canada's Rick Ley attacking Valery Kharlamov and Russian coach Boris Kulagin calling for Ley's jailing. The press warned of a bloodbath in game seven.

When Bill Harris was asked if his team could come back and win the final two games, he said, "We had to win tonight. It's hard to motivate players to win two games just to get a tie."

Game seven ended with Canada 4, Russia 4. "We won that game 5–4 and that's it," said Gerry Cheevers. "We lost at least four seconds when they let the clock continue running after that whistle in the third period and beside that, the red light went on and it couldn't flash if the green light was on."

With 1:28 left in the game, Cheevers noticed that a couple of seconds had ticked off after play had been halted. Canadian referee Tom Brown conferred with the time keeper and had him allow two seconds to elapse before restarting the clock.

In the waning moments of the game Bobby Hull took a pass from Paul Henderson and scored what was believed to be the winning goal. "I got the puck in the slot and let it go," said Hull. "I saw the puck go into the net and I looked up and saw the red light go on."

Referee Brown claimed that he did not see the red light go on, but in fact had seen the green light go on first to end the game. Team Canada's Ralph Backstrom was furious. "I asked the referee why he didn't allow the goal and he said he checked with the Russian linesman who told Brown that he had watched the clock run out. I don't know why he'd be watching the clock in that situation."

The Canadian ambassador summed up the feelings of Team Canada and of the entire country: "I'm distressed."

The dream of the WHA evaporated as the Russians won the eighth and final game, 3–2. Team Canada had contemplated a boycott of the last game because of the disallowed goal in game seven, but they eventually relented.

The Russians responded to the threat of a boycott by sitting out goaltender Vladislav Tretiak and four other star players for the final game. Unlike 1972, the Canadians returned home physically and emotionally drained. They had been beaten by a better conditioned team than themselves. Gordie Howe summed it up for Team Canada 1974: "God, I'm tired."

Yet Howe was one of the better performers, game in and game out, proving that his skills had a timeless quality. He was forty-six years old, yet performing against Soviet skaters half his age. "The abundance of Howe kept rolling up, accretions of memory, skills of the buffeting years," said Dick Beddoes of the *Toronto Globe and Mail*. "His themes are great ones: a boy's child-play, a man's life, the gladiatorial fight with time."

But the Canadians, as a group of hockey players, were losing that fight to the Soviets. And with each year another major stride was made by the European stick handlers. In 1976 two significant international hockey events were held involving the NHL's best and those from the continent. One of them was an eight-game tour of NHL cities by two Soviet hockey teams who played against select major league clubs.

In the past the NHL's rationale for not trouncing the Soviets was simply that they never seemed to have enough time to prepare for the events, whereas the Russian skaters were playing together as a team for several months. This time, however, the Soviets would be playing against regular NHL clubs who had been together for a significant part of one season. The opening game of the tour was held at Madison Square Garden in New York City between the Rangers and the Soviet Army team.

With only twenty-one seconds elapsed in the first period, Steve Vickers of the Rangers scored. It was the one and only moment of exultation for the NHL team. In no time at all the Soviets revved up their attack and skated smartly to a 7–3 triumph. Veteran Ranger players were impressed with the Soviet style. "We would stand up to meet our man," said Rangers defenseman Doug Jarrett, "but by the time I'd hit him he'd drop the puck off to a trailer and suddenly he'd be my man—and past me. The Russians are like a pack of wolves the way they're always yelling out there. One yells and suddenly they're all on top of you."

Once again NHL prestige suffered. "For Shame New York Rangers, for Shame New York," was the banner headline over Dick Young's column in the *Daily News*.

Meanwhile the second touring Russian team, the Soviet Wings, had also begun its tour. In their first match, the Soviet Wings routed the Pittsburgh Penguins, 7–4, at the Civic Center in Pittsburgh. Again the NHL leaders were stunned by the Russian style. "They play," said Penguins coach Marc Boileau, "like no NHL team does."

When the Soviet Wings defeated the Chicago Black Hawks, 4–2, Chicago coach Billy Reay explained: "Ultimately, it was the Russians' ability to outskate us that proved the difference."

When the Soviet Army team beat the Boston Bruins, 5–2, Boston coach Don Cherry asserted, "They made a believer out of me."

The Russians were far from invincible. They were trounced, 12–6, in a match between the Soviet Wings and the Buffalo Sabres. And the Montreal Canadiens forged a 3–3 tie with the Soviet Army team in what was regarded as the best match of the tour. After the Soviet Wings defeated the New York Islanders, 2–1, goalie Glenn Resch of the Islanders accused the Russians of employing unfair tactics around the goal.

"It's irritating," said Resch. "You've got to put up with constant harassment. The Russians are masters of interference in front of the net the way they hook, grab, and hit you." In a sense, the Soviets got their comeuppance against the rugged Philadelphia Flyers who not only defeated them, 4–1, but gave the visitors a taste of hockey at its most violent. At one point the Soviet coach pulled his team off the ice in protest against the Flyers' vigorous play but then relented and allowed his club to finish the game.

The Flyers, unlike the other NHL clubs, believed that they had discovered a chink in the Soviets' armor. "The Russians do a lot of fancy passing," said Flyers' aide Marcel Pelletier. "They made six or seven passes right away but didn't go anywhere. It's like football. You can complete a lot of passes and still not gain anything. I knew we could score on them, expecially on rebounds. Their defensemen don't move guys out from in front."

Despite losses to the Sabres and Flyers, the Soviets emerged from the tour with more accolades than ever before. But the Russians were not alone.

The impact of Soviet-style hockey on the North American game has been powerful, but another European country also left an indelible impression upon the professional game as played in the United States and Canada. Sweden, long a professional hockey hotbed, began supplying talent to the NHL in the mid-sixties. One of the first players to crack an NHL team was Swedish ace Ulf Sterner, who skated for the New York Rangers in 1964–65. At the time the NHL was a tough six-team league, and Sterner soon found the heavy checking not suited to the European style. From time to time other Swedes were eyed by the NHL scouts, but the impetus for serious importation of stick handlers from Sweden developed once the expansion of the NHL took place in 1967, and again in 1972, when the arrival of the World Hockey Association decimated the player market in North America. Nevertheless, it was not until the 1973–74 season that it was proved that a top-ranked Swedish player actually could cut the competitive ice in the NHL, when the Toronto Maple Leafs dispatched scout Gerry McNamara to the continent to find fresh talent. He recommended Swedish defenseman Borje Salming and winger Inge Hammarstrom to the Toronto high command. Salming became an instant star. "It was Borje," said New York Islanders' defenseman Stefan Persson, "who paved the way for the rest of us Swedes to make it in the NHL."

Salming scored 5 goals and 34 assists for 39 points in 1973–74, his rookie NHL year; Hammarstrom's totals were 20 goals, 23 assists, and 43 points in 66 games. Although Hammarstrom remained a fringe forward, Salming quickly emerged as a legitimate ace and was named to the all-star second team both in 1974–75 and 1975–76. His star continued to rise—despite a serious eye injury during the 1978 playoffs—and indicated that the road to championships might be paved via Sweden. Certainly the Salming experience inspired other clubs, both in the WHA and NHL, to intensify their scouting of Swedish leagues.

The quest for "another Salming" paid dividends for some teams and drew a blank for others. The Islanders imported Persson for the 1977–78 season, immediately placed him on the point of the power play, and watched Persson ripen into a first-line defenseman from the Salming mold.

Meanwhile, the Winnipeg Jets of the World Hockey Association were beaming over the ease with which forwards Anders Hedberg and Ulf Nilsson had moved into their lineup, not to mention defenseman Lars-Erik Sjoberg. The Winnipeg Swedes, in their own speedy way, had become more attractive to some hockey analysts than Canadian-born skaters in the NHL.

On Thursday, May 12, 1977, a headline in the *Toronto Globe and Mail* sent unpleasant rumblings up and down the corridors of the NHL. Above an article written by James Christie, the big, black letters proclaimed, "Swedes and Hull Show NHL It's Dull!"

Christie then pointed out to NHL President John Ziegler and his confederates that the best hockey was *not* being played in the senior pro league. And, even worse, the best hockey players were not even Canadian born.

The skaters who captured Christie's imagination were Hedberg and Nilsson, who teamed with Bobby Hull to comprise the Winnipeg Jets' super scoring line. "The Swedes," according to a former WHA official, "actually carried Hull for two seasons."

In addition to Nilsson and Hedberg, Winnipeg boasted that Sjoberg, the Jets' captain, was the equal of Larry Robinson, Denis Potvin, and Ian Turnbull of the NHL. In fact, this Swedish triumvirate could very well comprise the best players of the 1977–78 season.

Center Nilsson was described by Hull as the team's "air traffic controller" because of Ulf's radarlike passes to his breaking wings—which was not to slight Hedberg, the right wing, who many believed should have been in the NHL long ago.

"Playing Hedberg in the WHA as long as they did," said Boston Bruins' coach Don Cherry, "was like running Secretariat at the county fair."

Cherry may have wished Hedberg and Nilsson had remained in the WHA. The two high-scoring forwards signed lucrative contracts with the New York Rangers and brought their act to Broadway and the NHL during the 1978–79 season. Nilsson was by far the best Ranger until he broke his ankle at midseason and ended the year fourth in club scoring, even missing several months of play. Although Hedberg did not storm the NHL with scoring feats, the slick-skating winger was the top Ranger point collector, with seventy-nine.

Detroit Red Wings' coach Bobby Kromm had the good fortune to coach the Swedes while Kromm still was the Jets' bench boss in the previous season. Kromm was especially impressed with Sjoberg's cerebral approach to the game. Lars-Erik even persuaded management that all bonus agreements should be based on team performance, not individual productivity.

"Sjoberg was in Winnipeg for a year," said Kromm, "and then he was voted captain. That tells you something about Sjoberg the man."

Like journalist Christie, Frank Orr of the *Toronto Star* was impressed by the Swedes when he saw them perform in the WHA playoffs against the Quebec Nordiques in 1977. "The best player on the ice was Sjoberg." wrote Orr. "He's small (5'9", 175 pounds) but his agility, intelligence, and puckhandling skills make him one of the best at that position."

The early reports had it that the Swedes were incapable of absorbing the rougher North American–style hockey for any length of time, but Hedberg, Nilsson, and Sjoberg dispelled that idea in 1976. Harry Heale, coaching the New England Whalers at the time, was one of Nilsson's biggest boosters.

"One night," Neale recalled, "Ricky Ley, one of the toughest defensemen on the Whalers, hit Nilsson with what might have been the most violent clean check I've ever seen. I mean, I thought Rickey had broken every bone in Nilsson's body. Well, Nilsson got up and got five assists against us." Unfortunately, Nilsson did not fare as well in a collision with the New York Islanders' Denis Potvin, the NHL all-star defenseman. Potvin rammed Nilsson against the boards, and the center crumbled to the ice with a broken ankle and torn ligaments.

A goalie's nightmare, Hedberg fired with unerring wristshot accuracy and had a knowledge of the game's defensive aspects. "Hedberg," said Kromm, "can do everything—kill penalties, work the power play, score goals, and check. During his first year of pro hockey in North America he had to make an adjustment. Now I rate him one of the top wingers in the world, with Guy Lafleur, Aleksandr Yakushev, and Aleksandr Maltsev. Hedberg scored seventy goals last year [1977] and not one of them was on a slapshot."

It is, of course, debatable whether Hedberg, Nilsson, and Sjoberg were as competent as their more widely touted countryman Borje Salming, the Toronto Maple Leafs' defenseman, who ranks among the most gifted players in the NHL.

Like the other Swedes, Salming once was regarded as a European who would wither under heavy pounding. Instead he weathered all storms and proved himself an offensive as well as a defensive ace.

"To give a good pass to somebody," said Salming, "and have them come in clear and score in a close game is super as far as I'm concerned. For me, it doesn't matter who scores. Winning the game is the most fun, especially close games."

If the Torontonians and the New Yorkers were tickled with their Swedish players, the Minnesota North Stars insisted that *their* Swede, Roland Eriksson, was the best of the lot. Eriksson led all rookie scorers in scoring for the 1977 NHL season with twenty-five goals and forty-four assists. Although he failed to win the Calder Trophy, Eriksson nevertheless won much acclaim. North Stars' general manager Lou Nanne argued that Eriksson was, by far, the best rookie in 1977.

"He didn't get enough ink in the early months," said Nanne, "otherwise Roland would have taken the prize. To my mind, the Swede is the best player I have ever had as a teammate with the exception of Gump Worsley. He makes an unbelievably accurate pass and he can score, too."

Eriksson accumulated only ten penalty minutes with Minnesota in his first season and was considered "shy" by some anti-Swede railbirds, but Nanne disagreed. He asserted that Eriksson was one of the most elusive players he had ever seen. "You couldn't hit the Swede," said Nanne, "if you were standing five feet away and tossed a handful of confetti at him."

Less agile, but no less mobile and efficient, was defenseman Thommy Abrahamsson of the New England Whalers. "Thommy" said Whaler manager Jack Kelley, "is one of the best skaters around."

These, of course, were some of the best Swedes playing big league hockey in North America. There were other good ones around: Bjorn Johansson, Inge Hammarstrom, Christer Abrahamsson, Dan Labraaten, and Willy Lindstrom, to name a few.

By the 1979–80 season it was evident that the Swedish invasion was permanent. Big leaguers such as Thommie Bergman, Per-Olov Brasar, Thomas Gradin, Rolf Edberg, and Lief Svensson—not to mention Hedberg, Nilsson, Salming, and Persson—had proved that smorgasbord-on-ice was a delectable treat in the NHL.

In addition to the Swedes, a number of players from Finland had proved themselves more than capable of playing in the NHL. These included forwards such as Jari Kurri of Edmonton and Ilkka Sinisalo of Philadelphia and myriad defensemen including Jari Eloranta of Calgary, Tapio Levo of New Jersey, Reijo Ruotsalaninen of the Rangers, Risto Siltanen of Harford, and Hannu Verta of Buffalo.

Perhaps the biggest surprise of all was the fact that players from behind the iron curtain had begun filtering into the North American professional leagues. The first two were Vaclav Nedomansky and Richard Farda, who signed on with the WHA after defecting from the Czechoslovakian national team.

Voted the WHA's Most Gentlemanly Player in 1976, Nedomansky continued his consistent scoring in his first full season with the NHL after joining the Red Wings in 1978. Nedomansky led Detroit with thirty-eight goals and seventy-three points while tying an NHL record by tallying two consecutive three-goal hat tricks.

In subsequent years Nedomansky didn't come close to his first-year totals again, scoring thirty-five goals in 1979–80 and then only twelve goals in the two successive seasons. In the 1980–81 and 1981–82 seasons, respectively, Nedomansky could only muster thirty-two and forty points. Nedomansky clearly was a disappointment by NHL standards.

By far the most impressive Czechs to graduate to the NHL have been the Stastny brothers: Peter, Anton, and Marian. The coming of the Stastny brothers to the NHL was a complicated mission. Gilles Leger, director of personnel for the Quebec Nordiques, went to Czechoslovakia to try to persuade the brothers to follow the Swedes and Finns who were playing so successfully in North America. At first, the Stastnys were unprepared to leave their native land.

Connections were made, however, and finally Peter and Anton called Quebec from their vacation spot in Innsbruck, Austria, to express their willingness to play for the Nordiques. Club officials immediately set off to meet them, and with Marian, who was studying to a lawyer, as their assistant, the younger pair agreed to an estimated salary of over $200,000 each a year for six years. Marian was told that he too could join the Nordiques, but he preferred to wait until the Czechoslovakian government would approve such a move.

The Stastnys were then taken to the Canadian embassy where a team of Austrian policemen ushered the group safely to a Montreal-bound flight.

Later Nordiques President Marcel Aubut would say that had he known of the dangers of the trip he would never have done it. This is debatable, considering the superb performance of the Stastnys for the Nordiques.

Peter Stastny is lauded for his shooting and play-making abilities. In his first year for the Nordiques he scored 39 goals and added 70 assists. The latter was an NHL record for a rookie, as was his point total of 109. He was awarded the Calder Trophy to cap off a tremendous rookie season.

Anton scored as many goals as his brother but collected only forty-six assists— still very impressive numbers for a rookie. The combination of the two was deadly. In one 9–3 victory over Vancouver both Stastnys had hat tricks, with Peter adding three assists and Anton getting two. The next game against Washington featured four goals and four assists by Peter, and three goals and five assists for Anton.

Meanwhile, back in Bratislava, Marian was not having an easy time. He quit his hometown team and then was suspended—with no reason given—from the Czech hockey federation. He was questioned as to his desire to leave the country, and when he said he would like to, he was promised an exit visa within one or two months. None ever came. He decided, that he, too, would have to leave without consent.

The Nordiques began to send cash to the stranded Stastny to help his exit, but Marian was still afraid. He planned to leave via Hungary, and he applied for and received three one-day passes to the neighboring country before deciding that such a strategy was safe and feasible.

On the fourth one-day pass, Marian with his family drove straight through Hungary to the Yugoslavian customs station where he showed some illegal papers he had obtained through the Nordiques' steady supply of cash. They were admitted into the country where the next stage of their operation required a fourteen-day pass to Vienna. When only a three-day transit pass was allowed, the Nordiques officials once again had to intervene. The Canadian immigration officials flew to Vienna to escort Marian and his family to North America.

Peter Stastny, despite his Calder Trophy, insisted that neither he nor Anton had fully adjusted to the North American style, but the addition of his older brother would help. "Now, we are ready," he announced, as the rest of the NHL shuddered. Nordiques coach Michel Bergeron joined in the praises of the forthcoming triple Stastny line. "Imagine how good they will be now that Marian has joined them. They have been one of the best forward lines in the world. They'll be just as good in the NHL."

Marian's first year was not as productive as had been hoped for, however. His year without hockey seemed to have hurt his reflexes, and he was not used to the lengthy NHL schedule. Still his total of eighty-nine points was not unimpressive and, more importantly, the Nordiques had their best NHL season ever, finishing with a record of 33–31–16.

Peter's 139 points on 46 goals and 93 assists put him third in the scoring race behind Wayne Gretzky and Mike Bossy. Marian's 35 goals was the third highest tally for a Nordique that season. And despite an injury that kept his playing down to sixty-eight games, Anton managed to get 72 points.

They were slated to face the Canadiens in the opening round of the playoffs, and Montreal coach Bob Berry admitted, "we have a fear of the Nordiques." The first game went to Les Habitants 5–1, but in the second game the Stastnys struck. Marian assisted on two of the goals that brought the Nordiques a 3–2 win in the battle for the province.

The series was tied at two games apiece, and the tie breaker was scheduled at the Montreal Forum. It took very little time for Anton to set up Wilf Paiement with the opening goal, and in the fourteenth minute Quebec was up by two, thanks to a goal by Anton. Two Canadien goals in the third period forced the game into overtime, but the Nordiques eventually won on a goal by Dale Hunter.

The next round was set against the Bruins with the opening two games on Boston's smaller rink. This alone gave the Bruins an edge in the series, but Peter Stastny emerged as a clubhouse cheerleader trying to give his team a more optimistic viewpoint. Despite his rallying, the Nordiques lost the first two games of the best-of-seven series in Boston.

The next two games at Le Colisée in Quebec City belonged to the Nordiques, though. The fourth game, in particular, was typical of the Stastny style of play. On one play, Marian recovered the puck in the Bruins' zone, passed it straight to Peter at the bottom of the right circle, then sprinted to the inside edge of the circle, took a pass and put a twenty-foot shot between the pads of goalie Mike Moffat.

Again the series went down to the final game. Peter scored the first goal and refused to let up, even after Boston had tied the score. Then in the third period he passed the puck to defenseman Dave Pichette on a power play for the game-winning goal.

The Nordiques thus qualified for the semifinal round against the Stanley Cup Champion New York Islanders. Although the Nordiques lost the series, a full-fledged rivalry had developed between Peter Stastny and Islander center Bryan Trottier. The two traded clean and some not-so-clean checks.

The third game of the series was Quebec's strongest. The game was sent into overtime when Peter Stastny, who had scored earlier, cruised in one on one against goaltender Billy Smith. Although he feinted and aimed for the opening in Smith's pads, the puck rolled wide, and two minutes later Wayne Merrick scored to give the Islanders a three-game lead in the series.

After the fourth game, which featured continued intrepid play from the brothers, particularly Peter, Bryan Trottier shook hands with Peter Stastny at center ice. Despite the four-game loss, Peter felt that they had proved they belonged in the top of the league.

Even off the ice the Stastnys have adapted well to Canadian life. Marian opened a disco-bar-restaurant in the classy part of Quebec City, and the three brothers feel very much at home. "Quebec reminds me so much of Bratislava," said Peter. "They are the same size and I felt right away this is just like Europe, and that helped me."

The influence of Europeans was profound. "By the start of the 1980s," said New Jersey Devils Director of Hockey Operations Max McNab, "the North American professionals were employing about 40 percent of the European techniques."

More than anyone, Herb Brooks, the 1980 American Olympic coach who took over the New York Rangers coaching job a year later, became the foremost exponent of European strategy in the NHL. Instead of relying on the standard professional method of having the forwards skate up and down their wings—and the center ice lane—in more or less fixed positions, Brooks broke dramatically with tradition.

Brooks eschewed the traditional NHL shibboleths. Instead his teams began exhibiting a swirling motion all over the ice with Ranger forwards exchanging roles rather than remaining in set forward positions at left wing, center, or right wing. Spectacularly swift, they used the criss-cross to great advantage. The left wing moved to the center. The center moved to the wing position. "The important thing," said critic Gerald Eskenazi of the *New York Times*, "was that once a man was switched, someone was ready to take his place. But there was more to the American (Brooks) style than mere duplication of European and Soviet technique. The Brooks blueprint used more of the ice to pass the puck, and he was not afraid to have his men pass the puck from behind their net or across their goal."

Again breaking with North American tradition that favored players in the 6-foot, 200-pound category, Brooks did not want behemoths. His Ranger team of the 1982–83 season was the smallest and lightest in the league—and one of the speediest. He obtained passers and skaters. The Rangers dazzled the foe with passes up to seventy feet straight out, up to the red line.

"Why shouldn't you use half the ice?" asked Brooks. "If you've got players who can do it, you should make the ice work for you."

Brooks synthesized the old with the new, still relying on bodychecking as much as possible but always retaining the flow. The Rangers' success under Brooks so impressed some of the NHL old guard that they began opting for the European-American style and by the early 1980s more teams than ever were switching to this modus operandi.

Under the orchestration of NHL President John Ziegler and Al Eagleson, head of the NHL players' union, international matches were encouraged. During the 1982–83 season another Soviet all-star team played a series of exhibition matches against several NHL teams.

The European hockey revolution had taken a firm hold on North American hockey teams and hockey people. By 1985–86, NHL teams were looking to Europe for talent as frequently as they were scouting in their own backyard. The success of the Edmonton Oilers' Jari Kurri and the Philadelphia Flyers' Pelle Lindbergh demonstrated that Scandinavians could play well at any big-league position in North America.

SEVEN DECADES OF INTERNATIONAL TOURNAMENTS

Les Avants, Switzerland, 1910: The first European Hockey championship was held at Les Avants, Switzerland, in 1910, with England capturing the title. Switzerland, the host country, finished fourth. Germany and Belgium finished second and third, respectively.

Berlin, Germany, 1911: England did not come to defend its championship. Without England present, Germany, the host country, was heavily favored to win the tournament, but a team representing the Austro-Hungarian province of Bohemia, competing for the first time, won the title. Germany once again finished second, the Belgian team third, the Swiss fourth.

Prague, Austria-Hungary, 1912: The tournament was reduced to three teams, two of which came from the Austro-Hungarian Empire; one from Bohemia (Prague) and the other, a newcomer from Austria (Vienna), and Germany. The Prague hosts beat the Austrians 7–2, and the Germans beat the first-timers 6–3. The Bohemian-German showdown ended in a 2–2 tie. Germany protested the match and no championship honors were bestowed.

Munich, Germany, 1913: Defending champions Austria-Hungary (Bohemia) did not lose a match, but neither did Belgium. The game between the two teams ended in a 4–4 tie, and Belgium was declared champion because of a better goal margin. Germany took the bronze medal, and the Austrians came in fourth.

Berlin, Germany, 1914: This was the last European championship before World War I. Austria-Hungary (Bohemia), Germany, and Belgium shared the gold medal.

Antwerp, Belgium, 1920: World War I caused a gap of six years between tournaments. The 1920 event, held in conjunction with the Olympic Games, is regarded as the first world championship that Canada and the United States took part in. Canada amassed a goal record of 29–1 in three matches, including their final 2–0 victory over the United States. The Americans recorded an incredible 52 goals for and 2 goals against in capturing the silver medal with a crushing 16–0 win over Czechoslovakia. The Czechs narrowly escaped with the bronze medal, topping first-time entrant Sweden 1–0. France, competing for the first time, Belgium, and Switzerland were the other contestants.

Stockholm, Sweden, 1921: Sweden won its first championship by defeating the only other competing country, Czechoslovakia, 6–4.

St. Moritz, Switzerland, 1922: It came down to the Czechoslovakia-Sweden match for the second year in a row to decide the champion. This time the Czechs prevailed, ousting Sweden as champs, 3–2. Switzerland, the only other participant, took the bronze medal.

Antwerp, Belgium, 1923: Antwerp became the first city to host the tournament twice. Sweden won the tournament for the second time in three years. France took the silver medal and the Czechs took the bronze. Belgium and Switzerland were the other participants.

Chamonix, France, 1924: The first winter Olympics were held and ice hockey was on the agenda. But a world championship was also held, and Canada and the United States were once again the class of the tournament as they had been four years previously. Canada was represented by a club team, the Toronto Granites, who won the gold medal with an even more awesome goal ratio than their predecessor Winnipeg Falcons did in 1920. Their final total was 132 goals for and 3 against in six games. Included in that figure were a 30–0 victory over Czechoslovakia and a 22–0 whitewashing of Sweden. The United States tallied an 84–6 goal ratio to gain the silver medal. England won the bronze medal, and Sweden came in fourth.

Milan, Italy, 1924: Besides Olympic Games and the world championship, a separate European championship was held. France and Sweden made it to the finals, with the French winning 2–1. No bronze medal game was held, but Switzerland and Belgium came in second place in their respective divisions. First-timers Italy and Spain finished last in their divisions.

Stbske Pleso and *Stary Smokovec, Czechoslovakia, 1925:* The Czechs playing in their homeland totally dominated the field. Not allowing a goal in any of their matches, they won the championship. Austria took the silver medal, and Switzerland the bronze. Belgium finished last.

Davos, Switzerland, 1926: The tournament was split into three divisions. Czechoslovakia, Austria, and Switzerland emerged as winners in their divisions, and

England was added to the final round of four for scoring the next most goals. England did not garner a point in this round, while the remaining three teams accumulated four points each and had to play another round sans England. In this round Switzerland, who had won only one match in its fifteen years of competition, won the gold medal. The Czechs finished second, and Austria third.

Vienna, Austria, 1927: Homestanding Austria won the championship for the first time, going undefeated in the process. Belgium took the silver medal and Germany the bronze. Czechoslovakia played surprisingly poor and finished fifth overall. This year's new entrant was Hungary, who lost all three of its games by a combined score of 16–0.

St. Moritz, Switzerland, 1928: The Olympic, world, and European championships were decided at the same time. Canada, the class of the field, reached the final round along with England, Sweden, and Switzerland. Canada annihilated them respectively: 14–0, 11–0 and 13–0. Sweden placed second in the tournament and thus became European champ. The Swiss were third and England fourth.

Budapest, Hungary, 1929: Czechoslovakia was once again supreme, winning their fifth title. Poland was second and Austria third.

Chamonix, France and *Davos, Switzerland, 1930:* Japan became the first team in the tournament's history to come from Asia, but they were never a factor. Canada beat Germany for the title, 6–1. Germany held on to beat the Swiss, 2–1, to take the silver.

Krynica, Poland, 1931: Canada once again won the world title, but met stiff opposition in the final game. After rolling through the preliminary rounds with a goal record of 22–0, the Canadians were held to a scoreless tie by Sweden. The United States came in second, the Austrians were third and captured their second European title.

Lake Placid, New York, 1932: The world championship and the Olympics were decided in this single event. It was the first time that a non-European country had hosted the event. Canada as usual was at home in any country, winning the overall title despite having to settle for a scoreless tie with the Americans, who took the silver medal, in their second encounter of the tournament. Germany took the bronze medal, and Poland, the only other competing country, took fourth.

Berlin, Germany, 1932: The European championship was held separately this year. Sweden managed to win a tournament that was highlighted by the competitiveness of the entrants. More than half the games' outcomes ended in ties. Austria took second place, and Switzerland third. This year's new entry was Latvia.

Prague, Czechoslovakia, 1933: The United States ruined the reign of Canada in the world championships that they had appeared in. The Americans won their first title by defeating the Canadians, 2–1. Czechoslovakia finished third, thus earning their sixth European title. Austria was fourth.

Milan, Italy, 1934: High competitiveness once again was the highlight of the tournament. The nine participants were bunched tightly, but Canada regained its position at the top. The United States finished second. Germany finished third for its second European title. Switzerland and Czechoslovakia finished next.

Garmisch-Partenkirchen, Germany, 1936: For the first time since they began to play in this tournament Canada fell prey to a European foe when England, whose team included several Canadian-born players, won the championship by beating the Canadians, 2–1. But England had to settle for a scoreless tie with the United States. But when the Canadians defeated the Americans, 1–0, England was assured the gold. Canada and the United States finished second and third respectively.

London, England, 1937: England was awarded the tournament coming off their previous year's championship. They responded by breezing through the preliminary rounds, outscoring their opponents 45–0. But in the final Canada shut them out, 3–0. Switzerland beat Germany, 6–0, for the bronze medal.

Prague, Czechoslovakia, 1938: Canada, represented by the Sudbury Wolves, reigned supreme again, but not before surviving some tough competition. They narrowly defeated Germany, 1–0, and then took England, 3–1, for the title. The Czechs beat Germany, 3–0, for the bronze medal. This year's first-timer was Lithuania.

Zurich and *Basel, Switzerland, 1939:* Canada, represented by the Trail Smoke Eaters, won the title, barely surviving a second round 2–1 victory over Czechoslovakia. After that match the Canadians were unbeatable, scoring forty goals and giving up none. The United States finished second. Switzerland finished third, thus becoming the European champs. Finland, a first-time entrant, did not win a single match. This was the last world championship for eight years because of World War II.

Stockholm, Sweden, 1949: Czechoslovakia won its second world championship, despite being beaten by the United States, in a tightly fought for title. The United States and Canada finished right behind the Czechs, accumulating six points each. Sweden and Switzerland were next with five points. There were ten competitors in the field, the only newcomer being Denmark, who lost to Canada 47–0 in the elimination round. This score is still a record for most lopsided victory in the history of the world championships.

London, England, 1950: Canada won the title once more. The United States took the silver. Switzerland, in the absence of Czechoslovakia, finished third, thus becoming European champ. Switzerland and England finished next.

Paris, France, 1951: For the first time in the tournament's history A and B divisions were set up to accommodate the large field of thirteen countries. No matter the system, Canada, represented by the Lethbridge Maple Leafs, clearly was the tournament's best team and won another title. Switzerland took the European title.

Oslo, Norway, 1952: Canada, represented by the Edmonton Mercury, won the title score once more. Their only blemish on an otherwise perfect record was a tie with the United States, which took second place. Sweden and Czechoslovakia finished tied for third. A separate game was played to determine the European champ, which Sweden won, 5–3.

Zurich and *Basel, Switzerland, 1953:* Czechoslovakia did not compete because of the death of their president. This cleared the way for Sweden to win its first title. Germany took the silver and Switzerland the bronze.

Stockholm, Sweden, 1954: The Soviet Union sent a team for the first time and immediately became a force to be reckoned with in international hockey, winning the world championship despite a tie with Sweden, which finished third. Canada finished one point behind the USSR and took the silver.

Krefeld, Dusseldorf, Cologne, and *Dortmund, West Germany, 1955:* Annoyed at their defeat at the hands of the Soviets the year before, the Canadians sent a very strong team, the Pentiction Vees, who regained the championship by knocking off the Soviets 5–0 in the final. Czechoslovakia took the bronze.

Cortina d'Ampezzo, Italy, 1956: The Soviet-Canadian hockey war continued, and this time it was the USSR's turn to reign supreme. The United States also outdid Canada, taking the silver medal in the process. Canada settled for the bronze.

Moscow, Russia, 1957: The Soviets were supposed to have a cakewalk without the presence of Canada and the United States to hamper them, but Sweden and Czechoslovakia saw to it that things worked out differently than planned. Both teams tied the Soviets, and Sweden did not lose another match in the tournament, thereby capturing its second world championship. The Czechs finished with the bronze. This year's newcomer was the DDR (East Germany).

Oslo, Norway, 1958: The Canadians and United States returned to action, and the Canadians came with a vengeance. Represented by the Whitby Dunlops, considered one of the best teams ever, the Canadians took the gold medal, amassing a goal record of 82–6 in seven matches. The Soviets took second and Sweden third.

Prague, Czechoslovakia, 1959: The Belleville McFarlands representing Canada skated away with the title and once more defeated the Soviets, who took the silver, 3–1. The Canadians only loss was to Czechoslovakia, 5–3, after the championship had been already decided. That victory enabled the Czechs to garner the bronze, edging out the United States.

Squaw Valley, California, 1960: The United States, playing in their homeland, captured their first Olympic gold medal for hockey. They defeated Canada 2–1 and the USSR 3–2 in their most important matches and remained undefeated in the rest of their contests. Canada took the silver and the Russians the bronze, but this was good enough for the European championship. Czechoslovakia and Sweden finished next.

Geneva and *Lausanne, Switzerland, 1961:* A record twenty countries took part, forcing the addition of a "C" division. Canada, represented by the Trail Smoke Eaters, won the gold medal despite a draw with Czechoslovakia, who took the silver medal and the European championship. South Africa sent a team.

Colorado Springs and *Denver, Colorado, 1962:* United States authorities refused visas to the team of East Germany (DDR). In protest the Czechoslovakian and Russian teams withdrew. The three best teams from the "B" division, Norway, Switzerland, and England, were promoted to the "A" division where they were promptly annihilated by superior teams from Sweden, Canada, and the United States. The big surprise came when Sweden trounced the Canadians and the Americans, who finished second and third respectively, for Sweden's third world championship.

Stockholm, Sweden, 1963: Bulgaria boosted the entrants to twenty-one. The Russians began a string of domination by winning the title with a better goal record than their competition. Sweden, who finished third, beat the Soviets 2–1 but did not have as good a goal record as the Soviets. Czechoslovakia's victory over Canada, and subsequent silver medal, left the Canadians without a medal for the first time.

Innsbruck, Austria, 1964: The Soviets again dominated play and won the title in this Olympic year. Sweden, Czechoslovakia, and Canada finished next.

Tampere, Finland, 1965: The Soviets made it their third championship season in a row. Meanwhile sound play by Czechoslovakia and Sweden, who won silver and bronze medals respectively, stopped the Canadians from gaining a medal for the third year in a row.

Ljubljana, Yugoslavia, 1966: Czechoslovakia seemed on course to undo the Soviet domination. They went to the final game without a single loss or tie. Meanwhile the Soviets had been tied by Sweden. But in the final game the Soviets showed their overall superiority by defeating the Czechs, who took the silver, 7–1. Canada took the bronze.

Vienna, Austria, 1967: The series held further significance than usual because the "A" division was to be expanded to six teams for 1969, and the teams that finished first to sixth in 1967 would go into that group. Canada sent an extremely strong team but were subdued nonetheless by the Soviets, 2–1. With that loss the Canadians seemed to let down, allowing Sweden to capture the silver medal by crushing them, 6–0, therefore falling to a bronze medal.

Grenoble, France, 1968: The Soviets continued their dominance but not without a little luck. The Czechs defeated them, 5–4, but lost later on to Canada, 3–2. When Sweden tied the Czechs and the Soviets remained undefeated the rest of the way, this gave the title to the Soviets. Canada came in third.

Stockholm, Sweden, 1969: Under the new format the old standby held true. The Soviets, in a close fight for the championship, won out once again. Sweden finished second and Czechoslovakia third. Finland beat the United States twice, thus dropping the Americans to the "B" division for the next tournament.

Stockholm, Sweden, 1970: The world championships were originally scheduled for Canada for the first time, but when they were made aware that professional players could not compete they withdrew totally from the tournament. The United States followed suit. Twenty-one countries still remained, and of these the Soviet Union proved superior once more. The champion East Germany and runner-up Poland from the prior year's "B" division were installed in place of the United States and Canada, but were not major factors. Sweden finished second and Czechoslovakia third.

Berne and *Geneva, Switzerland, 1971:* In a record field of twenty-two countries Czechoslovakia was able to tie the Soviets, 3–3, and defeat them, 5–2, but were beaten themselves by Sweden and the United States. Thus the USSR won another gold medal. Czechoslovakia was compensated with the European championship and Sweden took the silver medal.

Prague, Czechoslovakia, 1972: The Czechs, who had waited twenty-three years between titles, ended the Soviet's nine-year domination by winning the gold before their home crowd. The Soviets took second and Sweden third.

Moscow, Russia, 1973: The Soviets regained their title with a vengeance, outscoring the rest of the field 100–18. Sweden took the silver and Czechoslovakia the bronze.

Helsinki, Finland, 1974: The Soviets won the title once more but this time in a haze of controversy. A doping scandal, which remains unsolved to this day, reversed many of the decisions in the tournament's games. The Czechs took second and Sweden third. The East Germans were relegated to the "B" division to be replaced by the Americans who won that division.

Dusseldorf and *Munich, West Germany, 1975:* The Soviets dominated once more as they breezed through the tournament without as much as a tie. Czechoslovakia was equally impressive, finishing second, and Sweden finished third.

Katowice, Poland, 1976: This became the year to beat up on the Soviets. Not only did Czechoslovakia, who won the gold, and Sweden, who took the silver, defeat the USSR; but host country Poland, a team thought little of, also defeated the Soviets. The Soviets settled for the bronze.

Vienna, Austria, 1977: The Canadians returned to the international hockey scene, boasting a squad of NHLers and WHAers whose teams had not made the playoffs. But the Soviets badly beat this contingent nonetheless. Canada saved face by thrashing the rest of their opposition to gain the silver medal.

Prague, Czechoslovakia, 1978: The Soviets won the title in the last game against the Czechs, who had come in undefeated and with a 6–4 victory over the Russians; the Soviets scored, 3–1, and therefore won on a better goal differential. The Czechs took second and Canada third.

Moscow, Russia, 1979: The Soviets again totally dominated the play and won the championship. Czechoslovakia finished second, and the tournament's biggest surprise was Sweden's knocking off Canada for the bronze medal.

Gothenburg and *Stockholm, Sweden, 1981:* The world championship was not staged during the Olympic year of 1980, but the Soviets did not seem to miss a beat, though in a less dominant form. Sweden finished second and Czechoslovakia third. A Canadian team that even included Guy Lafleur and Larry Robinson could do no better than fourth place.

Helsinki and *Tampere, Finland, 1982:* Still awesome, the Soviet Union's representatives clearly established themselves as the world power. Czechoslovakia was runner-up, Sweden third. Once again the National Hockey League of Canada's entry was an embarrassing fourth.

Dortmund, Dusseldorf, and *Munich, West Germany, 1983:* At least the Canadians bettered themselves by one slot, finishing third. The Soviets maintained their iron grasp on the gold, while Czechoslovakia stayed in second and Sweden dropped to fourth.

Prague, Czechoslovakia, 1985: Gold medal-winners in 1984 Olympics, the Russians were stunned on their return to the world championship format. The Soviet Union, which had last missed first place in 1976, dropped to third place. The Czechs, who ironically won a gold medal in 1976, took the championship, followed by Team Canada in second place. After a promising start, the American team finished fourth.

ICE HOCKEY IN THE OLYMPICS

The purest, most competitive—and, in many ways, most interesting—form of hockey has been that played by amateurs in the Olympic games. Unfortunately, Olympic hockey has too often been marked by controversy, much of it dominated by conflicting political ideologies.

In 1920, when the first unofficial Olympic hockey games were held, at Antwerp, Belgium, the Olympic program still had not been divided into winter and summer games. Both the United States and Great Britain had hoped that the 1920 games would be recognized as official events, but the International Olympic Committee declined to give it such status. Nevertheless, seven nations—France, Sweden, Belgium, Czechoslovakia, Switzerland, Canada, and the United States—participated in the contests at the Antwerp Ice Palace.

"The Winter Olympic Games were not officially added to the program until 1924. In 1920 ice hockey and skating contests were held at Antwerp, Belgium, and publicized in both the American and European press as the Winter Olympics," said Donald M. Clark, an American hockey historian. "The results have never been recognized as official by the International Olympic Committee. The United States team was a pick of the best eligible players from the St. Paul, Pittsburgh, and Boston teams of the United States Amateur Hockey Association. The original intent was to arrange a four-team playoff among St. Paul, Pittsburgh, Boston, and Cleveland, and to send the winner to Antwerp."

The committee in charge decided it was impossible to assemble a representative team composed entirely of American-born players; consequently they chose the best players from the leading American teams of the time. Of the players chosen, only Frank Goheen, Anthony Conroy, J. Edward Fitzgerald, and Cyril Weidenborner, all of St. Paul, and George P. Geran and Leon P. Tuck of Boston were American-born and reared. Joe McCormick, Larry McCormick, Herbert J. Drury, and Frank A. Synott were born and reared in Canada but were imported to play in the United States. There developed a protest from the Canadian press regarding the eligibility of these players to compete for the U.S. team; however, they were allowed to compete.

A minimum of $10,000 was needed to cover expenses for assembling the club and making the journey to Europe. To raise the money, the American team played a series of exhibition games in Pittsburgh against teams from Winnipeg, Hamilton, and Toronto.

On April 7, 1920, the American team sailed from Hoboken, New Jersey, well aware that their keenest competition would come from their brethren north of the border. Canada's representative, the Winnipeg Falcons, dominated by players of Icelandic descent, was favored to win the tournament principally because of their excellent forward, Frank Frederickson.

Both Canada and the United States were impressive in their opening matches, played according to the old seven-man rules. The American team routed Switzerland, 29–0, while the Canadians took the measure of Czechoslovakia, 15–0.

Commenting on conditions at the first international match of its kind, Frederickson observed: "We played indoors on a rink that wasn't full-sized by our standards, but was big enough. Unfortunately, the boards weren't really boards but rather wood panelings of a delicate nature and sometimes we'd bounce a hard carom off them and smash them to smithereens. Some of the teams were relatively new to hockey and showed it, even their gear. The Swedes wore ordinary leg pads and their goaltender had on his cricket pads. We loaned him one of our goalie's extra pads and he was very grateful.

"There were some pretty poor players on teams representing the weaker countries. Some were so bad they didn't even know how to stop—they just skated headlong into the boards!"

The major test was between the Americans and Canadians, in the semifinals. Canada prevailed, 2–0, and then defeated Sweden, 12–1, in the final match. The United States defeated Czechoslovakia, 16–0, to finish second, and the Czechs edged Sweden, 1–0, for third place.

Frederickson said, "Winning the Olympic championship was quite a feather in our cap and gave us a lot of publicity. I had the world at my feet. In time I received an offer of $2,500 to play twenty-four games in the Pacific Coast League. It was big money then and I accepted."

When the 1924 Olympic Games took place, professional hockey had become well established on both sides of the border. The NHL was in full bloom and growing fast, and there was considerable interest in the matches played at Chamonix, France, starting January 27, 1924.

The 1924 Olympic hockey games—now considered official—featured eight teams rather than seven, since Great Britain had joined the action. (Austria would have been the ninth team in the tournament but defaulted.) "The United States was represented by a ten-man team picked from the Boston, Pittsburgh, and St. Paul clubs of the United States Amateur Hockey Association," said Donald M. Clark. The American players were as follows:

Alphonse LaCroix	Newton, Mass., Boston A.A.
Irving Small	Winchester, Mass., Boston A.A.
Clarence "Taffy" Abel	Sault Ste. Marie, Mich., St. Paul A.C.
George P. Geran	Holyoke, Mass., Boston A.A.
Justin McCarthy	Arlington, Mass., Boston A.A.
Frank A. Synott	Chatham, New Brunswick, Boston A.A.
Williard Rice	Newton, Mass., Boston A.A.
Sharkey Lyons	Arlington, Mass., Boston A.A.
Art Langley	Melrose, Mass., Melrose
Herb Drury	Midland, Ontario, Pittsburgh A.A.
William Haddock, manager	Swansea, Wales, Pittsburgh A.A.

One-sided victories, such as Canada's 33–0 lashing of Switzerland and England's 20–0 whipping of Belgium, dominated the tournament, with Canada and the United States easing their way to the finals. The Americans—led by the tournament's leading goal scorer, Herb Drury (twenty-one goals) of Pittsburgh, and a defense that had not allowed a single goal thus far—hoped to defeat a powerful Canadian team and win the gold medal. But the Canadians overwhelmed the Americans, 6–1, in a well-played, hard-hitting finale. Drury and one other player—defenseman Clarence "Taffy" Abel, who tallied fifteen goals in the tournament and later played on the 1927–28 Stanley Cup champion New York Rangers—moved on to successful National Hockey League careers.

Unlike the 1924 games, the 1928 Olympic hockey tournament featured bitterness instead of hockey, as far as the United States was concerned. As Donald M. Clark said:

> Among the teams approached regarding sending a team were: University Club of Boston, Harvard University, University of Minnesota, Augsburg College of Minneapolis, and Eveleth (Minn.) Junior College. Either for the lack of finances or the opportunity. Augsburg formulated plans to attend, but General Douglas MacArthur, chairman of the American Olympic Committee, refused to approve them as a choice. He termed the Minneapolis college, led by the Hanson brothers, as "not representative of American hockey." University Club of Boston had a strong team made up of such stars as George Owen, Jack Fitzgerald, Sykes Hardy, Ed Mullowney, John Chase, Clark Hodder, Doug Everett, Myles Lane, Ken Marshall, and John Mansur. This team played a two-game series against the Toronto University Grads, 1928 Olympic Champions. They split, winning 1–0 and losing 2–1. Because of the lack of finances the University Club of Boston could not attend the games.

In the absence of an American team, the Canadian team (the Toronto University Grads) promptly swept its way to the gold medal, outscoring its opponents 38–0. The United States was disappointed at not having sent a team, and internationally U.S. hockey was at a standstill until the next Olympiad.

The 1932 Olympic Games—in Lake Placid, New York—brought forth an exciting and competitive four-team hockey tournament, along with an opportunity for the Americans to redeem themselves from the 1928 debacle. As Clark said, "The United States' team was under the auspices of the Amateur Athletic Union. Since the mid-twenties, when the once-strong United States Amateur Hockey Association degenerated into a weak body due to the encroachment of professional hockey, ice hockey in the United States had meager leadership and governing. With the 1932 Olympics scheduled to be held in this country, the United States Olympic Committee in 1931 induced the Amateur Athletic Union to step in and take charge of ice hockey in order to insure the United States a strong entry in the games."

The United States team hoped that several European countries would send teams to Lake Placid for the ensuing winter games. Ultimately Poland and Germany were the only European entries. With Canada and the United States, they played a double round robin series for the Olympic medals.

The American players were:

Osborne Anderson	Swampscott, Mass.
John P. Bent	New York, N.Y., Yale
John P. Chase	Boston, Mass., Harvard
Douglas N. Everett	Boston Mass., Dartmouth
Franklin Farrell	New York, N.Y., Yale
Joe F. Fitzgerald	Boston, Mass., Boston College
Edward M. Frazier	Stoneham, Mass.
John B. Garrison	Newton, Mass., Harvard
Gerald Hallock	New York, N.Y., Princeton
Robert C. Livingston	New York, N.Y., Yale
Winthrop Palmer, Jr.	Warehouse Point, Conn., Yale
Gordon Smith	Winchester, Mass.
John F. Cookman	New York, N.Y., Yale
Francis A. Nelson	New York, N.Y., Yale
Rufus Trimble, manager	New York, N.Y., Columbia
Alfred Winsor, coach	Boston, Mass., Harvard
Gil Gleason, assistant coach	Boston, Mass.
Tom Murray, trainer	Boston, Mass.

On the first day of the tournament, the Americans were locked in a tough battle with Team Canada, their rivals. Doug Everette, a star from Dartmouth College, scored midway through the second period to put the United States ahead, 1–0. The lead lasted until the final two minutes of the contest. As the United States hung on to its slim lead, Canada's center, Vic Lindquist, took the puck at center ice and plowed through the U.S. defense. Sweeping down the side boards, he managed to take a shot on net while sliding on his back! The U.S. team watched helplessly as the puck entered the net, tying the game, 1–1. Overtime came next, and more disappointment for the Americans.

With the United States shorthanded two men, Canada's Hack Simpson beat U.S. goaltender Frank Farrell with a hard shot to Farrell's glove side after ten minutes had expired in the extra period, giving Canada the first victory of the tournament. Germany defeated Poland, 2–1, in the second game that same day.

The United States rebounded in their second hockey match of the tourney as John Cookman converted a pass by John Bent thirty-five seconds into the second period, for what proved to be the winning goal in a 4–1 U.S. victory over Team Poland. It was a game in which Polish goaltender Josef Stogowski played spectacularly as he prevented a total blow-out by the Americans.

The Americans and Canadians again dominated the rest of the tournament: The United States defeated Germany twice, 7–0 and 8–0, and Canada beat Poland, 10–0, and Germany, 5–0. As usual it was the United States and Canada in the finals, with the United States needing to win two successive games against Canada in order to win the gold medal. All the Canadians needed was a tie.

Through a blistering snowstorm, the game was played in front of a standing-room-only crowd that included New York City Mayor Jimmy "Beau James" Walker. The United States was playing to assure an overall victory in the Olympic Games by Team USA. Unaware of the U.S. victory in the 50-kilometer ski race that had already given the United States first place, the American hockey team felt that the overall standing rested on its shoulders.

Quickly the Americans struck first. Ding Palmer rushed up ice and into the opposing team's zone. As he carried the puck behind the Canadian cage, he spotted teammate Doug Everett and fed him the puck. Everett slapped it home, and the United States went up, 1–0. But the lead didn't last long. Canada came soaring back and pressured the United States until it got the equalizer late in the first period, just as a U.S. penalty had expired. Score tied, 1–1.

In the second period the United States pressured Canada with excellent teamwork and perfect execution. Canada's goalie, Cockburn, would not relent a goal until two-and-a-half minutes remained in the period. Leading, 2–1, and with only one period left in the game, the United States looked as if it would finally capture the gold medal from the Canadians' grasp.

In the third period, the United States cleared the puck down the length of the ice, time after time frustrating the Canadians. The task of tying the game became even more frustrating when U.S. goaltender Frank Farrell turned away any opportunity the Canadians had. But the inevitable happened again. With only thirty-three seconds remaining in the game, Romeo Rivers—who had played an outstanding tournament—whacked at a bouncing puck in front of Farrell that wound up in the net and tied the score, 2–2.

During overtime the Canadians preserved a tie by playing safe hockey. They made no mistakes in winning their fourth straight gold medal.

The 1936 winter games were held under the most unpleasant circumstances in the history of the games. Adolf Hitler and the Nazi party had been in power for four years when the games began in the German winter resort, Garmisch-Partenkirchen.

The American sextet, comprising mostly collegians, with two members of the Boston Olympics of the Eastern Amateur Hockey League (Tom Moone and Gord Smith) added, opened the tournament against the German squad.

The American squad included:

Thomas H. Moone	Lexington, Mass., Boston Olympics
Francis Shaugnessy	Montreal, Que., McGill University
Gordon Smith	Winchester, Mass., Boston Olympics
Francis J. Spain	Newton, Mass., Dartmouth University
Paul E. Rowe	Arlington, Mass., Boston University
Frank R. Stubbs	Newton, Mass., Harvard University
Eldridge B. Ross	Melrose, Mass., Colgate University
John C. Lax	Arlington, Mass., Boston University
Phillip LaBatte	Minneapolis, Minn., Minnesota University
John Garrison	Newton, Mass., Harvard University
Malcolm McAlphin	Montclair, N.J., Princeton University
Francis F. Baker	Clinton, N.Y., Hamilton College
Walter Brown, manager	Boston, Mass.
Albert Prettyman, coach	Clinton, N.Y., Hamilton College

In the opening event, the American team defeated Germany 1–0, thanks to the goaltending of Tom Moone. Incredibly and ironically, the star of the German squad was a Jew, Rudi Ball, who kept the otherwise inept German forwards in the game. The sole American goal was scored by Gordon Smith on a pass from Captain Jack Garrison, at 14:02 of the first period. The Americans then stalled for the rest of the game to achieve their victory. The game was played in a blinding snowstorm.

A major controversy erupted over the eligibility of the powerful British team, which was made up totally of Canadian-born players. Canadian officials claimed that two players, goalie James Foster and Alexander Archer, had played illegally in Great Britain and were subsequently suspended by the Canadian Amateur Hockey Association. Canada claimed they were ineligible to play in the Olympics, but Great Britain insisted that the players had not violated any rules and that a

C.A.H.A. ruling had no bearing on the Olympics. A vote was taken and the British players were unanimously ousted. The Canadians then withdrew their charges after the vote, allowing the players to participate. The Canadians maintained that they wanted to establish a principle. This infuriated the European teams who argued that the players should not be playing. Threats of boycotts erupted throughout the tourney.

The first round was highlighted by two major upsets. First it was the Americans falling to Italy, 2–1. The game was marred by dirty play on both sides. The deciding goal was scored with two minutes left in the second overtime, after the Americans had blown a 1–0 lead late in the third period.

In the other upset Great Britain defeated Canada, 2–1. James Foster—the British goalie Canada had hoped to have suspended—was the star of the game, repeatedly holding off Canadian rushes in the last two periods as he protected the slim lead. Neither upset, however, was disastrous to the respective teams as both advanced to the final round.

In the final round, the Americans defeated Czechoslovakia, 2–0, held Great Britain to a 0–0 tie, and lost to Canada, 1–0.

As often was the case in the winter Olympics, the most fascinating game pitted the Americans against the Canadians. In 1936, with Adolf Hitler looking on, Don Neville of the Canadian team broke through the American defense and beat Goalie Tom Moone. It was the only goal the Canadians needed, as they defeated the American sextet, 1–0.

But the most astonishing aspect of the tourney was the emergence of Great Britain as the winner.

The British, having defeated the Canadians in the second round, then tying the United States and crushing the Czechs in the final round, were given the championship on the basis of total points. The Canadians finished second, and the Americans grabbed third place,.

The next winter Olympics were scheduled for 1940 but were canceled because of the outbreak of World War II, as were the 1944 events. The winter Olympics were next held in 1948 at St. Moritz, Switzerland. Once again controversy dominated the tournament even before it began. Because a dispute between the United States Olympic Committee, the International Ice Hockey Federation, and the Amateur Hockey Association of the United States, two American teams were sent to the Olympics.

During the 1932 and 1936 games the Amateur Athletic Union controlled amateur hockey in the United States and in turn sanctioned the United States Olympic hockey team. After World War II, the Amateur Hockey Association of the United States (AHAUS) became the governing body of ice hockey in the United States and was recognized by the International Ice Hockey Federation. But the United States Olympic Committee still recognized the Amateur Athletic Union as the only governing body in United States hockey. Thus two United States teams were sent to Switzerland, one by the AHAUS, one by the AAU.

The Swiss Organizing Committee voted to allow the AHAUS team to compete, over the objections of the United States Olympic Committee and the International Olympic Committee. The AAU team did not compete in a single game.

Nine nations—Canada, Czechoslovakia, Switzerland, United States, Sweden, Great Britain, Poland, Austria, and Italy—were entered in the 1948 tournament at St. Moritz. Canada regained the title it had lost in 1936 by defeating Switzerland, 3–0, in their final game. The Canadians actually would up in a first place tie with Czechoslovakia, both teams going 7–0–1. But Canada was awarded the gold because of a higher goal quotient. This figure is obtained by taking a team's total "goals for" and dividing it by their total "goals against." The Canadians outdid the Czechs by 13.88 to 4.44.

Considering the problems the United States had experienced with ice hockey in the 1948 Olympic Games, it seemed that it might not send a team to the 1952 games in Oslo, Norway. The United States Olympic Committee and the Amateur Hockey Association of United States had to iron out their differences.

A compromise calling for an eight-man committee was reached by Walter Brown, representing the AHAUS, and Avery Brundage and Asa Bushnell of the USOC. The committee would have four members from each group and would be completely independent and outside the framework of either organization. They called it the United States Ice Hockey Committee. The quartet sent by the USOC was made up of Daniel J. Ferris, New York; Asa S. Bushnell, Princeton; W. E. Moulton, Providence; and Edward Jeremiah, Hanover, New Hampshire. The AHAUS sent Walter A. Brown, Boston; Robert B. Riddler, St. Paul; Fred W. Edwards, Minneapolis; and Leonard Fowle, Boston.

The purpose of the committee was to select and organize a team representing the United States at Oslo in 1952. Robert Riddler of St. Paul was chosen team manager and John Pleban of Eveleth, Minn., coach.

Walter Brown held the eastern tryouts in Boston, while the western tryouts were taking place in Minneapolis. By January first a full team was assembled in Boston. Eight players came from Minnesota, six from Massachusetts, and one player from Rhode Island. They embarked on a series of thirteen exhibition games against the best teams of the East, resulting in a 10 and 3 record. On January 20, they left for Europe for a series of pre-Olympic games in England, France, Switzerland, Germany, and Belgium.

The United States sent a strong team to Oslo. The sextet made a formidable showing, finishing second, one game behind the Canadian team. The only loss in the series was a 4–2 defeat to Sweden. In the final game of the Olympics, the Americans tied the Edmonton Mercurys, Canada's representatives, 3–3. After the games, the United States embarked on an additional series of exhibition games against the best teams of Europe. Their overall record was fourteen wins, five ties, and only eight losses.

The 1952 Olympic team was made up of:

Allan Van	St. Paul, Minn.
James Sedin	St. Paul, Minn.
James "Ken" Yackel	St. Paul, Minn.
Arnold C. Oss, Jr.	Minneapolis, Minn.
John Noah	Crookston, Minn.
Robert Rompre	International Falls, Minn.
Andre Gambucci	Eveleth, Minn.
Ruben Bjorkman	Roseau, Minn.
Joe Czarnotta	Wakefield, Mass.
Leonard Ceglarski	East Walpole, Mass.
Clifford Harrison	Walpole, Mass.
Dick Desmond	Medford, Mass.
Don Whiston	Stoneham, Mass.
John Mulhern	Boston, Mass.
Jerry Kilmartin	Providence, R.I.
Robert Riddler, manager	St. Paul, Minn.
John E. Pleban, coach	Eveleth, Minn.
John Semple, trainer	Lynn, Mass.

The 1956 Olympic Games in Cortina, Italy contained what had become the usual share of controversy. But this time the problems centered on Canada. For the first time since 1936, the Canadian sextet finished not in first place but in third, behind Russia and the United States. This prompted Jimmy Dunn, president of the Canadian Amateur Hockey Association, to state that in the future Canada should send a real all-star team rather than the best team in the country.

Dunn made his remarks after watching the Kitchener-Waterloo Dutchmen, Canada's representatives, lose 2–0 to the champion Russians. Even Bobby Bauer, coach of the Dutchmen, agreed with Dunn, since every other country at the games was represented by an all-star team.

The selection format used by the 1952 U.S. Ice Hockey Committee was followed again in 1956. Robert Riddler once more was team manager, but the new coach was John Mariucci of Eveleth, Minnesota. The twenty-two players finally chosen held their final training in Duluth, and after several exhibition games in the States, left for pre-Olympic exhibitions in Italy and Germany.

The U.S. team was considered one of the finest ever assembled for Olympic competition. The team was especially strong up the middle, with centers Bill Cleary, John Matchefts, and John Mayasich. Likewise, the goaltending tandem of

Don Rigazio and Willard Ikola was considered excellent. The highlight of their appearance was a 4–1 victory over Canada.

The complete team consisted of:

Wendell Anderson	St. Paul, Minn.
F. W. Burtnett	Cambridge, Mass.
Eugene Campbell	Minneapolis, Minn.
Gordon Christian	Warroad, Minn.
William Cleary	Cambridge, Mass.
Dick Dougherty	International Falls, Minn.
John Mayasich	Eveleth, Minn.
Willard Ikola	Eveleth, Minn.
John Matchefts	Eveleth, Minn.
Dan McKinnon	Williams, Mass.
Richard Meredith	Minneapolis, Minn.
Francis O'Grady	Stoneham, Mass.
Weldon Olson	Marquette, Mich.
Kenneth Purpur	Grand Forks, N.D.
Donald Rigazio	Cambridge, Mass.
Dick Rodenhiser	Malden, Mass.
Ed Sampson	International Falls, Minn.
Jack Petroske	Hibbing, Minn.
Ben Bertini, trainer	Lexington, Mass.
John Mariucci, coach	Eveleth, Minn.
and Robert Riddler, manager	St. Paul, Minn.

The surprising performances by the USSR and U.S. teams brought about two interesting responses in the States. The Cleveland Barons of the American Hockey League were so impressed with the goaltending performance of Russian netkeeper, Nikolai Puchkov, that they offered him a two-year contract at $10,000 a year. Puchkov had three shutouts during the Olympic series, including two successive ones over the United States and Canada. In five games, he allowed only five goals. This was the second time ever that a North American professional club had approached a European hockey player.

The other development stemming from the 1956 games was more realistic. The series marked the first time in the history of the Olympics that the hockey games were of major interest in the United States. Newspapers featured the team on the front page and the U.S.–USSR game was broadcast across the country. Lynn Patrick, manager of the Boston Bruins, said, "Mariucci and his players have probably done more for amateur hockey in this country than all the other Olympic hockey teams we've ever had combined." The professional hockey teams also took notice of the amateur squad, which in previous years they had almost ignored.

Mayasich, Ikola, and Cleary were all placed on the negotiating lists of professional clubs. The respectable showing by the U.S. team and the heightened interest in amateur hockey across the nation set the stage for the 1960 Olympic Games in Squaw Valley, Idaho.

The prospects of an American team winning an Olympic gold medal were always remote, particularly in the post–World War II era when the Russians were getting stronger, along with the Scandinavian countries. Canada was always a formidable foe. Yet in 1960 Uncle Sam iced a solid team led by Ken Yackel, Bill Christian, goalie Jack McCartan, John Mayasich, and Tommy Williams.

The coach who shepherded the American team to Squaw Valley was Jack Riley. "We were definitely underdogs," said Riley, who was selected to head the U.S. club after guiding the Military Academy sextet at West Point. "We couldn't possibly win a gold medal. At least that's what they all said before we hit the ice."

Riley's 1960 Olympians did more to bolster the prestige of American hockey than any other team since the 1938 Chicago Black Hawks, a club sprinkled with Americans, which won the Stanley Cup. Their formidable opponents would be the Russians and the Canadians. It was not considered remotely possible for the Americans to topple either of these strong teams.

Riley's first challenge was the Swedish national team, traditionally a strong-skating, hard-shooting club. The favored Swedes were routed, 6–3. Murmurs about the American squad began filtering around Olympic Village. The murmuring grew louder after the U.S. skaters demolished Germany, 9–1.

The Americans were next scheduled to meet Canada's national team for the first time. Incredibly, the Americans defeated the Canadians, 2–1. Then they knocked off the Russians, 3–2, followed astoundingly by wins over Czechoslovakia, Sweden, and West Germany. Suddenly the Americans found themselves unbelievably within grasp of a gold medal. They had three games, three obstacles, ahead of them: Canada, Russia, and Czechoslovakia, all of whom they'd already beaten once.

The Canadians looked the better team, as they poured volley after volley at goalie Jack McCartan. "All I could see," said McCartan "were streaks of green Canadian jerseys."

McCartan made thirty-nine saves, most of them difficult, and allowed only one goal. The Americans scored twice, winning the match, 2–1. On Saturday, February 27, the Americans faced off against the Soviet team. More than ten thousand spectators jammed Blyth Arena for the contest, while millions watched the game on television.

After two periods, the clubs battled to a 2–2 draw. But most important, the Americans proved they could skate with the fleet Russians. For nearly fifteen minutes of the final period, the rivals tested goalies McCartan and Nikolai Puchov, and neither gave an inch until 14:59 of the last period.

Roger Christian and Tom Williams united, feeding the puck to Billy Christian who found himself one-on-one with goalie Puchov. "When the goalie came out of the net to cut down the angle," recalled coach Riley, "Billy outsmarted him and slid it in. That was it, because McCartan wasn't going to let the Russians score again."

The final score was United States 3, Soviet Union 2. Only one more opponent blocked America's bid for a gold medal: Czechoslovakia. For a time it appeared that Riley's stickhandlers would blow it all on the final day of the championship. They tied the Czechs, 3–3, after the first period, but fell behind, 4–3, in the second. At that point a strange twist of fate helped the Americans. Nikolai Sologubov, a crack defenseman for the Russian National Team, visited the American's dressing room and offered Riley some advice. "He suggested that our players take oxygen to restore their pep," Riley recalled. "As it turned out, some of our guys took his advice."

Whether the oxygen did the trick or not will remain a point of debate for hockey historians as long as the 1960 Olympics are discussed. Whatever it was, the Americans stormed onto the ice and nearly knocked the Czechs off their skates.

Roger Christian alone accounted for three goals in the last period. He tied the score, 4–4, at 5:50 of the period. Then Bill Cleary put the Americans ahead, 5–4, and followed that with a power-play goal. Within a thirty-eight-second span, Roger Christian and Billy Cleary scored, and then Christian closed the scoring at 17:56 for the sixth and final goal of the period for Uncle Sam's skaters. The final score was 9–4 for the United States. America had won its first Olympic gold medal in hockey.

"We had become a team of destiny," said Riley. "We won because of conditioning, spirit, and a real desire to bring home the gold medal. The players had a deep belief in the old adage: 'There's no substitute for victory.' "

In the 1964 Olympic Games in Innsbruck, Austria, the Americans did not have the luxury of playing at home.

The Americans played poor defensive hockey in Innsbruck, finishing the tourney with a 2–5 record for fifth place overall. This time the Soviet team won the gold medal, and they did it in the most convincing fashion. They were the only unbeaten team, at 7–0, outscoring their opponents 54–10. Sweden defeated Czechoslovakia, 8–3, for the silver, as Canada finished fourth.

Soviet domination of Olympic hockey lasted through the 1976 winter games. In the 1968 tourney in Grenoble, France, the Soviets clinched the gold when Czechoslovakia failed to produce a win in their 2–2 tie with Sweden on the last day of the tournament. The Soviets' only loss came at the hands of Team Czechoslovakia, 5–4, in their final match. But their overall 6–1 record was the best of the pack. Czechoslovakia, 5–1–1, had to settle for the silver, and Canada, 5–2, took the bronze. Team USA finished sixth with a 2–4–1 record. The team, which included future U.S. Olympic coach Herb Brooks, received some criticism. Clark said, "There was some criticism levied against the team's performance in Grenoble; however, the caliber of ice hockey in countries such as Finland, Sweden, Czechoslovakia, Russia and East and West Germany, continues to improve at a rate far greater than in the United States. The reasons for this are, primarily, more participants and more interest in the welfare of the national ice hockey team, on a year-to-year basis."

At Sapporo, Japan, in 1972, the Soviet team won its third consecutive Olympic gold medal in hockey. The task was, as predicted, an easy one for the Soviets. Canada was absent for the first time ever, but it was the Americans who drew attention in the tournament, as they surprised everyone by finishing ahead of Czechoslovakia for second place and the silver medal. Said Clark, "The young American team, averaging twenty-two years of age and sparked by goalie Mike Curran, a native of International Falls, Minnesota, catapulted the team to a surprising second place finish. After an opening loss to Sweden, the United States upset Czechoslovakia, 5–1. In their third game the Americans were defeated, 7–2, by the championship-bound Russians but rebounded to defeat Finland, 4–1, and Poland, 6–1. Although tying in the final standings, the United States was awarded second place by virtue of having defeated the Czechs."

Internationally, everyone was chasing the Soviets, and it was clearly evident that no one was going to catch them in the 1976 winter games at Innsbruck, Austria. Of the countries competing in the tourney, only Czechoslovakia challenged the Soviets in an intensely played 4–2 hockey game that the Soviet Union won.

Team USA again impressed people with a strong showing in the games. Jim Proudfoot of the *Toronto Star* was quoted as saying: "Judged by performance related to sheer ability, the U.S. hockey players have been outstanding athletes at the twelfth winter games. Their unexpected wins over Finland and Poland have been occasions for rejoicing. And their spirited, never-say-die tenacity in losses to the Soviets and the Czechs won them even more admirers." Even though Team USA did not produce a medal (they finished fourth), they still generated optimism. And although Canada failed to send a hockey team for the second successive winter Olympics, the American amateur hockey players, as whole, were improving. This became an understatement when the Olympic Games moved on to Lake Placid, New York, in 1980.

The expectations for the 1980 winter games remained the same. In amateur hockey, the Soviet Union had displayed relentless domination, and they were getting better. A year earlier they had soundly beaten a team of National Hockey League all-stars in a best-two-of-three playoff called the Challenge Cup series. After the series the NHL insisted that their team did not have ample time to practice and form a more cohesive club. But the fact remained: the Soviet Union was now the best hockey force in the world. How could anyone think they would not win the gold medal?

Herb Brooks, once head coach at the University of Minnesota, led a group of talented hockey players onto the ice at Lake Placid. Brooks secretly harbored the notion that they might win the gold medal, but he let very few people know— especially his players. Brooks did everything possible to keep each player from inflating his own ego. After all, as Brooks stated to his players: "You don't have enough talent to win on talent alone." Rated a strong underdog behind the Soviet Union, Czechoslovakia, Sweden, and Finland, the Americans took the ice for the first game of the tournament.

After one period of play the United States found themselves down, 1–0 to Team Sweden. They had been badly outplayed by the Swedes, as goaltender Jim Craig had to turn away seventeen shots to keep them in the game. After the period a shouting match erupted between coach Brooks and player Rob McClanahan. Paradoxically, the team burst onto the ice for the second period, a whirlwind of inspiration. The game ended in a tie as Bill Baker blasted a fifty-foot drive into the Swedish net with only twenty-seven seconds left in the game. At the moment it was only a tie, but it came against a team judged superior to the Americans.

Czechoslovakia, with the soon-to-be-Quebec-Nordiques Stastny brothers, was the next mighty opponent the underdog Yanks faced. Going into the second period tied, 2–2, the United States scored twice, taking a 4–2 lead while everyone's anxiety level mounted. As the third period began experts expected the Americans to go into a defensive shell. Instead they opened the game up, producing the first genuine shocker of the tournament by whipping the Czechs, 7–3. Later U.S. player Jack O'Callahan would call it the best game Team USA played all year.

After the stunning victory over the Czechs, Brooks and the Americans found themselves looking at the tournament in a different light. No longer underdogs for upcoming contests against Norway, Romania, and West Germany, Brooks feared a let-down.

Following a sluggish first period that saw the U.S. team fall behind, 1–0, to Norway, the Americans rebounded on goals by Mike Eruzione, Mark Johnson, and Dave Silk and solid goaltending by Jim Craig to take a 3–1 lead after two periods. Mark Wells and Ken Morrow iced the contest with third-period scores.

Despite the comfortable 5–1 victory, Brooks was dissatisfied. "I'd better take the whip to these guys. Some of them are backing up to the pay window."

The combination of a recovered Jack O'Callahan and a weak Romanian squad produced a 7–2 victory for the Americans in their next game. O'Callahan had injured a knee in the team's final pre-Olympic exhibition against the Russians at Madison Square Garden, missing the first three games of the tourney.

Buzz Schneider, Steve Christoff, Rob McClanahan, and Wells led the scoring parade, while Craig once again turned in a strong effort in the net.

Next for the United States would be a team that had always given them trouble in past Olympiads—West Germany. In the 1976 Olympics, the Americans had needed a win or tie over West Germany to secure a bronze medal. The United States had lost 4–1, and since then American–West German contests took on an added perspective. In 1980 a win was not needed against the West Germans, since the United States had advanced to the medal round by virtue of Sweden's upset over the Czechs earlier that day. Still, it was a game, and the Americans wanted to win very badly.

West Germany jumped to a 2–0 lead in the first stanza. McClanahan and Neal

Broten evened the score for the United States in the second period. Once again Brooks's club showed the benefits of a grueling training camp as they dominated the West Germans in the final stanza. McClanahan picked up the game winner, and Phil Verchota added an insurance tally to give the United States a 4–2 victory. After the game, the medal pairings were announced: Sweden would meet Finland and the United States would play Russia.

Many U.S. players had been watching the Soviets play and felt there were signs that the Russians could be defeated. One, Eric Strobel, observed at the time, "They looked slow sometimes. We thought they were a bit too old." The Russians had struggled in previous matches against the Finns and the Canadians. The U.S. team now looked forward to meeting the Soviets and the chance to hand them their first Olympic defeat since 1968.

In the early moments of the contest, Jim Craig assisted the Yanks' lackluster defense with several outstanding saves. The Russians drew first blood, however, as Vladmir Krutov deflected a slapshot by Aleksei Kasatonov midway through the first period. The U.S. team bounced right back to tie it as Buzz Schneider, on a pass from Mark Pavelich, beat the outstanding Vladislav Tretiak with a slapshot on the glove hand side of the Russian goaltender. At 17:34 Sergei Makarov scored on a pass from Vladmir Golikov, giving the Russians a 2–1 lead in the final minutes of the period. The Americans evened the score with but one second remaining on the clock, as Mark Johnson slid the rebound of a Dave Christian shot past Tretiak.

In the second period Russia regained the lead and held on to it throughout the period. The U.S. defense was weak and another Russian victory seemed imminent as the Americans struggled to even the score.

At 8:39 of the final period, the Americans knotted the score at three apiece on Mark Johnson's second goal of the game. Less than two minutes later, captain Mike Eruzione scored the go-ahead goal for the Americans and gave them their first advantage of the contest.

With ten minutes remaining in the game, the Russians tried to wear out the Americans with line changes every forty-five seconds. Brooks responded, telling his charges, "Play your game. Play your game." Whenever the Americans would play defensively Brooks would pull them from the ice and put on another line. This strategy worked, and it was the Russians, not the Americans, who were on the ropes now, as the Russians lost their composure and began dumping the puck in.

At the final buzzer the score read U.S.—4, USSR—3. The Russians had been defeated, and the underdog American squad became the Cinderella team of the century.

In their final game, the U.S. team faced a tough Finnish squad and needed a win for the gold medal. In the first period of the game Jukka Porvari scored, giving Finland a 1–0 lead—the sixth time in seven games that America trailed and had to come from behind to win. The United States evened it on Steve Christoff's backhander, then gave the lead back to the Finns, as Mikko Leinonen (who would one day play *for* Herb Brooks as a New York Ranger) potted a power-play tally. At the end of two periods, the Americans were down, 2–1.

Two and a half minutes into the third period, Dave Christian split the Finnish defense and passed to Phil Verchota who powered a drive past the Finnish goaltender. Less than four minutes later Rob McClanahan scored the go-ahead goal giving the Americans a 3–2 lead. For the remainder of the game Jim Craig's goaltending held the Finns scoreless, and America rallied once more to make the final score, 4–2. America had won its second gold medal in hockey, dethroning the Soviets who had not lost a championship since 1960, the year Herb Brooks had been the last player cut from the U.S. Olympic squad.

The miracle at Lake Placid in 1980 fostered some false feelings of grandeur in the American ranks, particularly after the United States defeated the Soviet Union in a pre-Olympic, six-game exhibition series in 1984. The U.S.–Soviet series started at Lake Placid—the perfect place to launch such a campaign—and the teams traveled across the country. Uncle Sam's skaters won the series, three games to two with one tie. But once the 1984 Olympics began, Team USA was outclassed by teams from the Soviet Union, Czechoslovakia, Sweden, and Canada.

The Soviets had rebounded from their embarrassing 1980 loss to the young Americans by replacing some oldtimers such as Valeri Vasiliev, the peerless defenseman, and forwards Boris Mikhailov, Vladimir Petrov, the late Valeri Kharlamov and Alexander Maltsev.

This U.S. team was even younger than the 1980 gold medalists, the players averaging 20.7 years. Their top scoring threat was the so-called Diaper Line with center Pat LaFontaine, 18, right-winger David A. Jensen, 18, and left-winger Ed Olczyk, 17. Against the Soviet Selects, the Diaper Line accounted for eight of nine U.S. goals in one stretch.

Once the Olympic competition began it became apparent the American team was doomed. Team U.S.A. lost, 4–2, to a Canadian sextet which, ironically, had been counted out of medal contention in the pre-Olympic polls, 4–2, on opening day.

Two days later, Czechoslovakia beat the Americans, 4–1, to all but seal Team U.S.A.'s fate. When Team U.S.A. managed only a 3–3 tie against the weak Norwegian outfit, the Star-Spangled Skaters were eliminated from advancement to the medal round. Team Canada rallied to beat the Finns and moved into the final round with an 8–1 win over Norway.

As expected, the Soviets marched through the A Pool without any problems, undefeated after four starts. The Russians continued their superior play in the medal round, eventually winning the gold, by defeating Canada 4–0, Czechoslovakia (the eventual silver medal winner), 2–0, and Sweden (the eventual bronze medal winner).

EQUIPPING FOR HOCKEY

Thanks to manufacturers who have spent a great deal of time and money on research over the past ten years, today's hockey player is able to purchase lightweight equipment that offers protection, safety, and comfort.

But make no mistake about it, outfitting a hockey player is not cheap, with the over-the-counter costs of equipping a forward or defenseman from head to toe, helmet to skates, ranging from $200 to $600. Goalie equipment is more expensive, with prices in the $500 to $1,000 range. Custom-made equipment naturally costs more.

Among the current major manufacturers, there are thirteen makers of sticks, eight of skates, and six of general equipment—pads, gloves, helmets, masks, uniforms, and incidentals. It is obvious that the hockey industry in the United States and Canada is healthy enough to keep all these manufacturers in business. But how does a consumer know which product to purchase?

It was interesting to learn the answer from pro shop owners/managers, who say that the success of the skate and stick manufacturers can be traced directly to their advertising and to which National Hockey League player endorses the product. The more popular the player, the greater probability the consumer will ask for the product. But pro shop people are quick to point out that while the popularity of a player endorsing a product may result in a sale, the most important thing is that the item fits the player correctly and that it is comfortable, offering the maximum in protection and safety. One key point to keep in mind when buying full equipment is that each piece should meet the next piece, that is, shoulder pad to elbow pad, shin pad to top skate, and so on. This allows for the greatest protection while maintaining mobility.

169

SKATES

A popular myth about skates must first be laid to rest: "My kid can't be a good skater because he has weak ankles." There is no such thing as weak ankles (unless an actual physical disability is involved). Poorly fitting skates and/or not knowing how to lace the skates properly are the reasons one invariably experiences difficulty with skating. Poor skating also results from parents' making the mistake of buying for a youngster skates that are one or two sizes larger than his or her regular shoes. They reason that the child can wear extra socks to make the skates fit, hoping to stretch usage through more than one season. Nothing could be worse! Skates must always fit properly, and for a growing youngster, never expect the skates to fit more than one season.

There are two important points to remember when purchasing a new pair of ice skates. First, never buy skates that are oversized, and second, when fitting the skates wear only one pair of socks similar to those to be worn while skating.

Boots

Two types of boots are made for hockey skates: stitched (leather and nylon) and molded (plastic), and the correct size for each is different. The stitched boot should be one-half to two sizes smaller than the regular shoe size, and the plastic boot should be one-half size *smaller*, depending on the manufacturer. The boots should fit snugly with the ball of the foot in the wide area of the skate boot, leaving only one-eighth to one-quarter inch of room in length for growth.

While the choice of whether to purchase a stitched or molded boot is a case of personal preference, many experts opine that a new skater gets more support from the molded boot. Since it wears so well and always retains its shape, it can be passed along to a younger player or resold. One manufacturer has developed a plastic *and* leather boot, combining the good features of both. The leather boot is fused to the plastic outer boot. The boot can be softened and remolded wherever there are pressure points. The boot is very expensive at this time, and most youngsters can get along adequately with earlier and less expensive models.

Blades

Just as boots have changed in recent years, skate blades have new types of blade holders, and the stainless steel blade has arrived on the scene.

The new blade holders are light, made of either polycarbonate plastic or a new material from DuPont called Zyte. Until recently, blade holders were black, but

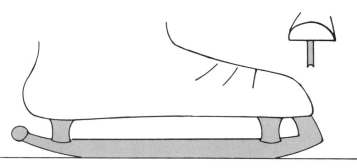

4-1   *Forward's skate and blade. Note that the forward's skate blade is highly "rocked" so that little of the blade actually touches the ice, enabling the forward to skate and turn faster. The term* rock *also means the radius or contour of the blade.*

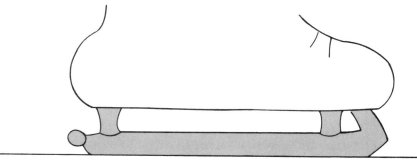

4-2   *Defenseman's skate and blade. More of the blade actually touches the ice than that of a forward's skate blade. Thus, the blade had less "rock" to it. While this means less speed, it also means greater stability.*

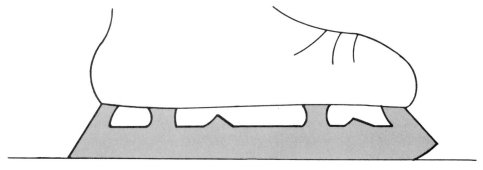

4-3   *Goaltender's skate blade. Nearly the entire length of the blade is on the ice surface, and the top of the blade is designed to prevent pucks from passing between the blade and the skate boot.*

4-4 *A regular hockey skate of stitched leather and nylon. Note that the blade holders are of the new polycarbonate plastic.*

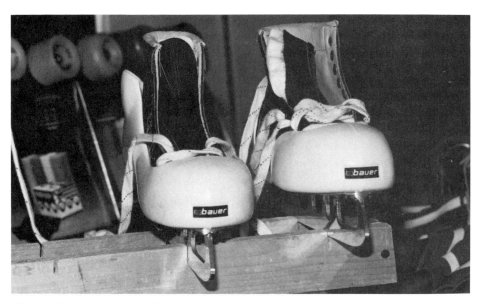

4-5 *The goalie skate is encased in a plastic protective coating. Look closely and note that the blade has very little "rock" to it and the blade itself has very little hollow ground into it.*

new ones produced in white and blue to contrast with the black boot are becoming very popular.

The new stainless steel blade has caused arguments among old timers who still favor the carbon steel blade, claiming it will hold an edge better than the stainless blade.

The cracking or breaking of the new blades and holders has been a bit of a problem, but the manufacturers are working to correct this defect and find fewer and fewer complaints.

Goalie Skates

The boots for goalie skates are basically the same as those for skaters. Both stitched and molded models are available, and all have extra protection built in. Goalie blades, however, are quite different: they are constructed so a puck cannot slip through while the goalie is making a skate save, and they are heavier and usually flat without much radius, to give better balance.

Care of Skates

It is of the upmost importance that boots and blades receive proper care at all times. After every practice or game the blades must be wiped dry, and then the inside of the boots must completely dry out (and not in a skate bag because they get musty). Let the boots dry naturally; *never* put them on a radiator or other heating element. Skate guards should be used when walking in any part of an arena without rubber matting, but should not be used when storing skates because condensation will cause the blades to rust.

Skate Sharpening

Skates should achieve the greatest speed with optimum control, which comes through proper skate sharpening by a professional. In discussing skate sharpening, three terms are used: radius, edge, and hollow. The radius, sometimes called "rock" or "contour," refers to the curve of the blade from toe to heel and affects the speed-control relationship. If the curve of the blade from toe to heel is flatter to the ice surface (that is, more blade touching ice surface), more speed will be gained with less effort. On the other hand, maneuverability is increased with less blade touching the ice. The edges of the blade are very important. The sharper the edges, the more they will cut into the ice, and they must always be free of nicks and rough spots.

The hollow is the ground-out section of the blade between the two edges. The deeper the hollow, the more the edges bite into the ice. This increases control, but reduces speed. When skates are sharpened with a shallower hollow, speed is increased, but there is more chance of skidding because the edges won't bite into the ice as much.

With hockey skates, a player will often have the radius of the blade changed to suit the position he plays. Slightly more blade will be sharpened off the front of the blade for a forward, while a bit more is taken off the heel for a defenseman. Usually it is best to have a little more radius added each time the skates are sharpened until the skater feels he has good balance and speed and maneuverability.

If the skates chatter or jump when stopping after they have been sharpened, they may be too sharp. Just take a skate guard or a soft piece of wood and rub it against the edges of the blade. If the blades skid when stopping, ask the skate sharpener to add more hollow the next time the skates are sharpened. Plan on at least one practice after having skates sharpened before using them in a game.

With goalies, whose skate blades are wider than the other players, the preference is for a flat grind. This gives the goalie better balance and allows him to skate from side to side smoother and faster. Some goalies, however, do have some hollow ground into their skates.

STICKS

Hockey sticks have come a long way since the days when players fashioned sticks from trees they chopped down themselves. Sticks now come in a selection of colors, weights, and "lies" (angles) and are manufactured in combinations of different materials.

The first two questions usually asked by a new hockey player when purchasing a stick are: "Am I a left-hand or right-hand shot?" and "What should be the length of the stick?"

The first question can best be answered by placing a stick on the floor and asking the player to pick it up and hold it as he would to shoot the puck. Whichever hand is placed nearest the blade end of the shaft dictates whether the player is a left- or right-handed shot; that is, if he grasps the blade end of the shaft with the left hand, he is a left-handed shooter.

As for the length of the stick, this question has caused more than a few arguments among hockey people. Some say the stick should reach the player's chin when he's wearing skates, while others say it should be chin high when he's not wearing skates. There are also those who believe the stick should be chest high, and

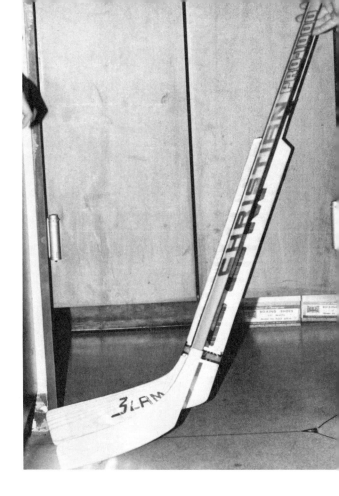

4-6 *A regular hockey stick rests in front of a goalie stick, showing the difference in construction and size. The "lie" of a hockey stick is the angle of the shaft to the blade. A high "lie" means the shaft is straighter to the blade and the puck will be carried more closely to the body. Defensemen usually like a higher lie while forwards prefer a lower one giving them longer reach and greater power behind a shot. The back stick in this photo is about average (5 or 6).*

still others who think nose high is best. Actually, the best length is the one most comfortable to the player. The player must be able to swing the stick freely from side-to-side without its striking his body and, most importantly, be able to switch from his forehand to his backhand and vice-versa without getting all tied up. When measuring for a stick, it should also be remembered to consider whether the player skates in an erect position or in a crouch. It is advisable for the younger player to purchase a junior-size stick rather than cutting down a regular size stick.

Another thing to keep in mind when purchasing a stick is the lie (angle) of the stick. The lie is designated by numbers, with 5 or 6 being the most popular. As the numbers increase, the angle of the stick to the ice increases, too. This means that if a player wishes to carry the puck close, making it easier to stickhandle or dig the puck out from between skates, a high number lie would be best, but if he wishes to carry the puck away from himself, achieve greater reach, or get more power into a shot, a lower number would be desirable. Forwards generally choose sticks with lower lies, whereas defensemen opt for higher lies.

Most sticks are manufactured in wood—usually ash, although birch, elm, and hickory are also good and sturdy. Synthetics such as fiberglass, plastic, and graphite are also used. Even though a hockey stick is strong, it can break, a fact that some hockey people feel should happen under certain conditions to prevent a player from being impaled. An unbreakable stick was manufactured at one time, but it proved much too heavy. Sticks with aluminum shafts and wood blades are gaining in popularity. If the blade breaks, it can be replaced, easily attaching to the shaft.

Specific measurements for sticks are listed in the National Hockey League rule book:

> No stick shall exceed fifty-five inches in length from the heel to the end of the shaft, nor more than twelve and one-half inches from the heel to the end of the blade.
> The blade of the stick shall not be more than three inches in width at any point, nor less than two inches. All edges of the blade shall be bevelled. The curvature of the blade of the stick shall be restricted . . . not to exceed one-half inch.

And for goaltenders' sticks:

> The blade of the goalkeeper's stick shall not exceed three and one-half inches in width at any point, except at the heel where it must not exceed four and one-half inches in width; nor shall the goalkeepers' stick exceed fifteen and one-half inches in length from the heel to the end of the blade.
> The widened portion of the goalkeepers' stick extending up the shaft from the blade shall not exceed more than twenty six inches from the heel and shall not exceed three and one-half inches in width.

The blade of a hockey stick should be taped to protect it from cracks and moisture and, because tape acts as a cushion for the puck, to help control the puck better.

Either black friction tape or white adhesive tape can be used. The adhesive tape is not as sticky (treat the friction tape with powder to eliminate stickiness), adheres better to the stick, and lasts longer. Tape as much of the blade as is comfortable, but when taping, start at the toe of the blade and work back to the heel.

After taping, the player can lay the blade of the stick on the floor and gently step on the blade so it picks up dirt from the floor, which will also eliminate stickiness. For a better grip when holding the stick with one hand or to more easily pick the stick up if it falls to the ice, a tape knob for the top of the stick can also be made.

Goalies' sticks come in a wide variety of weights and lies. The correct way to measure a goalie for a stick is to have him stand with skates on, trying different sticks until he finds that one with the most comfortable lie, allowing for maximum coverage.

A goalie should tape an extra-large knob on the butt-end (top) of the stick so he can pick it up easily if it falls to the ice. The taping of the blade should be done from the shaft of the stick to the blade, but not on the heel.

Although it is not common and not recommended, some goalies, usually those who are good shooters, use a stick with a curved blade.

As with all hockey equipment, care must be taken with the storage of sticks. Wood dries out and becomes brittle, so it is best to store sticks in damp places, such as laundry rooms, basements, or garages.

Remember there is no returning a hockey stick to the pro shop or store once it has been used, so before making a purchase inspect it carefully. Certain defects are easy to spot, such as a lamination that is not glued properly, a knot in the laminated wood, or gaps in the fiberglass covering.

PUCK

The puck, made of vulcanized rubber, is one inch thick and three inches in diameter. It weighs between five and a half and six ounces.

HELMETS

Although it has been around since 1894, the hockey helmet has recently revolutionized the equipment market because only NHL professionals who signed contracts before 1979 are permitted to play without wearing one. But make no mistake about it, today's helmets are certainly not like the originals in either comfort or protection.

Helmets, which must pass rigorous government tests, are manufactured with a hard outer shell to give protection from a sharp blow and a special padded lining to absorb and distribute shock. The shell of the helmet is subjected to a force of twenty foot-pounds being dropped on the top, back, and sides, and it must not crack to the outer edge of the shell nor can a crack penetrate the thickness of the material. It is also tested to make sure that nothing, including a stick blade, can penetrate the openings and that the chin strap will hold the helmet in place. Most helmets are injection-molded with a polycarbonate or Zytel shell, the same material used in skate blade holders.

4-7 *A hockey helmet with full protective wire mask (often worn by goalies today). Note the good fit—tight but not too tight, down to eyebrow level, with protective chin pad and strap.*

All the protection a helmet affords is virtually useless unless it is fitted properly and the player feels comfortable with it on. The helmet should come to within three-quarters of an inch from the eyebrow and fit snugly. Parents should not—just as with skates—plan to buy an oversize helmet for a young player to "grow into." If the helmet moves freely as the head moves, then it is too loose. If any part of the outside or inside of the helmet appears damaged, be sure to have it corrected immediately. Never leave a helmet in the trunk of a car because any chemical, even on a rag, can damage it.

FACE PROTECTORS

Along with the helmet, face protectors have become mandatory up to the junior level and have been showing up among professionals in greater numbers of late. There is little doubt that the face protector has prevented a lot of permanent eye damage and cut down on dental bills.

There are two types of masks—clear plastic and polycarbonate visors and the wire cage. The clear plastic visor has a tendency to fog up, and although manufacturers are working on this problem, so far nothing satisfactory has come along to prevent fogging. Players with the polycarbonate visors must not keep the protector in a vinyl skate bag or leave them on vinyl car seats over a long period of time because the plastic in vinyl reacts with the polycarbonate, producing stress marks that weaken the visor and can cause it to break. As with the helmet, a polycarbonate visor should never be left in the trunk of a car.

The problem with the wire cage is that the bars interfere with vision. This can be overcome if the youngster wears the cage mask while watching television. In time, the lines of the bars will fade from sight until they are hardly noticeable.

Goalie Masks

It is virtually impossible today to find a single goalie playing—on any level—who does not wear a mask. It is now just as much a part of his equipment as goalie pads.

There are two types of masks—solid, molded fiberglass that fits flush to the face, and the wire cage attached to a helmet. The latter is now very popular. A piece of plastic that hangs down and protects the throat area can now be added to the cage mask.

MOUTHPIECE

The mouthpiece is another item of protection being used by more and more players. This is a piece of plastic worn in the mouth that covers the teeth and prevents the player from biting his tongue. It is very similar to the mouthpiece worn by boxers. The once common sight of toothless players is rapidly becoming a rarity.

GLOVES

Skaters can choose between an all-leather glove or a nylon-with-leather-palm glove, with the nylon glove being much lighter as well as washable.

All gloves are well padded to protect the back of the hand, thumb, and fingers, and have a cuff that extends the protection to slightly above the wrist. The fit of

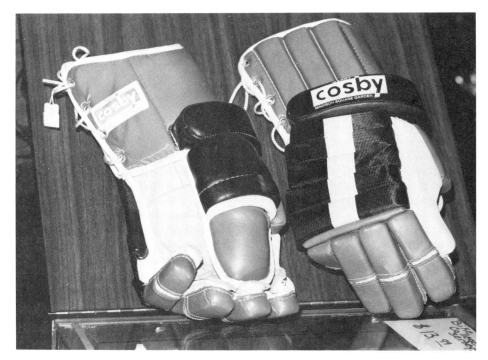

4-8   *Regulation hockey gloves with leather pads and fingers and nylon backing and cuffs. There is extra-heavy protection on the thumb and the backs of the fingers.*

4-9   *The goalie's "blocker" is almost a smaller, square version of an ancient gladiator's shield. Behind the thick blocking back is the glove, with a well-protected thumb.*

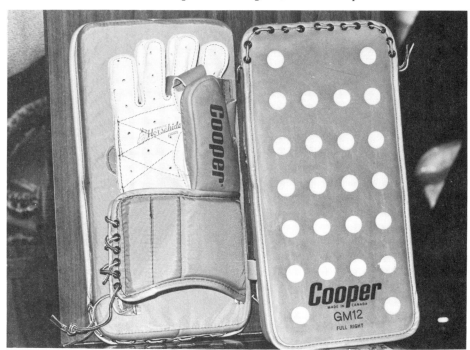

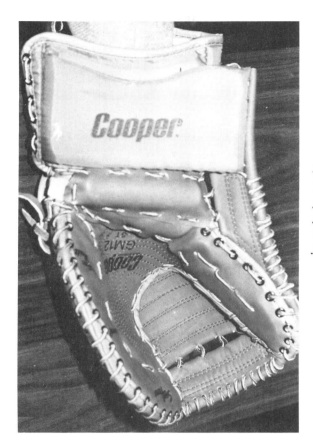

4-10
The goalie's "trapper" looks a great deal like a baseball glove, with wider webbing between thumb and fingers and fewer fingers.

gloves is important: gloves that are too small do not give the proper protection; those that are too big do not give the player the proper "feel" of the stick. Gloves have to be broken in, and the best way to accomplish this is to wear them while doing push-ups.

Goalie gloves are quite different than those worn by skaters. The glove worn on the stick hand is called the "blocker" and comes with a wide and sturdy protective back that permits the goalie to get more leather on the puck. The other glove, the "trapper," is very similar to a first baseman's mitt, giving the goalie a better chance to catch the puck. It has a long cuff that extends above the wrist.

To break in a "trapper," either mold the center of the pocket around a few pucks and tie up the glove, or use a mallet and hammer the pocket to soften it up.

PADS

Shoulder Pads

Today manufacturers are marketing shoulder pads that are less cumbersome, give better protection, and absorb less perspiration, thanks to a new honeycomb material.

Forwards and defensemen usually wear different types of pads, which must fit properly while protecting the upper arm and chest. Pads for defense usually extend farther down the abdomen, but all shoulder pads are made to take "add-ons," in order to satisfy any player's desire for more protection.

A goalie's shoulder pads have padding extending down the arms, and additional padding can be added if necessary. In addition, a goalie wears a chest protector that can be ribbed, paneled, or tufted, and made out of felt or foam (some claim that felt absorbs more shock than foam). It should fit so that it does not restrict the goalie's movements.

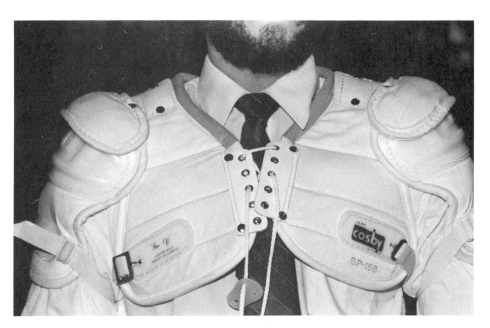

4-11 Shoulder pads for a forward, which allow for easy movement of the arms. The shoulders are protected with heavy plastic. Proper fit can be achieved with the adjustable elastic straps.

4-12   The padding for a goalie's upper body, to be worn under the jersey. This set is almost entirely heavy cotton padding, with extra thickness on the chest and shoulders.

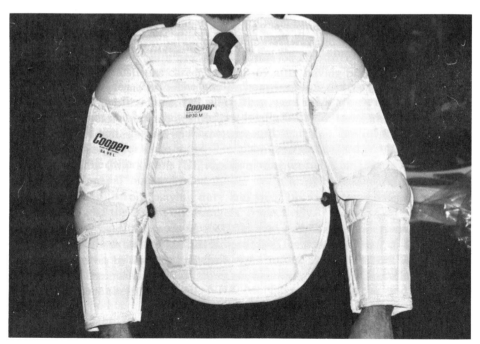

4-13   This padding for a goalie's upper body covers the shoulders and elbows with heavy plastic instead of cotton padding. The chest protection is of slotted foam.

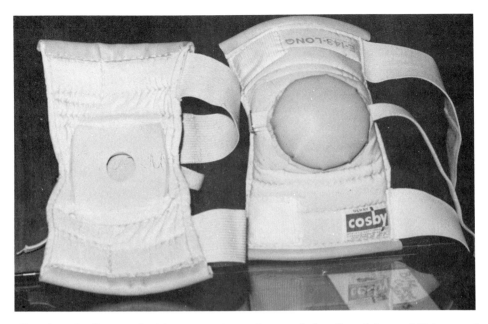

4-14   The player's elbow pad with a protective pad around the elbow joint and Velcro and elastic adjustable straps.

Elbow Pads

Elbow pads are a must. The newer models, which offer protection with less weight, are either the slip-on variety or have a Velcro closing. One pad, a solid, heat-molded plastic foam "donut," is claimed by its manufacturer to be over 90 percent lighter than the multilayered Rubatex pad.

NOTE: When fitted properly, the shoulder pad, elbow pad, and the cuff of the glove protect the entire arm.

Goalie Pads

Goalie pads, which should be as light as possible, are very expensive and fitting them is extremely important.

The pads should fit from four to six inches above the player's knees and not be too wide as to impede free movement or to have the knees bumping against each other. If the pads are too long, the goalie will have a problem crouching.

The better and more expensive pads are usually stuffed with deer hair, but there is never a guarantee that each pad will weigh or measure the same, although manufacturers try to avoid this as best they can. All goalie pads are designed to take additional padding on the inside if the player decides more is necessary.

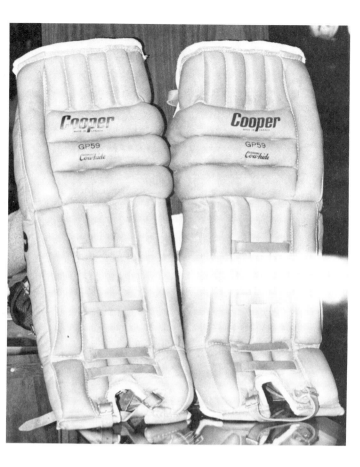

4-15

The goalie pads are made with a ribbed leather covering. The bottoms of the pads fit around the goalie's skates by a toe strap.

When putting on the pads, the goalie should tie up the toe straps first, then work up the leg. Toe straps are easily lost or misplaced, so be sure to carry extra sets. It is not recommended that the pads be treated with oil, since that adds weight.

GUARDS

Shin Guards

This extremely important piece of equipment comes in models for defensemen and forwards, and players must be present when the pads are purchased.

Measuring the pad, from the center of the knee to about one inch above the foot where the skate should start, is critical, as the pad must protect the whole knee beyond any question.

Pads for defensemen differ in that some have "wings" that wrap around the back of the leg and others have a plastic protector extending out further from the shin to radiate the shock of a shot.

There is an adjustable shin guard on the market that allows a youngster to use the pads for more than one season before outgrowing them.

Ankle Guards

Ankle guards are available for those wishing more protection in that area. Defensemen usually add this piece of equipment to their skates, although forwards have also been known to wear them. As new improvements for better ankle protection are built into skates, ankle guards will no longer be necessary.

CLOTHING

Sweaters

Originally sweaters, or jerseys as they are also called, were made of wool to keep a player warm while playing hockey outdoors. Today, however, with most games played indoors, the manufacturers are marketing nylon sweaters lighter in weight and designed not to absorb perspiration. They have increased ventilation to permit the rapid evaporation of perspiration, are easily washed, and dry quickly. Remember, always follow the manufacturer's washing instructions that come with the sweater.

Socks

Either single-knit or double-knit stirrup (footless) hockey stockings are worn over regular athletic socks (the same as those worn when being fitted for skates). Wash stockings and socks frequently—preferably after each use—but be careful since the stockings tend to shrink in the drier.

Pants

With the introduction of hockey pants that resemble warm-up pants, a revolution of sorts is taking place. The new design is being worn more and more, at the expense of the traditional short pants.

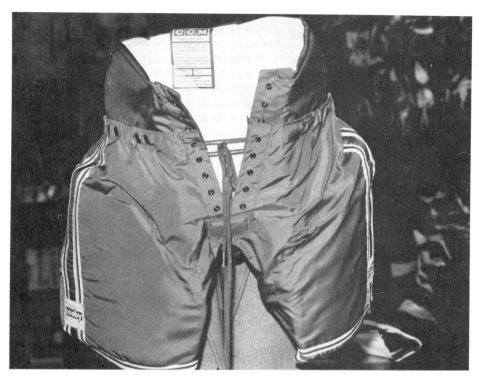

4-16   The traditional player's short pants (Bermuda shorts length) are often made of heavy-duty nylon with thick padding underneath around the thighs and kidneys. The player also wears a garter belt and long sport hose that go from the thigh into the boot.

An athletic supporter and cup, which must be worn, are separate from the pants. In the Cooperall (longpants) System, the girdle is held in place by "friction-fit"; in the Pro-Pac (short pants) System, the girdle has a cinch-up strap. Suspenders hold up the pants, which are made of nylon and are washable.

The only complaint with the new-style pants is that they tend to become hot. But the Philadelphia Flyers, the first NHL team to adopt the new pants (the Hartford Whalers came next in 1982–83), say that the new girdle in the pants has greatly decreased the number of groin injuries.

When purchasing a pair of traditional short pants, it is wise to check that the kidney protection fits correctly and that there is total protection of the thigh. If the pants are too small, there will be an unprotected area between the pant leg and shin pad. Fit is all-important. Small and medium-sized players should wear pants about six inches larger than their waist size; heavier players should wear pants about eight inches larger in the waist. The pants, which can be held up with either a belt or suspenders, are made of nylon and are washable.

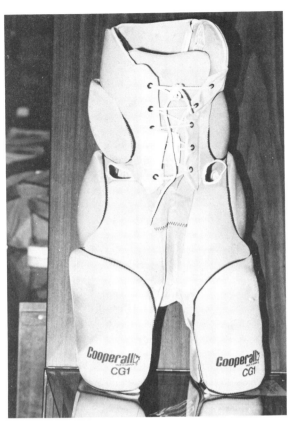

4-17 *The new Cooperall girdle that is worn un-*
der the new long pants. The unit features
all-in-one thigh, hip, and kidney pads, as
well as special groin protection in the front
of the abdominal area, which short pants do
not have.

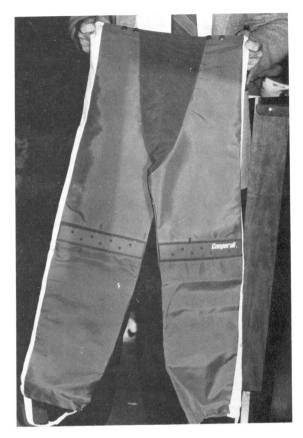

4-18 *The new long pants are worn over the new*
one-piece girdle unit and regulation shin
guards. Note the bottom strap that goes
around the foot, as in ski pants, and pre-
vents "creeping." The only real complaint
about the new pants (other than many play-
ers simply feeling strange in them) is that
they are warmer than the old, short pants.

Underwear

Because an undershirt and long underwear are easy to wash and can prevent skin irritation, they are usually worn. The combination can also keep a player warm, but care should be taken. A player's strength can rapidly be sapped if he becomes overheated.

OTHER EQUIPMENT

Athletic Supporter and Cup

As stated before, the supporter and cup are separate from the pants. No youngster, except the very young who can get by with Jockey shorts, should ever play without an athletic supporter and cup.

Garter Belts

Players who don't want their socks falling down while on the ice use a garter belt. For some players, a garter belt is hard to adjust, so help may be needed the first few times it is worn. Always wear a garter belt; never use rubber bands or tape to hold socks up, because they can cut off circulation.

The Brad Hall Super Support System is a new completely washable garter belt, athletic supporter, and cup all in one that is very easy to put on without any assistance.

Kim Crouch Collar

For the protection of a goalie's neck line, there is the Kim Crouch Collar. Considered cut-proof, the collar fits around the neck like a turtleneck and offers some chest protection as well. Players other than the goalie are also starting to use the Kim Crouch Collar.

5

TRAINING
AND CONDITIONING
FOR HOCKEY

Every training and conditioning program should start with the mouth—and what a player puts into it. Diet is an essential concern and is generally acknowledged to be a key to building stamina, strength, and bulk. Any youngster or professional athlete should be considering what he or she eats in terms of balance, quality, type, and amount.

According to Bob Williams, Physical Therapist for the New York Rangers, many athletes today are underweight for the amount and type of work they do while participating in sports.

"We have to increase their caloric intake," explains Williams, "in order for them to play a full season, exhibition games, and possibly the playoffs. Carbohydrates make an excellent pregame meal, and to build up muscle, we bulk them up on proteins. But there is no substitute for a balanced diet from the four main food groups: meats, grains and breads, fruits and vegetables, and dairy foods."

Interestingly, Williams also says that the ethnic background of a player has to be considered in diet plans. "Chris Kotsopoulas (of Greek extraction) may be used to spicy Greek foods, and an Italian player may crave lots of pasta. I think it's wrong to force them away from food prepared the way they've had it all their lives, so we work to balance the diet rather than change it."

Trainers Ron Waske, Craig Smith, and Gary Ball all recommend a well-balanced diet for the average player. They recommend food from all the basic food groups, with a heavy dose of carbohydrates (pasta is a favorite) prior to the games.

Smith comments, "It's hard to tell a grown man what to eat. All players are given a suggested nutritional plan prior to training camp. This makes them aware of their needs over the long NHL season. We try to get the players to stay away from junk food, but it is difficult, especially on the road."

Ideally a player should have a substantial pregame meal four to six hours before a game. Foods served should be easily digestible and high in carbohydrates and protein.

For many years an important and often overlooked aspect of the game of hockey was the amount of training and conditioning that should be put in before a player laces up his skates. But concern over health and exercise from the general American public combined with the strenuous training and conditioning programs instituted by the eastern European countries, have forced the North American hockey coaches and players to totally rethink their systems for preparing athletes. Off and on the ice, players should perform regularly a series of fairly rigorous exercises designed to keep them in shape, protect them from injuries, and improve their playing ability. Naturally the nature and amount of these exercises vary for different age levels.

PRETEEN YEAR-ROUND TRAINING AND CONDITIONING

For youngsters between the ages of nine and twelve, drills must be designed to hold their interest long enough for them to complete the training. Training for the young player should not only develop muscles and flexibility, but also instill a sense of purpose and goals—all the while being interesting and fun.

Tag is one drill that holds the interest of youngsters and helps them get ready for the hockey season. There are many varieties of the game: it can be played with a basketball or a medicine ball (but nothing heavier), or in pairs, with the youngsters holding hands.

Running in a circle is useful for developing skill and coordination. Again, there are many varieties of this exercise. Players can run in different directions, trying to avoid hitting each other. They can play leapfrog, hop on one leg or two, run sideways or backwards, or otherwise enliven the drill. They should also be encouraged to think creatively about their drills.

Follow the leader is another way to get young players to exercise. Agility and acrobatics—such as handstands and tumbling—can be stressed, and often the players will try to outdo one another in the difficulty of their respective moves.

Obstacle courses are useful in keeping youngsters fit while also aiding in coordination. Jumping rope—it can be done in a number of ways, singly or doubly—is an excellent means of developing muscle control and coordination.

Basic hockey drills should not be neglected, even off the ice. Stickhandling can be practiced with a baseball, or even with two baseballs. Combination drills are useful, with a player stickhandling a baseball and kicking a soccer ball at the same time, or simultaneously dribbling a basketball and kicking a soccer ball. Soccer and basketball are excellent sports for helping the aspiring hockey player, as is dryland hockey.

PRESEASON TRAINING FOR PRETEENS

When the hockey season nears, training should be concentrated more on the dry land imitation of hockey skills. Puck handling, shooting, and passing should be practiced with a variety of drills using one or more pucks. Weighted pucks are not recommended. Even skating can be practiced off the ice, as explained throughout in this section.

YEAR-ROUND TRAINING
FOR TEENS AND ADULTS

Unlike the younger player's conditioning, where agility and coordination are emphasized, drills for older players should aim more at speed, cooperation, and further agility. Daily basic calisthenics should be introduced to players between the ages of thirteen and fifteen, so that it becomes a lifetime habit. Toe touching, push-ups—sometimes with the feet raised on a block—sit-ups, and so on, should all be part of the daily regimen.

One series of exercises can be done with partners. A pair of players face each other standing over a horizontal hockey stick, and try to drag each other over the "line." They may also lock hands and try to push each other backward. This drill can also be done with the players back-to-back. Players can try to lift each other up back-to-back, or simply carry their partners.

Another useful drill is to have players jog in a large circle with hockey sticks and try to imitate all sorts of hockey movements. Running is always a good idea, but there are many ways of going about it. Agility running can be done in small groups. To emphasize speed, sprints should be done from a variety of positions: players should start from a sitting position or from lying on their backs or stomachs.

Shorter drills include jumping from or over chairs and benches and jumping rope. Players can be attached by their suspenders to a pole and do stickhandling exercises from that position. Basketball dribbling and moves with a medicine ball should also be included.

The imitation of hockey skills off the ice should be maintained, with stickhandling, shooting, and passing done at high speeds. Checking drills can easily be performed on dry land, and hockey skills can be imitated with a basketball. Again, basketball, street or roller hockey, and soccer are always good practice for the aspiring hockey player, and can even be played with hockey formations and rules.

PRESEASON TRAINING FOR TEENS AND ADULTS

As the season looms, training must of course be intensified. Short runs of about a mile are good, as are sprints and relay races. Once direct shooting and passing have been mastered, these skills should be practiced with obstacles, such as players blocking others, or from uncomfortable positions.

OFF-ICE TRAINING DURING THE SEASON

One set of exercises that should be performed during the active season, the preseason, and the off-season are stretching drills. It has become almost universally accepted that flexibility is a major factor in injury prevention, as well as in the development of stamina. Stretching should be performed before and after every game or practice, but slowly—to eliminate bouncing or jerking movements. Flexibility exercises should always be done gradually: stretching slightly, holding the position until the muscles begin to relax, and then stretching just a bit further. Even without straining himself, a player develops limberness and flexibility from repeated stretching.

The following are a number of stretching exercises that are generally accepted and can be done by players of virtually any ability, from teenage through old age. Each exercise should be done initially ten times (for each limb or in each direction) unless otherwise specified.

1. While lying prone, bend one knee, clasp both hands around the knee, and pull it toward the chest, keeping the head on the mat. Then do the same ten more times, but attempt to touch the head to the knee. Perform both variations with both legs. This basic exercise is excellent for anyone with chronic lower back problems and can even be done—in bed—by a person currently in the throes of a mild back spasm. This, of course, pertains only to muscular strains and spasms. Never exercise with back problems related to disks or vertebrae unless under a doctor's constant supervision. Also, do not lift the head to touch the knee if suffering lower back spasm.

2. Lying prone with the arms out to each side, lift one leg straight up, pause, lower the leg to the opposite fingers (left leg over to right hand), pause and hold, bring leg back to vertical, then lower.

3. Lying prone, with arms extended down and a few inches from the sides, slowly raise both legs, keeping them straight, all the way over the head and attempt to touch the toes on the floor behind the head. Pause, then slowly raise the legs all the way back and down. Caution: If the player cannot control the descent of the legs behind the head, do not let him or her simply flop them down. Not only could he or she actually strain the back but might also have insufficient strength or control to raise the legs back up, and he or she will simply have to roll out of the predicament, totally defeating the purpose of the stretching drill. Instead, have the player raise the legs up and back only as far as he or she can do comfortably, stopping when the back and arms can no longer control and counterbalance. The person should try to get the legs further and further back over the head each time, but always with control.

4. Lying face down, raise one leg and grasp the ankle with the opposite hand (the leg may be bent). Try to straighten the leg as much as possible while grasping it (do not jerk), then lower the leg slowly to the floor.

5. Sitting up (torso straight; never slouch), place the right hand on the left heel and gradually pull that leg up toward the chest and hold for several seconds, then lower it slowly. Repeat with left hand or right heel.

6. Sitting on the floor, both feet are pulled into the crotch until the soles touch, keeping the hands on the ankles. Then bend slowly over and attempt to touch the head to the feet. The aim is to stretch further and more comfortably each time, but never to bounce or jerk.

7. While sitting on the floor, legs extended in front, each leg is stretched to the side as far as comfortable, keeping them straight. Arms are straight to each side at shoulder height. Then bend toward one toe, with the arms brought together to touch that toe while the head touches the knee.

Many male athletes are well trained in strength, speed, and stamina drills of the conventional sort, but until recently they were not well versed in flexibility exercises. It cannot be stressed strongly enough that these bending and stretching exercises should be done without bouncing or jerking. The first tendency in exercise 7 is to bounce or jerk in order to get the head to touch the knee. But that tendency must be fought, as there can be severe strain or pull as a result of bouncing or jerking.

8. Stand with the feet approximately shoulder width apart, hands on hips. Bend over slowly, take one hand off one hip and touch that hand to the opposite toe, straighten up, then touch both hands (or fingertips, or even just as far toward the floor as possible!) between the feet, straighten up then touch the other hand to its opposite toe. Keep the nontouching hand on the hip while doing this drill and don't bounce!

9. Step forward with one foot, bending the knee as much as possible, then stretch the other leg as far as possible behind, keeping the foot flat on the floor. Hold, then push up on the forward leg slowly, then back down.

Exercises that are more familiar but also good for flexibility are: squats (feet about twelve to fourteen inches apart, squat until the buttocks almost touch the heels, then rise), trunk twists (feet slightly apart, arms extended out front at shoulder height, then turn torso to each side, moving arms to that side at the same time, attempting to move arms further to each side with each repetition), arm circles (stand straight, feet slightly apart, arms to each side at shoulder height, then move arms in tiny circles for ten rotations, then large circles, then both tiny and large circles in other direction), and head circles (standing straight, turn head in complete rotation twenty times, clockwise and counterclockwise).

During the active season, players should supplement daily stretching with a variety of other dry land drills. Basic calisthenics such as pushups, pullups, and situps are highly recommended. Shadow boxing and wrestling help develop coordination, as will all of the team sports mentioned before. Games help make the team cohesive and enhance the cooperation between players. All of the dry land stick-handling, dribbling, and kicking exercises should be maintained.

Aside from ability, coordination, and flexibility, the player should be performing regularly exercises that strengthen the heart and lungs, thereby increasing overall stamina. Any regular form of running, walking, swimming, bicycling, or jumping rope will increase stamina. Overall stamina for the legs, which do the most continuous work in hockey, can be enhanced through the forementioned activities, as well as by water skiing, snowskiing, snowshoeing, skateboarding, and surfing.

The only way to increase body strength and muscle size, whether specifically or in general, is through a program of weightlifting. This can be as simple as hefting large cans (there are a host of Canadian hockey players who come from the farmlands of Alberta and Saskatchewan, their muscles enhanced by years of tossing hay and lifting bales), or as complicated as working out in a gymnasium with Nautilus machines or the Universal Gym.

Here are some general guidelines for weightlifting:

1. Have a good physical first, and then get into a coached or guided program.
2. Start small and work up to larger weights. The rule of thumb is that when it is possible to lift a weight easily more than twelve times, it is time to increase the weight.
3. Do all lifting exercises smoothly and slowly. Don't move right into any fancy "jerks" or any advanced weightlifting techniques until the basic "range of motion" skills have been learned thoroughly.
4. Pause briefly at the start of a repetition and at the contracted position in the exercise.
5. Do all exercises with a controlled counting system, as in a two-count to raise and a four-count to lower.
6. Always learn the proper breathing technique for the weightlifting exercise being performed.

DRY LAND TRAINING FOR GOALTENDERS

Drills designed for goaltenders differ slightly from those for other members of the team. Some exercises should be done with full equipment; others, without.

Goaltenders should go through the same basic stretching exercises recommended for other players, but these should be supplemented with other forms of exercise. Jogging in a small area, with a variety of movements, is recommended. Goalies should practice hopping up and down on one foot and jogging in place sideways from right to left. Hopping should also be done in a lateral direction on each foot, as well as jumping rope and forward and backward rolls. All these moves should be started and ended in the basic goaltender stance with knees bent, leaning slightly forward.

Still in the classic stance, the goaltender should work on his coordination by bouncing a tennis ball in his catching hand or by juggling two or three balls. Two players can also toss one or more tennis balls back and forth to each other. Goaltenders can also practice by kicking a soccer ball or tennis ball against a well while still retaining the classic stance.

Team drills can further enhance coordination. One fairly complicated drill involves one goaltender doing forward rolls or jogging with his blocking glove, catching glove, and a supporter with a cup. A partner should hit tennis balls to him, which he should deflect with his blocker.

Simpler games can be done with partners, including table tennis and handball. A variation of the "catch" drill can be performed by slapping one or more tennis balls between partners. Goaltenders can also play catch while moving from the squat position, putting one leg out, moving to the butterfly position, standing up and then crouching again. Throwing a medicine ball back and forth while moving through these steps is a good drill.

Not only is handball a good exercise, but the hockey equivalent of it—using the back of the blocker glove to hit the ball against the wall—is even better. Bouncing a tennis ball while moving from the crouch position, to throwing out one leg and then the other, will also improve coordination and timing.

Kangaroo jumps from a squatting position should be done backwards and forwards, preferably while bouncing a tennis ball from one hand to the other during the jumps. A goalie can also jump straight in the air and take off for a short spring immediately upon landing, and this can be done backwards or forwards. From a standing position the goaltender can jump as far to the right or left as possible, landing on only one foot—which can also be done while tossing a tennis ball from one hand to the other.

The butterfly position should become natural to any goaltender: knees in, toes out, and the insides of the feet flat on the ground. From this the goaltender should practice moving from the squatting position to a semisquat and back. Catching a tennis ball while moving from the butterfly to a crouch and throwing each leg out will stretch the necessary muscles while also increasing dexterity.

There are several drills involving use of the goalie's stick. One involves a partner placing tennis balls on the floor as quickly as possible, which the goaltender must clear with his stick (he can also practice kick-saving these balls). Tennis balls, handballs, or baseballs can also be rolled rapidly toward the goalie, or the goalie can swing his stick in a circle along the ground while one or two others try to jump over it (when done on the ice, this exercise is a good balance drill for the skaters jumping). One exercise that can be used for the stick or the blocker and glove has a partner standing behind the goalie, throwing balls over his shoulders and head. Without turning, the goalie must either catch these and clear them or stick-save them out of the way.

Arm strength can be improved by having two goaltenders toss a bar back and forth, both underhand and overhand. They can also carry each other over their shoulders while trying to take long strides, both forward and backward.

Goaltenders may also try guarding the net with ten-pound weights in their hands. These weights should be donut-shaped, and the goaltender should have the backs of his hands facing the shooter. First tennis balls can be bounced toward the goalie, but after a while, they can be *hit* toward him with a tennis racket. Again using the blocker and stick, one goalie can guard the net while a second, also with stick and gloves, screens him, and a third tries to bounce a tennis ball into the net.

Goalies can hit tennis balls back and forth—keeping them in the air if possible—

and they can vary this by practicing on one leg. Or standing on a mat, they can throw a volleyball at each other, with the catcher required to dive for the ball. One-on-one variations of soccer and basketball are helpful for goalies.

A tennis racket in the hands of a coach can help in developing a goaltender's hand–eye coordination. The coach moves the racket in different directions as quickly as possible, and the goalie mimics the moves with his stick (these are often called "shadow drills"). A variation of this drill is for the coach to use the handle of the racket in the same moves, while the goaltender tries to contact the racket with his stick and the coach tries to move the handle out of the goaltender's way. Moving back about fifteen feet, the coach can then try to hit tennis balls up around the goaltender's hands, straight or on the bounce.

New York Islander goalie Billy Smith recommends video games as an added exercise for hand-eye coordination. This is one drill few players would be reluctant to perform!

Wearing full equipment, a goaltender can also go through a complete exercise routine. Standing approximately ten feet from a wall, with a partner behind him, the goalie catches or deflects tennis balls thrown at the wall by the partner. Again, if a partner is equipped with tennis ball and racket, a goalie can practice fending off angle shots, screen shots, and deflections.

ON-ICE WARMUP DRILLS

Before any game or practice session, certain warm-up exercises should be done on the ice to further loosen up the muscles and prevent injury. At least twenty minutes should be spent doing these stretching exercises.

The groin muscles should be given special attention before games. There are several ways to stretch out and loosen the muscles. One is to glide forward on one skate with the knee bent as much as possible and the other leg extended in back with the skate blade flat on the ice. The stick should be on the ice in front, held in the same hand as the front foot. The head must be up and the torso erect, although the back will be very slightly curved.

Another groin exercise starts with the player moving down ice, feet shoulder width apart and stick above his head. The player then separates his legs as far as comfortably possible, pressing on the skates' inside edges, and bends over, placing his stick against the toes of his skates (see photo 5-1). The player then should snap his feet back to their original position and bring the stick up again. The hamstring muscles can be stretched by performing the same exercise without separating the legs, and the drill can also be performed while skating backwards.

5-1   These Pee Wees are warming up by doing toe touches.

Arm, shoulder, waist, and back muscles can be loosened through alternating toe touches, skating with the feet shoulder width apart and the stick across the back of the shoulders (see photo 5-2). With skates on inside edges, the player should attempt to touch his right hand to his left foot and vice versa. With the stick in the same position a player can stretch his upper torso muscles by twisting the shoulders from side to side while staying erect. This should be done with the skates on the inside edges, and must be performed smoothly without any jerking motions.

5-2   Pee Wee Paul Galletta performs the alternate toe touch as an on-ice warmup.

Groin, hamstring, and quadricep muscles can also be loosened by on-ice leg lifts. These involve holding the stick out front at shoulder height and kicking each leg up to touch the stick. Players should be watched carefully to ascertain that they are now lowering the stick to their foot instead.

Goaltenders have their own variety of warm-up exercises to perform, in addition to the regular player drills. One of these is kneeling in the butterfly position, leaning back until the head touches the ice and then pulling back up again, keeping the spine straight (see photo 5-3).

The split position is often painful for many goalies, and virtually impossible to do right away. The player should lower himself to the ice as slowly as possible *without bouncing*. This cannot be stressed enough! Bouncing improperly into a split can result in *permanent* damage to the groin and thigh muscles. If it is too difficult to rise from this position, the goalie should simply sit sideways. If the goalie can get all the way down to the ice, however (there are few today who can do a genuine split), he should try to bring his forehead to rest against his knee.

The one-pad stretch is another useful warm-up for goaltenders. Extending one leg with the blade of that skate on the ice, the goalie rests on the knee of the other bent leg. This is one of the best groin exercises. Groin muscles can also be loosened by side leg lifts. The goalie lies on his side, pelvis at right angle to the ice, with one leg on top of the other, so that the pads are "stacked." The top leg is raised slowly and then lowered, but not all the way to the other leg (see photo 5-4). Keep both legs straight throughout the drill.

After these warm-up drills, a player should exercise to enhance balance and agility. A figure skating maneuver is good: "Shooting the Duck." The player simply glides down ice in a squatting position, on one skate, with the other foot held straight out in front.

Another good balance drill is to skate down ice on one foot while holding the stick out in front in both hands, at about shoulder height. The player then lifts one leg—keeping it as straight as possible—first to the back, then the side, and finally to the front.

Since hockey is, after all, a strenuous contact sport, the player must remember to "practice" getting knocked down and regaining his feet. One good drill is to set up two cones, with a stick balanced on top of them. The player should then slide under the stick on his stomach, while keeping his head up. Immediately after passing under the stick between the cones, the player should get back on his feet. Random skating by a large group of players in a relatively confined area (the area between the blue line and the red line, for instance) will aid in avoiding unwanted contact. Drop rolls are an effective way for players to regain their feet if hit. Skaters glide across the ice, drop to one knee, switch to the other, and then rise as quickly as possible. This is also a good drill for defensemen who spend a fair amount of time blocking shots on one knee.

5-3   *The butterfly squat as a warmup exercise for the goaltender.*

5-4   *One warmup for goaltenders is the side leg lift.*

Jumping may seem like a skill confined to figure skaters, but nothing could be further from reality. All hockey players can be confronted with prone bodies, sticks, or other assorted pieces of equipment scattered about the ice, and the only way the player can avoid injury is by jumping that object. Young players should begin by jumping over a hockey stick lying on the ice, progress to a stick laid across horizontal cones, and finally be able to jump over a stick placed on top of two vertical cones.

One of the dangers of a book about a sport that is geared to "everybody" is that it is usually either too complicated for the novice and too simple for the more advanced athlete. Obviously a final word about training and conditioning should be directed to parties at both ends of that spectrum: Always approach training and conditioning with a sense of perspective. The beginner should start slowly and work up to more repetitions of ever more complicated exercises, and under proper supervision whenever possible. For the more advanced athlete: of course, there are myriad more and more difficult drills to perform. The general rules that apply across the spectrum is to find out one's own needs, weaknesses, and strengths, then to regularly perform an array of drills that will push toward one's limit, but never beyond it.

6

HOCKEY MEDICINE
AND INJURY PREVENTION

Hockey is a team sport that incorporates speed, muscular endurance, heavy body contact, and a continuous expenditure of energy. Those who have played or watched the game know that it is one of nonstop action with constant directional changes and challenges for possession of the puck. Thus, hockey makes great demands on players' bodies over the course of a sixty-minute game.

Hockey is the only major sport requiring the use of an artificial arm (a hockey stick) and artificial feet (skates) while being played on an artificial surface (ice).

The sport requires endurance, speed, tenacity, and the ability to keep up with rapid changes in pace. The physiological intensity places enormous strain on the muscular, nervous, cardiovascular, and respiratory systems. Almost all the muscles of the body are employed during a game. Some of the muscles work to provide flexibility to the hockey player, but the muscles of the legs and hips perform the greatest amount of hard work. Quick acceleration, use of the body, and the constant stop-and-go of hockey action requires the player to be in peak physical condition.

Today's hockey training programs stress cardiovascular endurance, muscle flexibility, and strength. Training of this nature better conditions the player for the rigors encountered over the duration of a long season.

Fitness provides a strong defense against injury. Well-conditioned players do not tire as rapidly nor as easily and are therefore less susceptible to injury caused by slow reactions to injury-provoking situations.

"The more flexible you are, the more stress you can absorb," explains Ron Waske, trainer for the four-time Stanley Cup-winning New York Islanders. "When somebody hits you, if you have the flexibility, your muscles don't tear as much. Ligaments and joints give a little bit more, too."

Conditioning as a means of injury prevention is a relatively new concern of modern professional hockey. In fact, for twenty years physiotherapist Bill Head, who founded a conditioning clinic for the Canadiens in Montreal's Forum arena, was the sole source of ideas on prevention and rehabilitation. Players from the other NHL teams would visit Head's clinic with their problems whenever their team played in the Forum. Then the Soviet Union arrived with its highly conditioned players, and after a steady stream of coaches and trainers visited the Soviet Union, clinics and programs sprang up throughout the NHL. Now every NHL team has its own training, conditioning, and rehabilitation program.

MINOR HOCKEY INJURIES

Although a hockey player can attempt to prevent injuries through sound, intelligently planned conditioning programs, it would be totally unrealistic to believe that hockey can be played as an injury-free sport. Given the circumstances of play, the speed of the game, and the intensity of the players' effort, injuries are inevitable. However, most hockey injuries fall into the category of wounds, cuts, and lacerations. These injuries are common in virtually every action-oriented team sport.

Probably the most common injury in hockey is the incision (cut) or laceration. The majority of these wounds occur in the facial area, and although they are usually not considered a major injury, they are a regular occurrence in the professional game. Craig Smith, head athletic trainer for the New Jersey Devils, says, "a cut a game is not unusual in the NHL."

The basic on-the-spot treatment for lacerations is to first stop the bleeding with direct pressure and then to clean and bandage the wound. A more serious cut or incision should be given professional attention, since this type of wound might need one or more sutures to be closed properly. Waske and Smith estimate that the average NHL team totals between 150 and 200 stitches during a season. These sutures are administered by the team physician. Estimates are that during the season each player has one incident which requires stitches.

Lacerations, especially those of the face, have been reduced dramatically on the amateur, scholastic, and collegiate level by mandatory use of the helmet and face mask.

Another common minor injury is contusions, also known as bruises. This injury's symptoms include pain, swelling, and discoloration. With constant, nonstop action, crunching body checks, swinging sticks, and a rubber disc traveling at high speeds, bruises are a way of life for the hockey player. Ice is the major treatment for most bruises.

MAJOR HOCKEY INJURIES

The most serious injury for the hockey player is the knee injury. With the hockey player in constant motion during the course of a game, tremendous strain is put on the knee. This type of injury can range from the sprained or bruised knee to the most serious injuries—torn ligaments, cartilage damage, and dislocation of the knee cap.

According to Sandy MacDonald, manager of the McCann Ice Arena in Pough-keepsie, New York, a former hockey player and an instructor of many young skaters, "the new hockey [the "constant motion" technique described in the chapter on tactics] entails so much crossing over that there's a much higher incidence of knee injuries."

Treatment for the bruised or sprained knee begins with ice and careful stretching, then progresses to flexibility exercises. Possibly the greatest stride forward in sports medicine has been in the development of the Cibex. The Cibex is a diagnostic system that uses a series of degree and graph printouts to give the trainer a reading on the injured athlete's range of motion, thus enabling him or her to plan a better course of rehabilitation.

Used in conjuction with the Cibex is the UBX table. On this device all joints of the body can be tested for their range of motion and flexibility. These readings help the athletic trainer determine to what degree the athlete has recovered and to what level or percentage he can perform.

The Orthotron system is another recent development available to today's athletic training staffs. The Orthotron is a hydraulic system providing resistance to input. It is a system that rehabilitates injuries involving flexibility and range of motion.

According to Gary Ball, director of the Athletic Training Program at Kean State College of New Jersey, rehabilitation is only possible if the athlete cooperates with and understands the role of the trainer. "Many strides have been made in the field during the past five to ten years," says Ball. "The athlete should be aware that today's trainer can rehabilitate injuries and get him or her back in the lineup faster and in better condition."

Another common serious injury is the muscle strain, pull, or tear. Areas most affected by this type of injury are the groin and hip muscles. NHL trainers Waske and Smith agree that muscle problems and their rehabilitation are dictated by the severity of the injury. Electrical and ultrasound muscle treatments are used to speed the body's rehabilitation process. Rest is basically the best cure for muscle difficulties. Smith adds that to rush a player back from an injury of this type can result in more problems: "Rushing a player back too soon usually results in a more severe reoccurrence, sometimes even leading to a player being out of the lineup three times longer."

OTHER HOCKEY INJURIES

The majority of hockey injuries come as a result of body contact. Fractures are not as regular an occurrence in the NHL as one would think, according to the Islanders' Waske. "A team during an average season may have one or two fractures. Those would most likely be in the facial area—nose, cheek, and jaw. Another trouble spot is the wrist. These fractures usually are caused as a player attempts to brace himself during a fall. Facial fractures are caused by high sticks, elbows, and the puck."

The incidence of concussion has been reduced with the use of the helmet in all levels of the sport. However, despite the protection, head injuries still occur. The Devils' Smith delineates the procedure for determining the seriousness of a head injury: "First we check the player's neurological signs—sight, smell, touch, and so on. The orientation of the player is then checked—does he know where he is, who he is? Finally, the injured's diagnostic signs are reviewed: grip strength, eye contact, and reaction. If there is any doubt as to the player's health, we send him off to the hospital for X-rays and observation."

Internal injuries are not common in hockey because of the development and improvement in protective equipment worn by today's player. From head to toe, the hockey player benefits from years of research by manufacturers, trainers, and physicians. A major advance has come in the design of hockey pants. Kean State College's Ball cites the development of the girdle for the decline of hip, thigh, and buttock injuries: "Players are now outfitted in a football-type girdle with all the pads enclosed. This way the pads don't shift and slide around as with the old pants." Smith also feels that despite complaints of violence in hockey, certain acts, such as spearing, are no longer prevalent in the game.

The popular picture many people have of the classic hockey player includes the gap-toothed smile. But that picture is changing. Many older players lost a number of teeth before arriving in the NHL, but today's younger players are better protected with the advent of face masks and mouth guards. Ron Waske commented that "most of the Islanders have their own teeth—I would say that seventy-five percent of the team uses mouth guards. The mouth guard has become standard equipment for today's hockey player."

Foot problems in hockey are serious, since a player makes his living with his feet. Most foot problems are congenital in nature. Others are caused by ill-fitting skates, bunions, and calluses. "The one thing most players are good at, concerning health, is taking care of their feet," said Waske.

A new health problem that has become a concern for players and trainers alike is the "crud" or "gunk," a rash which appears on the skin of a minority of players. Tom Reid, a former NHL player for the Minnesota North Stars, actually had to retire because of the "gunk."

The rash usually shows up on the hands or arms and was thought to develop from the players contact with gloves and other equipment. Islander trainer Waske has his own opinion. "The medical staff and I feel that this condition is a nervous condition and should be treated as such."

Today's hockey player is blessed by developments in equipment, athletic training methods, improved facilities, and the growing field of sports medicine. As is the case with other big league sports, today's hockey player is bigger, stronger, and faster than those before him. By all reports, he is also smarter. The modern athlete realizes that good physical conditioning and sound preventive medicine can prolong a career as well as improve performance.

Gary Ball makes a good point on where sports medicine is today. "In the past a person would put a cold, raw steak on a black eye and the swelling would go down. No one cared why the eye got better, as long as it did. The modern athletic trainer and the modern athlete is now aware of not only what can help him, but also why."

Research and development continues to improve the field of sports medicine. New, sophisticated operations are beginning to be used, such as carbon development—where a carbon filament is attached to a torn or weak muscle, allowing damaged fiber to redevelop stronger than originally.

Hockey is a violent sport and injuries will always be part of the game, but with the participants following correct training methods and rehabilitation procedures, the number of serious injuries have been and will continue to be noticeably limited.

7

GIRLS AND WOMEN IN HOCKEY

Although there is some recent indication of a trend or return toward conservatism in this country, it is still true that women's sports is one of the most rapidly developing and changing aspects of our society. Men have lessened their marathon time by only an average of about eight or nine minutes in almost two decades, but women have decreased their records by almost an hour. A few decades ago women were not even allowed to run the mile in world competition, but they are now getting ever closer to that fateful four-minute mark. Twenty years ago exceptional women athletes were as scarce as the proverbial hen's teeth, but today women regularly grace the main sports page in the papers—albeit mostly for tennis and golf.

It is also a fact today that thousands of young women (and some not-so-young too) are playing hockey. And in hockey, as well as all other major sports, interesting changes are taking place.

Women have always been considered more injury prone than men, because they have less flexibility and smaller musculature. And it was true that women's injuries were much more prevalent when they first began to play organized hockey (always remembering, of course, that throughout the fifties and sixties women, for the most part, played with *no* protective equipment). It looked as though all those nasty predictions would come true: hockey was too tough (even without body contact for girls), and women were just too weak to play the game. Worse yet, because of the higher injury rates, women in the game would cost more money.

As more and more girls began to play the game, and, more significantly, as they began to get the proper training, conditioning, and equipment, their injury rate remained about the same. This means in reality a significant drop in the number of injuries to girls and women, when one considers that now thousands more are playing with little increase in the rate.

Using injuries as an excuse to keep women and girls from playing hockey is even more absurd from the viewpoint of the organized physical activities in which both women and men have performed for a long time. In figure skating, experts say that there is a higher injury rate for men than for women. This sounds wonderful as a case for the women's side, until one considers that this is in part due to the retention of "macho" attitudes in figure skating as elsewhere. In other words, the men have more injuries because they are constantly being pressured to jump and turn higher or further or more, whereas women figure skaters (at least here in the United States) are expected to display more finesse, grace, and fluidity. Nevertheless, injuries as a statistic to be used against a sex in a sport simply do not apply in figure skating. It is an important Olympic and world sport in this country, and since both women and men perform, the injury factor and its cost is simply something to live with, not to be held against someone.

The same applies to ballet. Women and men have performed in this highly physical art form for more than a century, and the injury rate differential between men and women is a nonsense statistic. The probability is that men have a higher injury rate as in figure skating, since here, too, they are pressured to jump higher and perform more turns, whereas women are encouraged from a different viewpoint. Both men and women are essential to the art, and the possibility of injury is ever present, and accepted. If a performer, regardless of sex, has not maintained a high level of training, practice, and conditioning, and then suffers an injury, he or she may be judged lacking. But women ballet dancers are expected to devote as much time, energy, heart, and soul to their craft as men—and they do.

Another judgment made against women playing hockey concerns the *kind* of injury to which they are prone. Women, because of their lesser flexibility, are said to be more prone to knee and other joint injuries, which often shorten a career and cost huge amounts in therapy and rehabilitation as opposed to a simple fracture or contusion.

This, too, is a myth. The fact is that the sports world does not have a realistic idea at this moment just how much women can increase their flexibility with regard to playing hockey—largely because so few have been encouraged to enter concentrated flexibility programs. A look at the NHL gives some indication of how much women's joint injuries may eventually be curtailed when one notes how much they have *increased* on certain NHL teams. For instance, the New York Rangers, under the guidance of Olympic medal-winning coach Herb Brooks, have begun to concentrate on the "constant motion" or European or Soviet type of hockey. This technique requires that any player on the team, whether defenseman or forward, scorer or utility man, be able to play the off-wing, shoot and pass from any place on the ice, and most of all, skate a constant crossover kind of game.

This type of game renders the skater more susceptible to being hit from the side or generally subjects him to more strain on the joints and ligaments than in the old technique of "straight-up-and-down-the-alley" hockey. And the team has had the injuries to prove the point. Ironically enough, the onlooker can almost tell when the team begins to "gel," since in order to really practice the technique Brooks preaches, the injury rate initially soars. This is partly due, no doubt, to the fact that many of today's NHL players refuse to take seriously the year-round training and conditioning programs which coaches, including Brooks, are pressuring their players to adopt along with the new playing method. As the dirty, blind side check grows more rare in the league and as NHL players adapt better to constant flexibility training, the injury rate will drop again.

Injuries, then, reflect in part a player's effort to change and develop, and must be expected, not held against the player by reason of sex.

It would be more to the point if hockey coaches and trainers who work with girls and women began to think constructively in terms of the difference in musculature. It is known, for instance, that women tend to have more stamina than men because of their bodies' ability to convert their greater proportion of fat into energy. This factor could lead to a totally different structure of the game—put women on for longer shifts and see what happens. Or, ponder the unfortunate fact that women's hockey allows no body contact except inadvertently. With their added padding on the lower body, think of what women could do with a hip check. And it is also true that much of the body contact in hockey is not so much based on "amount of meat, but what is done with it." Women might be capable of developing whole new checking techniques, where simple leverage and the application of torque are needed (look at karate or Ju Jitsu, in which women can be the virtual equals of men since the art relies on concentration, technique, and leverage rather than brute strength).

There are, of course, other myths that have been erected as stumbling blocks to women entering sports, and the myth of the menstrual cycle has been one of the worst. It has now been proved again and again that well-trained women athletes can perform at any and all stages of their menstrual cycle with no observable loss of ability.

Then there is the "loss of femininity" myth. Using sexual preference or "masculinity" as a means of repressing women's athletic prowess is one of the more unfortunate ploys in the history of sports. First of all, it has long been a not-very-well-kept-secret that homosexuality occurs in some men's locker rooms throughout sports, but no one has decided to cancel professional teams. While the macho image of the hockey player is probably stronger than in any other professional sport, the fact is that if a woman plays hockey, sexual preference or masculine characteristics will not "rub off." One has only to look at Chris Evert Lloyd or Evonne Goolagong Cawley to see that a player will be as feminine or as masculine as she feels comfortable being, regardless of the type of sport or who else is playing it.

The most important thing for any young girl or older woman to remember about playing hockey is to play as hard, as well, as diligently, as enjoyably as she is willing to. Judging from women's activity in other major sports, women in hockey will one day be a relatively common sight, subject of course to the special factor of limited

210

and costly ice time, which make it more difficult for women to find both time and space to learn the sport.

SOME SPECIFIC TRAINING FOR WOMEN

Since women tend to have smaller muscles than men, particularly in the upper body, the system of training and conditioning for women should involve developing those areas, along with the abdominal and thigh muscles.

In addition to the upper body, abdominal and thigh exercises, women should work to develop the strength of their wrists and lower arms. Shooting skills are a must and wrist/lower arm muscles in most male hockey players are unusually well developed.

Weightlifting has become popular for women and is no longer considered too "masculine." An intense weightlifting program (under supervision, of course), concentrating on the wrists, shoulders, deltoids, abdomen, and thighs is recommended for the aspiring female hockey player.

The comment most heard around the rink after a women's hockey game is that it is "so much slower" than men's games. Part of this is because women *are* slower, but this is no reason not to work on speed in skating. One has only to look at women marathon runners to see that women are perfectly capable of cutting down the time differential between men and women considerably—and in a relatively short time. In 1966, when women began running marathons (illegally), the initial (and unofficial) time—3:20—of Roberta Gibb was far behind the leading Kenji Kimihara (2:17:11). Yet in 1982 Grete Waitz won the New York City Marathon women's division (time: 2:27:14) and ran with the leading men nearly all the way, finishing only 17 minutes and 55 seconds behind Alberto Salazar.

The same can be done with women's skating: sprints and power skating technique can increase women's speed enormously. The women's game as currently played is slower than the men's version, however, since there is no body contact allowed. It may seem illogical that in fact lack of body contact should slow the game up. But think a moment: a game played on ice with skates is by definition a fast sport and one with lots of body contact. But if a player knows she is not to hit another player along the boards, she won't skate in as fast. It actually takes time and slows down a skating game when one has to avoid body contact whenever possible. Perhaps with the new protective gear and the realization that women's abilities far exceed previous estimates (women played half-court basketball for many years because it was believed they didn't have the strength and stamina to play a full-court game), young girls will eventually be taught how to body check.

The game will only change in the senior levels if women who have learned the skills when young and have practiced them at length arrive in the older leagues to prove they can perform with body contact.

One of the specific aspects of training that should be taught to girls in hockey is motivation, drive, and teamwork. Because girls and women have not had the money, attention, and expertise lavished on them that boys have had, they tend to discount their own abilities and contributions. Looking again to sports that have long included a women's version, we see that the intangible or mental aspects of the sports have been developed along with the physical. Women swimmers are fierce competitors: women track and field competitors practice and strive as hard as the men.

It is a fact that professional sports (and even World or Olympic level amateur sports) have long presented men with an opportunity for fame or money, or as a means of rising socially. When girls and women perceive the same opportunities available to them in a sport (as in tennis and golf—even, to some extent, basketball), they will begin to make huge strides in performance, skill, strength, and speed.

THE HISTORY
OF GIRLS AND WOMEN IN HOCKEY

It was 1956 when "defenseman" Abby Hoffman made headlines across Canada, and it was largely because of a proposed swimming party. Abby Hoffman was, in fact, a nine-year-old girl who had just been selected to play in the Timmy Tyke minor hockey tournament, and the swimming party was proposed for the "boys" of the team after the tournament.

Hoffman had managed to disguise her sex throughout the season by dressing at home, which most of the kids did, and by wearing her hair in a boyish close crop. But the proposed swimming party, combined with the necessity for producing a birth certificate (which would clearly show her sex as female) in order to participate in the tourney, was Abby's downfall. However, determined to play in the league and the tournament, Abby and her family took hockey off the ice and into the courts. But the Ontario Supreme Court ruled against Abby, and she remained banished from the league. Undaunted, Abby went on to a distinguished track career, competing in four Olympics, the British Empire Games, and the Pan American Games.

In April 1982, in remembrance of Hoffman's struggle to play hockey, the Ontario Women's Hockey Association (OWHA) played their first annual Abby Hoffman Cup in Brantford, Ontario—a national women's tournament. In truth, though, Abby Hoffman had not forged a new trail for women in the ice sports, nor was the Abby Hoffman Cup Tourney the first truly national women's hockey tournament. Women are known to have played hockey as far back as the nineteenth century.

From a copy of OWHA's newsletter, a faded picture of the Ottawa Canadian Banknote team of 1905 shows six ladylike players dressed in ankle-length skirts, turtleneck sweaters, and tassled toques. Peeking out from under one long flowing skirt, however, is a pair of genuine *hockey* skates, not figure skates. As one looks at this aged testimony to women's hockey, one must remember that at that time men did not wear any significant protective gear when they played the game, either. In fact, women's hockey was a popular and avidly played sport throughout the 1920s and 1930s in Canada and small, isolated sections of the United States. Women's hockey leagues in Ontario attracted both media attention and spectator interest through the 1920s. There was even an East-West (national) championship annually in Canada. Canada at that time was a nation of small towns connected by the national railroad system, and the women's hockey tourney would take off in railroad cars and live in them (on sidings) until the tourney was over. Of course this meant that the East-West tournament always had to take place between towns that were connected by the railroads.

The games took place on outdoor ice, and records indicate that over 3,000 people watched one East-West tourney in Fort William, Ontario. In the 1930s the Preston (Ontario) Rivulettes were the winningest and best-known women's hockey team in all of Canada, with an astounding record of only two losses in more than 350 games. The Rivulettes were the Canadian women's hockey champions for an entire decade, from 1930 to 1940—something even the fabled Montreal Canadiens cannot claim.

The history of women's hockey, both in Canada and the United States, parallels the status of women overall. Women achieved great strides in civil rights and cultural freedom prior to World War II, culminating with a huge influx of women into the job market when the men went off to fight from 1940 through 1945. After the war, however, the men returned, women were forced back into the home, and a new era of conservatism toward women and their role in society began, which extended into the mid-1960s. The rise and fall and further rise of women's hockey echoes this history. Participation and interest in women's hockey waned during the war years (reflecting what was happening at the highest levels of professional men's hockey), and women's hockey of the fifties and early sixties reflected the prevalent attitude toward women: they should be feminine, weak, frivolous, and decorative. Women no longer used hockey skates, but darted about, giggling and flirting, on white figure skates, wearing no protective equipment whatsoever. Stories of the time dealt more with hair styles and fashion than with skating prowess or stickhandling, and one "cute" story—with voluptuous starlet Jayne Mansfield on ice wielding a hockey stick and a vacuous smirk—personified the devaluation of women's participation in all sports.

This is why Abby Hoffman's effort to play hockey in a boys' league in 1956 was so astounding. At a time when other girls and women were hastening to appear as useless and feminine as possible, Hoffman played as an equal with boys her age, and succeeded.

Arnold Bruner, then of the *Toronto Daily Star*, described a typical women's hockey game of the period: "It was a gentlemanly—oops—ladylike game of hockey with the girls, some wearing no more protective equipment than flimsy blouses, doing everything they could to keep from bumping into each other."

By the mid-1960s, reflecting the activism of the times, women's hockey began to take on a more serious nature. In British Columbia, Jack Campbell and Doug Dionne wanted to get ice time for their daughters and other interested girls, and at the beginning of the 1963–64 season they received *one* hour of ice *per week* from the Killarney Community Centre Association. In Burnaby (a suburb of Vancouver) a women's softball team became a hockey team when ice time became available. By 1965–66 there was a five-team girls' league, and age divisions of junior, intermediate, and senior were formed. Within a couple of years there were twenty-five teams in the lower British Columbia mainland and twelve teams on Vancouver Island. Soon teams from the interior of the province began to join what is now the B.C. Girls' Ice Hockey Association. By the 1970s girls teams from British Columbia were traveling to the eastern provinces on tours, one team went to Finland for exhibitions, and another traveled to Japan for a tourney.

British Columbia and Ontario were not the only hotbeds of women's hockey, however. In Saskatchewan one story has it that NHL greats Max and Doug Bentley's earliest (and stiffest) competition came from their own sisters. Besides Max and Doug, the Bentley's sent four other brothers from their Saskatchewan home into professional hockey. But according to Bill Bentley, the family's father, it was not the boys but the girls, seven sisters in all, who were the family's better hockey players when young.

"The girls had a hockey team when they were kids," explained Papa Bentley, "and they could beat the blisters off the boys nine times out of ten!"

Likewise, in traditional U.S. hockey areas such as Massachusetts, women's hockey flourished. Leagues grew in the late sixties and early seventies, with women's rediscovery of "liberation."

"You don't find the 'dollies,' the ones with the heavy eye shadow and makeup, the ones who wouldn't wear a helmet because it would mess up their hair," said Ronnie Horne, a player for the Milton (Ontario) Senior team. "The players today are more natural girls, the type who wear just a little makeup, but go more for the scrubbed look. They look healthy and care about their bodies—that's why they play."

Ironically, the image of the women hockey player began to reverse, and as the women's movement began to be labeled "lesbian," the women's hockey world began to backpedal on the image of its members, fearing the same label. Frank

Champion-Demers, president of the Ontario Women's Hockey Association, worried about the image of women's hockey. "We still have this stigma that only toughies play hockey," he said. "But women's hockey is really recreational hockey, as it should be. They're having a good time. And hockey is an excellent team sport. We want to make it a female sport."

Although women rushed to join girls' and women's teams and leagues, they were isolated women who tried to join the men's teams, like Abby Hoffman before them. Gail Cummings, eleven, tried out for the goalie slot on a Huntsville Minor Hockey Association all-star team, and in October, 1976, she signed a Canadian Amateur Hockey Association player registration certificate and played four games with the Atom All-Stars team before she was notified by coach Barry Webb that her certificate had been rejected. Like Hoffman, Gail and her family took the matter all the way up to the Ontario Supreme Court where she was ultimately rejected. Before Gail, Karen Koch, then nineteen, had tried to play for a Senior A men's club in Michigan and had actually played goal for a Northern Michigan University fraternity team. Karen even moved to Toronto in an effort to find a men's team that would let her play, but there was an Ontario Hockey Association rule prohibiting women's playing on men's teams, and that was the end of Karen Koch's hopes. For a short time, in 1970, Jane Yearwood, ten, played goal for a boy's team in an organized league in Edmonton, Alberta. Jane was remarkable in that she had been playing goal since the age of five, and did so without a mask.

More than a decade later a high school senior in the unlikely town of Oyster Bay, Long Island, New York, won a discrimination suit against the town, and Barbara Broidy could officially play with the boys in the town's high school ice hockey league. Unfortunately for Barbara, the lengthy battle was won just as she was about to go off to college, and her chance to play with the boys had passed almost completely by.

Whatever the image, the fears, and the difficulties, by 1982 there were more than 12,000 girls and women playing hockey in the Canadian province of Ontario alone. And registered with the Amateur Hockey Association of the United States (AHAUS) women's division were 116 teams covering the spectrum from Squirt (twelve years and up) through Senior A (women twenty and older), including 35 women's and girls' teams in Massachusetts alone. Alongside this is the women's collegiate circuit, which plays with the rules of the NCAA rather than AHAUS and includes college teams throughout the United States. As with U.S. men's amateur hockey, the collegiate circuit is most active in the Northeast, particularly among the Ivy League colleges, as well as in Minnesota and Colorado. AHAUS women's teams include a 24-team enclave in the state of Michigan (the Upper Peninsula of that state and the Detroit area have long been hockey crazy).

Women's hockey equipment has changed with the times, and the female branch of the hockey family tree has gone from long skirts and toques, through see-through blouses and figure skates, into equipment identical to that of the men, with two notable exceptions. Shoulder pads include a breast protector, and a relatively new women's pelvic protector has already been dubbed the "Jill strap."

Women and girls play the men's rules consistently, whether they are CAHA, AHAUS, or NCAA teams, except one difference pertains throughout: no body-checking. Actually, the no bodychecking rule (No. 640 in the AHAUS manual) is only required of women ages nineteen and below, which means that senior teams, the highest level for women's amateur hockey, could have body checking if they so chose. But like most men's senior teams, they have never learned body checking (men can have body checking from the Bantam level up, and those men who do not make the jump from Bantam and Junior into professional hockey have usually not mastered proficient body checking, either). Further, many women have outside careers and families to which they must return after playing a game—usually in the middle of the night because of the difficulty in getting ice time at the local rink.

8

HOCKEY SKILLS

Whether a person is planning a hockey career as an amateur or a professional, or simply wants to play recreational hockey, the prerequisites as well as the basic skills to be learned are the same. Without a doubt, skating is the single most important skill required to play the game of hockey. "Power skating" is the term used today, a term relatively new to the hockey scene, and what it means in a nutshell is proper use of inside and outside edges when skating.

OFF-ICE DRILLS

To get the feel of new skates—which have been properly fitted and laced up (see the chapter on equipment)—the potential skater should walk around the rink area where rubber mats have been laid down, or even walk around the house, with the scabbards on.

When the skater feels confident of maintaining balance, he or she should then stand with knees well bent, feet shoulder width apart, and toes pointing forward. This is called the proper hockey stance and should include a straight torso with the weight balanced on the balls of the feet (see photo 8-1). Do not lean forward, but do keep the head up. The skater should then slowly lean the feet in toward each other slightly: don't just cave in the ankles, lean from the knee down, thus the knees will be closer together than in the normal stance. The skate blades are now on their *inside* edges. By then leaning the feet out (remember, the toes stay forward; this is all being done by leaning the feet from side to side without changing the toe

8-1   The proper hockey stance.

direction), the skate blades will then be on their *outside* edges. This sounds simple, but it is in fact difficult to develop into habit and is simultaneously the single most important thing the skater can learn about skating.

Once accustomed to the feel of the edges, the skater can then move on to another off-ice balance drill that helps in making turns. Assuming the basic hockey stance (knees always somewhat bent, blades about shoulder width apart, head up, torso upright), the skater should balance on the *outside* edge of one skate blade and raise the other leg so that the knee comes as close to the chin as possible (see photo 8-2). Lower the raised leg, place it forward of the other on its *outside* edge, and raise the other leg. This should be done at length, alternating legs and performing the exercise in both clockwise and counterclockwise directions.

The next off-ice drill introduces the skater to crossovers, which are used to

8-2 *Pee Wee Steve Brown performs a knee lift off-ice.*

8-3 *Pee Wee Scott Brown demonstrates the crossover off-ice.*

maintain speed and augment power and balance while skating in a curve. A crossover is performed using both the *inside* and *outside* edges in the following manner: with toes pointing forward and the left skate on its *outside* blade edge, the skater lifts the right skate just high enough to allow it to cross over the left skate. The right skate is then placed on its *inside* edge (see photo 8-3) and the left skate is then brought forward even with the right. The skater then alternates skates, continuing the drill in circles both clockwise and counterclockwise.

These off-ice drills should be continued until the skater has attained good balance and confidence on skates, and is ready to move on to the ice. Many skating instructors feel a youngster should get on the ice as soon as possible, because they will grasp the demonstration of a drill more quickly on ice than in a classroom lecture. However, off-ice practice should always be performed first.

ON-ICE DRILLS

Beginning hockey skaters can go out on the ice in full equipment, but should absolutely not be given a stick or a puck. A stick will be used as a "crutch" by the beginner, to maintain balance, and proper techniques might never be learned. At the same time, a puck is also a real distraction from the skating.

Most instructors agree that the best way for a skater to become accustomed to the ice surface is for him or her to first walk or glide (without raising the blades from the ice). The stride, based on power skating principles of edging, will be learned later.

An important lesson to be learned at the outset is that falling is natural for any skater, no matter how expert. The would-be player should relax and never be embarrassed by a fall.

The instructor should first demonstrate how to fall. When about to fall, the skater should attempt to get into a sitting position and land on the backside, sliding until coming to a halt. Next, the skater puts both hands on the ice, stretches out one leg and bends the other, so that the body is supported on three points. Next, the skater bends the outstretched leg in toward the body, with the blade on the ice, and when in a comfortable position, presses up slowly while placing the leg with the blade on the ice on its outside edge (see photo 8-4). Carefully, the skater now rises into a standing position. This technique will eliminate the skidding, slipping, and rolling around common with beginners who fall.

With these ice skills mastered, the skater has reached a crucial point: this is where many youngsters are now allowed a stick. A stick held in the hands (but not allowed to touch the ice yet) *can* aid balance without being a crutch. This must be left to the discretion of the instructor, but if the skater immediately and continually puts that stick on the ice to aid in balance, it should be taken away.

The two most basic on-ice drills, leg lifts and crossovers, are identical to those practiced off-ice. Before beginning the drills, however, it should be stressed that anything learned on the ice must always be learned forward and backward, as well as both clockwise and counterclockwise. Many recreational skaters cannot skate in a clockwise direction, since in the United States, most rinks have counterclockwise skating only.

For leg lifts, the skater begins by crossing the *width* of the ice surface, lifting one leg then the other. When the skater reaches the opposite boards, the drill is continued, this time moving backward (see photo 8-5). As this drill, which is a tremendous confidence builder, is repeated over and over, the knees are raised higher and the action becomes crisper.

The faceoff circle is the ideal place to teach the clockwise and counterclockwise stationary crossovers. With the toes pointed straight toward the faceoff dot, and the

8-4
Keenan MacDonald, age 5, is about to get up from a fall, but meanwhile he balances himself.

8-5 *These young skaters are performing leg lifts without sticks.*

entire blade of the skate on the ice, the skater does crossovers all the way around the circle, first in one direction, and then in the other—always keeping the toes pointed straight at the faceoff dot.

THE STRIDE

During the first on-ice drills, the skater will begin to develop his or her own style of gliding over the ice surface. Because they "walked" the first few times they went on the ice, most beginning skaters think that skating is similar to walking or running. In fact, it used to be fairly common to see even NHL skaters making a windmill sort of churning as they attempted to get started up the ice. Jim "The Chief" Nielson, a defenseman for the New York Rangers for years, was one with such a distinctive takeoff. Unfortunately, it was symptomatic of poor skating habits. A skater goes virtually nowhere unless he or she grasps the importance of edges and how they are best used.

So, while the first-time skater is encouraged to "walk" or glide without lifting the feet, the basic power skating stride must be learned as soon as the skater has developed some confidence in basic balance on skates.

There are two absolute musts to learning the stride in hockey skating, and they sound as though they are the reverse of what the skater should do. These two musts are: keep the weight balanced on the balls of the feet; and when the stride is executed, push the skate and leg to the side. That's right; to the side.

If the skater puts the weight on the toes—which is the initial inclination—and does not thrust the skate to the side, the entire power and thrusting ability of a skate edge is lost.

Thus, the skater should first assume the proper stance: head up, torso erect, skates shoulder width apart, weight evenly distributed on the balls of the feet, and knees well bent. Next, he pushes off on the *inside* edge of the right skate, thrusting the leg to the side as far as possible, so that the blade of the skate is at about a 45° angle to the opposite blade (see photo 8-6). As soon as that stride has been completed, return the right skate, placing it on the ice even with the left. For the first few times the skater should, at this point, glide for the count of two, to give himself the opportunity to get the weight evenly distributed on the balls of the feet again. Then the drill is repeated with the other skate.

Once the skater is confident that he can balance evenly between strides, he should then switch from one foot to the other without the two-count, but always remembering to have both blades on the ice at once before pushing the next foot to the side on an inside edge.

8-6 *Pee Wees practice the basic stride. Note the thrusting feet pushing to the side on the inside edges.*

It should be pointed out here that this book deals with hockey and the *basics* of its history, skills, tactics, and so on. Although good skating is absolutely essential to good hockey—particularly in today's game, which emphasizes a return to skating excellence and finesse—it is not possible here to enter into every single power skating drill generally in use today. As an example, after the skater learns the basic stride and before he moves on to stops and turns (let alone stickhandling and shooting), the following nuances to the stride should be mastered and practiced for lengthy periods of time along with the basics already covered.

223

Forward Inside Edges—Two Feet

From the proper stance, point the toes out, with the skates on their inside edges, etching semicircles on the ice. Keep the skate blades on the ice throughout the drill, but as the toes begin to point in at the end of the semicircle, bring the heels in, too, so that the skates are in the original position with the toes straight forward. The trick to this drill is to bring the heels in line with the toes very sharply.

After mastering this drill the skater should then perform the same exercise, thrusting with one foot (called by some power skating instructors "half" edges) instead of both, but keeping both skates on the ice. The toe of one skate turns out on an inside edge and executes the semicircle, while the nonthrusting skate remains stationary on a very slight inside edge (for stability). The drill should be performed with a short thrust and quick heel return, as before.

Forward Inside Edges—One Foot

Although the name sounds almost like the two previous drills, it differs quite a bit. The skater should push off with one inside edge, then raise that skate and keep it raised slightly, against the boot of the other skate, which is stationary. The shoulder above the thrusting skate is slightly back.

Forward Outside Edges—One Foot

It might seem that once the skater has mastered the concept and feel of edges, these drills will come easily. But most skaters have great difficulty with the outside edges, and this drill is a toughie for skaters of all ages.

After the skater has taken several proper strides down ice, he should then lift one skate slightly and cross it in front of the other, putting the blade down on an outside edge, with the shoulder above that skate slightly forward. As that blade touches, the skater then thrusts with the back *outside* edge of the trailing skate, executing a semicircle. Immediately after the thrust, the trailing skate should then be brought forward, crossed over, and placed down on an *outside* edge.

Forward Edges—Inside to Outside

The skater should stride down ice and at a signal place the weight on one *inside* edge, with the opposite shoulder slightly back, executing the now-familiar semicircle. However, at the end of the semicircle, the skater should, while remaining on the same skate, switch to the outside edge of that skate (with the opposing shoulder now slightly forward), which results in a semicircle in the other direction.

The above drills are only the forward drills and must also be learned skating backwards. This gives some indication of how really complicated proper skating skills are. At every moment of these drills, the torso should remain erect, the head up, the knees bent, and the shoulders should move correctly relative to the edges and the drill, but without jerking or bobbing up and down.

It is obvious that while every hockey team has a myth or legend about one of its superstars who went out on a backyard pond at the age of three in his brother's size twelve skates and became the best skater in the NHL, the reality for the vast majority of aspiring hockey players is that they should make sure they get a really good skating experience and education before they try to score fifty goals.

STOPS

Before moving on to various types of turns, the skater would do well to master stopping. The first stop taught to virtually every novice skater is absolutely similar to the snowplow stop taught the novice skier, and is called, identically, the *forward snowplow stop*. After striding down ice, the skater gets into the proper stance with both blades on the ice and the weight evenly distributed, then applies pressure evenly to *both inside* edges (see photo 8-7). The tendency here is to put the weight on the toes, or simply to turn the toes inward without putting pressure on the inside edges—either of which will lead to disaster. If the weight is shifted to the toes, the

8-7 In the forward snowplow stop, notice that Steve is applying pressure to both inside edges, but happily does not shift his weight to his toes.

skater will pitch forward; if the toes are turned without edging, the skater (1) will not stop and (2) might well sit back and fall.

In the *one-foot snowplow stop,* the skater strides, then places one skate slightly ahead of the other, putting pressure on the *inside* edge. The trailing skate should also remain on a very slight inside edge for balance.

Next, the skater should learn two more one-foot stops, which are not performed in the snow plow fashion. The *one-foot stop on inside edges* is better described by what the head and shoulders do than what the skates do. After skating down the ice, the skater should turn the head in one direction, bringing the opposite shoulder forward. This, in turn, causes the hip on the same side as that shoulder to follow immediately. As the hip follows the shoulder, the blade of that skate should press hard on its *inside* edge. The skate not being pressured should be lifted off the ice.

The *one-foot stop on outside edges,* also called the "T-stop," is hard to learn because it entails the outside edges. But it is important because it is the stop most commonly used by hockey players when leaving the ice, as well as by players in the face-off circle. This stop will be described here with the left skate doing the edging, but must, of course, be learned both ways, with either skate. To execute the stop, the skater places the right skate on the ice with the toe straight forward. Then the left skate is lifted and placed perpendicular, immediately behind the right skate, toe pointing left, on its *outside* edge. As the left skate is placed on its outside edge, the right skate is then lifted, and as the stop is completed, the weight shifts onto the left skate (see photo 8-8).

Because this stop is so difficult, in order to get the feel of the stop, the skater can first *drag* the left skate along the ice on its *outside* edge, rather than placing it definitively behind the right skate.

The *hockey stop* is the most important stop for the hockey player to learn and must be learned in both directions. This stop can be best described by following the motion of the head. When ready to make the stop, the skater turns his head in the direction intended for the stop (our example is to the left). Turning the head left brings the right shoulder forward, followed by the right hip and skate. As the right skate comes around, it should be pressed hard on its *inside* edge, while the left skate remains on the ice on its *outside* edge. The stop leaves the skater's weight on the right foot, which enables a rapid takeoff if needed (see photo 8-9).

BACK STOPS

There are various back stops, but the easiest is the *back snowplow stop.* It is also the quickest way to stop while skating backwards, leaving the player free to keep an eye on the puck as well as on the attacking skater. Quite simply, with the torso leaning

8-8   David Bell performs the one-foot stop on the outside edges, or T-stop, most commonly used by hockey players when leaving the ice.

8-9   As these youngsters perform the classic hockey stop, throwing up ice in the process, their weight is on the right (rear) foot, enabling a quick takeoff.

slightly forward, the skater applies pressure to *both inside* edges, executing the stop.

In the *one-foot back snowplow stop* pressure is applied (keeping the weight on the ball of the foot, not the toe) on the *inside* edge of one skate while the other skate remains on the ice near the edging skate but forward of it and on a slight *inside* edge.

The movement of the upper body is crucial to the *back hockey stop*. Skating backward rapidly, the player presses the right shoulder back and the right hip and skate follow, with the right skate on an *inside* edge, and the left on an *outside* edge. The stop concludes when the weight is over the left skate.

Notice that there is no mention of turning the head in the back hockey stop. This is because it is a stop normally made by defensemen while watching an attacker, and the head should remain forward. In fact, too many defensemen use the back hockey stop, wasting energy in doing so, when they would be better off using the faster and simpler back snowplow stop.

A variation of the back hockey stop is good for a player coming against another player along the boards, and is actually the method used for a hip check. The right shoulder presses back, followed by the right hip and the right skate on the inside edge, but the left skate is on its *inside* edge also. Needless to say, this variation should only be learned after the standard stop is first mastered.

TURNS

Like all other aspects of skating, turns can be broken down into very complicated maneuvers, and skating turns have been given some confusing names, such as "Mohawk," "Boston," and "rink" turns. But the coasting turn and the pivot are two basic methods of turning while skating that enable the player to change direction without really stopping.

The Coasting Turn

When speed is not of the essence, this is the correct turn to employ. In a left turn the skater lowers the left shoulder, leans to the left, and digs the *outside* edge of the left skate into the ice, causing the left knee to bend and the right leg to follow the turn (see photo 8-10).

The Pivot

With shoulders straight and knees bent, the player leans to the left, digs the *outside* edge of the left skate and the *inside* edge of the right skate into the ice and points the toes in the direction of the turn. This can be done rapidly and without much loss of speed, allowing the skater to keep up with the action.

8-10 *Steve Brown completes the coasting turn, with the left shoulder down and the outside edge of the left skate digging into the ice.*

STICKHANDLING

Stickhandling is the transference of the puck from backhand to forehand and back again, in order to maintain control of the puck and confuse the opposition as to whether the puck carrier's intention is to retain the puck or pass it off.

Before discussing the basics of stickhandling, the proper technique of grasping the stick should be reviewed. The stick is held with the fingers and thumbs wrapped around the shaft—not in the palms of the hands. The top hand should be firm on the stick, not on the butt end, while the bottom hand should be from a foot to 18 inches down the shaft, unless leaning into a shot, when it can be lowered further (see photo 8-11). It is essential not to change the grip, whether stickhandling, passing, or shooting.

8-11   *These youngsters show how to hold the hockey stick properly before stick handling begins.*

In the forehand position, with both hands on the stick and the blade of the stick slanted in slightly, the puck is "cradled" in the center of the blade, just slightly toward the heel of the stick. Now the skater moves forward slowly and quietly (fast and noisy stickhandling is not the mark of a good hockey player as some novices think; rather it is energy-wasting and dangerous), moving the puck from the forehand to the backhand, while extending the arms as far as possible from side to side without losing balance (see photos 8-12, 8-13, 8-14). The only time the two-

8-12   *Stick handling. In the forehand position, with both hands on the stick and the blade of the stick slanted in slightly, the puck is "cradled" in the center of the blade.*

8-13   *The skater moves forward slowly, moving the puck from the forehand to the backhand.*

8-14   *As the player moves the puck to the backhand, the arms should be extended as far as possible.*

hand grip on the stick should ever be abandoned is if the puck carrier uses one arm to block his checker, which obviously should only be done by the expert player, skater, and stickhandler.

Two excellent stickhandling drills can be practiced in conjunction with the pivot turn. Cones are set up on the ice, and the player skates toward the cone, stickhandling at the same time. As he or she approaches the first cone, the puck should be cradled on the stick and a pivot turn executed, handling the puck around the turn. Then the skater moves to the next cone, but lets the puck slide off the stick as he executes the pivot turn, and picks the puck up after the turn, on either the forehand or the backhand. A most important aspect of stickhandling is the ability to do it without looking down, and the goal of every skater should be to carry the puck down the length of the ice, moving it from forehand to backhand without looking at the puck once.

One skill the skater should attempt to develop—both for stickhandling and passing—is "split vision." This is the ability to see both the puck and the other player (whether it is an opponent to be circumvented with the puck or a teammate about to receive the pass) almost simultaneously. When stickhandling, the player should attempt to carry the puck slightly out in front, so that he can see puck and opponent at once. If he finds he is carrying the puck too close to be seen with the bottom of his vision, he might want to change the lie of his stick, so that it cradles the puck slightly further out.

Faking, Feinting, or Deking

A variation of stickhandling, this maneuver should be performed slowly at first. If the skater wishes to *fake* a move to the right, he should dip his head and shoulder in that direction, move the puck to that side and shift the weight slightly to that bent knee (see photo 8-15). Having established the appearance of moving to the right, quickly swing the puck to the left, push off the right skate and take off to the left (see photos 8-16, 8-17). If the opponent is standing still or rushing at the puck carrier, he is easier to fake. If the opponent is backing up as the "deker" nears, and does not commit himself to the fake, the puck carrier must be prepared to pass or shoot when his deceit fails.

After acquiring the aptitude for stickhandling, the player should then remember certain basic rules that accompany the skill: stickhandling should be saved for the opponent's end of the ice; the opponent easiest to fake is the one rushing straight at the puck carrier; the opponent should be tricked into committing before the puck carrier actually skates around him; and, last of all, passing will get the puck further and faster than stickhandling.

8-15 *"Deking" to the left. The skater fakes a move to the right, dipping his head and shoulder in that direction.*

8-16, 8-17 *Having established the appearance of moving to the right, quickly swing the puck to the left, push off the right skate, and take off to the left.*

PASSING

Moving the puck toward the opponent's net is the name of the game, and one of the quickest ways to press forward is to pass the puck. This is probably the newcomer's weakest skill, so it should first be practiced with the passer in a stationary position. Next passing should be practiced with two players moving very slowly, without any opposition, about twenty feet apart, taking turns passing and receiving.

A player must learn to know his teammates well, to anticipate their movements, in order to become an exceptional passer. But basic rules always pertain: keep the head up, an eye on the target, and *never* make blind passes.

Direct Passes

With head up and eye on the passer, the receiver slowly skates forward, keeping his stick square to the passer if possible. The passer, head also up and eye on the receiver, snaps his wrists slightly and tilts the blade over the top of the puck, releasing it near the toe of the blade. Stick and arms should follow through in the direction of the receiver, and the receiver should "give" slightly with his stick as he receives the puck, tilting the blade slightly to trap the puck.

Layup or Headman Pass

This pass is also known as "leading the man" and simply means that the basics outlined above are followed except the pass is made to a spot *ahead* of the stick of the receiver. The goal is to place the puck so that the receiver will not have to break stride to retrieve it, or reach back, or pick it up on his skates instead. It is therefore better to have slightly too much lead, rather than putting the puck too far back.

Flip Pass

When an opponent's stick is blocking forward movement, or when it is necessary to clear the puck against the boards into center ice, the flip pass is appropriate. The stick should be flicked rapidly by following through a bit higher than normal with the blade.

If the flip pass is used on the boards, the passer should always keep in mind that boards differ from rink to rink, and that the pass will come off the boards at the angle it approached. This pass is good for defensemen to use in their own zone, when passing off the boards behind their own net, from one corner to another.

SHOOTING

Ninety-nine times out of a hundred the puck enters the net as a result of a shot, so this skill warrants a great deal of practice. It is best to start shooting off-ice, firing the puck at a target from different distances and angles.

While practicing shots, the shooter would do well to review certain rules: always keep the head up and the eyes on a definite target. Remember that if the shooter watches the goalie instead of one of the corners of the net, the puck will invariably hit the goalie. Always follow through, but try to keep the follow-through low. If the shot is consistently high, consider cutting down on the amount of hook on the blade, or decrease the amount of wrist flick in the shot.

Wrist Shot

This maneuver requires strength in the hands, wrist, and forearms, but is excellent for deceiving the opponent into thinking that there is no shot coming, since it takes place with virtually no wind up.

With skates on inside edges, the puck is cradled on the stick blade, the lower hand over the top of the shaft and upper hand under. The wrists are rolled and then snapped forward as the puck is fired, while the weight shifts from the back foot to the front one, and the skates end up on their outside edges.

Flip Shot (Lifting the Puck)

This shot requires excellent timing and coordination and should be practiced on both the forehand and the backhand. Sliding a hand further down the shaft of the stick than normal, the shooter pulls the puck back on the toe of the blade, which should be opposite the toe of the rear skate. Rolling the wrists slightly to get the stick under the puck, the upward motion forces the puck into the air. In the follow-through, the weight is shifted from the rear skate to the outside edge of the front skate, to prepare for a possible rebound.

The flip shot is good for lifting the puck over the goalie when he is down. It is also used by defensemen to get the puck out of the defensive zone and by all players to flip the puck from center ice into the offensive zone. A goaltender sometimes loses sight of a flip shot, or it can take a crazy bounce and go into the net.

Slap Shot

The slap shot, while it may be the toughest for a goaltender to handle, is also the hardest shot to execute properly because it is difficult to control. Unfortunately, a wild "golf" swing at the puck is something virtually any skater can manage, so the slap shot has become very popular, to the detriment of other shooting skills.

There are two variations to the slap shot: the *standing* and the *skating slap shot.* For the standing slap shot, the puck should be on the blade of the stick lined up with the front skate, which is on its *outside* edge. Sliding the lower hand four to five inches down the shaft, the stick is drawn back, making sure the upper hand is no higher than hip level, the inside edge of the stick blade no higher than shoulder level and the arm of the lower hand straight. Bringing the stick forward as fast as possible, the shooter rolls the wrists (slightly—less than for any other shot) and strikes the ice slightly behind the puck, driving it forward. As the shooter follows through, the rear leg and skate come off the ice entirely.

The *skating slap shot* is executed in the same manner except the puck is allowed to slide in front of the shooter, who then takes a few strides before slapping the puck toward the target.

Though there is only a second for wind up, and it is necessary to have the head down and eyes on the puck to get off the slap shot, the player should try to take a quick glance at the target to ascertain whether the goalie has moved.

Tip In

For this shot, the shooter stations himself in front of the goaltender, facing a teammate who is preparing to take a shot. Pressing on both inside edges for balance, the potential shooter guards against an opposing defenseman tying up his stick. The goaltender will most likely be waiting for the shot from the teammate, so the player in front of the net watches the shot and uses the blade of his stick to change the direction of the puck, deflecting it into the net. Often the goaltender will not be able to react fast enough to make a save off a tip in.

Backhand Shot

This is a shot which should be used far more often, but it has become a lost art, and players waste precious time shifting the puck from their backhand to their forehand to take a shot. The same procedure is followed as for the forehand shot, with the shooter making certain to lean hard in the direction of the shot follow through by pressing the stick hard against the ice (see photos 8-18, 8-19, 8-20).

8-18 *Pee Wee Coach Sandy MacDonald, Director of the Mid-Hudson Ice Arena in Poughkeepsie, New York, demonstrates the backhand shot.*

8-19 *The backhand shot procedure is the same as for the forehand shot.*

8-20 *The shooter should make certain to lean hard in the direction of the shot follow-through by pressing the stick hard against the ice.*

Breakaway/Penalty Shot (See Glossary for Definitions)

This is probably the most exciting play in hockey—one-on-one with the goalie. In this situation, the skater must decide beforehand which approach and shot he will try and then must stick to it. It is best to attempt to outsmart the goalie, but then that is exactly what he is attempting to do, too.

If the goalie chooses to stay in his crease (see glossary), the shooter would do best to skate to within twenty to thirty feet out and fire the puck as hard as possible at an open corner or a space between the goalie's pads, if there is one.

A good, experienced goalie will more likely move out to cut down the angle and challenge the player to make the first move, to commit himself. The skater should stickhandle to under twenty feet from the net and then fake a forehand shot. If the goalie takes the deke and goes down, the skater then veers slightly away from the net, quickly shifts to the backhand, and lifts the puck into an empty corner.

If, after faking the forehand shot, the goalie fails to go for the fake, the shooter would do best to stride on the forehand side, gaining the most net at which to shoot.

BODY CHECKING

Most simply defined, body checking is *cleanly* hitting the opponent off the puck and is a necessary skill for forwards and defensemen both. There are essentially two methods of checking: with the stick playing the puck and with the body playing the man. Players must also learn how to cover an opponent when he does not have possession of the puck. (See the chapter on tactics for more on checking.)

Hip Check

The hip check has become another of hockey's lost arts in recent years, because timing, the ability to execute backward pivots to perfection, and a lot of practice are required.

The defensive player skates backward on an angle, attempting to give his opponent the illusion of enough room to skate around him. When the two skaters are almost parallel to each other, the defender takes off an extended inside edge, going straight for the attacker and hitting him on the thigh with the hip.

Shoulder Check

Taking no more than two strides toward his opponent, the defender aims for the chest, and as contact is made with the shoulder, he straightens and lifts.

8-21   *The checker presses an opponent into the boards and then places a leg between his thighs to prevent his kicking the puck along the boards.*

Skating the Man Off

This is a good check for defensemen who should, as they skate backwards, get the puck carrier to think he can skate around the defenseman, along the boards. When the puck carrier makes his move, the defender takes off with the near leg, turns and skates forward with the opponent, angling him into the boards (see photo 8-21). The checker must keep his arms and a hip in front of the attacker, or he may break out of the check. If it is necessary to check the opponent into the boards from the rear, the defender should not simply crash him into the boards, but instead should get his stick on one side of the opponent's body and press him into the boards. Then the defender can grab the top of the boards and place a leg between the opponent's thighs, preventing him from kicking the puck along the boards.

Poke Check

This check is particularly good for forechecking forwards to pressure the opposing puck carrier into yielding the puck, or even forcing him to give up the attack and regroup. Whether the forward goes in after or waits for the puck carrier, the check is made when the forward fully extends the arm holding the stick, with the blade square to the puck, and pokes the puck off the attacker's stick. Once the poke check is completed, the player should put the other hand back on the stick in order to gain control of the puck. Contact between the two players often occurs, so there should be no holding or grabbing.

Backskating defensemen can use the poke check against a puck carrier in the defensive zone, and the poke check is also an excellent defensive weapon for any player killing a penalty.

Sweep Check

The sweep check is an effective forechecking maneuver. With one knee quite bent and balanced on the outside edge of the lead skate, the skater drags his other skate on an inside edge while the glove of the stick hand is down on the ice for balance. As he glides in this position toward the opponent, he sweeps his stick into the blade of the opponent's stick, knocking the puck off his stick (see photos 8-25 through 8-29). This check is rarely used while skating backward.

Press Check and Lift Check

Both of these checks involve use of the stick. To execute the press check, the skater places his stick on the opponent's lower arms, or against his stick, pressing as hard as possible. Hopefully, this maneuver may force the opponent off the puck or force it off his stick.

The lift check is used when the defender is very close to the puck carrier or one of his intended receivers. The defender's stick is placed under the opponent's stick and lifted off the ice and away from the puck.

The checker should always be careful when checking an opponent to observe the rules of clean checking—and never draw a penalty with the stick or the body, if possible.

8-22
Age and size do not hinder Jock Mac-Donald (age 7) from properly poke checking his younger brother, Kennan (age 6).

8-23
Whether the forward goes in after or waits for the puck carrier, the check is made when the forward fully extends the arm holding the stick.

8-24
When the blade of the stick is square to the puck the puck is poked off the attacker's stick.

8-25   *The sweep check is an effective forechecking maneuver.*

8-26   *With one knee quite bent, the skater balances on the outside edge of the lead skat*

8-27
The skater drags his other skate on an inside edge.

8-28
The glove of the stick hand is down on the ice for balance.

8-29
As the checker glides toward his opponent, he sweeps his stick into the blade of his opponent's stick, knocking the puck off his stick.

9

GOALTENDING

When youngsters begin to play hockey, the coach all too often relegates the poorest skater to the goaltender's position. If a team makes such a move it makes a tremendous mistake, because the goalie should be an excellent skater—certainly no worse than any other teammate.

A goalie is no different from any other skater on the team and must practice *all* the on- and off-ice skating drills outlined in the chapter on skills. A goaltender must, in fact, be able to skate backward as well as the defensemen. He will, however, be required to learn other skating skills discussed in this chapter.

The goalie should never be excused from *any* skating drill and should wear full equipment when participating. One note of caution: when wearing the equipment, the goalie should warm up properly before any vigorous skating, otherwise he could easily pull a groin muscle.

Beyond the ability to skate well, the desire to be a goaltender, coupled with certain physical and mental attributes, must be considered.

Physically, size is not all that important, but good eyesight, good concentration, quick reflexes, better than average muscular coordination, and the ability to stand up to the tremendous checking and jostling, "courtesy" of opponents who park themselves in the crease, are necessary.

Mentally, a goalie must not fear the puck, which will be fired at great speeds from many different angles. He must make his teammates believe he is the last line of defense and will stop anything coming his way. He must be confident he can perform the job. Finally, he must not fluster easily and must learn to forget the last goal scored against him.

STANCE

"Stance" is the position the goalie assumes before a shot and is taken regardless of the style or styles of goaltending he uses.

For the proper stance, the goalie should line his skates up evenly (staggered pads cover a narrower area), a shoulder width apart (for better balance and because it is easier to close the pads than open them), slightly on the inside edges of the skates, weight evenly distributed along the blades of the skates or slightly forward. The knees should be bent, chest a bit forward, and head held in a comfortable position (see photo 9-1). Never keep the legs straight because quick leg action depends on flexed knees. When the goalie straightens up, the spring in his legs is lost.

The stick should rest about one to two inches in front of the skates, with the blade either flat on the ice or riding the heel. "Heelriding" is a more comfortable way to hold the stick, and the goalie is usually able to lower the stick quickly if the puck is shot along the ice. The stick should be held in a relaxed grip.

The hand holding the stick can be just above the widened portion of the stick or slightly higher, if the goalie is preparing for a poke check. The "trapper" glove should be held knee high at the side of the pads, about two inches out, or in front of the pads.

A tall goalie will stand a little more erect, while a smaller one may crouch a bit.

9-1   Pee Wee Marco Bertolozzi of the Dutchess Youth Hockey League, Dutchess County, New York, shows the ideal basic stance for a goaltender. Photo by Tim Hewitt.

STYLES

There are four basic goaltending styles and a goalie normally employs two or more during the course of a game. The body build and ability of a goalie dictates which style a coach encourages.

The Standup Goaltender

With this style, the goalie—usually tall and rangy—stays on his skates and only leaves his feet when it is absolutely necessary to smother the puck. The advantage with this style is that it keeps the goalie in front of the puck and in position to make the save. The weakness is that saves on shots along the ice aimed for the bottom corners of the net are difficult to make (see photo 9-2).

The Angle Goaltender

If the goalie is agile, quick, a good skater, and has a small physique, he can be an angle goaltender. For this style, the goalie may move from two to five feet out in front of the crease as the play comes into the defensive zone, or make the move to that position as the puck is shot. The weakness of this style is that while the shooter can see very little of the net, the goalie may lose his relationship to the net, giving the shooter an opportunity to deke or to pass around him. It is also difficult to control rebounds using this style (see photo 9-3).

The Flopping Goaltender

The flopping goaltender must be quick enough to accurately time his "flop," which he must do the moment the puck is shot, in order to smother it or feed it into a corner. The plus of this style is that every inch of the goal mouth is covered when the goalie is down, while the obvious weaknesses are that he cannot handle a rebound or stop a high shot (see photo 9-4).

9-2   *This standup goalie has just missed a bottom corner shot. Photo by Tim Hewitt.*

9-3   *The angle goaltender in this photo, after making one save, is unable to stop a rebound shot. Photo by Tim Hewitt.*

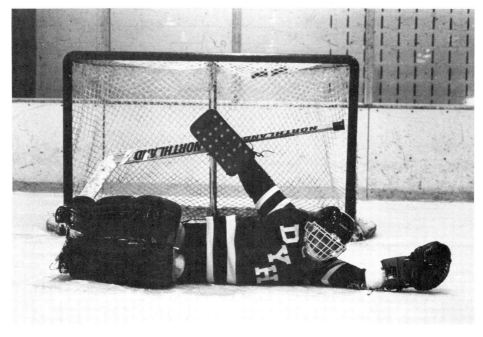

9-4   The flopping goaltender completely covers the goalmouth, but is prey to a high shot. This example also shows "stacking the pads." Photo by Tim Hewitt.

The Back-In Goaltender

This is an excellent style for the big, hulking netminder who is fairly quick, but does not have great agility. With this style, the goalie does not cut down the angle, but stays back in the goal mouth covering the area from post to post. The back-in goaltender is aware of his relationship to the net, can line up the angle of the puck on the goal line, has a bit more time to make a save, and is not bothered as much by the opposition jostling in front of the net. The one problem with this style is that the shooter has more open net at which to fire, unless the goalie is built along the lines of "Perfect Pierre LaFong," who was described by Quincy, Massachusetts, hockey writer Roger Barry as the ideal size for a goaltender—five feet tall by five feet wide. Unfortunately for the Boston Bruins fans of that day (the 1950s Bruins were at an all-time low), "Mr. Five-by-Five" LaFong was a figment of Barry's fertile imagination.

PLAYING THE ANGLE

No matter what style a goalie employs, he must line the puck up at the correct angle, yet take care when "cutting down the angle" not to give the shooter too much open net. How does the goalie "play the angle?" He must keep his eyes on the puck, but he can glance down or split his vision to check his position in his crease and line up that way. Or he can tap the posts with either the "trapper" or the knob of the goalie stick. At first, playing the angle is tough, but as the goalie gains experience, he'll be able to sense where he is nearly every minute. The three basic "laws" of cutting the angle must become second nature to a goaltender: cut down the amount of net the shooter can see, never let the shooter gain the "short" side, and always play the puck, not what the shooter is doing with his body (see photo 9-5).

9-5 *Playing the Angle. Notice the tape ribbons coming from the goal posts to the camera. These show how thoroughly the goalie has cut down the angle, leaving the shooter virtually no place to put a shot. Photo by Tim Hewitt.*

SKATING IN THE CREASE AREA

The goalie must learn special skating skills. The following descriptions are based on the goalie being righthanded, that is, he holds the stick in his right hand. As with all skating skills whatever is done moving to the right must also be done moving left.

The Slide

This maneuver is used to get the goalie from the left side of the net to the right while keeping his body in front of the puck at all times. The goalie must be able to perform a *long* slide that allows him to move completely across the goal mouth in one motion, and the *short* slide that lets him shift his body just a bit to cover a change in puck direction.

With the blade of the right skate pointed toward the blue line and knees slightly bent, push off on the *inside* edge of the left skate. When the move is performed correctly, the right skate scrapes along the ice, which is one reason why a goalie only has a slight edge on his skates.

The Glide

With the blade of the right skate turned *parallel* to the blue line and both knees slightly bent, push off on the *inside* edge of the left skate. The *inside* edge of the same skate is dragged to stop, and the goalie is ready to assume the basic stance (see photo 9-6).

Another drill is for the goalie to push off on the *inside* edge of either skate and when ready to stop use the *outside* edge of the other skate and shift his weight back on that skate.

Skating to the right or left is what the goalie must do in order to protect the goal posts when there is action to the side of the net. When protecting the left post, the left skate is held tight up against the post, left arm hooked around the post, head turned toward the puck and stick ready to block any pass from behind the net (see photo 9-7). If the goalie is protecting the right post, the right skate is tight up against the post, right arm hooked around the post, left arm on the top of the crossbar, eye on the puck, and stick ready to block a pass (see photo 9-8).

9-6　*The glide. With the blade of the right skate turned parallel to the blue line and both knees slightly bent, push off on the inside edge of the left skate. Drag the inside edge of the same skate to stop, and the goalie is once more ready to assume the basic stance. Photo by Tim Hewitt.*

9-7　*Protecting the left post. Photo by Tim Hewitt.*

9-8　*Protecting the right post. Photo by Tim Hewitt.*

Skating Out (Forward variation of glide)

To propel himself forward, the goalie can flex either knee, whichever feels more natural, and push off the *inside* edge of that skate. To stop, the goalie uses the snowplow, described in the chapter on skills. The goalie must remember, when skating out to cut down the angle, to resume the proper stance once he has stopped.

Skating Back In

With a quick twist of his rear end, the goalie pushes off the *inside* edge of either skate, and he moves back into the crease, or net. To stop, the goalie uses the one-foot backward snowplow. (See skills, page 228).

NOTE: Another way of performing these moves is to skate out by pressing hard into the ice with both the *inside* edges and then turning the toes of the skates in to stop. You perform the same move skating backward but turn the heels of the skates in to stop.

The Skate Save

The skate save is one of the most difficult and least recommended moves for a goalie, because when attempting it the center of the goalie's body is opened up and the puck must be stopped with the skate blade, a very small surface. The save should only be used when it is impossible for the goalie to get his entire body in front of the puck.

To make the save, the goalie, with the entire right skate blade on the ice parallel to the blue line, points the tip of the blade toward the right boards and stretches. The goalie stays up and does not go down all the way on the left knee.

When the maneuver is done to the left, the goalie, if he is righthanded, has the option of placing the stick in front of the skate.

Fielding the Puck

Many times a goalie skates behind the net to stop a puck that is "wound around" the boards. Of course, no opponent should be near when the goalie makes his move. While the goalie must be able to skate left or right, it is wise for him to return to the net on the same side he left.

The goalie can expedite things for the defensemen if, after fielding the puck behind the net, he skates it up to the goal line so the defensemen won't have to move it away from the boards. Of course, this is only done if there is no danger of being checked by an opponent.

Using the Stick

The stick is an important part of the goalie's equipment, for he must be able to use it for stickhandling, passing, and making saves. As is the case with team skating drills, the goalie must participate in stick drills and work as diligently as the other skaters in using the stick and learning to stickhandle and pass on both his forehand and backhand.

Stickhandling

A goalie stickhandles in many different situations, including leaving the net to pick up a loose puck and then controlling it and carrying the puck around the back of the net to set up a teammate or firing the puck out of the defensive zone.

Passing

The goalie will employ the pass when opponents are pressing, and he can shoot the puck into a corner. Or, when no opponent is near, he can pass the puck to a teammate in the clear. The goalie's passes should be as crisp and accurate as any other team member's.

The Stick Save

There are many times during a game when the goalie uses his stick to make a save, but he must learn to "angle" the puck away from the front of the net.

A goalie on the left side of the crease when the puck comes at him should turn the tip of the stick toward the left post, deflecting the puck into the left corner of the boards. A right corner stick save would be the reverse.

One trick used by a goalie is to tilt the blade of the stick backwards and angle the puck over the net behind him, out of the rink. However, deliberately shooting the puck out of the rink can result in a penalty (two minutes for "deliberately shooting puck out of the rink").

Clearing the Puck

A goalie can use his stick to clear the puck once the save has been made. If the goalie is to the right side of the crease, he can, with his stick hand, *sweep,* not shoot or bat, the puck on his backhand into the right corner, or he can place his left hand on the widened portion of the stick to assist the right hand. The latter method is easier for the goalie, but slower to perform.

Kicking the Stick

If there are opponents near the net and a slow shot comes along the ice, the goalie can kick his stick as the puck hits the blade and steer the puck out of danger. The potential problem is that the goalie may lose his balance and, as he kicks the stick, the puck could sneak under the blade of the stick into the net.

Batting the Puck

After catching the puck, the goalie may elect to toss it in the air and bat it with the stick into a corner. There are also times when a shot about shoulder high can be batted away with the stick without the goalie first catching it. The maneuver is done by simply batting the puck with the widened portion of the stick, always remembering to keep an eye on the puck, of course.

Using the Pads

Another piece of important equipment is the goalie's pads, which are used for safety and defense.

The Kick Save

For the righthanded goalie the kick save can be used to stop a fast shot to the goalie's right. Keeping an eye on the puck, the goalie snaps the right pad up and out at a forty-five degree angle to stop the puck. Since this type of save opens up the entire center of the pads, the goalie should not use it unless it is impossible for him to shift his body to get in front of the puck. The same maneuver should be practiced with the left pad, but only to develop strength in both legs since any puck to the goalie's left should be caught with the "trapper" (see photo 9-9).

The Half Split

This is another maneuver used to make a save on a fast shot. The goalie turns the blade of the left skate parallel to the blue line and thrusts the left leg out until the

9-9   *The kick save. Photo by Tim Hewitt.*

9-10   *The half split. Photo by Tim Hewitt.*

right knee touches the ice. Correctly executed, the split will have the calf of the right leg and the right skate blade as flat as possible on the ice surface (see photo 9-10). When attempting the half split, the goalie should place the "trapper" *or* the stick in the crotch area to cover the opening. To recover from the half split, the goalie should snap or pull the legs together, or rise from the left knee.

The Full Split

Exactly the same as the half split except the goalie extends down to the crotch area with the calves of both legs on the ice. This is a very difficult move to learn, but it covers a wide area and is an excellent defensive maneuver.

Dipping the Pads

This is a good move because it can be executed quickly yet still allows the goalie to maintain his balance. When a shot is coming in knee high, the goalie dips both knees inward and the gap between the pads is closed (see photo 9-11). Also, when the goalie goes all the way down on the ice he can use the stick to draw the puck into his pads, stopping play. (If the goalie happens to land on his rear end, the pads can be lifted slightly and placed on top of the puck.)

9-11   *Dipping the pads. When a shot is coming in knee high, the goalie dips both knees inward and the gap between the pads is closed. Photo by Tim Hewitt.*

Stacking Or Decking the Pads

This is a desperation move for the goalie and should only be done when the puck is less than six feet away. To "stack" to the right, the goalie slides to the right, tucking his left leg behind the right and gliding on his left hip. As his hip glides along the ice, he then kicks the left leg forward, which completes the "stack." The goalie recovers by pushing up on his left arm, on to his left knee, and up.

The "V" Save

A lot of practice is required for this popular save. To perform it, the goalie directs both skates to the posts and turns both knees inward as he drops to the ice (see photo 9-12). The inside edge of both pads are flat on the ice with the body erect and the stick out in front in the normal position. Timing is very important, as the goalie must go down in time to get the pads on the ice, but not so soon as to allow the opponent to shoot for the upper part of the net.

9-12   The "V" save. The goalie directs both skates to the posts and turns both knees inward as he drops to the ice. Photo by Tim Hewitt.

9-13   The inside pad dip. Photo by Tim Hewitt.

The Inside Pad Dip

This move can be made to the right or left, but always in conjunction with the stick. If a fast shot comes along the ice to the goalie's right, he quickly slides the right skate, perpendicular to the blue line, to the right. The inside edge of the right pad is then lowered to the ice by turning the right knee inward and lowering the body to rest on the left knee (see photo 9-13). The save can then be made with either the pad or stick.

Using the Trapper

The "trapper" is a glove similar to the one worn by a first-baseman and is designed to catch the puck. It can also be used to sweep the puck away in front of the net, smother the puck, shovel the puck into a corner, or pick the puck off the ice. All the maneuvers should be practiced over and over to develop proficiency. Most experts believe a goalie should use the "trapper" as often as possible during a game. (See photo 9-14.)

Using the Blocker

This is a glove backed with a thick block of leather worn on the stick hand and is useful when the goalie can get the "blocker" on the puck and deflect it. (See photo 9-15.)

258

9-14 Using the "trapper," a glove similar to the one worn by a first baseman and designed to catch the puck. Photo by Tim Hewitt.

9-15 Using the blocker, a glove backed with a thick block of leather worn on the stick hand and useful for deflecting the puck. Photo by Tim Hewitt.

Screen Shots

When the goalie has difficulty seeing the play because teammates and opponents block his vision, he should crouch as low as possible and look for the puck between the skaters' legs. He must also move away any opponent parked in or near his crease. If a shot is taken that the goalie cannot see, he can go down in a "V" save position to cover most of the net or lower the shaft of the stick to cover a shot along the ice. Of course, by using either or both of these maneuvers the goalie is betting the shooter won't aim for the upper part of the net. If the goalie has any doubts, he can maintain his basic stance and try to locate the puck after the shot has been made.

Flip Shot

This shot can be difficult for the goalie. He can lose sight of the puck in the lights or background or it can take a crazy bounce when it hits the ice. The goalie has several options on a flip shot. He can skate out of the net and catch the puck, or he can get his body in front of the puck and block it. No one can predict what a puck will do after it bounces off the ice, so the goalie must be extra careful, remembering that it is easy for the puck to bounce past him and into the net.

Tip-Ins

Good, sound, basic goaltending is the key here. The goalie must keep an eye on the puck even when it deflects off a skate, a stick, or a body, while maintaining balance and the ability to move in any direction to stop the puck.

Breakaways and Penalty Shots

The goalie should skate out of his net to cut down the shooter's angle, but as the skater gets closer the goalie should begin to skate back, still keeping the angle cut down. The closer the shooter gets to the net the better chance the goalie has of making the save. Let the shooter make the first move. Some goalies don't like to come out too far, because they feel vulnerable to low shots while backing into the net.

If an opponent is on a breakaway, there is always the chance a teammate will check him as he moves laterally in an attempt to deke the goalie. Of course, the goalie won't have the benefit of a teammate on a penalty shot. It's only him against the shooter.

Rebounds

Goalies must work diligently at controlling rebounds. As discussed, a goalie can catch the puck, deflect it into a corner, or smother it. But when rebounds occur, and they will, it is best for the goalie to maintain his basic stance and stay in front of the puck to make a second save.

He can further control a rebound by raising his buttocks slightly, thereby straightening the angle of his pads, which in turn gives the puck a soft or "dead" rebound off the pads.

One of the reasons a goalie may give up a lot of rebounds is a stiff, too rigid grip on the stick. It is recommended that a goalie always hold the stick with a relaxed grip, which gives the puck a soft or "dead" rebound.

A WORD ABOUT POSITIONAL PLAY

Positional play is just as important for a goalie (maybe more so) as it is for any other team member, but is simply different. For instance, rule of thumb for the goalie is to take up his stance at the front corner of the crease to whichever side the puck carrier swerves around the defense, heading for one of the face-off circles. This position cuts down the angles from both corners and forces the puck carrier (usually) deeper, whereupon the goalie can back into his net until hugging the post of that same side.

If the goalie takes up his position at the outer edge of his crease (always in relation to the puck carrier), he can then (1) glide out and into a shot after it has been taken, to further cut down the angle, or (2) glide back into his net in several directions in relation to the shooter.

When the puck is behind the net and to one side, the goalie always plays as closely as possible to the goal post on that side. If the puck is on the "trapper" side, drop the trapper alongside the pad, with the thumb turned out, which puts the trapper in catching position. If the puck is on the stick side, turn the blade of the stick over so that the puck cannot bounce in front of the net. Make sure to play the puck on the stick side before it crosses the goal line.

FACE-OFFS

Without any question a goalie can be faulted if an opponent scores directly off a face-off. It should never happen!

The goalie should face the puck on an angle with pads slightly open, allowing no room on the *short* side (that's the stick hand side), and coming out just enough to cut down the angle on the *long* side. The "trapper" should be at his side.

The face-off should be set up so that no teammates screen the goalie. A sharp eye should be kept on how the opposition is lining up for the face-off. That indicates what they may do if they gain control of the puck.

HELPFUL HINTS

1. Stay on foot as much as possible. Don't flop.
2. There are two basic methods to use to rise after falling to the ice: by using just one leg, or by using the *inside* edge of both skates and springing up.
3. Shots *off* net (off target) should not be played, unless they might rebound dangerously.
4. Practice without a stick to develop good footwork and an excellent "trapper."
5. Study and learn opponents' shooting styles.
6. Remember, when the goalie is out of the crease, he is fair game.
7. When play is at the other end of the ice, stand erect and take as relaxed a position as possible, but keep an eye on the puck, and if the puck advances out of the offensive zone, assume the basic stance, ready for a shot.
8. If the opposition succeeds in a two-man—or even three-man—rush, the goalie should always cut down the angle on the puck carrier, not attempting to play the other opponents, unless the puck is passed to them.
9. Be alert for a penalty call against the opposition. If play continues (until opponent touches puck), the goalie can be "pulled" from his net for an extra skater, without fear of a goal being scored against.
10. If it is late in the game and the team is behind, the coach may want to replace the goalie with an extra skater. Keep an eye on the bench to see what the coach wants to do.

10

TACTICS AND SYSTEMS OF PLAY

POSITIONAL PLAY AND TEAM PLAY

The object of the game of hockey is to score goals, but even more basic to the sport is the concept of teamwork. Unless the player truly understands and plays with a deep sense of what teamwork is all about, those goals will not be scored. There have been many losing teams in the NHL with high goal scorers, but without the network or support system that is teamwork.

Unfortunately, the glamorous side of hockey—the offense—has taken such precedence over solid defensive play that the notion of teamwork has become skewed, with many teams simply becoming puck-feeding mechanisms for their offensive stars. But if one looks at the teams that have won the Stanley Cup in the past decade—or throughout the history of the award—one sees that there are few champion teams that didn't have that perfect mesh of teamwork and balanced positional play.

There are certain basics to remember about teamwork and positional play. Perhaps the first and most basic is the proverb, "no man is an island." Each player (no matter how many goals he or she scores) is as important as his or her teammates, but no more. In fact, when skating down the ice with or without the puck, a player would do well to remember constantly that the rest of the team is more important than he is—after all, there are five of them.

Next in importance for team play is to learn the team's system, totally, and then try to integrate that philosophy and methodology completely. On offense, know the team's theory of play, on defense, adhere completely to the team's defensive system. This sounds a bit simple-minded, but in fact it is one of the hardest principles of team play to learn. Many a youngster—even a pro—loses touch with the team philosophy at the sight of a loose puck, and with personal glory in mind takes off without his mates, only to find himself up-ice without a mate to pass to.

Speaking of the lone breakaway: It looks flashy, but it really is not good for overall team play. The offensive player should at all times be trying to create a two-on-one situation; in other words, a potential for give-and-take.

Another important principle for the offensive team member to keep in mind is that if a teammate has the puck, the offensive player should try to position himself to receive a pass, redirect the puck, take a shot, or simply pass again to a mate who is in a better goal-scoring position. The puck carrier should try never to give it away or throw it away. Far too much offensive play simply consists of dumping the puck over the opponent's blue line, which totally defeats the purpose of the advance up-ice and too often yields control of the puck to the opponent.

For the defensive player, variations of the same rule apply: to remember that he is still playing a hockey game when he does not have the puck or the man he is covering does not have it either. Keep working, continue to cover the man, look for a loose opponent, try to recover the puck. Most important for the defensive player is to remember that the defense is as important as the offense. The great Bobby Orr (Boston Bruins and Chicago Black Hawks) started a trend of offensive, goal-scoring defensemen who have turned every youngster's head, unfortunately. The day of the defensive defenseman has virtually passed, and the game is in dire need of good, solid defensemen who don't lead rushes up-ice every time the puck arrives in their zone.

Positional play has changed greatly in the past decade and a half of professional hockey in North America. First, the development of the offensive defenseman, along with the "non-alley" offensive style currently in vogue, has completely altered the concept of positional play.

Despite the changes that have taken place, there still exist today—at least in name—a center and two wings (left and right), who comprise the forward offensive unit, and the defense consists of a left and right defense, with a goalie as the last line of defense.

It once was true, though, that when a team got the puck and moved it up to the forwards, the classic situation was that the center would take the puck up the center zone, then pass off to one of the wingers as they skated up their "alleys" or lanes over the opponent's blue line. Wingers were encouraged to rigid positional play, and spent most of their careers skating up and down their "alley" faithfully, without deviating, if possible. A wandering winger was considered a problem case, and if he couldn't maintain his position, was often trade bait.

The Center

The center is traditionally known as the playmaker. An excellent skater, the center is required to pass either from the forehand or backhand position, to either wing. The center is expected to pass the puck ahead to his wingers as much as possible, yet he is to take the lead in forechecking. If the winger crosses the opponent's blue line first, however, the center should take up the winger's position. More than any other position, the center should follow the puck at all times. Even in traditional positional hockey, the center is allowed leeway to cover the entire offensive zone in order to follow the puck.

Right and Left Wings

Traditional wingers are expected to skate up and down their alleys, a lane no wider than twenty or twenty-five feet from the boards. Wingers check their opposing wingers and should be able to stay ahead of their opponents when skating back to their own end of the ice. Hopefully, wingers are also capable of skating backwards when necessary, switching roles when necessary. In the offensive zone they should play the puck, finishing the plays started by the center; but in their defensive zone, they should play the man, just as the defenseman does. Like the center, the winger must be a good skater and excellent passer.

Traditionally, left shots played left wing and right shots played right wing. (See page 174 for definition of left-hand and right-hand shot.) This was seemingly logical, since this meant that the winger was then taking passes on his forehand. But when the puck is in the offensive zone, it also means that the winger has the puck on his board side, which is a difficult position from which to shoot. "Playing the off-wing" is becoming more and more common today. This simply means that a right shot plays left wing, and the reverse, too. This enhances the possibilities for wingers scoring from better angles. It also means that a player, of necessity, must learn how to take a pass on the backhand. With the modern system of play, which is almost constant motion, there is less stopping of the forwards to retrieve passes or switching of the puck from backhand to forehand to set up shots or other passes.

Defensemen

One of the worst aspects of traditional hockey—strict positional play—was that since the defensemen rarely led rushes up-ice nor scored often, they were often poor, or at least slow, skaters. The primary requirement was the ability to skate backwards and play the man. The ability to move sideways, or laterally, was another must.

Even though the whole basis for positional play is changing today, there are still certain dos and don'ts for defensemen. When the defenseman is the only player left between the opposition in possession of the puck and his net, he must never stickhandle the puck; "play the man" is the absolute bottom line. Nor should the defenseman pass blindly out of his own zone. The blind pass more often than not simply yields the puck back to the opposition. Not only should the defenseman not make blind passes, but he should be master of quick, short passes to his forwards.

Another indicator of why the defenseman should be a better skater than was expected a few years ago, is the fact that the defenseman should be capable of moving with the play, rather than simply standing guard between his blue line and the opponent's blue line. The defenseman should follow his forwards over the opposing blue line, taking up the "point" position just inside the line (this term is most often heard when referring to the power play, when the "point" position is crucial). Then, if the opposition regains the puck and breaks out, the defenseman must be able to move backwards rapidly, hopefully in tandem with his defensive partner.

The two defensemen should stay relatively close together—no more than twenty feet apart—as they move back, but once the opposition has moved into their defensive zone, they should split their duties—one playing the puck if possible, while the other takes up a position directly in front of the net, in order to check or remove the opposing forwards.

Defensemen must be well-versed in various methods of checking, as discussed in the chapter on skills, but some coaches believe they must also be adept at blocking shots in front of their own net—a rough assignment. Very simply, when the defenseman senses a forthcoming shot right on net, he skates (or glides) somewhat closer to the shooter and then, at the last second, drops to one or both knees, taking the shot in the knees, thighs, or chest. Naturally, if the shooter looks as though he's about to blast off a slap shot that will rise to waist height, dropping to the knees is suicidal—no defenseman is expected to take a blast in the face. So, estimating the shot, the power of the shot, and the height of the shot is difficult but crucial when blocking. Long practices with tennis balls (softer and less scary for younger players) being shot at the net can develop the defenseman's skill at blocking shots.

RECENT CHANGES

Since the late 1960s the game of hockey has been revolutionized with regard to positional play. While there had been offensive defensemen before Bobby Orr, such as Red Kelly in the fifties, Eddie Shore in the twenties and thirties, and Lester Patrick before that, it was really Orr who freed the modern defenseman to lead rushes and score goals. Now, as often as not, it is a good skating and stickhandling defenseman who leads the team up the ice, while the forwards do more lateral skating in the neutral zone, preparing to receive passes or to scoot across the opponent's blue line once the defenseman has carried the puck through the neutral zone.

But besides Bobby Orr, there has been the Russians. "The Russians" has become a catch-all phrase for an entire system of hockey training as well as playing technique and philosophy. The Russians have been most adept at the new system and have developed much of the style, but it is really best called the "European Method," since it is now employed by the Czechs, Swedes, Finns, and virtually all European teams.

Basically, the style and technique is motion, motion, motion. Instead of a lot of stoppage of play—for setting up passes, for hard (and often illegal) checking, for setting up shots—the game is one of constant motion. Plays are set up in such a way that instead of stopping to receive a pass, a player is constantly attempting to be in position to receive a pass without pausing (another example of why playing off-wing is so important today), to shoot on the fly, never to "dump" the puck over the opponent's blue line, to stickhandle right up to the opponent's net, not to freeze the puck in the corners. Passing—almost a lost art ten years ago—has become the name of the game, and defensemen are expected to be adept at lateral passing as well as the traditional forward pass to the center.

Such style and technique requires incredible stamina. Furthermore, the small, agile player is making a comeback in North America, thanks to the "European technique."

North American hockey had crystallized into a dogged system of "brawn over brain" until international competition level forced the NHL to rethink its game. Although the small, fast-skating stick artist had been an accepted part of hockey years ago, NHL hockey had become "Americanized" since the early sixties. This is not to say that Americans were actually playing the game (this has only happened in the last few years), but that the "American way" had come to pervade the thinking about the game. The "policeman," a respected member of every team, evolved from being the protector of the little guys on the team, to a huge, brawling goon, or hit man, often sent out gratuitously to remove, maim, or otherwise terrorize the opposition. Team size as a whole increased enormously, and the average hockey team began to look like an American football team. The small player virtually disappeared, and it was even whispered that anybody less than 5'10" and around 180 pounds couldn't really play NHL hockey.

Then the NHL played the Russians (see the chapter on history), and although the NHLers pounded them into oblivion in their first few confrontations, the Russians just kept skating, passing, and scoring. The level of conditioning, the stamina, the passing ability, the outstanding stickhandling began to make an impression. Canadian and American coaches began traveling (and working) in Europe, to learn the year-round conditioning and training techniques. It was only a matter of time before the "control through motion" would return to North America.

Yes, that's the right word, "return." Because the fact is, this style of hockey is a modernized adaptation of what was played in North America thirty, forty, and fifty years ago. Herb Brooks, coach of the gold medal–winning U.S. Olympics hockey team and most recently coach of the New York Rangers, is a big proponent of the European style and imported many small players to the Rangers. It was he who observed, "If we persist in the 'motion technique' here in North America, soon we'll be playing the way it was done in the thirties!"

Thus it is that positional play and team play in North American hockey are undergoing total revision. With new legislation against violence, the goon is slowly disappearing back into the minor leagues. The small player is having a renaissance, and everybody on the team, including the defensemen, is required to think of passing, passing, passing—moving, moving, moving.

THE FACE-OFF

No matter how adept a team becomes at the new system of controlling the puck through constant motion, getting the puck in the first place is absolutely essential. The face-off and controlling the face-off is the first step toward controlling the game. If one were to study the statistics of a typical game, invariably the team who wins the game is the team that dominates the face-off circle. In fact, many NHL teams have "face-off specialists." If a face-off specialist also happens to be a good goal scorer, then he's nearly perfect. Philadelphia's Bobby Clarke is the ideal example. Despite diabetes, Clarke is an absolutely devoted, deeply talented player who is the scourge of the face-off circle. Traditionally the player who "took the draw" was (and often still is) the center, since he was the playmaker for the line anyway. This makes sense because the player taking the draw is also responsible for placing all the rest of his teammates around the face-off circle. The player taking the draw in a face-off is the hockey equivalent to the quarterback in football.

There are certain basic rules which pertain to any face-off, anywhere on the ice and there are rules that apply to certain face-offs in certain areas. The primary goal, of course, is control of the puck. How this would best be done depends on the score of the game, the time of the game, who is participating in the face-off, and where the face-off is taking place.

Technique, speed, and intelligence can be virtually everything in a face-off. The player taking the draw must not only be able to position his teammates best (and instruct them how to block or hold up the opposition), but he must also be able to accurately assess the strengths and weaknesses of his opponents, patiently take his time to structure the face-off to his own designs, and *never* remain in position in the circle if his opponent is not in proper stance and readiness. In fact, if the opponent is improperly positioned, the player *must* withdraw from the circle or face sure defeat and outmaneuvering. The face-off player must also anticipate the official's moves, move with lightning speed and accuracy, and yet avoid too much repetition of his moves, to prevent stereotyping or telegraphing his technique to the opposition. Finally, he should have beforehand a precise idea of what he intends to do with the puck if he gains control of it.

Generally, the player taking the draw should hold his stick in the normal position (some players take a reverse grasp with their lower hands in order to pull to their backhand—Bobby Clarke is a notable exception who gets away with this maneuver), because doing otherwise will simply telegraph the intention to the opposition. Place the stick lightly on the ice where the puck will be dropped and keep the toes straight ahead with weight balanced evenly on both skates. The player doesn't look at the face-off circle, but keeps his head in position to watch the official's hands, ready to deal with the fact that many officials drop the puck so violently that it takes a large bounce.

The first face-off in any game is at center ice, and the standard move would be for the center to draw the puck back (on his backhand) to a defenseman. As the face-off man sends the puck back to the defenseman, the other forwards should "screen" their opponents, giving the defenseman time to take over the puck, and begin the offensive move out of the neutral zone. The advantage to this move is that the opposition must remain behind the center line until the puck is dropped.

Occasionally the man on the draw wants to shoot the puck rapidly toward the opposition end of the ice, in which case the winger on the side to which the puck is shot would move rapidly in that direction to force action on the puck. If the man on the draw cannot get control of the puck immediately, but it remains in the face-off area, he should instantly attempt to hold up his opponent, allowing a teammate (usually a winger) to enter the circle and steal the puck.

If the puck is successfully sent back to the defense, the face-off player can simply wait for a return pass from the defenseman, or skate to one of the wing positions, allowing that winger to skate in for the return pass from the defenseman. It is generally desirable to first send the puck back to the defenseman when taking a face-off in the neutral or defensive zones; since the opposition's defense is ready, before the red center line or their blue line, it is entirely possible that they could gain possession and shoot the puck back into the defense zone. Giving possession to the defense gives a team time to set up its offensive strategy.

Some think the difference between neutral and offensive zone face-offs and those taken in the defensive zone is the difference between winning and losing. In other words, in the neutral and offensive zones, always plan a face-off to be won. In the defensive zone, plan the action as though the face-off could be lost. While the hope is to win, strategy should be structured as though the face-off will be lost. Basically this means setting it up so that every opposing member of the face-off will be checked; concentrate on playing the man rather than the puck.

There are several schools of thought on the strategy of the defensive zone face-off: one, as described above, recommends approaching it as though it can be lost; but another says, no, *never* plan a strategy as though a face-off can be lost, in fact, the defensive zone face-off is a *must-win* situation.

In the most recent Amateur Hockey Association of the United States (AHAUS) *Intermediate Coaches Manual,* the offensive and defensive zone face-offs are categorized as "win-only" strategies, whereas the neutral zone face-off is described more as a "check and control" situation. No matter how simple the strategy of a sport, there are philosophies for every level, coach, and league!

The following diagrams explain the most common face-off situations and how they would be handled in any zone and under any game conditions.

SYMBOLS FOR FACEOFF DIAGRAMS

Home team ◯   Player skating ◯→

Opposition ✗   Screening opposition ◯-(

Puck traveling --→

ADDITIONAL SYMBOL FOR BREAKOUTS

Player skating with the puck ◯〜→

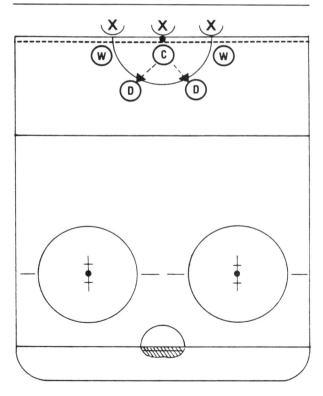

Diagram A

The center-ice faceoff *The center-ice faceoff takes place at the beginning of each period and after each goal is scored. The object of the faceoff is to gain contrtol of the puck and proceed with an offensive attack. The standard move is for the center to play the puck back to one of his defensemen. While the defenseman gets the puck under control, the center and the two wingers screen the opposing forwards.*

Variation: Occasionally the center may want to shoot the puck into the opponent's end of the ice and quickly forecheck. After the center shoots on his forehand, the winger on that side should break in to force the puck.

Once the standard pass back to the defense has taken place, there are a couple of basic possibilities for beginning an attack. If the center allows the opponent to skate by him toward the defenseman with the puck, he can then simply wait in the faceoff circle for a return pass from the defenseman, at which point he takes off. Or the center can skate one opposing winger off to one side and allow one of his wings to skate into the middle for the defenseman's return pass.

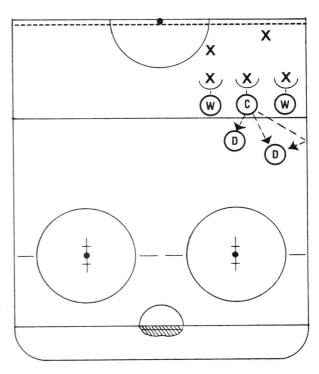

Diagram B

Faceoff At One's Own Blueline *Since this situation takes place at or just outside one's own defensive zone, the object is to gain quick control of the puck and to begin a drive up ice out of this area. As with the center-ice faceoff, the standard move is to play the puck back to a defenseman and then screen the opposing forwards until the puck is under control.*

Variation: Another option is to play the puck forward to a designated fast-breaking wing. However, this is frequently "read" and interrupted by an opposing defenseman, and should be done only with extreme caution.

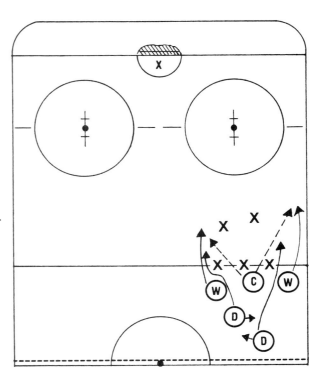

Diagram C

Faceoff At the Opposing Blueline *It is somewhat less expensive to lose a draw in this area, so the center may want to play the puck ahead into his offensive zone (Remember, this is the opponent's* defensive *zone!) There is always the conventional option of sending it back to one of the defensemen in order to gain control.*

Note in Diagram C that the center can play the puck forward to either wing, and as the puck is dropped the defenseman on that wing will speed ahead and get into position to screen the opposing defender. The other defenseman falls in behind the center as the offensive attack proceeds.

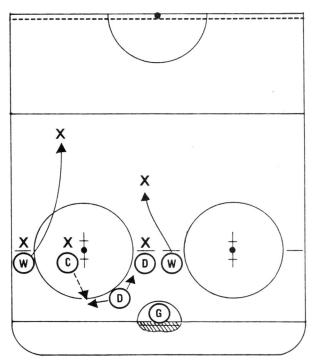

Diagram D₁

Faceoffs in the defensive zone *(Diagrams D₁, and D₂) These situations are where the most disagreement exists as to what the object of the faceoff should be for the defending team. Some say a team should always set themselves up as though they will lose the draw, but others say this is the absolute "must win" instance. In any case, there are two basic setups in the defensive zone, in which the opposing team will most likely dictate the face-off structure and the "home" team will set itself up as a response to the opposition.*

In Diagram D₁, while the center attempts to get the puck back to the defenseman in front of the goal, the wingers instantly skate up-ice to cover the opposition "points," and the other defenseman prepares to cover the opposing wing nearest the goal crease.

The defensive zone faceoff should always be taken by the team's best faceoff expert, but if it is impossible to gain control of the puck, the goal is to clear it and prevent a shot on goal.

Diagram D₂

In Diagram D₂ the defensive center once again tries to send the puck back to the defenseman nearest the goal, but in this case the opposition has placed a wing in the slot position on the outer parameter of the faceoff circle. The defending wing near the faceoff circle must then be prepared to do two things: either cover that opposing wing in the slot, and/or skate out to check or screen the opposing defenseman on the point.

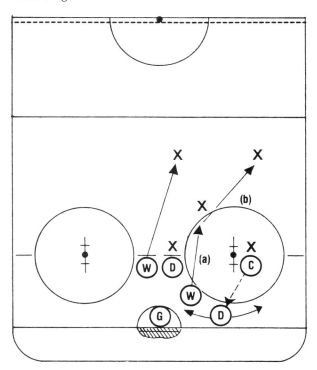

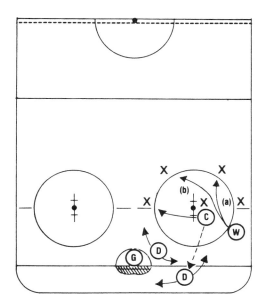

Diagram E₁

Short-handed faceoff in the defensive zone
(Diagrams E₁, E₂, and E₃)

In this situation the primary goal is to get the puck and either clear it or "rag" it (skate with the puck, keeping it away from the opposition), when the equally important problem of covering the opposition while down a man must also be considered. The basic plan must be to set up the few players at hand in such a way as to cover the opposition through several possible combinations. Diagrams E₁ and E₂ show possible moves for each defending player, depending on which opposition player gets the puck, while diagram E₃ shows a less conventional option. Note that in E₃ one defenseman is taking the faceoff, contrary to the standard practice of using one's best center for the crucial draw.

Diagram E₂

The theory behind this instance is that it is most important to cover the potential opposition scorers as quickly as possible. And since if the puck goes behind the circle there is little chance of a goal's being scored from there, a defenseman is not really needed behind the circle. Instead he takes the draw, leaving opportunity for the two forwards to move out as quickly as possible to deal with the slot and/or the points. The plan also enables the defending team to set up the box zone defense most easily while playing in its own end.

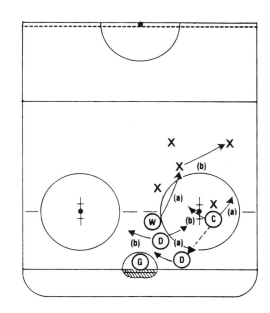

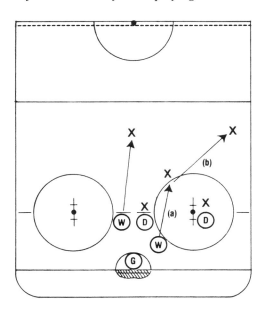

Diagram E₃

Defenseman taking the draw while short-handed in the defensive zone

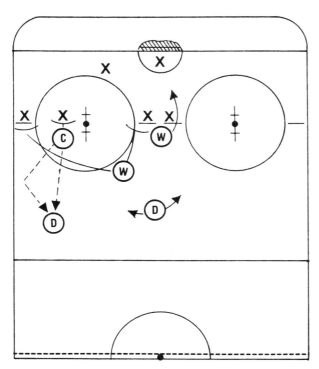

Diagram F

Faceoff in the offensive zone *When facing off in the offensive zone, the thought is always to win or at least get a shot on goal. Even if the draw is lost, the opposition has a long skate to get into scoring position!*

In Diagram F the center plays the puck back to the point for a shot on goal. One wing breaks to the net for a possible rebound or deflection. The other wing (and/or the center) screens the opposition, allowing time for the shot. The other defenseman will play the blueline as the shooting defenseman follows his shot in.

Variation The center can also play the puck back to the top of the faceoff circle for a quick shot, or he can shoot on goal himself.

OFFENSIVE TEAM PLAY

Bringing the Puck Out of the Defensive Zone

There are two basic ways a team can bring the puck out of its own defensive zone—the controlled break-out and the breakaway. In the controlled break-out, the entire team moves at the same speed out of the zone. Usually the defensive squad assumes control of the puck after an opponent has shot it in. Remember first and foremost that many goals are scored by the opposition after they yield the puck when the defense makes an error while in possession, attempting to set up a controlled break-out.

The following diagrams describe several options for setting up a controlled break-out, depending on the opposition's method of forechecking.

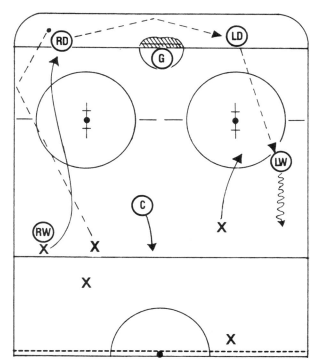

Diagram G. Breakouts

In Diagram G the opposing team dumps the puck into the offensive zone (the "home team's" defensive zone). The right defenseman sees the oncoming check and plays the puck off the backboards to the left defenseman. He in turn quickly passes it ahead to the left wing, who skates it out of the zone.

Diagram H

In this instance the opposition is employing the 2–1–2 system of forechecking, in which the two opposing wings forecheck the two defending rearguards and the opposing center hangs back, looking for a pass. The opposing defensemen play the point positions.

The left defenseman, under pressure, passes the puck to the right defenseman, who plays it up to the center, near the middle. The center passes to his right wing and the winger is off in a controlled breakout.

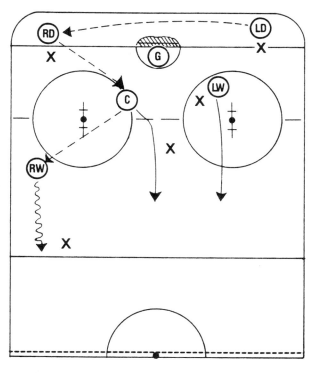

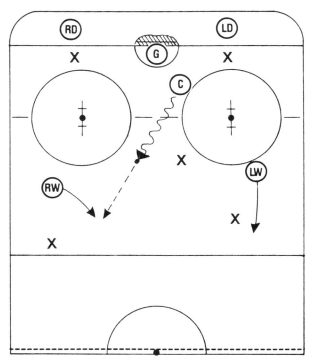

Diagram I

In Diagram I the opposition again employs the 2–1–2 forechecking mode, but this time the left defenseman cannot pass to the right defenseman, because he is too heavily checked. Not only that, the left defenseman is about to be hit himself, which will leave a loose puck around the net. Instead, he rapidly passes forward to the center, who then puckhandles until he, too, meets a forechecker. At that precise moment, the center passes off to the right wing, who has been moving toward center.

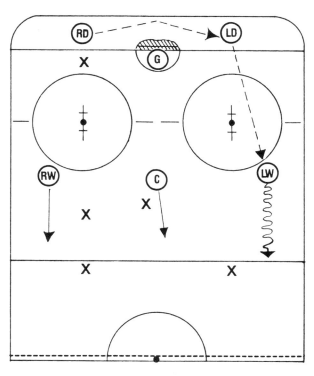

Diagram J

Using the 1–4 method of forechecking, the lone opposing forechecker is deep in the defensive zone, forcing the right defenseman to pass behind the goal cage to the left defenseman. Left defense sends the puck ahead to the left wing, who then attempts to "muscle" it up along the boards. Since the center ice area is clogged with four opposition players, passing among the forwards in this instance is not only difficult but dangerous.

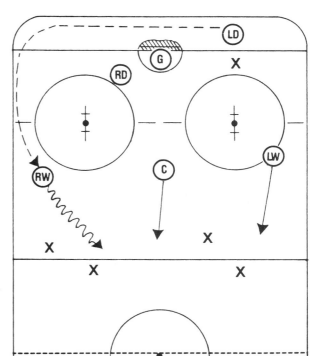

Diagram K

Once again breaking out against a 1–4 forechecking system, the left defenseman caroms the puck all the way around the boards to the right wing, who skates rapidly toward an opening at center ice.

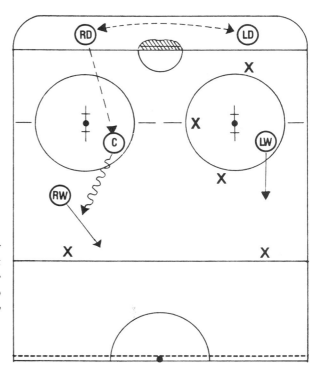

Diagram L

Breaking out against a 2–3 forechecking system, the left defenseman passes the puck to the right defenseman. Right defense sends the puck forward to the center, who then crisscrosses with the right wing, as they skate up the weak side of the opposition.

Offensive Play

Obviously, if a team has made a breakaway out of their defensive zone, they have the advantage of numbers, and taking advantage of those numbers should head immediately into the offensive zone and set up a scoring situation. The breakaway, however, is not the standard situation when a team in control of the puck nears center ice. Often there is some sort of "regrouping" necessary in the neutral zone before skating into the offensive zone.

The first play, one that every team *with* the puck should try to avoid but every defending team should try to accomplish, is when the defense stands its ground before its blue line and the puckhandler cannot find a way to get the puck across that line except for "dumping." Even when it is necessary to shoot the puck into the offensive zone, the puck carrier (usually the center) should at least attempt to shoot the puck in such a way that it will carom off the back boards at an angle the winger can deal with, hopefully by a shot on goal. Today's motion offense often makes it impossible for the defending team to simply plant itself at its blue line and "stonewall" the team with the puck. If a team is constantly looking for ways to move the puck forward, it is extremely difficult for the defending team to forecheck thoroughly, and the defense cannot stand implacable at the blue line.

One on One

Virtually the only way for the puck carrier to get around the lone defender is by forcing him into making a mistake. There are several ways of tempting him into a slip.

The first rule for the puck carrier is never to skate directly at the defender. He should first try to make him look at the puck—stickhandling rapidly or making it look almost as though he "giving" the defender the puck on his stick. If the defender slips, looking at the puck or moving for it, the puck carrier skates right around him.

Faking or deking can also cause the defender to slip up. By shifting his weight to one skate, or slipping the puck between the defender's legs, the puck carrier then skates to the opposite side and continues on. The attacker may drop the puck back on his stick, dip that shoulder, and, when the defender moves, straighten up and move out. A fake shot—usually a slap shot—can make the defender pause, enabling the attacker to move around him.

Two on Two

This is basically a double one-on-one situation, and the offense should try to turn it into a two-on-one if possible. The best move would be for the puck carrier to move toward one defenseman and then treat the situation as though it were two-on-one, which follows.

Two on One

This situation occurs most frequently in hockey, and there is no reason why it should not culminate in a shot on goal. It is thus a situation that a team should work to perfect. The puck carrier is the key player on the two-on-one.

In the classic two-on-one situation, the puck carrier takes the puck around the lone defender, who tries to stay between the two attackers, backing slowly toward his net. The puck carrier should try to make the defender commit himself, and if he drives close enough to the net, the defenseman has no alternative but to move slightly toward him. If the defenseman commits himself, the puck carrier should immediately pass over, or back, to the other attacker, then continue moving in toward the net, to nab a possible rebound. If the defenseman refuses to commit, the puck carrier has little alternative but to take a shot on goal, attempting to do so before he loses the angle completely. Both attackers should still continue in toward the net for rebounds or forechecking, should the defenseman or goalie recover the puck. In traditional two-on-one the rule was never make more than one pass, but with today's constant motion schools of hockey, this rule has gone bye-bye.

Another technique would be for the two attackers to constantly pass between each other as they drive hard at the defenseman. As the defenseman attempts to follow the rapid passing done at high speed, he may falter, move toward one or another attacker, or simply move out of the center position between them, giving one attacker the angle and a clear shot.

A faked shot by the puck carrier followed by a drop pass to his trailing partner is sometimes successful. The former puck carrier would then continue into the opponent's defensive zone to screen or check the defenseman, to pick up the rebound or deflect a shot.

Finally, if a winger is the puck carrier, he may skate (passing back and forth with other attackers until they are over the opponent's blue line) to a designated spot (determined by long and intense practice sessions) and quickly turn *toward* the boards, pivoting away from the commited defenseman and pass quickly to the other attacker who is now centered and right on goal.

Three on Two

In the speed and passion of a hockey game it is often difficult to realize that one's team has a three-on-two about to happen, and it is essential to have some kind of a team signal system. Then the squad would do well to set itself up in the neutral zone, primarily to get the puck centered, so that offensive play can go to either side of the opponent's goal.

Again, in the three-on-two situation, the attackers are striving to create a two-on-one someplace near the goal where a lone defender is stuck with two attackers.

If the centerman takes the puck in, the two wings should skate in with him as far as possible, thus cutting down the possibility of a defender taking out two men. The center skates toward one defender and attempts to draw him out of position. If he succeeds, he then passes to the wing on the side that no longer has a defender. If he cannot draw a defenseman out of position, the center must shoot while the wings go in for the rebound.

The center can also stop with the puck just inside the opponent's blue line, in the hope that a defender will come out to get him. If this happens, the center then passes to the wing who is not being checked. If the defenseman does not come out, the puck carrier passes to one of the wings who continues on toward the goal or takes a long shot.

If one of the wingers is the designated puck carrier, he should still skate in, as far as possible from the centerman, even if the defenseman drives him into the boards, since the puck will often still continue into the offensive zone. But if the wing stays wide and takes one defender with him, the other defenseman is now confronted with a two-on-one, and the puck-carrying wing should pass off to the center or far wing, whoever is open for the shot.

Three on One

This is one occasion that should never arise in a hockey game, but when it happens, the offense should be happy. Even when a team suddenly gets a three-on-one situation, it more often than not flubs it. The whole on-ice squad should be made aware of the opportunity with a designated signal, and whoever is the puck carrier when the situation arises must not hog the puck, which is the most immediate tendency. With all that ice and only one defender before the opposing goal, it is difficult not to skate blithely away, attempting to do it solo. But the puck carrier should always remember that centering the puck for the optimum number of moves and passes to be made down ice is always the best first move. Then simply make whatever moves are necessary from all of the foregoing in order to create the best shot or shots possible.

Some general rules apply to attacking play in the offensive zone. A team in possession of the puck must always think offensively, but it is essential at the same time to keep one player from the forward line in a position to back-check and aid the defense if the puck should be lost. Simultaneously it is to a team's advantage to keep a forward planted in front of the net, thereby occupying one whole defender and putting a man in position for a quick shot. If things are too crowded in front of the net, the attackers may put a man in the "slot." (Many people mistakenly think that the "slot" is the spot right in front of the net. Wrong. The "slot" is midway between the two face-off circles.) Or they may place two men on or near the two face-off circles, setting up several pass and shooting options.

When the area around the net and the end boards is too crowded and neither shot nor lateral pass is recommended, this usually means that the two attackers back at the blue line (if they are actually across the opponent's blue line, they are "point" men) may be in the clear. A pass back to one of the points would open up shooting options.

Only years of game experience can give a player that sense when one more pass will be too many and when the moment is ripe for the shot on goal. One problem today with the increased use of the quick lateral pass is that forwards often do too much passing in the offensive zone, missing shots. Or they pass for too long and the pressure they put on the defense reverses: they finally blow a pass, lose the puck, and find themselves with all their forwards caught up-ice—potential disaster.

Forechecking

Forechecking is a pressing defensive system that takes place in the opponent's defensive zone. The object of forechecking is (1) to prevent the opposition from mounting an attack while still behind its own blue line, and (2) to regain control of the puck, thereby resuming the offense in the opponent's end of the ice.

Basically there are two setups that employ two men forward and three men back and one basic strategy that employs one man forward and four back. In all cases, as long as the puck remains behind the blue line, the five attackers remain inside the blue line also.

The first two-man-forward system is as follows: As the winger covering the puck carrier moves in to play the man, the center also moves in, at an angle, to stop the pass.

The defenseman on that side is back, but moves forward slightly to check his wing, while the other winger stays at the top of the face-off circle, ready to move in for a shot if the puck is regained or to check the opposing center if he moves out. The last defenseman is positioned at the blue line, ready to cover the center or the remaining opposing winger.

This forechecking system leaves everyone several options depending on what the opposition does, and they can respond by either checking or moving into attack and shoot positions.

The next two-man-forward strategy is basically man-to-man coverage. The wingers cover the opposing defense, the center covers the opposing center, and the defensemen cover the opposing wings. The winger who is covering the puck-carrying defenseman moves in to play the man (not the puck), while the other wing also moves in but will block his check from receiving a pass. The defensemen both move in to check the opposing wings, also to prevent them from receiving a pass. Again, the situation is "play the man not the puck," where it is essential to keep the wings from breaking out. The center must cover the opposing center and also be ready to move back and cover for either of the defensemen.

The one-man-forward system, or 1–4, is as follows: Center in front of goal, wingers covering wingers, and defense either lined up near the blue line ready to cover the center in any fashion or lined up behind center, prepared to do the same.

General rules to follow in forechecking include working diligently and constantly to develop all of these strategies and being prepared to switch to any system, depending on the speed and abilities of the opposition, the time, and the score. Developing the forechecking capabilities of forwards is often neglected today, but think of it this way: if a team forechecked perfectly, the opposition would never get the puck out of its own end.

DEFENSIVE SITUATIONS

One on One

As the offense moves down-ice, the first thing the defenseman must do is check, as he skates backwards, to make sure that the opposing wings are being covered. If they are, a defenseman can concentrate on the puck carrier and the general center zone of the ice. If not, he *cannot* commit himself.

As play moves into the neutral zone, the defenseman skates backwards, stick extended, attempting to force the puck carrier into committing a particular move without doing so himself. No matter what, the defenseman is looking at the man, never the puck, He can watch the puck carrier's face and eyes to see if he will telegraph a move, but as they near the defender's blue line, he should begin to watch the puck carrier's mid-body area—which also telegraphs moves.

If the defender in question is alone, he should try not to body check the puck carrier, because a miss leaves the puck carrier all alone with only the goalie to go.

Another rule of thumb is not to body check the opponent if he has his head up (as he should); do so only if he has his head down and the check is a certain hit.

The primary thing to remember in defending in a one-on-one situation is that it is a situation between equals. The thought that being on the defensive is "inferior" to being on the offense can do the most harm. If, however, the puck carrier succeeds in getting around the defenseman, the defender can still attempt a check as a last resort. If beaten, the defenseman should attempt to skate directly to the goal, trying one more time to cut off the puck carrier or a shot.

A last rule for the defense to remember is never to back too far in toward the goaltender, which screens him from possible shots. At the same time it is important to back up at an angle *slightly* toward the goaltender, in an attempt to keep the puck carrier screened from the goal at all times.

Two on Two

This situation would basically be a double one-on-one were it not for the fortunate fact (for the defenders) that the goalie gives the defending team a one-man advantage. But the defensemen still each takes one offensive player and remembers (1) not to back in too far and screen the goalie, and (2) to back up at an angle that keeps the puck carrier outside.

If the puck carrier switches sides, the defensemen should then switch the player each is covering, rather than one defenseman crossing in front of his partner to chase the puck carrier. All of this should be done with a maximum amount of communication between defensive partners—yell at each other if necessary.

If the puck carrier takes a shot, the defenseman covering him should play the body and stop him from continuing toward the net, while the other defender should go immediately for the puck, preferably pivoting in front of the opponent to beat him to the puck.

The general guidelines, then, are to play the situation man-to-man, with the defenseman farthest up-ice playing the body no matter what, and the trailing defenseman going for the puck, switching to zone defense only if the attackers switch sides.

Two on One

This situation is dangerous for the defense, but it can be played successfully. Obviously it often is, since it is the most common situation, yet we don't see scores of 20–0. The strategy simply requires quick thinking and coordination between goalie and one defender (defender rather than defenseman, since it sometimes occurs that the defense has been stranded up ice, and the lone defender is a backchecking forward, God forbid). Again, if the defender simply remembers that there is a goalie, then it is not really a two-on-one situation, but a two-on-two.

The general strategy is for the goalie to play the puck carrier, by coming out and cutting down on the angles. Once the goalie has committed himself to the puck carrier, it is absolutely essential that the defender (1) prevent a pass from being made to a second attacker and (2) set up the worst possible shooting angle for the puck carrier. The lone defender should attempt to stay in the middle and not make an irreversible commitment to an attacker.

Finally, if the puck carrier succeeds in making a pass to the trailing attacker, the defender should then check that player, leaving the goalie to cover any shots. There are several possible variations to this situation (see offensive play), but two basic rules apply throughout: try to prevent passes while checking the most dangerous attacker and set up the worst possible shooting angles, while keeping the best possible defensive position—middle of the defensive zone—without getting caught too far up or too far back.

Three on One

This situation is the nightmare of any defenseman and the only hope is to center himself on the three attackers, not make a fatal commitment, and attempt once again to prevent passes while creating poor shooting angles. The goalie is often the life-saving factor in the three-on-one dilemma, and he must coordinate as much as possible with the lone defender. The biggest problem in this situation is that the three attackers are able to pass back and forth at will, since the defender and the goalie both are better off trying to stay centered as much as possible, to avoid commitment. If, however, play nears the net, and the defender has backed into the net as far as is safe, then the ultimate move is to play the two *non*–puck carriers and leave the puck carrier to the goalie. Any way it's played, it's rough.

Three on Two

In this situation all of the forwards have been caught up-ice, and the defensive team must stop three attackers. Again, if one remembers the goalie, the situation is virtually equal, but it is a difficult moment for the defense, nonetheless. The ideal would appear to be to stop the attack at the blue line. This is, in fact, a dangerous approach to take. If that check at the blue line should fail, a three on one has been set up in the defensive zone.

As the attack moves into the defensive zone, the defense must attempt the usual—stay as close together in the center as possible so that the attack doesn't split the defense. Once the wings have gone outside and the center has positioned himself in the slot, there is little more the defense can do. Ultimately the defense will have to play the wings and pray that a forward can get back soon enough to pick up the player in teh slot.

If the puck comes down with one of the attacking wings, that defenseman (the onside defenseman) should play the puck carrier, while the other defenseman plays the other attackers as a two-on-one (setting up bad angles or preventing shots).

If the puck is carried in by the center, one defenseman can move up to cover the center, while the other moves back, staying in the center, to cover passes or shots.

If the center brings the puck down, stops and then the wings do a criss-cross, the defense covers the lane, or zone, rather than switching to cover the same wings. One defender should play the wings as a two-on-one, while the other stays slightly behind to cover all other contingencies.

Three on Two—with Two Backcheckers

This situation actually has more defenders than attackers and should definitely be played at the blue line. If one defender (assured that the attacking wings are covered by backchecking forwards) moves up on the puck carrier and forces him to make a move, there is a good possibility that the attacking wings will go offside. If not, there is also a good chance that the puck carrier will be forced to simply "dump" the puck, since he has no teammate to pass to. Once again, the burden of responsibility lies with the backchecking forwards: they should always leave the center zone to the defense and this usually means leaving the puck carrier to the defense, while they check the attacking wings.

One on Two

This situation seems like the ideal one for the defense, since there are two defenders and only one attacker, but again, it can be muffed unless early action is taken. One defender should move up on the puck carrier quickly and "play the man," preventing the possibility of the puckcarrier waiting long enough for a teammate to arrive.

To many a new fan who watches that first hockey game, it looks as though the game is completely without a "system." It appears almost as though every move is simply a reaction to the moment, without plan. But this is absolutely not true, and the first real line of any defense is to know the team's system—that way every player knows exactly what position—what role—to play, no matter what situation arises. On defense, attitude can be as important as action: the defensive player should never think of "being on the defensive" as being inferior. He should feel as confident as when playing offense and always cover his man or his zone looking for the break.

There are several general guidelines for play in the defensive zone: The defenseman should try to keep track of the puck but never lose his check. Don't screen the goalie, and if the opponent gets to the puck first, take him out with the body. Never let both defensemen chase the puck behind the net, and if the puck is in the corner, one defenseman should play the puck carrier, while the other stays in front of the goal. Never let an attacker park in the slot or near the crease. When covering the attacker in the slot, always be in touch with his body when trying to watch the puck. If the going simply gets too rough—the opposition is swarming all over—then force a face-off. This at least gives the defending squad a chance to regroup and maybe even change lines. And if the defenders should regain the puck, they must think before they move or pass—always knowing where everybody is on the ice.

As for tactical systems in the defensive zone, they are basically three: In one system, the center would have the responsibility for covering the "points." Whichever point attacker is on the same side as the puck is the center's check, and if the puck moves to the other side of the net, the center moves to cover the other point. The wings cover the down-ice attackers, one defenseman covers the corner puck carrier, and the other defenseman covers the net. In another system the wings would cover the points, the center covers the slot, and the defensemen would do the same as in the previous system. The third system leaves the center free to cover the puck in the defensive zone, hoping to gain possession and form a quick attack. In this case the defense is basically the same—one on the puck carrier and one on the net. The winger on the puck side would cover the point, while the "off" winger would cover both the slot and the "off" point in case of a pass to that position.

THE POWER PLAY

The power play—setting up an offense when the opposing team is one or more men short due to penalties—is a very specialized system in hockey today. Professional teams, who have ample manpower to specialize, usually have certain players who go on ice for the power play. Since the point positions can be of such importance when the power play reaches the opponent's defensive zone, there is usually a strong forward with a powerful shot and good passing abilities who can also handle defensive play, to take one point position. Then on the other point, the defenseman with the best shot and stickhandling talent takes over. Since injuries and penalties take their toll in any game, however, it is always best to have every team work constantly on the team's power play system during practice.

The power play actually begins the second the penalty takes place, because as soon as the referee raises his hand to indicate an infraction, the team about to have the player advantage should try to pull their goalie and put the extra skater on the ice. As long as the offending team does *not* touch the puck, the referee cannot whistle the end of play. Thus, the first maneuver in a power play situation is to keep possession of the puck and get the extra skater on the ice—even if it means skating all the way back into their own defensive zone to set the play up. After all, the opposition cannot score, because as soon as they touch the puck, the whistle blows.

Once the whistle has blown and the power play is under way, the most basic plan is for the attackers to set up the puck in their own end. Since the penalty killers can shoot the puck all the way into the attackers' end of the ice without "icing" being called, the power play most often begins behind the attackers' own net.

The classic initial move behind the net is for one defenseman to remain behind the net with the puck, the center (or best puck carrier and passer) to skate behind the net to pick up the puck, and begin the procedure up-ice. If the center is immediately checked by an opposing penalty killer, he can pass back to the defenseman, and begin the play again. The wings should come back with the center and start the move up-ice with him—not ahead of him. This is to avoid making long passes, because if the opposition picks up one of these long passes, they can kill the entire penalty simply skating and passing ("ragging") the puck among themselves.

If the opposing forechecker is spotted before he corners the center behind the net, the defenseman should *not* pass the puck up to the center as he comes behind the net, but let him skate by. When the center has passed behind the net and is about halfway to the sideboards, he should turn and begin to skate up-ice. At the same moment, the wing on that side begins to skate up-ice and the defenseman moves from behind the net on the same side, which *should* draw the forechecker to him. Just as the forechecker reaches the defenseman, he should then pass off to the center, thus neatly moving the puck beyond the forechecker. As this happens, the defenseman in front of the net should take care not to interfere with the forechecker, which would extract a penalty and lose the player advantage.

If there is no forechecker, but the opposing forwards simply move up-ice with the attacking wings, then the best option is to position both point men behind the net, one directly behind with the puck and the other in a corner. When the center picks up the puck behind the net, the point man who passed it to him moves from behind the net, trails the center in the center zone, and covers any checks or "lost" pucks. The point man in the corner begins to move out behind the wing on that side, and when the wing gets about halfway to the blue line, he skates toward the center as though to take a pass from the center. Hopefully, his check moves with him, leaving the point man behind him open for a pass from the center. This point man should be a good offensive player with speed and stickhandling abilities, or the whole aim of this move will be lost. Having moved the opposition out of his way, this player should then be able to accelerate quickly and take the puck out of the zone.

If the puck carrier finds the opposing defense standing up to him at the blue line, he should wait for his forwards to catch up, then pass off to one who can stickhandle past the defense. Only as a last resort should the puck be "dumped" into the opponent's defensive zone, since the probability is that they will immediately blast it all the way down-ice forcing the power play attack to begin again. If it is necessary to "dump," then it should be done as near as possible to a teammate who can skate after the puck and forecheck fiercely.

Once in the opponent's defensive zone, many moves can be made, but they all have one primary objective—to pull the defenders out of position and set up a shot. The classic defensive stance for penalty-killing is the "box" zone defense.

There are two basic means of shattering the "box." One is to place an attacker at the center of the box, forcing one defender to leave a corner of the box, opening up the situation. The second system is to set up an imbalance on one side of the box. If there are three attackers on one side of the box, this forces two corners of the box to move out of position and commit themselves. In this instance the point man on the "heavy" side of the box passes in to a forward, and as the two defenders move out of position to cover the puck carrier and onside wing, the point man would then move into the slot and take a pass, for a fair shot.

Most important is the theory that quick moves and quick passes will eventually pull the "box" apart. With the overload method, the passing triangle that destroys the box has the advantage of being possible from any side, and short passes are the key.

Power Play with a Two-Man Advantage

If the attacking team has a two-man advantage, there is little problem in moving the puck to the defending blue line, since the defending team is unlikely to have a forechecker. Once in the attacking zone, the defense most often sets up a three-cornered defense, or triangle, with one man up-ice. This defender is responsible for covering both points, and quick passes back and forth between the points may pull this defender out of position, to one side. If the man farthest up-ice gets moved out of position, then one of the defenders at the bottom of the triangle must also move out of position to cover, and there is an optimum chance for a clear shot. When the top man has been drawn out of position, a quick pass to the opposite point is a good bet, or the center can move in to screen the top defender. Again, the opposite point or opposite wing has a clear shot at the goal.

PENALTY KILLING

This term is self-explanatory and is the opposite side of the power play. When killing a penalty, playing one or two men short, attitude is again the first line of defense. Think positively, and while playing defensively try to find a way to regain the puck: statistics in professional hockey show that teams that score while shorthanded often go on to win the game. Kill the penalty as aggressively as possible and try the utmost to regain possession of the puck. Even if unable to score a shorthanded goal, keeping the puck ("ragging") can negate the opposition's power play.

If, however, the attack arrives at the penalty killer's blue line with the puck, the best option is the forementioned zone or "box" defense. If one man short, there are basic rules to this box system that must be remembered at all times. The penalty killer should never chase the puck, which would mean, of course, being pulled out of position and thus opening up one end or side of the box defense. Always play the zone and the most threatening attacker in that zone (usually a man in the slot or an unchecked point man). The wings or forwards should move as aggressively as possible toward the points, to force bad shots or bad passes, while the "bottom" of the box should force the attacking wings outside, as far from the crease as possible. The best hierarchy of defending is to watch the zone first, the man next, and the puck last, in that order. While the puck can legally be whacked all the way down-ice by a shorthanded team, possession is better if it can be maintained. If the defensive squad is tired or highly pressured and it's near the end of the penalty, they should try to get a face-off.

Remembering the old adage that the best defense is a good offense, the team that excels in forechecking often begins penalty killing with this tactic. Aggressive forechecking (*if* the team is good at it, fine; if not, they shouldn't do it, or their forwards might be caught down-ice, and the defense might be stuck with a dangerously top-heavy situation at their own blue line) can often blow an opponent's whole power play in their end of the ice.

If a team uses two forecheckers in penalty killing, the first forechecker usually goes deep, attempting to make the puck carrier stop and reverse with the puck, behind his own net. At that moment, the other forechecker moves in to force the reversing puck carrier to change directions again. Even if the puck carrier ultimately breaks out or succeeds in passing the puck out, this has usually lost them precious moments in trying to set up their power play. Aggressive forecheckers must stay in position to get back if the puck carrier breaks out or passes out—either to check the new puck carrier or to get all the way back and help the defense at the blue line. If the first forechecker succeeds in making the puck carrier pass, the second forechecker can often check the attacker receiving the pass.

The most common form of penalty killing is called the wing-on-wing, which is simply that—without forechecking—the wings allow the opposing wings to come down-ice, covering them as they progress, until the blue line, where the defense stands up to them and tries to force them into dumping the puck, rather than handling it across the blue line.

Another possibility is for the penalty killers to set up a triangle zone in the neutral zone, with the fourth man in the attacker's defensive zone. The defender in the attacker's defensive zone tries to stop passing and stickhandling, forcing the attackers to virtually dump into the neutral zone. Failing that, the wings attempt the same thing in the neutral zone: to actually stop play and force dumping.

Finally, the man at the bottom of the triangle, behind the defending blue line, picks up anything dumped over the line, along with the goaltender. This tactic is seldom used and works only as a surprise tactic or against a team that is unusually bereft of good passers and stickhandlers.

Penalty Killing—Two Men Short

As described in the power play section, the only standard defense for a team playing two men short is the triangle defense, and the only rule is to avoid doing what the opposition wants—to get suckered or faked into moving out of zone or position. If the top man gets pulled to one side, the back defender on the same side of the puck must move to the point, while the trapped forward goes back as fast as he can to become one of the "bottom" corners of the triangle.

Pulling the Goaltender

This is done normally only as a last resort. Pulling the goalie, unless done to put an extra skater on ice before the referee blows the whistle for a delayed penalty, is used only when a team is down by a goal or more and the game is within moments of ending. Logically, if the team can't score again it loses, so risking the opposition scoring again can't make it any worse.

There are two schools of thought as to the best moment to pull the goalie. Some think the best time to pull the goalie is while play is still underway, when the opposition may miss the fact that the goal is empty and the extra man is on the ice. But whether the goaltender is pulled while the play goes on or at the face-off, the primary concern of the team with the extra skater is to keep the opposition from getting the puck and, of course, to keep the puck in the opponent's defensive zone.

If a team waits for a face-off to pull the goaltender, obviously they've made an announcement to the opponent, and the necessity for gaining possession is all the greater. The standard setup for the face-off is to put in a team's ace face-off expert, a player in the slot, and another as near the goal as possible for deflecting or tipping in a shot or screening the opponent's goalie. The men playing the points will also attempt a shot as quickly as possible, as this is a last-ditch attempt to score a tying goal.

11

NCAA RULES

Rule 1

THE RINK

The Rink
Section 1.
Ice hockey shall be played on an area of ice called a rink.

Rink Dimensions
Section 2.
- **a.** As nearly as possible, the dimensions of the rink shall be 200 feet [61.0m] long and 90 feet [27.4m] wide. The corners shall be rounded in the arc of a circle with a radius of 20 feet [6.1m].
- **b.** The rink shall be surrounded by a wooden or fiberglass wall or fence known as the "boards" which shall extend not less than 40 inches [101.6cm] and not more than 48 inches [121.9cm] above the level of the ice surface. The ideal height of the boards above the ice surface shall be 42 inches [106.7cm].

    Except for the official markings provided for in these rules, the entire playing surface and the boards shall be white in color except the kick plate at the bottom of the boards, which shall be light yellow in color.
- **c.** The boards shall be constructed so that the surface facing the ice shall be smooth and free of any object that could cause injury to players.

    All doors giving access to the playing surface must swing away from the ice surface.

    All glass, wire or other types of protective screens and gear used to hold them in position shall be mounted on the boards on the side away from the playing surface.

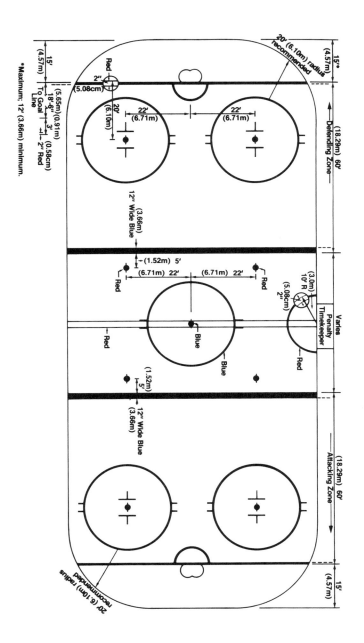

Goal Posts and Nets

Section 3.

a. Fifteen feet [4.57m] from each end of the rink and in the center of a red line two inches [5.08cm] wide, drawn completely across the width of the ice and continued vertically up the side of the boards, regulation goal posts and nets shall be set in such a manner as to remain stationary during the progress of a game. The goal posts shall be kept in position by metal rods, pipes or similar means affixed in the ice or floor.

The goal line shall be placed on the ice surface a maximum of 15 feet [4.57m] and a minimum of 12 feet [3.66m] from the end of the rink.

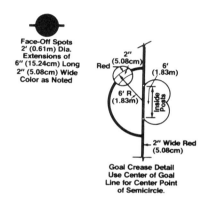

Face-Off Spots
2' (0.61m) Dia.
Extensions of
6" (15.24cm) Long
2" (5.08cm) Wide
Color as Noted

Goal Crease Detail
Use Center of Goal
Line for Center Point
of Semicircle.

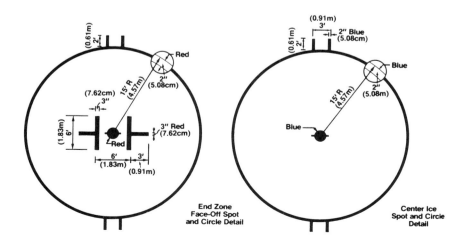

End Zone
Face-Off Spot
and Circle Detail

Center Ice
Spot and Circle
Detail

293

b. The goal posts shall be of approved design and material, and shall extend vertically four feet [1.22m] above the surface of the ice. They shall be set six feet [1.83m] apart, measured from the inside of the posts. A crossbar of the same material as the goal posts shall extend from the top of one post to the top of the other.

c. A net of approved design shall be attached to each goal frame.

d. The goal posts and crossbar shall be painted red. All other exterior and interior surfaces shall be painted white.

e. The red line, two inches [5.08cm] wide, between the goal posts on the ice and extending completely across the rink, shall be known as the goal line.

f. The goal area, enclosed by the goal line and the base plate of the goal, shall be painted white.

Goal Crease
Section 4.

a. In front of each goal a goal crease area shall be marked by a red line two inches [5.08cm] in width.

b. The goal crease shall be formed by drawing a semicircle, six feet [1.83m] in radius, on the ice using the center of the goal line as the center point.

c. The goal crease area shall include all the space outlined by the crease lines and extending vertically four feet to the level of the top of the goal frame.

NOTE: *The rectangular goal crease (four feet [1.02m] × eight feet [2.43m]) may also be marked on the ice surface.*

Division of Ice Surface
Section 5.

a. The ice area between the two goals shall be divided into three parts by lines 12 inches [30.48cm] in width and blue in color, drawn 60-feet [18.29m] out from the goal lines, extending completely across the rink parallel with the goal lines, and continuing vertically up the side of the boards. (Blue line and goal line extended are included in 60-foot [18.29m] measurement.)

b. That portion of the ice surface in which the goal is situated shall be called the defending zone of the team defending that goal, the central portion shall be known as the neutral zone and the portion farthest from the defending goal shall be known as the attacking zone. The zone line shall be considered part of the zone that the puck is in.

c. There shall also be a line 12 inches [30.48cm] in width and red in color, drawn completely across the rink in center ice, parallel with the goal lines and continuing vertically up the side of the boards, known as the "center line." This line shall contain at regular intervals markings of a uniform distinctive design which will easily distinguish it from the two blue lines; the outer edges must be continuous.

Center Ice Spot and Circle

Section 6.

A circular blue spot two feet [0.61m] in diameter shall be marked exactly in the center of the rink; and with this spot as a center, a circle of 15 feet [4.57m] radius shall be marked with a blue line two inches [5.08cm] in width.

Two blue lines two feet [0.61m] long and two inches [5.08cm] wide, parallel to the blue lines, shall be marked on the ice extending from the outer edges of both sides of the face-off circle. These lines shall be three feet [0.91 m] apart, 18 inches [45.72cm] on each side of the center of the face-off spot and circle.

Extending from each end of the face-off spot and parallel to the boards shall be a blue line six inches [15.24cm] long and two inches [5.08cm] wide.

Face-off Spots in Neutral Zone

Section 7.

Two red spots two feet [0.61m] in diameter shall be marked on the ice in the neutral zone five feet [1.52m] from each blue line. The spots shall be 44 feet [13.4m] apart and each shall be a uniform distance from the adjacent boards.

Extending from each end of the face-off spots and parallel to the boards shall be a red line six inches [15.24cm] long and two inches [5.08cm] wide.

End Zone Face-off Spots and Circles

Section 8.

a. In both end zones and on both sides of each goal, red face-off spots and circles shall be marked on the ice. The face-off spots shall be two feet [0.61m] in diameter. Extending from each end of the spot and parallel to the boards shall be marked a red line six inches [15.24cm] long and two inches [5.08cm] wide.

   The circles shall be two inches [5.08cm] wide with a radius of 15 feet [4.57m] from the center of the face-off spots. Eighteen and one-half feet [5.65m] and 21½ feet [6.55m] from the goal line and parallel to it, two red lines two feet [0.61m] long and two inches [5.08cm] wide shall be marked on the ice extending from the outer edge of both sides of each face-off circle.

   Parallel to the goal line and equidistant from and on opposite sides of the center of each end face-off spot, two red lines six feet [1.83m] long and three inches [7.23cm] wide and six feet [1.83m] apart shall be marked on the ice. Perpendicular from the center of these lines and extending away from the center face-off spot is drawn a line three feet [0.91m] long and three inches [7.62cm] wide. (The effect of these lines is to produce a 'T' on opposite sides of the center face-off spot.)

b. The location of the face-off spots shall be fixed in the following manner:

   Along a line 20 feet [6.10m] from each goal line and parallel to it, two points shall be marked 22 feet [6.71m] on both sides of the straight line joining the centers of the two goals. Each such point shall be the center of a face-off spot and circle.

Players' Bench
Section 9.

a. The rink shall be provided with seats or benches for the use of players of both teams and should accommodate at least 20 persons of each team. The benches shall be placed immediately alongside the ice in the neutral zone, convenient to the dressing rooms. Benches for the two teams should be separated by a substantial distance.

   Where physically possible, each players' bench shall have two doors opening in the neutral zone. All doors opening to the playing surface shall be constructed so that they swing away from the ice surface.

b. Only players in uniform and five additional team personnel shall be permitted to occupy the bench area.

Penalty Bench
Section 10.

a. The rink must be provided with benches or seats to be known as the penalty bench. It is preferable to have separate penalty benches for each team separated from each other and substantially separated from either players' bench. The penalty bench(es) shall be situated opposite the players' bench(es) in the neutral zone. The penalty bench(es) are for the exclusive use of the timekeeper, the penalty timekeeper, scorer and penalized players. No other person shall be allowed in the penalty bench(es).

b. On the ice immediately in front of the penalty timekeeper's seat, there shall be marked in red on the ice a semicircle of 10 feet [3.0m] radius and two inches [5.08cm] in width, which shall be known as the referee's crease. (See diagram of rink.)

Signal Timing Devices
Section 11.

a. A suitable sound device must be provided for the use of timekeepers.

b. An electrical clock, or other timing device, shall be provided for the purpose of keeping the spectators, players and game officials accurately informed as to all time elements at all stages of the game, including the time remaining to be played in any period.

   Time recording for both game time and penalty time shall show time remaining to be played or served.

   NOTE 1: A backup timing device must be available.

c. Behind each goal, electric lights shall be set up for the use of the goal judges. A red light will signify the scoring of a goal. Where automatic lights are available, a green light will signify the end of a period or a game.

NOTE 2: *A goal cannot be scored when a green light is showing.*

NOTE 3: *Goal judges' boxes should be properly isolated so that there will be no interference with the activities of the judges.*

Goalkeeper's Privileged Area
Section 12.

The goalkeeper's privileged area is an area bounded in the rear by his end of the rink, in front by an imaginary line connecting the special spots, and on the sides by imaginary lines from the special spots to the end boards.

Rule 2
TEAMS

Composition of Team
Section 1.

a. A team shall be composed of six players: goalkeeper, right defense, left defense, center, right wing and left wing.

b. Each player and each goalkeeper listed in the lineup of each team shall wear an individual identifying number at least 10 inches [25.40cm] high on the back of his sweater and at least four inches [10.16cm] high on the front or on both sleeves. All players of each team shall dress uniformly.

It is recommended that the visiting team wear colored jerseys and stockings and the home team white.

NOTE: *When wearing long pants, it is recommended that the visiting team's pants be dark and the home team's pants be light in color.*

Captain of Team
Section 2.

a. One captain shall be appointed by each team, and he alone shall have the privilege of discussing with the referee any questions relating to interpretation of rules that may arise during the progress of a game. He shall wear the letter "C," approximately three inches [7.62cm] in height and in contrasting color, in a conspicuous position on the front of his sweater.

If the captain is not available because of injury or an imposed penalty, another player may be designated to act as captain.

A complaint about a penalty is not considered a matter "relating to the interpretation of the rules," and a minor penalty shall be imposed against any captain or other player making such a complaint. If such complaints continue, a misconduct penalty shall be imposed.

> **b.** The referee and official scorer shall be advised prior to the start of each game of the name of the captain of the team and the designated alternate.
>
> **c.** No goalkeeper shall be entitled to exercise the privileges of captain.
>
> **d.** Only the playing captain of either team may talk or confer with a referee. A playing captain may not dispute judgment decisions of the referee. For an infraction of this rule, a misconduct penalty shall be imposed.

Players in Uniform
Section 3.

> **a.** At the beginning of each game, the coach of each team shall list the players and goalkeepers who shall be eligible to play in the game. A maximum of 18 players, plus not more than three nor less than two goalkeepers, shall be permitted; and a captain shall be designated.
>
> *NOTE: Only players from each team shall participate in the pregame warm-up. The 18 players and not more than three goalkeepers participating in the pregame warm-up do not necessarily have to be the same players listed on the official game report form. It is mandatory, however, that the 18 players and goalkeepers listed on the official game report form are the players who will dress for the game.*
>
> *Should more than 18 players and three goalkeepers participate in the pregame warm-up, the offending team shall be assessed a minor penalty for delay of game.*
>
> **b.** A list of names and numbers of all eligible players and goalkeepers must be handed to the referee or official scorer before the game. No changes or additions may be made to the list after the game begins.
>
> **c.** Each team shall be allowed one goalkeeper on the ice at one time. The goalkeeper may be removed and another "player" substituted.
>
> **d.** A substitute goalkeeper shall be on the bench at the start of the game and shall at all times be fully dressed and equipped ready to play. When the substitute goalkeeper enters the game, he will take his position without delay.
>
> **e.** Except when all goalkeepers are incapacitated, no other player shall be permitted wo wear the equipment of the goalkeeper.

Starting Lineup
Section 4.

> **a.** Prior to the start of the game, at the request of the referee the coach of the visiting team is required to name a starting lineup to the referee or the official scorer. At any time in the game at the request of the referee made to the captain, the visiting team must place a playing lineup on the ice and promptly commence play.
>
> **b.** Prior to the start of the game, the coach of the home team, having been

advised by the official scorer or the referee the names of the starting lineup of the visiting team, shall name the starting lineup of the home team; this information shall be conveyed by the official scorer or the referee to the coach of the visiting team.

NOTE 1: Coaches shall provide their lineups immediately following the pre-game warm-up.

c. No change in the starting lineup of either team as given to the referee or official scorer, or in the playing lineup on the ice, shall be made until the game is actually in progress. For an infraction of this rule, a bench minor penalty shall be imposed upon the offending team provided such an infraction is called to the attention of the referee before the second face-off in the first period takes place.

d. Following any stoppage of play, the visiting team shall promptly place a lineup on the ice ready for play, and no substitution shall be made from that time until play is resumed. The home team may then make any substitutions that do not result in a delay of the game. For an infraction of this rule, a bench minor penalty shall be imposed upon the offending team.

If there is any undue delay by either team in changing lines, the referee shall order the offending team or teams to take their positions immediately and shall not permit a line change.

NOTE 2: When a substitution has been made under the above rule, no additional substitution may be made until play commences.

NOTE 3: If prior to competitions, the name of the home team has not been established, the competing teams will decide which is to be the home team by mutual agreement; that is, by the flip of a coin or some similar method.

e. Teams shall be on the ice ready to play promptly at the beginning of each period. The home team shall take the ice first. For an infraction of this rule, a bench minor penalty may be imposed upon the offending team.

Change of Players
Section 5.

a. Players may be changed at any time from the players' bench provided that the player or players leaving the ice always be at the players' bench and out of the play before any change is made.

A goalkeeper may be changed for another player at any time under the conditions of this section.

NOTE 1: When a goalkeeper leaves his goal area and proceeds to his players' bench for the purpose of substituting another player, the referee or linesman shall be responsible to see that the substitution is not illegal because of the premature departure of the substitute from the bench (before the goalkeeper is at the bench). If the substitution is made prematurely, the referee or linesman shall stop the play immediately by blowing his whistle unless the nonoffending team has possession of the puck, in which event the stoppage will be delayed until the puck changes hands. There shall be no time penalty assessed the team making the premature substitution, but the resulting face-off will take place at the center "face-off spot."

b. A player serving a penalty on the penalty bench, who is to be changed after the penalty has been served, must proceed at once by way of the ice and be at his own players' bench before any change may be made. For any violation of this rule, a minor penalty shall be imposed on the player relieving.

NOTE 2: The number of times any particular player may be substituted (i.e., withdrawn from, or returned to, the game within the same period, or otherwise) is not limited. A substitute player is not required to notify the referee or assistant referee before engaging in play; and, while the officials shall not begin play with extra players on either team, the responsibility of the proper number rests with the teams. Officials and coaches are requested to see that substitutions are made without undue loss of time and that players leave and enter the rink promptly.

c. A player who has received a time penalty or one who is serving for a disqualified player, must remain in the penalty box until his time is completed. For an infraction of this rule a minor penalty shall be imposed on the offending player. The offending player must serve the balance of his initial penalty, plus an additional minor penalty.

d. When a penalized player or his immediate substitute, either from the penalty box or the players' bench, returns to the ice, he shall not be eligible to play any puck coming from his own defensive zone until he has returned to his own defensive zone or until possession and control of the puck have been gained by another player in the neutral zone or in the attacking zone of the penalized player.

PENALTY—Last play face-off.

e. On any face-off, if a team starts play with fewer players than entitled to, any subsequently entering player shall not be eligible to play any puck coming from his own defensive zone until he has returned to his own defensive zone or until possession and control of the puck have been gained by another player in the neutral zone or in his own attacking zone.

PENALTY—Last play face-off.

f. If at any time a team plays too many men, it shall immediately withdraw the extra player or players. For an infraction of this rule a bench penalty shall be imposed for each additional player.

If an extra player from the bench or the penalty box prevents or tries to prevent a breakaway attempt at a goal, there shall be a delayed whistle.

For an infraction of this rule a penalty shot and misconduct penalty shall be imposed.

Injured Players
Section 6.

a.   When a player other than a goalkeeper is injured or compelled to leave the ice during a game, he may retire from the game and be replaced by a substitute; but play must continue without the teams leaving the ice.

b.   When a team has fewer than six substitutes available and none is in goalkeeper's equipment, and it becomes necessary to substitute for the goalkeeper because of his incapacitation by injury, breaking a skate or receiving a time or misconduct penalty, a reasonable length of time shall be allowed for the substitute to change into his equipment. If a goalkeeper sustains an injury or becomes ill, he must be ready to resume play immediately or be replaced by a substitute goalkeeper.

When a substitution for the regular goalkeeper has been made, such substitute must play in goal until the first stoppage of play thereafter. When the regular goalkeeper returns, he shall not be allowed any warm-up.

c.   If a penalized player has been injured he may proceed to the dressing room without taking a seat on the penalty bench. If the injured player receives a minor and/or major penalty, a substitute player shall be placed immediately on the penalty bench and shall serve the penalty without change. No other replacement for the penalized player shall be permitted to enter the game except form the penalty bench. For violation of this rule, a minor penalty shall be imposed.

The penalized player who has been injured and been replaced on the penalty bench shall not be eligible to play until his penalty has expired.

d.   When a player is injured so that he cannot continue to play or go to his bench, play shall not be stopped until the injured player's team has secured possession of the puck. If the player's team is in possession of the puck at the time if injury, play shall be stopped immediately, unless his team is in scoring position.

e.   When there is a stoppage of play due to an injury to a player other than the goalkeeper, the injured player must leave the ice until the next stoppage of play.

NOTE: In the case where it is obvious that a player has sustained a serious injury, the referee or linesman may stop play immediately.

Rule 3

EQUIPMENT

Sticks

Section 1.

a. The sticks shall be made of wood or a combination of wood and aluminum. Adhesive tape of any color may be wrapped around the stick at any place for the purpose of reinforcement or to improve control of the puck.

b. No stick shall exceed 58 inches [147.32cm] in length from the heel to the end of the shaft nor more than 12½ inches [31.75cm] from the heel to the end of the blade. The blade of the stick shall not be more than three inches [7.62cm] or less than two inches [5.08cm] wide at any point. All edges of the blade shall be beveled.

The curvature of the blade of the stick shall be restricted in such a way that the distance of a perpendicular line measured from a straight line drawn from the base of the heel to the base of the toe and the point of maximum curvature shall not exceed one-half inch [1.27cm].

c. The blade of the goalkeeper's stick shall not exceed 3½ inches [8.89cm] in width at any point except at the heel where it must not exceed 4½ inches [11.43cm] in width; nor shall it exceed 15½ inches [39.37cm] in length from the heel to the end of the blade.

The widened portion of the goalkeeper's stick extending up the shaft from the blade shall not extend more than 26 inches [66.04cm] from the heel and shall not exceed 3½ inches [8.89cm] in width.

d. A minor penalty shall be imposed on any player or goalkeeper who uses a stick not comforming to this rule.

e. When a formal complaint is made by the captain of a team about the dimensions of any stick, the referee shall make the necessary measurements immediately. Measurement of a challenged stick is to be made at first stoppage of play (or during the stoppage of play when the challenge is made). If a player's stick is found to be illegal, the minor penalty begins immediately. If a player's stick is found to be legal, the challenging team will receive a bench minor penalty for delay of game.

If a goal is scored with an illegal stick and the stick is found to be illegal before play resumes following the goal, the goal is disallowed and a minor penalty is assessed and begins immediately.

If a player breaks or has his stick broken intentionally or changes his stick before a measurement can be made, he will receive a minor and misconduct penalty; and any goal scored with that stick will be disallowed.

NOTE: It is the responsibility of the home team to provide a current copy of the NCAA Men's Ice Hockey Rules and a stick-measurement device at the penalty bench.

Skates
Section 2.

Skates shall be free from points or dangerous extensions. It shall be considered dangerous if the blade extends more than three-fourths of an inch [1.91cm] beyond the shoe at either toe or heel. The ends of the skates (both toe and heel) shall be rounded and blunt so that there are no points which might cause injury. All skates of players and officials shall be equipped with approved safety heel tips.

NOTE: From the standpoint of safety, it shall be the duty of the players, coaches and officials to see to it that the provisions of this rule are carried out prior to the game. All players must wear skates.

Goalkeeper's Equipment
Section 3.

a. With the exception of skates and stick, all the equipment worn by the goalkeeper must be constructed solely for the purpose of protecting the head or body, and he must not wear any garment or use any contrivance which would give him undue assistance in keeping goal.

b. The leg guards worn by goalkeepers shall not exceed 10 inches [25.40cm] in extreme width when on the leg of the player.

NOTE 1: Before the game starts, the referee should measure the pads upon request. He should not permit a goalkeeper to wear or use any equipment or garment which would give him undue assistance. Aprons or webbing extending more than three inches [7.62cm] below the crotch are not permitted. Protective padding attached to the back or forming a part of goalkeeper's gloves shall not exceed eight inches [20.32cm] in width nor more that 16 inches [40.64cm] in length at any point.

c. It is compulsory for all goalkeepers to wear full face masks.

d. A minor penalty shall be imposed on any goalkeeper using illegal equipment in a game.

NOTE 2: It is recommended by the NCAA Men's Ice Hockey Committee that goalkeepers wear a throat protector.

Protective Equipment
Section 4.

a. All protective equipment, except gloves, helmets, and goalkeeper's leg guards, must be worn under the uniform. A glove from which all or part of the palm has been removed or cut to permit the use of the bare hand shall be considered illegal equipment.

b. It is compulsory for all players, including goalkeepers, to wear helmets with chin straps securely fastened. Football helmets may not be worn.

NOTE 1: The intent of this rule is to have the entire head covered. A combination of mask and helmet covering the entire head is permissible for a goalkeeper.

NOTE 2: Helmets displaced during play must be replaced at first whistle. If a goalkeeper's mask and/or helmet is displaced, there shall be an immediate whistle.

c. All players including goalkeepers are required to wear an internal mouth-piece which covers all the remaining teeth of one jaw.

d. It is compulsory for all players other than goalkeepers to wear face masks that have met the standards established by the HECC-ASTM F 513-77 Eye and Face Protective Equipment for Hockey Players Standard.

NOTE 3: It is recommended that all players, including goalkeepers, begin wearing face masks that have met the new standards established by the HECC-ASTM F513-81 Eye and Face Protective Equipment for Hockey Players Standard. Beginning with the start of practice for the 1984-85 season, it will be mandatory for all players, including goalkeepers, to wear face masks that have met those new standards.

NOTE 4: Players, including goalkeepers, who violate any of this section, shall not be permitted to participate in the game until their equipment has been corrected or removed. Second offense by the same player in the same game constitutes a misconduct penalty. Third offense by the same player in the same game constitutes a game misconduct.

Dangerous Equipment
Section 5.

a. The use of pads or protectors made of metal, or of any other material likely to cause injury to a player, is prohibited.

NOTE: The NCAA Men's Ice Hockey Committee recommends the use of any protective equipment that is not injurious to the player wearing it or other players.

Puck
Section 6.

The puck shall be black and shall be made of vulcanized rubber, or other approved material, one inch thick [2.54cm] and three inches [7.62cm] in diameter, and shall weigh between $5\frac{1}{2}$ [155.92g] and six ounces [170.1g]. Any logo placed on a puck shall be situated in the center of the puck, and the diameter of the logo shall not exceed $1\frac{3}{4}$ inches [4.45cm].

NOTE: *It is recommended that pucks be chilled before being put into the game. It is also noted that pucks with raised identifying labels attached to them may not slide as well as pucks without such labels.*

Rule 4
PENALTIES

Penalties
Section 1.

Penalty time served shall be actual playing time and penalties shall be divided into the following classes:

a. Minor penalties
b. Bench minor penalties
c. Major penalties
d. Misconduct penalties
e. Disqualification penalties
f. Penalty shot

Where coincident penalties are imposed on players of both teams, the penalized players of the visiting team shall take their positions on the penalty bench first in the place designated for visiting players, or where there is no special designation, on the bench farthest from the gate.

Minor Penalties
Section 2.

a. For a "minor penalty," any player, other than a goalkeeper, shall be ruled off the ice for two minutes, during which time no substitute shall be permitted.

b. A "bench minor penalty" involves the removal from the ice of one player of the offending team for a period of two minutes. Any player except a goalkeeper of that team may be designated to serve the penalty by the coach through the playing captain, and such player shall take his place on the penalty bench promptly and serve the penalty as if it were a minor penalty imposed upon him.

c. If the opposing team scores a goal while a team is "short-handed" by one or more minor or bench minor penalties, the first of such penalties shall automatically terminate.

   If the referee signals an additional minor penalty against a team that already is short-handed because of one or more minor or bench minor

Blowing the Whistle

Holding

Clasp wrist of whistle hand with the other hand well in front of the chest

Hooking

A series of tugging motions with both arms, as if pulling something toward the stomach

Interference

Crossed arms with fists clenched stationary in front of chest

Misconduct

Hands should be moved once from sides down to hips. Thus, point to player first, hands to hips second

Delayed Calling of Penalty

Referee points with open palm, fingers together, once with free hand (without whistle)

Icing

The back referee signals the icing situation by fully extending his free arm (without whistle) over his head

The front referee (or linesman) will then indicate the icing is completed by extending his free arm over his head, up straight

The back referee (or linesman) will then signal the play (blow whistle) move to the face-off spot where he will cross arms to indicate the icing

The front referee will not give the cross arm signal when retrieving

Delayed or Slow Whistle

Use arm in which whistle is not held (raising straight up). If play returns to Neutral Zone without stoppage, arm is drawn down the instant the puck crosses the line

"Wash-Out"

Both arms swung shoulder height, not waist height

1. When used by the referee it means "no goal" and "no high-sticking the puck"

2. When used by linesman it means "no icing" and/or "no high-sticking the puck" only

Boarding

Strike the clenched fist of one hand into the open palm of the other hand directly in front of the chest

Tripping

Keep both skates on the ice when signaling, using right hand on right leg

High-Sticking

Placing both clenched fists, one immediately above the other, above the forehead

penalties, and a goal is scored by the nonoffending team before the whistle is blown, the goal shall be allowed, the delayed penalty shall not be assessed, and the first of the minor penalties already being served shall terminate automatically. If any other fouls are committed on the same play or after the referee has stopped play, the offending players shall be penalized.

NOTE 1: "Short-handed" means that the team must be below the numerical strength of its opponents on the ice at the time the goal is scored. The minor or

Slashing

A single chopping motion with the edge of one hand across the opposite forearm extending in front of the chest

Charging

Rotating clenched fists around one another in front of chest

Cross-Checking

A single forward and back motion with both fists clenched in front of the chest

Elbowing

Tapping either elbow with the opposite hand

Illegal Use of Hands

Grasp the wrist and place open palm of hand straight ahead (as if giving a "stop" signal)

Roughing

Fist clenched fully extending arm in front of the body

Butt-Ending

A crossing motion of the forearms, one moving under the other

Spearing

A single jabbing motion with both hands together, thrust forward in front of the chest, then dropping hands to the side

Kneeing

A single slapping of the right palm to the right knee, keeping both skate blades on the ice

Penalty Shot

Arms crossed (fists clenched) above the head

Hitting from Behind

Arm placed behind the back, elbow bent, forearm parallel to the ice surface

Grasping the Face Mask

A single or double motion as if grasping a face mask and pulling it down

bench minor penalty that terminates automatically is the one that causes the team scored against to be short-handed. Thus, coincident minor penalties to both teams do not cause either side to be short-handed.

NOTE 2: When coincident minor penalties are called involving a player from each team and then one team has an additional minor penalty called against it, the player receiving the additional minor penalty is designated as the first player for release if a goal is scored by his opponent.

307

When two minor penalties are called on one player at the same time and the opposing team scores a goal before expiration of the first minor, the remaining time on the first minor is eliminated and the time on the second minor immediately begins. This rule shall not apply when a goal is scored on a penalty shot.

When the minor penalties of two players of the same team terminate at the same time, the captain of that team shall designate to the referee which of the players will return to the ice first and the referee will instruct the penalty timekeeper accordingly.

When a player receives a major penalty and a minor penalty at the same time, the major penalty shall be served first by the penalized player.

> NOTE 3: *This applies to the case where BOTH penalties are imposed on the same player. See also* Note *to Section 8 of this rule.*

Major Penalties
Section 3.

For any major penalty, the offender shall be ruled off the ice for five minutes, during which time no substitute shall be permitted.

When a major penalty is imposed upon a goalkeeper, the time penalty shall be served by the offending goalkeeper, but a substitute player in goalkeeper's equipment shall be allowed in the game replacing some other player. Another player without goalkeeper's equipment shall go the the penalty bench with the goalkeeper and shall go on the ice in place of the penalized goalkeeper when the penalty time has expired. The penalized goalkeeper may not go on the ice unitl his teammate with goalkeeper's equipment has left the ice.

Misconduct Penalties
Section 4.

    a. A misconduct penalty involves the removal of a player, including a goalkeeper, from the game for a period of 10 minutes, but a substitute is permitted to replace that player immediately. A player whose misconduct penalty has expired shall remain in the penalty box until the next stoppage of play.

        A misconduct penalty is imposed upon players when:

1. They use foul or abusive language to a referee or in other ways attempt to influence;
2. A player has interfered with a penalty shot try;
3. A player persists in disputing decisions, showing disrespect for a referee or in not going directly to the penalty bench;
4. The "kick shot" is used;
5. An extra player from the penalty bench or players' bench prevents a breakaway attempt at a goal;

6. A player throws a stick or a portion of a stick among the spectators;
7. Any player or players who, except for the purpose of taking their places on the penalty bench, enter or remain in the referee's crease while he is reporting to or consulting with any game official, including the referee, timekeeper, penalty timekeeper, scorer or announcer.

If a minor and/or major penalty is imposed on the same player in addition to the misconduct penalty, the 10-minute misconduct penalty is to be served in addition to the minor and/or major penalty; but a substitute must enter the penalty bench along with the player receiving the misconduct penalty. The substitute may enter the game when the time penalty has elapsed, but the offending player must remain in the penalty box until the expiration of both penalities. If no other penalty has been imposed in addition to the misconduct penalty, a substitution may be made immediately.

b. A game misconduct penalty involves the suspension of a player for the balance of the game, but a substitute is permitted to replace that player immediately.

Disqualification Penalties
Section 5.
a. A disqualification penalty, consisting of suspension for the remainder of the game and a major penalty, shall be imposed upon any player who fights, attempts to injure an opponent or commits other serious penalties as outlined in these rules before the start of the game, during or after the game.

    The offending player may not go to the penalty bench and may not, while in uniform, occupy any area designated or reserved for players. A substitute, other than a spare goalkeeper, must enter the penalty bench immediately in the place of the disqualified player and enter the game after the five-minute penalty has elapsed.

    When coincident disqualification penalties are imposed against an equal number of players of each team, the penalized players shall leave the game; and each team then shall be permitted substitutions on the ice for the penalized players.

b. The progressive game disqualification structure will be as follows:

1. First disqualification penalty—that game plus one.
2. Second disqualification penalty—that game plus two.
3. Third disqualification penalty—that game plus three.
4. Fourth disqualification penalty—that game plus four.

(The progression will continue after the fourth disqualification penalty.)

NOTE: This disqualification structure is for the current season only and does not carry over to the next season.

c. The team of the disqualified player or players will not be permitted to dress a substitute player or players (equal to the number of disqualified players) in the next scheduled game whenever the team is playing the same opponent in consecutive games at the same location.

If a different team is scheduled as the next opponent, the offending team will be permitted to dress a substitute player or players.

Penalty Shot

Section 6.

a. Any infraction of the rules that calls for a penalty shot shall be handled as follows:

The referee shall cause to be announced over the public address system the name of the player designated by him or selected by the team entitled to take the shot (as appropriate). He then shall place the puck on the center face-off spot and the player taking the shot will, on the instruction of the referee, play the puck from there and attempt to score on the goalkeeper. The player taking the shot may carry the puck in any part of the neutral zone or his own defending zone; but once the puck has crossed the attacking blue line, it must be kept in motion towards the opponent's goal line. When the puck is shot the play shall be considered complete. No goal can be scored on a rebound of any kind, and any time the puck crosses the goal line the shot shall be considered complete. Only a player designated as a goalkeeper or alternate goalkeeper may defend against the penalty shot.

b. The goalkeeper must remain in the crease until the player taking the penalty shot has touched the puck; he must remain in the goalkeeper's privileged area until the completion of the play. In the event of violation of this rule or any foul committed by a goalkeeper, the referee shall allow the shot to be taken, and if the shot fails he shall permit the penalty shot to be taken over again. The goalkeeper may attempt to stop the penalty shot in any manner except by throwing his stick or any object, in which case another penalty shot shall be awarded.

c. When a penalty shot is awarded under 6-9-c (deliberately displacing goal post), 6-22-e (interference), 6-26-g (illegal entry into game), 6-41-a (throwing stick) or 6-45-b (fouling from behind), the referee shall designate the player who has been fouled as the player who shall take the penalty shot.

When a penalty shot is awarded under 6-13-c (falling on the puck in the crease) or 6-41-c (goalkeeper's stick deliberately left on ice), the captain of the nonoffending team shall designate any player who is not serving a penalty at that time to take the shot.

If because of injury the player designated by the referee to take the penalty shot is unable to do so within a reasonable time, the captain shall designate any player who is not serving a penalty at that time to take the shot.

d. If the player designated to take the penalty shot commits a foul in connection with the same play or circumstances, either before or after the penalty shot has been awarded, he shall be permitted to take the shot before going to the penalty bench unless his penalty is a game misconduct or disqualification penalty. In that case, the penalty shot shall be taken by a player selected by the captain of the nonoffending team from the players who are not serving a penalty at that time.

If, at the time a penalty shot is awarded, the goalkeeper of the penalized team has been removed form the ice to substitute another player, the goalkeeper shall be permitted to return to the ice before the penalty shot is taken.

e. While the penalty shot is being taken, players of both teams shall withdraw to the sides of the rink beyond the attacking blue line.

f. If any player of the opposing team interferes with or distracts the player taking a penalty shot and thereby causes the shot to fail, a second attempt shall be permitted and the referee shall impose a misconduct penalty on the offending player.

g. If a goal is scored from a penalty shot, the puck shall be faced at center ice in the usual way. If a goal is not scored, the puck shall be faced at either of the end face-off spots in the zone in which the penalty shot was tried.

h. If a goal is scored from a penalty shot, a further penalty to the offending player shall not be applied unless the offense for which the penalty shot was awarded was such as to incur a major or misconduct penalty. In that case, the penalty prescribed for the particular offense shall be imposed.

If the offense for which the penalty shot was awarded was one that normally would incur a minor penalty, no further minor penalty shall be served regardless of whether a goal was scored on the penalty shot.

i. If the foul upon which the penalty shot is based occurs during actual playing time, the penalty shot shall be awarded and taken immediately in the usual manner even if a slow whistle permitting the play to be completed results in the expiration of the period.

The time required for the penalty shot shall not be included in the regular playing time or any overtime.

Goalkeeper's Penalties
Section 7.

a. A goalkeeper shall not be sent to the penalty bench for an offense which incurs a minor penalty. Instead, the captain of the offending team shall designate another member of his team who was on the ice when the offense was committed to serve the penalty, and such substitute shall not be changed.

b. If a goalkeeper incurs a major or misconduct penalty, he shall serve the time penalty; but a substitute player in goalkeeper's equipment shall be allowed in the game replacing some other player. Another player without goalkeeper's equipment shall go to the penalty box with the goalkeeper and shall go on the ice in place of the penalized goalkeeper when the penalty time has expired. The penalized goalkeeper may not go on the ice until his teammate with goalkeeper's equipment has left the ice.

c. If a goalkeeper, in goalkeeper's equipment, participates in the play in any manner when he is beyond his attacking blue line, a minor penalty shall be imposed upon him. However, he may proceed without participating in the play to his player's bench if it is beyond the blue line.

d. Within the rectangular area bounded in the rear by his end of the rink, in front by an imaginary line connecting the special spots and on the sides by imaginary lines from the special spots to the end boards, the goalkeeper has certain privileges. (See diagram of rink.) When he is outside of this area, however, he must play the puck in the same manner as that prescribed for other players and is subject to the same penalties.

Delayed Penalties

Section 8.

a. If a player is penalized while two players of his team are serving penalties, the penalty time of the third player shall not commence until the penalty time of one of the other two players has elapsed. The third player penalized must proceed at once to the penalty bench, but may be replaced by a substitute until the penalty time of the penalized player begins.

b. When any team has three players serving penalties at the same time and, because of the delayed penalty rule, a substitute for the third offender is on the ice, none of the three penalized players on the penalty bench may return to the ice until play is stopped. When play is stopped, the player whose full penalty has expired, may return to the play.

However, the penalty timekeeper shall permit a player or players to return to the ice in the order of the expiration of their penalties when, because of such expiration, the penalized team is entitled to have more than four players on the ice.

Example 1: Players A1, A2 and A3 receive consecutive minor penalties of two minutes each. A1 leaves the ice at 1:25—time up at 3:25. A2 leaves the ice at 1:30—time up at 3:30. A3 leaves the ice at 1:50—A3's time will begin at 3:25 when the first penalty time expires and will run to 5:25. A4 takes the ice for A3 so that Team A shall not have fewer than four men on the ice. A1's penalty expires at 3:25, but he may return to the ice only at the first stoppage of play. When A2's penalty time expires at 3:30, A1 may return immediately to the ice, even if A4 or another player has not left the ice, because Team A is now entitled to five men. When A3's penalty time expires at 5:25, A2 may return immediately to the ice, even if no other Team A player has left the ice, because Team A is now entitled to six men. But A3 may not return to the ice until the next stoppage of play. In case of simultaneous penalties, the team captain shall designate players A1, A2 and A3.

Example 2: Player A1 receives a two-minute minor penalty at 1:40, to end at 3:40; A2 receives a five-minute major penalty at 1:55, to end at 6:55; and A3 receives a two-minute minor penalty at 2:15, postponed and not due to start until 3:40 when A1's time expires. At 2:50, a goal is scored against Team A and A1's time automatically expires. A3's time begins at 2:50 and will run to 4:50.

c. In the case of delayed penalties, the referee shall instruct the penalty timekeeper that players whose penalties have expired shall only be allowed to return to the ice when there is a stoppage of play.

When the penalties of two players of the same team will expire at the same time, the captain of that team will designate to the referee which of the players will return to the ice first and the referee will instruct the penalty timekeeper accordingly.

When a major and a minor penalty are imposed at the same time on players of the same team, the penalty timekeeper shall record the minor as being the first of such penalties.

NOTE: This applies to the case where the two penalties are imposed on different players of the same team. (See also 4-2-Notes 2 and 3, regarding minor penalties.)

Calling of Penalties
Section 9.

a. If an infraction of the rules calling for a minor, major, misconduct, or game misconduct or disqualification penalty is committed by a player of the side in possession of the puck, the referee shall blow his whistle immediately and award the penalties.

The resulting face-off shall be made at the place where the play was stopped unless the stoppage occurs in the attacking zone of the player penalized, in which case the face-off shall be made at the nearest face-off spot in the neutral zone.

b. If an infraction of the rules calling for a minor, bench minor, major misconduct, game misconduct or disqualification penalty is committed by a player of the team NOT in possession of the puck, the referee shall signify the calling of a penalty by pointing his open hand to the player to be penalized and immediately upon completion of the play by the team in possession, blow his whistle and award the penalty to the offending player.

The resulting face-off shall be made at the place where the play was stopped, unless during the period of the delayed whistle, the side in possession ices the puck or shoots the puck from its defensive zone so that it goes out of bounds or is unplayable. In that case, face-off following the stoppage shall take place in the neutral zone near the defending blue line of the team committing the foul.

If the penalty or penalties to be imposed are minor penalties and a goal is scored on the play by the nonoffending side, the first minor penalty shall not be imposed; but major and disqualification penalties shall be imposed in the normal manner regardless of whether a goal is scored. If any other fouls are committed on the same play or after the referee has stopped play, the offending players shall be penalized.

NOTE 1: "Completion of the play by the team in possession" in this rule means that the puck must have come into the possession and control of an opposing player or goalkeeper or has been "frozen." This does not mean a rebound off the goalkeeper, the goal or the boards or any accidental contact with the body or equipment of an opposing player.

NOTE 2: If, after the referee has signaled a penalty (but not before the whistle has been blown) the puck enters the goal of the nonoffending team as the direct result of the action of a player of that team, the goal shall be allowed and the penalty signaled shall be imposed in the normal manner.

c.   THE REFEREE SHALL DESIGNATE AND PENALIZE OTHER IM-PROPER PLAY OR CONDUCT NOT HEREIN MENTIONED, AND AT HIS DISCRETION MAY INCREASE ANY PENALTIES IN THESE RULES, ESPECIALLY FOR ANY PARTICULARLY DELIB-ERATE INFRINGEMENT THEREOF (AS MAY BE SHOWN BY A REPETITION OF ANY OFFENSE).

NOTE 3: A goal should not be awarded as a penalty for any offense, such as throwing a stick to prevent a goal or otherwise.

d.   The referee shall use a "delayed whistle" when a foul is committed against the team in possession of the puck, thereby postponing the stoppage of play until the offending team shall have possession and control of the puck.

Rule 5

OFFICIALS

Appointment of Officials
Section 1.

The officials of a game shall be a referee, an assistant referee, a linesman, a game timekeeper, a penalty timekeeper, an official scorer and two goal judges. All officials should be supplied by the home team, or assigned by league.

NOTE: Unless otherwise determined, the officials shall toss a coin to determine which shall be the referee in charge.

Three-man Officiating System (Two Referees, One Linesman)
Section 2.

a. The referees' duties are as follows:

1. The referee and, subject to him, the assistant referee, shall have general supervision of the game and shall have full control of all game officials and players during the game, including stoppages. In case of any dispute, their decision shall be final and there shall be no appeal. They may change their own decision or that of any other official, provided they do so before play is renewed following rendition of the original decision.

   The referees and the linesman should arrive on the ice together and shall remain on the ice at the conclusion of each period until all players have proceeded to their dressing rooms.

2. The referees and linesman shall be garbed in black trousers and official sweaters.

   They shall be equipped with whistles and a metal tape measure with a minimum length of six feet [2m].

3. The referees are not required to confer with coaches during the game or its intermission periods.

4. The referees shall order the teams on the ice at the appointed time for the beginning of the game and at the commencement of each period. Teams shall be notified three minutes before play is to start following each intermission.

5. When a referee becomes aware of any lack of conformity to the regulations on equipment, it shall be his duty to see that the required equipment is in use.

6. The referees shall, before starting the game, see that the appointed game timekeeper, penalty timekeeper, official scorer and goal judges are in their respective places and satisy themselves that the timing and signaling equipment is in order.

7. It shall be their duty to impose such penalties as are prescribed by the rules for

infractions thereof, to stop play for any other infraction of the rules and to give final decisions in the matters of disputed goals. The referees may, in matters of disputed goals, consult with the linesman and/or goal judge before making a decision.

8. The referee shall announce to the official scorer or penalty timekeeper all goals and assists legally scored, as well as penalties, and for what infractions such penalties are imposed.

   The name of the goal scorer and any player entitled to an assist will be announced on the public address system. If a goal is disallowed for any violation of the rules, the referees shall report the reason for the disallowance to the official scorer, who shall announce the referees' decision correctly over the public address system.

   The infraction of the rules for which each penalty has been imposed will be announced over the public address system.

9. If a referee or linesman should accidentally leave the ice or receive an injury which incapacitates him from discharging his duties while play is in progress, the game shall be stopped immediately by one of the other two officials, unless one of the teams has the puck in a scoring position, in which case the play shall be allowed to be completed. If it is obvious that the injury sustained is of a serious nature, play shall be stopped immediately.

   If a referee or linesman is unable to continue to officiate for any reason, the other two officials shall continue to officiate the game using the two-man officiating system. (See 5-4.)

10. If, in the opinion of the referees, the conditions among the players become unsatisfactory during the course of the game, they may call the game at any time. It shall be "no game" unless two periods have been completed. Whenever a game is interrupted because of events beyond the control of the responsible administrative authorities (i.e., not involving the players), it shall be continued from the point of interruption, unless the teams agree otherwise or there are conference, league or association rules to cover the situation.

b. The linesman's duties are as follows:

1. The linesman shall determine infractions of the rules concerning offsides (see 6-29) or preceding the puck into the attacking zone (see 6-31).
2. The linesman shall stop the play:
   (a) when the puck goes outside the playing area (see 6-33-a),
   (b) for premature substitution for a goalkeeper (see 2-5-a, NOTE 1),
   (c) when an ineligible player plays the puck coming from his defending zone (see 2-5-d,e).
3. The linesman shall conduct all face-offs in the neutral zone, including the faceoffs at center ice at the beginning of the game and after each goal is scored. If in the last five minutes of regulation play the score is tied or one

goal separates the two teams, he will take any face-off on the special spots. This also will apply for the overtime period.

4. The linesman shall, when requested to do so by the referee, give his version of any incident that may have taken place during the playing of the game.

5. The linesman shall not stop the play to impose any penalty except for violations of too many players on the ice (see 2-5-f), and he shall report such violations to a referee who shall impose a bench minor penalty against the offending team.

He shall report immediately to a referee his version of the circumstances with respect to deliberately displacing the goal post from its normal position (see 6-9-c).

He shall report immediately to a referee his version of any infraction of the rules constituting a major, disqualification or game misconduct penalty or any conduct calling for a bench minor or misconduct penalty under these rules.

Two-man Officiating System (Two Referees)
Section 3.

The referees' duties are as follows:

a. The referee and, subject to him, the assistant referee, shall have general supervision of the game and shall have full control of all game officials and players during the game, including stoppages. In case of any dispute, their decision shall be final and there shall be no appeal. They may change their own decision or that of any other official, provided they do so before play is renewed following rendition of the original decision.

The referees should arrive on the ice together and shall remain on the ice at the conclusion of each period until all players have proceeded to their dressing rooms.

b. The referees shall be garbed in black trousers and official sweaters.

They shall be equipped with whistles and a metal tape measure with a minimum length of six feet [2m].

c. The referees are not required to confer with coaches during the game or its intermission periods.

d. The referees shall order the teams on the ice at the appointed time for the beginning of the game and at the commencement of each period. Teams shall be notified three minutes before play is to start following each intermission.

e. When a referee becomes aware of any lack of conformity to the regulations on equipment, it shall be his duty to see that the required equipment is in use.

f. The referees shall, before starting the game, see that the appointed game timekeeper, penalty timekeeper, official scorer and goal judges are in their respective places and satisfy themselves that the timing and signaling equipment is in order.

g. It shall be their duty to impose such penalties as are prescribed by the rules for infractions thereof, to stop play for any other infraction of the rules and to give final decisions in the matters of disputed goals. The referees may, in matters of disputed goals, consult with the goal judges before making a decision.

h. The referees shall announce to the official scorer or penalty timekeeper all goals and assists legally scored, as well as penalties, and for what infractions such penalties are imposed.

The name of the goal scorer and any player entitled to an assist will be announced on the public address system. If a goal is disallowed for any violation of the rules, the referees shall report the reason for the disallowance to the official scorer, who shall announce the referees' decision correctly over the public address system.

The infraction of the rules for which each penalty has been imposed and reported by the referee will be announced over the public address system.

i. If a referee should accidentally leave the ice or receive an injury which incapacitates him from discharging his duties while play is in progress, the game shall be stopped immediately by the other referee unless one of the teams has the puck in a scoring position, in which case the play shall be allowed to be completed. If it is obvious that the injury sustained is of a serious nature, play shall be stopped immediately.

j. Should one of the appointed referees be unable to act at the last minute or through sickness or accident be unable to finish the game, the other referee shall have the power to appoint a replacement, if he deems it necessary.

k. If, in the opinion of the referees, the conditions among the players become unsatisfactory during the course of the game, they may call the game at any time. It shall be "no game" unless two periods have been completed. Whenever a game is interrupted because of events beyond the control of the responsible administrative authorities (i.e., not involving the players), it shall be continued from the point of interruption, unless the teams agree otherwise or there are conference, league or association rules to cover the situation.

Three-man Officiating System (One Referee, Two Linesmen)
Section 4.

a. The referee's duties are as follows:

1. The referee shall have general supervision of the game and shall have full control of all game officials and players during the game, including stoppages. In case of any dispute, he may change his own decision or that of any other official, provided he does so before play is renewed following rendition of the original decision.

The referee and linesmen should arrive on the ice together and shall remain on the ice at the conclusion of each period until all players have proceeded to their dressing rooms.

2. The referee and linesmen shall be garbed in black trousers and official sweaters.

They shall be equipped with whistles and a metal tape measure with a minimum length of six feet [2m].

3. The referee is not required to confer with coaches during the game or its intermission periods.

4. The referee shall order the teams on the ice at the appointed time for the beginning of the game and at the commencement of each period. Teams shall be notified three minutes before play is to start following each intermission.

5. When the referee becomes aware of any lack of conformity to the regulations on equipment, it shall be his duty to see that the required equipment is in use.

6. The referee shall, before starting the game, see that the appointed game timekeeper, penalty timekeeper, official scorer and goal judges are in their respective places and satisfy himself that the timing and signaling equipment is in order.

7. It shall be his duty to impose such penalties as are prescribed by the rules for infractions thereof, and he shall give the final decision in matters of disputed goals. The referee may, in matters of disputed goals, consult with the linesmen and/or goal judges before making his decision.

8. The referee shall announce to the official scorer or penalty timekeeper all goals and assists legally scored, as well as penalties, and for what infractions such penalties are imposed.

The name of the goal scorer and any player entitled to an assist will be announced on the public address system. If a goal is disallowed for any violation of the rules, the referee shall report the reason for the disallowance to the official scorer, who shall announce the referee's decision correctly over the public address system.

The infraction of the rules for which each penalty has been imposed will be announced as reported by the referee over the public address system.

9. If the referee should accidentally leave the ice or receive an injury which incapacitates him from discharging his duties while play is in progress, the game shall be stopped immediately by a linesman, unless one of the teams has the puck in a scoring position, in which case the play shall be allowed to be completed. If it is obvious that the injury sustained is of a serious nature, play shall be stopped immediately.

If the referee is unable to continue to officiate for any reason, the two linesmen shall act as referees and continue to officiate the game using the two-man officiating system. (See 5-3.)

10. If, in the opinion of the referee, the conditions among the players become unsatisfactory during the course of the game, he may call the game at any time. It shall be "no game" unless two periods have been completed. Whenever a game is interrupted because of events beyond the control of the responsible administrative authorities (i.e., not involving the players), it shall be continued from the point of interruption, unless the teams agree otherwise or there are conference, league or association rules to cover the situation.

b. The linesmen's duties shall be:

1. Linesmen shall determine any infractions of the rules concerning offsides (see 6-29), preceding the puck into the attacking zone (see 6-31) or icing (see 6-21),

2. Linesmen shall stop the play:
   (a) when the puck goes outside the playing area (see 6-33-a),
   (b) when the puck is struck with a stick above the height of four feet [1.22m] (see 6-18-d),
   (c) when the post has been displaced from its normal position (see 6-9-c),
   (d) for offsides occurring at face-off circles (see 6-12-a),
   (e) for premature substitution of a goalkeeper (see 2-5-a, NOTE 1),
   (f) for injured player(s) (see 2-6-d, NOTE),
   (g) when an ineligible player plays the puck coming from his defending zone (see 2-5-d,e).

3. Linesmen shall face the puck at all times, except at the start of the game, at the beginning of each period and after a goal is scored. The referee shall call upon a linesman to conduct a face-off at any time.

4. Linesmen shall, when requested to do so by the referee, give their version of any incident that may have taken place during the playing of the game.

5. Linesmen shall not stop the play to impose any penalty except for violations of:
   (a) too many players on the ice (see 2-5-f) or
   (b) stick or puck thrown on the ice (see 6-1-h).

   They shall report such violations to the referee who shall impose a bench minor penalty against the offending team.

   They shall report immediately to the referee their version of the circumstances with respect to deliberately displacing the goal post from its normal position (see 6-9-c).

   They shall report immediately to the referee their version of any infraction of the rules constituting a major, disqualification or game misconduct penalty or any conduct calling for a bench minor or misconduct under these rules.

Goal Judge
Section 5.
The goal judge shall signal the referee when the puck enters the cage. The referee

320

may give the goal judge an opportunity to inform him as to the manner in which the puck was caused to enter the cage and whether the conditions of the goal-crease rule have been complied with. The final decision as to whether or not the goal shall be scored shall be made by the referee.

The goal judge shall judge at the same cage during the entire match.

NOTE: The goal judge should not talk to the goalkeeper. His duties are very important and should be handled by someone thoroughly competent and informed.

The NCAA Ice Hockey Committee recommends that the goal judges be isolated from the spectators. The goal judges should not smoke or converse. They should wear officials' sweaters.

Penalty Timekeeper
Section 6.

a.   The penalty timekeeper shall keep, on the official forms provided, a correct record of all penalties imposed by the officials, including the names of the players penalized, the infractions penalized, the duration of each penalty and the time at which each penalty was imposed. He shall report in the penalty record each penalty shot awarded, the name of the player taking the shot and the result of the shot.

b.   The penalty timekeeper shall check to be sure that the time served by all penalized players is correct. He shall be responsible for the correct posting of penalties on the scoreboard at all times, and shall promptly call to the attention of the referee any discrepancy between the time recorded on the clock and the official correct time, and shall be responsible for making any adjustments ordered by the referee.

He shall upon request, give a penalized player correct information as to the unexpired time of his penalty.

He shall notify the referee, when play is stopped, if a penalized player went on the rink before his penalty time was complete. In case of a delayed time penalty, he shall see that no penalized player returns to the ice until there is a stoppage of play or until a substitute has been removed.

NOTE 1: The infraction of the rules for which each penalty has been imposed will be announced twice over the public address system as reported by the referee. Where players of both teams are penalized on the same play, the penalty to the visiting player will be announced first.

NOTE 2: Misconduct penalties and coincident major penalties should not be recorded on the timing device, but such penalized players should be alerted and released at the first stoppage of play following the expiration of their penalties.

NOTE 3: If the penalty time is unexpired at the end of the period, the penalty carries over into the next regular or overtime period.

Official Scorer
Section 7.

a. Before the start of the game, the official scorer shall obtain from the coach of both teams a list of all eligible players and the starting lineup of each team. This information shall be made known to the opposing team's coach before the start of play, either personally or through the referee.

  The official scorer shall secure the names of the captain and designated alternate from the coach at the time the lineups are collected and will so indicate by placing the letter "C" or "A" opposite their names on the score sheet. This information shall be presented to the referee for his signature at the completion of the game.

b. The official scorer shall keep a record of the goals scored and who scored them and players to whom assists have been credited and shall indicate those players on the lists who have actually taken part in the game. He also shall record the time of entry into the game of any substitute goalkeeper. He shall record on the official score sheet a notation where a goal is scored when the goalkeeper has been removed from the ice.

c. The awarding of points for goals and assists shall be announced over the public address system, and all changes in such awards also shall be announced in the same manner.

  No requests for changes in any awarding of points shall be considered unless they are made by the team captain at or before the conclusion of actual play in the game.

d. The official scorer also shall prepare the official score sheet for the referee's signature.

Game Timekeeper
Section 8.

a. The game timekeeper shall signal the referee and the competing teams for the start of the game and each succeeding period, and the referee shall start the play promptly in accordance with 6-42.

  To assist in assuring the prompt return to the ice of the teams and the officials, the game timekeeper shall give a preliminary warning three minutes prior to the resumption of play for each period.

b. If the rink is not equipped with an automatic gong, bell or siren, or if such a device fails to function, the game timekeeper shall signal the end of each period by ringing a gong or bell or by blowing a whistle.

c. He shall cause to be announced on the public address system at the nineteenth minute in each period that there is one minute remaining to be played in the period.

d. In the event of any dispute regarding time, the matter shall be referred to the referee for adjustment; and his decision shall be final.

NOTE: *It is the responsibility of the home team to provide a current copy of the NCAA Ice Hockey Rules and a stick-measurement device at the penalty bench.*

Rule 6

PLAYING RULES

Abuse of Officials and Other Misconduct

Section 1.

a. A misconduct penalty shall be imposed on any player who uses obscene, profane or abusive language during the game, intermission or after the game, or to any person who intentionally knocks or shoots the puck out of reach of an official who is retrieving it, or who deliberately throws any equipment out of the playing area.

b. After a penalty has been called, a minor penalty shall be assessed to any player who challenges or disputes the rulings of any referee or fails to go directly and immediately to the penalty bench. If the player persists in such challenge or dispute, he shall be assessed a misconduct penalty; any further dispute will result in a game misconduct penalty being assessed the offending player.

c. A misconduct penalty shall be imposed on any player or players who bang the boards with their sticks or other instruments any time.

In the event that the coach, trainer or student manager commits an infraction under this rule a bench minor penalty shall be imposed.

d. Where coincident penalties are imposed on players of both teams, the penalized players of the visiting team shall take their positions on the penalty bench first in the place designated for visiting players or, where there is no special designation, then on the bench farthest from the gate.

e. Any player who persists in continuing or attempting to continue an altercation after he has been ordered by the referee to stop or who resists a referee in the discharge of his duties shall, at the discretion of the referee, incur a disqualification penalty.

f. A misconduct penalty shall be imposed on any player who, after warning by the referee, persists in any course of conduct (including threatening or abusive language or gestures or similar actions) designed to incite an opponent into incurring a penalty.

g. No coach, manager or other nonplaying person connected with a team shall use foul or abusive language to an official or otherwise try to influence him either while play is in progress or during an intermission. For violation of this rule a minor penalty shall be imposed.

NOTE: If an incident occurs during an intermission, the captain's choice shall be made from his team that started the game. Any announcement or recording should be designated as being against the offending person and not the team.

h. There shall be no whistles blown or other signals given by coaches, trainers or others than the officials, except for substitution when play is stopped. No coach or manager shall enter the rink, except by permission of the referee in case of injury to a player.

Activities of a coach during the progress of the game should be confined to the immediate area of the bench (this is to discourage walking up and down alongisde the rink to coach). For violation of this rule a minor penalty shall be imposed upon a player (his captain's choice) of the team then on the ice for whose benefit the offense was committed.

No coach, manager or other person connected with a team shall throw a stick or puck on the rink. If a puck is thrown onto the ice and definitely interferes with or confuses play, an immediate whistle should occur. If play is not interfered with or confused, a slow whistle is in order. For a violation of this rule a minor penalty shall be imposed upon a player (his captain's choice) of the team then on the ice for whose benefit the offense was committed.

i. A bench minor penalty shall be imposed against the offending team if any player, coach, trainer or student manager interferes in any manner with any game official, including referees, linesmen, timekeepers or goal judges, in the performance of their duties.

The referees may assess further penalties under 6-27 (Molesting Officials) if they deem them to be warranted.

j. A misconduct penalty shall be imposed on any player or players who, except for the purpose of taking their positions on the penalty bench, enter or remain in the referee's crease while the referee is reporting to or consulting with any game official, including the linesmen, timekeeper, penalty timekeeper, official scorer or announcer.

k. If a player persists in any course of conduct for which he was previously assessed a misconduct penalty, he shall be assessed a game misconduct penalty.

Adjustment to Clothing and Equipment
Section 2.

a. Play shall not be stopped nor the game delayed for adjustments to clothing, equipment, shoes, skates or sticks.

b. For infringement of this rule, a minor penalty shall be imposed.

c. The onus of maintaining clothing and equipment in proper condition shall be upon the player. If adjustments are required, the player shall retire from the ice; and play shall continue without interruption with a substitute.

d. No delay shall be permitted for the repair or adjustment of goalkeeper's equipment. If adjustments are required, the goalkeeper will retire from the ice and his place will be taken by the substitute goalkeeper immediately.

e. For an infraction of this rule by a goalkeeper, a minor penalty shall be imposed.

Attempt to Injure
Section 3.

a. A disqualification penalty shall be imposed on any player who deliberately attempts to injure an opponent. A substitute for the penalized player shall be permitted at the end of the fifth minute.

b. A disqualification penalty shall be imposed on any player who deliberately attempts to injure a referee, coach, student manager or trainer in any manner.

Board-Checking
Section 4.

A minor or major penalty, at the discretion of the referee based upon the degree of violence of the impact with the boards, shall be imposed on any player who body-checks, cross-checks, elbows, charges or trips an opponent in such a manner that causes the opponent to be thrown violently into the boards.

Pushing, charging or body-checking an opponent from the rear into the side- or endboards or goal/cages is a flagrant violation, and the offending player shall be assessed a major penalty.

NOTE: Any unnecessary contact with a player playing the puck on an obvious offside play that results in that player being knocked into the boards is "boarding" and must be penalized as such. In other instances where there is no contact with the boards it should be treated as "charging."

"Rolling" an opponent (if he is the puck carrier) along the boards where he is endeavoring to go through too small an opening is not boarding. However, if the opponent is not the puck carrier, then such action should be penalized as boarding, charging or interference; or, if the arms or stick are employed, it should be called holding or hooking.

Broken Stick
Section 5.

a. A player without a stick may participate in the game. A player whose stick is broken may participate in the game provided he drops the broken portion. A minor penalty shall be imposed for an infraction of this rule.

NOTE 1: A broken stick is one that, in the opinion of the official, is unfit for normal play.

b. A goalkeeper may continue to play with a broken stick until stoppage of play or until he has been legally provided with a stick.

c. A player whose stick is broken may not receive a stick thrown onto the ice from any part of the rink but must obtain a stick at his players' bench or be handed one by a teammate. A goalkeeper whose stick is broken may not receive a stick thrown onto the ice from any part of the rink but may receive a stick from a teammate without proceeding to his players' bench. A minor penalty shall be imposed on the player or goalkeeper receiving a stick illegally under this rule.

d. A penalty shot shall be awarded if a goalkeeper deliberately leaves his stick on the ice to prevent a goal.

e. A minor penalty shall be imposed on any player who shall kick, throw, hold or knock an opponent's stick for the purpose of keeping it from the possession of an opponent.

NOTE 2: A stick with a chipped or cracked blade shall not be considered a broken stick, provided such blade is entirely covered with tape and there are no projecting points. Sticks should be kept low at all times.

Charging
Section 6.

a. A minor penalty shall be imposed on a player who runs or jumps into or charges or pushes an opponent from behind.

b. A major penalty, at the discretion of the referee, shall be imposed on a player who charges or otherwise fouls a goalkeeper while the goalkeeper is within his goal crease. Exception: waving arms in front of goalkeeper—minor.

c. A minor penalty shall be imposed on a player who body-checks a goaltender in his privileged area.

NOTE 1: If more than two steps or strides are taken it shall be considered a charge. A fair body-check is one in which a player checks an opponent who is in possession of the puck, by using his hip or body from the front or diagonally from the front or straight from the side, and does not take more than two steps in executing the check.

NOTE 2: No player shall be checked from behind.

d. A minor penalty shall be imposed on a player making physical contact after a stoppage of play.

Cross-Checking and Butt-Ending
Section 7.

a. A minor or major penalty, determined at the discretion of the official, shall be imposed on a player who cross-checks an opponent.

NOTE 1: A cross-check is defined as a check delivered by extending the arms with both hands on the stick and making contact with the opponent above the waist.

b. A major penalty shall be imposed on any player who injures an opponent by cross-checking.

c. A disqualification penalty shall be imposed on any player who butt-ends or attempts to butt-end an opponent.

NOTE 2: An attempt to butt-end shall include all cases where a butt-end gesture is made regardless of whether body contact is made.

Deliberate Injury of Opponents
Section 8.

A disqualification penalty shall be imposed on a player who deliberately injures or attempts to injure an opponent in any manner.

Delaying the Game
Section 9.

a. A minor penalty shall be imposed on any player or goalkeeper who delays the game by deliberately shooting or batting the puck outside the playing area.

NOTE 1: This penalty shall apply also when a player or goalkeeper deliberately bats or shoots the puck outside the playing area after a stoppage of play.

b. A minor penalty shall be imposed on a player or goalkeeper who deliberately holds (freezes) the puck against the boards, cage or ice with his stick, skate, foot or any other part of his body for the purpose of delaying the game. (See also 6-13-b.)

NOTE 2: This rule does not apply to a stalled puck between two players, but it does apply when a player, obviously alone, deliberately stalls the puck. A stalled puck between two players at the boards should call for a fast whistle. The face-off following any stalling by an attacking team in its attacking zone should be in the neutral zone.

c. A minor penalty shall be imposed on any player (including goalkeeper) who delays the game by deliberately displacing a goal post from its normal position. The referee or linesman shall stop play immediately when a goal post has been displaced.

If the goal post is deliberately displaced by a goalkeeper or player during the course of a breakaway, a penalty shot will be awarded to the nonoffending team. The shot shall be taken by the player last in possession of the puck.

NOTE 3: *A player with a breakaway is defined as a player in control of the puck with no opposition between him and the opposing goal and with a reasonable scoring opportunity.*

d. A bench minor penalty shall be imposed upon any team that, after a warning to its captain by the referee, fails to place the correct number of players on the ice to commence play and thereby causes a delay by making additional substitutions, by persisting in having its players offside or in any other manner to cause a delay.

e. A minor penalty shall be imposed on any player who intentionally drops his gloves and/or stick.

NOTE 4: *This includes delay of the game by unnecessarily adjusting equipment or clothing, tying skates, conferring with coaches, players or others, or committing any act for the obvious purpose of stalling or delaying the game. (See also 6-34-b.)*

Elbowing and Kneeing

Section 10.

a. A minor penalty shall be imposed on any player who uses his elbow or knee in such a manner as to foul an opponent.

b. A major penalty shall be imposed on any player who injures an opponent as the result of a foul committed by using his elbow or knee.

Face Masks

Section 11.

a. A major penalty shall be imposed on any player who grasps the face mask of an opponent.

NOTE 1: *Grasping the face mask may also be treated as a "deliberate attempt to injure" under 6-3.*

b. Intentional placement or pushing of an open hand on the face mask shall be judged a minor penalty.

NOTE 2: *The inadvertent or accidental placement of an open hand on the face mask shall not be judged a penalty.*

c. A deliberate attempt to butt or spear an opponent by the use of the face mask shall be judged a major penalty.

NOTE 3: This attempt may also be treated as a "deliberate attempt to injure" under 6-3.

Face-offs
Section 12.

a. The puck shall be faced off by the referee or linesman dropping the puck on the ice between the sticks of the players facing off. Players facing off will stand squarely facing their opponent's end of the rink, approximately one stick length apart with the entire blade of their sticks on the ice.

When the face-off takes place in any of the end face-off circles, the players taking part shall take their positions so that they will have one skate in each side and clear of the line running through the face-off spot and both feet behind and clear of the line parallel to the goal line. The sticks of both players facing off shall have the blades on the ice in contact with the designated marking and entirely clear of the spot or place where the puck is to be dropped and parallel to the sideboards.

No other player shall be allowed to enter the face-off circle or come within 15 feet [4.57m] of the players facing off the puck and must stand onside on all face-offs.

If a violation of this subsection occurs, the referee or linesman shall re-face the puck.

b. If, after warning by the referee or linesman, either of the players fails to take his proper position for the face-off promptly, the official shall be entitled to proceed with the face-off.

c. During any face-off anywhere on the playing surface, no player facing off shall make any physical contact with his opponent's body by means of his own body or his stick, except in the course of playing the puck after the face-off has been completed.

For violation of this rule, the referee shall impose a minor penalty or penalties on the player(s) whose action(s) caused the physical contact.

NOTE 1: A face-off begins when the referee designates the place of the face-off and he (or the linesman) takes his position to drop the puck.

d. If a player facing off fails to take his proper position immediately when directed by the official, the official may order him replaced for that face-off by any teammate then on the ice.

No substitution of players shall be permitted until the face-off has been completed and play has been resumed, except when a penalty is imposed that will affect the on-ice strength of either team.

329

e. A second violation of any of the provisions of 6-12-a above by the same team during the same face-off shall be penalized with a minor penalty to the player who commits the second violation of the rule.

f. When an infringement of a rule has been committed or a stoppage of play has been caused by any player of the attacking team in the attacking zone, the ensuing face-off shall be made in the neutral zone on the nearest face-off spot.

NOTE 2: *This includes a stoppage of play caused by a player of the attacking team shooting the puck onto the back of the defending team's net without any intervening action by the defending team.*

NOTE 3: *This includes the stoppage of play caused by a player of the attacking team when the goal cage becomes accidentally dislodged.*

g. When an infringement of a rule has been committed by players of both teams on the play resulting in the stoppage, the ensuing face-off will be made at the point where the puck was when the stoppage occurred.

h. When a stoppage occurs between the end face-off spots and near the end of the rink, the puck shall be faced off at the end face-off spot on the side where the stoppage occurred, unless otherwise expressly provided by these rules.

i. No face-off shall be made within 15 feet [4.57m] of the goal or sideboards.

j. When a goal is illegally scored as a result of a puck being deflected directly from an official anywhere in the defending zone, the resulting face-off shall be at the end face-off spot in the defending zone.

k. When the game is stopped for any reason not specifically covered in the official rules, the puck must be faced off where it was last played.

l. When a team shoots the puck and it is deflected by a glove or stick protruding from the opponent's bench, the face-off shall be in the neutral zone face-off spot nearest the bench.

m. The whistle will not be blown by the official to start play. Playing time will begin at the instant the puck is faced off and will stop when the whistle is blown.

n. On any face-off, if a team starts play with fewer players than entitled to, any subsequently entering player shall not be eligible to play any puck coming from his own defensive zone until he has returned to his own defensive zone or until possession and control of the puck have been gained by another player in the neutral zone or in his own attacking zone. The penalty for violation of this rule is a last-play face-off.

o. If the goal cage is accidentally dislodged by a defending player, the face-off shall be at the near end face-off spot.

p. If the puck strikes an overhead obstruction, the ensuing face-off is a last play face-off.

NOTE 4: *If the stoppage of play is caused by an attacking player in his attacking zone, the face-off shall be at the zone line. If the stoppage of play is caused by a defending player in the defending zone, the ensuing face-off is a last-play face-off.*

q. If the referee mistakenly stops play, the face-off is at center ice.

r. When a stoppage of play in an end zone takes place and is followed by a gathering of players, no attacking player on the ice or other player coming from the bench shall enter the end zone further than the outer edge of the face-off circles nearest the blue line.

For violation of this rule, the ensuing face-off shall take place at the nearest neutral zone face-off spot.

Falling on or Diving for the Puck
Section 13.

a. A minor penalty shall be imposed on a player other than the goalkeeper who deliberately falls on or gathers a puck into his body.

NOTE 1: *Any player who drops to his knees to block shots should not be penalized if the puck is shot under him or becomes lodged in his clothing or equipment, but any use of hands to make the puck unplayable should be penalized promptly.*

b. A minor penalty shall be imposed on a goalkeeper who when his body is entirely outside the boundaries of his own crease area deliberately falls on or gathers the puck into his body or who holds or places the puck against any part of the goal or against the boards.

c. No defending player, except the goalkeeper, will be permitted to fall on the puck or hold the puck or gather a puck into the body or hands when the puck is within the goal crease.

For infringement of this rule, play shall be stopped immediately and a penalty shot shall be ordered against the offending team; but no other penalty shall be given.

NOTE 2: *This rule shall be interpreted so that a penalty shot will be awarded only when the puck is in the crease at the instant the infraction occurs. However, in cases where the puck is outside the crease, 6-13-1 still may apply; and a minor penalty may be imposed, even though no penalty shot is awarded.*

d. If a player leaves his feet to play the puck and does not make contact with the opponent, play shall continue.

NOTE 3: This section is intended to restrict the diving, rolling or sliding type of body block. It is not intended to restrict a player who has fallen to the ice from playing the puck or to prevent a player from going down on one or both knees to block a shot.

Fighting
Section 14.

a. A disqualification penalty shall be imposed on any player who starts fighting.

NOTE 1: This section shall include fighting, slugging with the fists, spearing, butt-ending or malicious use of the stick at any height, kicking or attempting to do so.

b. A minor penalty shall be imposed on a player who, having been struck, retaliates with a blow or attempted blow. However, at the discretion of the referees, a disqualification or a double minor penalty may be imposed if such player continues the altercation.

NOTE 2: The referee is provided very wide latitude in the penalties which he may impose under this rule. This is done intentionally to enable him to differentiate between the obvious degrees of responsibility of the participants either for starting the fight or persisting in fighting. The discretion provided should be exercised realistically.

c. A disqualification penalty shall be imposed on a player identified by the referees as being the instigator or the aggressor in an altercation.

d. A player who does not retaliate after being struck will not be assessed a penalty.

e. A disqualification penalty shall be assessed any player involved in fighting off the playing surface or with another player who is off the playing surface.

f. Any subsequent player(s) entering an altercation shall be subject to the same penalty(ies) as his teammate(s).

g. When an altercation occurs on the ice, all nonparticipating players, excluding goalkeepers, must proceed immediately and directly to their respective players' bench at the signal of the referee. Goalkeepers must remain in the immediate vicinity of their goal crease. For a violation of this rule, a minor penalty shall be assessed to every offending player.

Goals and Assists

Section 15.

a. A goal is made when the puck, entering from the front, passes between the cage posts below the top of the net and completely across the goal line. If the puck was last touched by a defending player before it entered the cage, the goal is allowed regardless of the manner in which the puck was caused to enter the cage, except that if an attacking player propels the puck other than with his stick, or illegally with his stick, and it bounds or deflects off the person or equipment of the goalkeeper or any other defensive player, the goal shall not be allowed.

An attacking player may score a goal when the puck was last touched by his stick, and then only if the stick was not more than four feet [1.22m] off the ice (height of the goal cage).

If the puck is deflected into the goal from the shot of an attacking player by striking any part of the person of a player of the same side, the goal shall be allowed. The player who deflected the puck shall be credited with the goal.

The goal shall not be allowed if the puck has been kicked, thrown or otherwise deliberately directed into the goal by any means other than a stick.

NOTE: If the puck is between the goalkeeper's pads or lodged in his equipment and is carried over the goal line by an opponent pushing the goalkeeper into the cage, the goal is not allowed. But if it is carried over by a teammate pushing the goalkeeper or if the goalkeeper himself propels it over the goal line, the goal is allowed.

b. A goal scored shall count one point for the team not defending the cage in which the goal is made.

c. A goal shall not be allowed in any of the following cases:

1. If the attacking team has committed a foul that assisted in the making of a goal.
2. If the attacking team had too many players on the rink at the time the goal was made.
3. If the goal was contributed to by a nonplayer.
4. If the puck hits an official and goes directly into the net.
5. If any member of the attacking team (other than the player in possession of the puck) was in or skating through the goal crease when the goal was made from outside the crease, unless the goalkeeper was outside the crease when the play was made (in which case the goal is allowed). (See 6-13-c.) (Exception 6-22-d.)

6. If a goal is made by an attacking player carrying the puck into the cage upon any part of his body, or kicking the puck into the cage.

7. If a goal is made after the referee, assistant referee or timekeeper has signaled play to stop.

8. If an attacking player propels the puck other than with his stick, or illegally with his stick, and it bounds or deflects off the person or equipment of any defensive player into the net.

9. If it is scored with an illegal stick.

d. A goal shall be credited in the scoring records to a player who propels the puck into the opponents' goal. If a goal is scored by a defensive player, credit shall go to the last offensive player to have touched the puck. Each goal shall count one point in the player's record.

When a player scores a goal, an assist shall be credited to the player or players taking part in the play preceding the goal, even though the play may originate in the defensive zone; but not more than two assists can be given on any goal. Each assist so credited shall count one point in the player's record.

For statistical purposes in the records, a save for a goalkeeper shall be credited only when the goalkeeper has prevented the puck from entering the net.

Game Misconduct
Section 16.

A game misconduct penalty involves the suspension of a player for the balance of the game, but a substitute is permitted to replace that player immediately.

NOTE: This is not to be confused with the disqualification penalty. A player receiving a game misconduct penalty is suspended for the remainder of that game only. He is allowed to play in the team's next scheduled game.

Handling the Puck
Section 17.

a. The puck may be stopped and carried or kick-passed by the skate. It may be stopped by any other part of the body, but not thus carried; nor may it be held. It may be stopped by the hand on or off the ice. It may be propelled by the hand or arm, even though in the crease, along the ice, but not thus passed to a teammate. If caught and held, carried or passed to a teammate by hand or arm, an immediate face-off must follow. The puck may be batted by the open hand, but the player who batted it must be the first to recover it for his team. (For the goalkeeper's exceptions, see 6-17-b below.)

If the puck, after being batted in the air by hand or stick or propelled by the hand along the ice, is first touched by an opponent (except a deflection off the goalkeeper), all players are eligible and play is not stopped. If the puck, after being batted in the air by hand or stick, or propelled by the hand along the ice, is first touched by a teammate except a sideward or backward bat from the goalkeeper, play must be immediately stopped. A face-off as provided in 6-12 shall follow. Penalties for violations of this section are specified under separate sections of this rule or elsewhere in the rules.

NOTE 1: If the puck is caught and dropped immediately, play shall continue.

b. A team shall have only one goalkeeper, with goalkeeper's equipment or privileges, on the ice at any one time; and only a player in goalkeeper's equipment is entitled to the privileges outlined below:

1. With his feet or stick, the goalkeeper may play the puck in any manner or direction (except by throwing his stick).

2. Within the privileged area bounded in the rear by his end of the rink, in front by an imaginary line connecting the special spots and on the sides by imaginary lines from the special spots to the endboards, the goalkeeper has certain privileges (see diagram of rink). When he is outside of this area, he does not have these privileges and must play the puck in the same manner as that prescribed for other players, and he is subject to the same penalties as other players.

(a) In stopping the puck, he may catch it, propel or bat it with his hands or stick in any direction. In clearing the puck, he may pick it up, carry it out of the crease or throw it toward his own end of the rink (but not forward). In doing these things, however, he shall not hold the puck more than three seconds. A goalkeeper, after initial warning, may be guilty of delay of the game by unnecessary holding of the puck and may be subject to a minor penalty.

(b) He may not deliberately conceal the puck in his equipment.

(c) He may not throw the puck toward his opponent's end of the rink.

(d) With his hands or arms, he may propel the puck on the ice or bat it in the air toward the opponent's end of the rink, but may not pass it to a teammate.

PENALTIES—(a) through (d)—Special spot face-off.
NOTE 2: If in the opinion of the referee such propelling or batting is done for the purpose of passing the puck to a teammate, and it is played by a

teammate, play should be stopped immediately and the puck faced off at the special spot.

    (e) He may not interfere with an opponent who is not playing the puck.

NOTE 3: Any minor time penalty incurred by a goalkeeper, whether for a foul within his privileged area or elsewhere, shall be served by a teammate on the ice at the time of the infraction and chosen by his captain.

    (f) He may play the puck with his stick at any height; but if injury results from the goalkeeper's high stick, he is liable to the appropriate penalty.

    (g) The goalkeeper shall not be body-checked in his privileged area.

NOTE 4: It is recommended that goalkeepers be urged to make all stops while standing on skates. The practice of diving for the puck and covering is dangerous and should be discouraged.

    (h) If the goalkeeper participates in the play in any manner when he is beyond his attacking blue line, a minor penalty shall be imposed upon him.

High Sticks
Section 18.

a. Carrying sticks above the height of four feet [1.22m], height of the goal cage, is prohibited; and a minor penalty may be imposed on any player violating this rule.

NOTE 1: It is strongly recommended that coaches discourage the use of the slap shot in which the stick is raised above shoulder height on the back swing preparatory to the shot.

b. A goal scored from a stick carried above the height of four feet [1.22m] shall not be allowed, except by a player of the defending team.

c. When a player carries or holds any part of his stick above the height of four feet [1.22m] so that injury to the face or head of an opposing player results, the referees shall have no alternative but to impose a major penalty on the offending player.

d. Batting the puck above the height of four feet [1.22m] with the stick is prohibited, and when it occurs there shall be a whistle unless:

1. The puck is batted to an opponent, in which case the play shall continue.

NOTE 2: When a player bats the puck to an opponent, the referee shall give the washout signal immediately. Otherwise he will stop the play.

2. A player of the defending team bats the puck into his own goal, in which case the goal shall be allowed.

e. When a player at any time causes a stoppage of play by striking the puck with his stick above the height of four feet [1.22m], the resulting face-off shall be made at one of the end face-off spots adjacent to the goal of the team causing the stoppage.

f. A major penalty may be imposed for any penalty involving the use of the stick for contact to the head or neck region of the opponent.

Holding an Opponent
Section 19.

A minor penalty shall be imposed on a player who holds an opponent with hands or stick or in any other way.

NOTE: This rule does permit the lifting of an opponent's stick for the purpose of obtaining the puck or preventing the opponent from playing the puck. It does not include the use of the stick in a reversed position, in pressing down against the ice and thereby holding the stick of an opponent. Such pressing down of the stick of an opponent who is playing the puck, with a stick held in its usual position, is permitted.

Hooking
Section 20.

a. A minor penalty shall be imposed on a player who impedes or seeks to impede the progress of an opponent by hooking with his stick.

b. A major penalty shall be imposed on any player who injures an opponent by hooking.

Icing the Puck
Section 21.

a. For the purpose of this rule, the center line will divide the ice into halves. Should any player of a team, equal or superior in numerical strength to the opposing team, shoot, bat or deflect the puck from his own half of the ice beyond the goal line extended of the opposing team, play shall be stopped and the puck faced off at the end face-off spot of the offending team, unless on the play the puck enters the net of the opposing team, in which case the goal shall be allowed.

For the purpose of this rule, the point of last contact with the puck by the team in possession shall be used to determine whether icing has occurred or not.

Icing the puck shall occur the instant the puck crosses the opponent's goal line extended.

NOTE 1: If, during the period of delayed whistle due to a foul by a player of the team NOT in possession, the team in possession ices the puck, then the face-off following the stoppage of play shall take place in the neutral zone near the defending blue line of the team committing the foul.

NOTE 2: When a team is short-handed as the result of a penalty and the penalty is about to expire, the decision as to whether icing has occurred shall be determined at the instant the penalty expires; and if the puck crosses the opponent's goal line after the penalty has expired, it is icing. The action of the penalized player remaining in the penalty bench will not alter the ruling.

NOTE 3: When the puck is shot and rebounds from the body or stick of an opponent in his own half of the ice so as to cross the goal line extended of the player shooting, it shall not be considered icing.

b. If the puck was so shot by a player of a team below the numerical strength of the opposing team, play shall continue and the face-off shall not take place.

c. If, however, the puck goes beyond the goal line extended at the opposite end of the ice directly from either of two players facing off, it shall not be considered a violation of the rule.

d. If, in the opinion of the referees, a player of the opposing team excepting the goalkeeper, is able to play the puck before it passes his goal line extended, but has not done so, the face-off shall not be allowed and play shall continue.

e. If the puck touches any part of a player of the opposing team or his skates or stick or touches the goalkeeper or his skates or stick at any time before crossing his goal line extended, it shall not be considered icing the puck and play shall continue.

f. If the referees err in calling an icing the puck infraction (regardless of whether either team is short-handed), the puck shall be faced on the center ice face-off spot.

Interference

Section 22.

a. A minor penalty shall be imposed on a player who interferes with or impedes the progress of an opponent who is NOT in possession of the puck, or who deliberately knocks a stick out of an opponent's hand, or who prevents a player who has dropped his stick or any other piece of equipment from regaining possession of it or who knocks or shoots any abandoned or broken stick or illegal puck or other debris towards an opposing puck carrier in a manner that could cause him to be distracted.

NOTE 1: The waving of arms in front of a goalkeeper by an opponent is interference.

NOTE 2: The last player to touch the puck, other than the goalkeeper, shall be considered the player in possession. In interpreting this rule, the referee should make sure which of the players is the one creating the interference— often it is the action and movement of the attacking player that causes the interference since the defending players are entitled to stand their ground or shadow the attacking players. Players of the team in possession shall not be allowed to run interference deliberately for the puck carrier.

b. A minor penalty shall be imposed on any player on the players' bench or on the penalty bench who, by means of his stick or his body, interferes with the movements of the puck or of any opponent on the ice during the progress of play.

c. Unless the puck is in the goal crease, a player of the attacking team may not stand on the goal-crease line or in the goal crease, or hold his stick in the goal-crease area or skate through the goal crease while the attacking team has possession of the puck. For violation of this rule or if the puck should enter the goal while such conditions prevail, a goal shall not be allowed and the puck shall be faced off at the nearest neutral zone face-off spot.

A player of the attacking team may stand or stay in the crease when the puck is in the crease or when he is actually in possession of it.

The provisions of this rule will apply only while the goalkeeper is inside the crease. If he is not in the crease, the rule becomes inoperative.

d. If a player of the attacking team has been physically interfered with by the action of any defending player so as to cause him to be in the goal crease, and the puck should enter the net while the player so interfered with is still within the goal crease, the goal shall be allowed.

e. When a player controlling the puck in his attacking zone and having no opponent to pass other than the goalkeeper is interfered with by a stick or part thereof or any other object thrown or shot by any member of the defending team, a penalty shot shall be awarded to the nonoffending side.

NOTE 3: The attention of the officials is directed particularly to three types of offensive interferences that should be penalized:

1. When the defending team secures possession of the puck in its own end and the other players of that team run interference for the puck carrier by forming a protective screen against forecheckers.

2. When a player facing off obstructs his opposite number after the face-off when the opponent is not in possession of the puck.

3. When the puck carrier makes a drop pass and follows through so as to make bodily contact with an opposing player.

   Defensive interference consists of bodily contact with an opposing player who is not in possession of the puck. A player may, however, guard, cover or maintain his position against an opponent not playing the puck by standing in front of him, even touching the opponent with some part of his body.

f. If in the last two minutes of the game, there is a deliberate illegal substitution (too many men on the ice), a penalty shot shall be awarded against the offending team. No additional penalty shall be assessed.

Interference by Spectators
Section 23.
a. Any player who physically interferes with a spectator shall automatically incur a game misconduct penalty.
b. In the event that objects that interfere with the progress of the game are thrown onto the ice, the officials shall blow the whistle and stop the play; and the puck shall be faced off at the spot where play is stopped.

   NOTE 1: *The band(s) will not be allowed to play while the game is in progress. After a warning, a bench minor penalty may be assessed against the offending team's band.*

   NOTE 2: *If the fans continue to throw objects on the ice after being warned, a bench minor penalty may be assessed against the offending teams' fans for delay of game.*

Kicking a Player
Section 24.
A disqualification penalty shall be imposed on any player who kicks or attempts to kick another player.

Kicking the Puck
Section 25.
a. Kicking the puck shall be permitted in all zones, but a goal may not be scored by the kick of an attacking player.

b. The puck may not be played by the so-called "kick shot" which combines the use of the leg and foot driving the shaft and blade of the stick and producing a very dangerous shot. A misconduct penalty shall be imposed for an infraction of this section.

Leaving Players' Bench or Penalty Bench
Section 26.

a. No player may leave the players' bench or penalty bench at any time during an altercation. Substitutions made prior to the altercation shall be permitted provided the players substituting do not enter the altercation.

b. For violation of this rule, a major penalty shall be imposed on the player or players who leave the players' bench or penalty bench during an altercation, except that if more than five players from a team leave their players' bench during an altercation, a maximum of five players, as designated by the referee, shall be assessed disqualification penalties and no additional major penalties under this rule shall be assessed.

c. Except at the end of each period, or on expiration of a penalty, no player may at any time leave the penalty bench.

d. A penalized player who leaves the penalty bench before his penalty has expired, whether play is in progress or not, shall incur an additional minor penalty, after serving his unexpired penalty.

e. If a player leaves the penalty bench before his penalty is fully served, the penalty timekeeper shall note the time and signal the official, who will stop play immediately.

f. A player who returns to the ice before his time has expired because of an error of the penalty timekeeper is not to serve an additional penalty, but he must serve his unexpired time.

g. If a player in possession of the puck is in such a position as to have no opposition between him and the opposing goaltender, and, while in such position, he is interfered with by a player of the opposing team who has illegally entered the game, the referee shall award a penalty shot to the offended player and assess a misconduct penalty against the offending player.

Molesting Officials
Section 27.

Any player who intentionally makes physical contact with an official shall receive a disqualification penalty. The use of a substitute for the player disqualified shall be permitted after the major penalty has expired.

Obscene or Profane Language or Gestures
Section 28.

a. Players shall not use obscene gestures or profane language on the ice or anywhere in the rink, before, during or after the game. A misconduct penalty shall be imposed for the violation of this rule. If such a violation occurs during a penalty situation, a minor penalty shall be imposed; if violation continues, misconduct penalties shall be imposed.

b. Coaches, managers, trainers or other nonplaying persons connected with a team shall not use profane language to an official or otherwise try to influence him either while play is in progress or during an intermission. A minor penalty shall be imposed for a violation of this rule.

NOTE 1: The minor penalty is upon a player (his captain's choice) from his players on the ice at the time of the incident. If the incident occurs during an intermission, the captain's choice shall be made from his team that started the game.

NOTE 2: Any announcement or recording should be designated as being against the offending person and not the team.

Offsides
Section 29.

a. The position of the player's skates and not that of his stick shall be the determining factor in all instances deciding an offside. A player is offside when both skates are completely over the outer edge of the blue line involved in the play at the instant the puck completely crosses the outer edge of that line.

NOTE 1: A player is onside when either of his skates is in contact with or on his own side of the line at the instant the puck completely crosses the outer edge of that line regardless of the position of his stick.

NOTE 2: It should be noted that, while the position of the player's skates is what determines whether a player is offside, nevertheless the question of offside never arises until the puck has completely crossed the outer edge of the line, at which time the decision is to be made.

b. If, in the opinion of the official, an intentional offside has been made, the puck shall be faced off at the end face-off spot in the defending zone of the offending team.

NOTE 3: An intentional offside is one that is made for the purpose of securing a stoppage of play regardless of the reason, or in which an offside play is made under conditions where there is no possibility of completing a legal pass.

c. If the official errs in calling an offside infraction, regardless of whether either team is short-handed, the puck shall be faced on the center ice face-off spot.

   d. Whenever a defensive player gains possession of the puck on the infraction of zone play by the opponents, play should not be stopped when that player has a clear opening for advancing the puck. Should the puck cross an imaginary line that joins the edges of the special spot circles and extends to the boards or not leave the defensive zone immediately, the offside should be called without further delay.

Passes

Section 30.
   a. The puck may be passed by any player to a player of the same team within any of the three zones into which the ice is divided. (See 2-5-d, e.)
   b. Should the puck, having been passed, contact any part of the body, stick or skates of a player of the same team who is legally onside, the pass shall be considered to have been completed.
   c. The player last touched by the puck shall be deemed to be in possession. Rebounds off the goalkeeper's pad or other equipment shall not be considered as a change of possession or the completion of the play by the team when applying 4-9-b (Calling of Penalties).

Preceding Puck into Attacking Zone

Section 31.
   a. Players of an attacking team must not precede the puck into the attacking zone.
   b. For violation of this rule, the play is stopped and the puck shall be faced off in the neutral zone at the face-off spot nearest the attacking zone of the offending team, if the puck was "carried" offside. The face-off shall be at the origin of the pass, if passed offside.

   NOTE: A player in full control of the puck who crosses the blue line ahead of the puck shall not be considered offside.

   c. If, however, the puck is cleanly intercepted by a member of the defending team at or near the blue line and is carried or passed by his team into the neutral zone, the offside shall be ignored and play permitted to continue, even if a menber of the attacking team has preceded the puck into the attacking zone. (Officials will carry out this rule by means of the slow whistle.)
   d. If a player legally carries or passes the puck back into his own defending zone while a player of the opposing team is in that defending zone, the offside shall be ignored and play permitted to continue. (No slow whistle.)

Protests

   Section 32. It is the policy of the NCAA Men's Ice Hockey Committee not to recognize or allow protests.

Puck Out of Bounds or Unplayable
Section 33.

a. When the puck goes outside the playing area at either end or either side of the rink or strikes any obstacles above the playing surface other than the boards, glass or wire, it shall be faced off from where it was shot or deflected, unless otherwise expressly provided for in these rules.

b. When the puck becomes lodged in the netting on the outside of either goal so that it is unplayable or if it is frozen between opposing players intentionally or otherwise, the official shall stop the play and face off the puck at either of the adjacent face-off spots, unless in the opinion of the official the stoppage of play was caused by a player of the attacking team, in which case the resulting face-off shall be conducted in the neutral zone.

NOTE: This includes stoppage of play caused by a player of the attacking team shooting the puck onto the back of the defending team's net without any intervening action by the defending team.

The defending team or the attacking team may play the puck off the net at any time. However, if the puck remains on the net for longer than three seconds, play shall be stopped and the face-off shall take place in the end face-off zone except when the stoppage is caused by the attacking team, in which case the face-off shall take place on a face-off spot in the neutral zone.

c. A minor penalty shall be imposed on a goalkeeper who deliberately drops the puck on the goal netting to cause a stoppage of play.

d. If the puck comes to rest on top of the boards surrounding the playing area, it shall be considered in play and may be played legally by hand or stick.

Puck Must be Kept in Motion
Section 34.

a. The puck must be kept in motion at all times.

b. A minor penalty shall be imposed on any player, including the goalkeeper, who holds, freezes or plays the puck with his stick, skates or body along the boards in such a manner as to cause a stoppage of play, unless he is actually being checked by an opponent.

Puck Out of Sight and Illegal Puck
Section 35.

a. If a scramble takes place or a player accidentally falls on the puck and the puck is out of sight of the official, he shall immediately blow his whistle and stop the play. The puck shall then be faced off at the point where the play was stopped, unless otherwise provided for in these rules.

b. If at any time while play is in progress a puck other than the one legally in play shall appear on the playing sufrace, the play shall not be stopped but shall continue with the legal puck until the play then in progress is completed by change of possession.

Puck Striking Official
Section 36.

Play shall not be stopped if the puck touches an official anywhere on the rink, regardless of whether a team is short-handed.

Refusing to Start Play
Section 37.

There shall be no refusal to obey the decision of the referee. For violation of this rule the penalty shall be a forfeiture and the score shall be 1 to 0, unless the decision of the referee is accepted within three minutes, in which case a major penalty shall be added to the original penalty.

NOTE: This rule includes refusing to start play at the request of a referee.

Slashing
Section 38.

  a. A minor or major penalty, at the discretion of the referee, shall be imposed on any player who impedes or seeks to impede the progress of an opponent by slashing with his stick.

  b. A major penalty shall be imposed on any player who injures an opponent by slashing.

  NOTE: In administering the slashing rule, officials will penalize any player who swings his stick at any opposing player (whether in or out of range) without actually striking him or who on the pretext of playing the puck, makes a wild swing at the puck with the object of intimidating an opponent.

  c. Any player who swings his stick at another player in the course of any altercation shall be subject to a disqualification penalty.

Spearing
Section 39.

A disqualification penalty shall be imposed on a player who spears or attempts to spear an opponent.

NOTE 1: Spearing shall mean stabbing an opponent with the point of the stick blade while the stick is being carried with one hand or both hands.

NOTE 2: Attempt to spear shall include all cases where a spearing gesture is made regardless of whether bodily contact is made.

Start of Game and Periods

Section 40.

a. The game shall commence at the scheduled time by a face-off in the center of the rink and shall be renewed promptly at the conclusion of each intermission in the same manner.

No delay shall be permitted by reason of any ceremony, exhibition, demonstrations or presentation unless consented to in advance by the visiting team.

The home team shall have the choice of ends to start the game. The home team players' bench shall be nearest the end selected.

b. The teams shall change ends at the beginning of each subsequent regular period. If, in the opinion of the official, conditions are more favorable to play at one end of the rink than at the other, he may equalize opportunities by having teams change ends at the middle of one or all three regular and overtime periods, but not in only two regular periods. The official must rule that this change is to be made before the commencement of the game or period.

NOTE 1: The intent of this section is that no team shall play under unfavorable conditions throughout an entire period or, when ends are changed at the middle point, two successive half-periods.

c. During the pregame warm-up (which shall not exceed 20 minutes in duration), each team shall be allowed to skate on the entire ice surface until such time that one team assumes its own end. At that time, each team must confine its activity to its own end of the rink for the duration of the warm-up.

Throwing Stick

Section 41.

a. No player, including the goalkeeper, shall throw his stick in any zone. If the stick is thrown to prevent a goal, a penalty shot will be awarded. If thrown, but not to prevent a goal, a minor penalty shall be awarded.

b. No player shall throw a stick or portion of a stick from the playing surface. It must be dropped to the ice immediately. For a violation of this rule, a misconduct penalty shall be awarded.

c. A penalty shot shall be awarded when a goalkeeper deliberately leaves his stick on the ice to prevent a goal.

NOTE: When a player discards the broken portion of a stick by tossing it to the side of the ice (and not over the boards) in such a way that it will not interfere with play or opposing players, no penalty will be imposed.

Time of Match

Section 42.

a. The time allowed for a game shall be three 20-minute periods of actual play with recommended rest intermissions of 15 minutes between each period. The duration of the match includes all intermissions.

Officials' duties and powers continue during intermissions and until all players have left the ice.

b. The team scoring the greatest number of goals during the three 20-minute periods shall be the winner.

c. If any unusual delay occurs in the first or second periods, the official may order the next regular intermission to be taken immediately and the balance of the period will be completed on the resumption of play with the teams defending the same goals. The teams will change ends and play the following period without delay.

d. The rules committee recommends that all secondary school matches be limited to regular periods of not less than 15 minutes. It is recommended that penalty times be reduced in the same proportion that length of period played is to a 20-minute period. Example: With 10-minute periods played, a misconduct penalty will be five minutes; with 15-minute periods played, misconduct penalty will be 7½ minutes; a minor penalty will be 1½.

e. If, at any time during the course of the game, the official believes that the playing conditions or the conditions among the players have become unsatisfactory, he may call the game; and the score of the game shall be what it was when the game was called. It shall be "no game" unless two periods have been completed.

NOTE: Whenever a game is interrupted because of events beyond the control of the responsible administrative authorities (i.e., not involving players), it shall be continued from the point of interruption, unless the teams agree otherwise or there are conference, league or association rules to cover the situation.

Tied Games

Section 43.

a. If the score is tied at the end of three regulation 20-minute periods, the following shall take place:

   1. The teams shall not change ends.

   2. A 10-minute period shall be played.

   3. The team that scores first wins and the game is ended. If no goal is scored in the 10-minute period, the game shall be declared a tie.

b. Any overtime period shall be considered part of the game and all unexpired penalties shall remain in force.

c. If either team declines to play in the necessary overtime period, the game shall be declared a loss for that team.

NOTE: If, in the opinion of the officials, the ice surface is unplayable, the ice will be resurfaced. The normal intermission shall be in effect. All tournament games will be played under the discretion of the tournament committee.

Timeouts

Section 44.

Each team shall be permitted to take one timeout of one-minute duration during the game and which must be taken during a normal stoppage of play. The timeout may be used for warming up the substitute goalkeeper or for any other purpose.

Tripping

Section 45.

a. A minor penalty shall be imposed on any player who places his stick, knee, foot, arm, hand or elbow in such a manner that it causes his opponent to trip or fall.

NOTE 1: If, in the opinion of the officials, a player on a sweep or hook-check is unquestionably playing the puck and obtains possession of it, thereby tripping the puck carrier, no penalty shall be imposed unless the tripping is flagrant.

b. When a player in control of the puck in his attacking zone is tripped or otherwise fouled, thus preventing a reasonable scoring opportunity, a penalty shot shall be awarded to the nonoffending team. However, the official shall not stop the play until the attacking team has lost possession of the puck to the defending team. If a goal is scored by the nonoffending team, no penalty shot is awarded.

NOTE 2: The intention of this rule is to restore a reasonable scoring opportunity that has been lost because of a foul from behind when the foul is committed on the opponent's side of the attacking blue line.

"Control of the puck" is defined as the act of propelling the puck with the stick. If, while it is being propelled, the puck is touched by another player or his equipment, hits the goal or goes free, the player no longer shall be considered "in control of the puck."

Unnecessary Roughness

Section 46.

A minor penalty may be imposed on any player deemed guilty of unnecessary roughness, at the discretion of the referee.

NCAA VERSUS IIHF PLAYING RULES

The following is an outline of the more significant rule differences between the IIHF and NCAA playing rules. There are other differences of a more technical nature which are not mentioned because they are unnecessary to consider for the purpose of a one time friendly exhibition game.

INTERNATIONAL ICE HOCKEY FEDERATION (IIHF)	NATIONAL COLLEGIATE ATHLETIC ASSOCIATION (NCAA)

Goal Crease

Rectangle	Semi-circle

Goalkeeper's Privileged Area

He may play the puck up to the center red line.	He may not fall on the puck outside of the area bounded by an imaginary line connecting the end zone face-off spots and from the face-off spots to the end boards.
He may be bodychecked outside of the goal crease provided he has possession and *control* of the puck.	He may not be bodychecked *anywhere*.

Deliberate Illegal Substitution

Penalty shot if in the last two minutes of the game.	No rule

Players in Uniform

20 including 2 goalkeepers	18 excluding goalkeepers

Too Many Men

A bench minor (1) regardless of how many extra players.	A minor penalty to each extra player.

Penalized Player Returning to Play

Only the offside pass rule applies.	The returning player is not eligible to play the puck in the neutral zone or his attacking zone unless he skates into his defensive zone or the puck is played by another player in the neutral zone.

Injured Player

An injured player that has been assessed a penalty must be replaced on the penalty bench immediately.

If an injured player has been assessed a major penalty, his team is not required to place a substitute on the penalty bench until just before the penalty expires.

Warm-up of Substitute Goalkeeper

Not permitted

One minute—once per game

Illegal Stick

Minor penalty

Misconduct Penalty

Stick Measurement Request

Bench minor on the team if they request a measurement and stick is legal.

Bench minor on *second* request and both sticks are legal.

If the player refuses to give the referee his stick for measurement—minor plus misconduct. Any goal scored is allowed.

Misconduct only—any goal scored is disallowed.

Facemasks

Optional unless dangerous to other players.

Mandatory in ECAC, only

Scoring a Penalty Shot on a Shorthanded Team

A minor penalty is terminated.

Minor penalty does *not* terminate.

Goalkeeper—Major or Misconduct Penalty

Served by another player on the ice.

Goalkeeper must serve.

Game, Gross Misconduct, or Match Penalty

Game Misconduct — Suspended for the balance of the game and subject to further suspension.
Gross Misconduct and Match Penalty — Balance of the game and cannot play again until his case has been reviewed.

Disqualification Penalty

Suspension for the balance of the game and the next game of his team.

Goalkeeper's Action on a Penalty Shot

May go out to the red line. If he throws anything, a goal is awarded.

Must stay in "privileged" area. If he throws anything, another penalty shot is assessed.

Designation of a Player to Take a Penalty Shot that is Awarded to the Team or a Player that is Injured

Player on the ice

Any nonpenalized player

Goalkeeper Participating in the Play

Up to the center red line

Up to his attacking blue line

Awarding of a Goal

When the goalkeeper has been removed and:

1. An opposing player on a breakaway is fouled from behind.

2. An illegal player interferes with the puck or an opponent.

3. Any member of his team throws any object at an opponent on a breakaway thereby preventing a shot on the open goal.

No such rule

Penalized Player not Going Directly and Immediately to the Penalty Bench

Bench minor to the team

An additional minor penalty to the player

Any Player or Team Official Throwing Something onto the Ice

Bench minor

Minor penalty to a player on the ice

Team Official Going onto the Ice

Game misconduct to offender

Minor penalty (captain's choice) to player on the ice

Misconduct of Team Official

Game misconduct

No rule

Butt-end or Spearing or Attempting to Do So

Minor *or* major plus misconduct
If injury results—match penalty

Major plus disqualification

Roughing

Minor or double minor penalty

Minor penalty

Player(s) Intervening in an Altercation

Game misconduct to first player in

Same penalties as original offenders

Players to Benches During an Altercation

No such rule

At the signal of the referee, all nonparticipating players except the goalkeepers shall go to their players bench. A minor penalty for a violation of this rule.

Goalkeeper Throwing Puck Forward

Minor penalty to goalkeeper

End zone face-off

Hand Pass to a Teammate

Last play face-off if deliberately batted to a teammate, otherwise play continues.

Last play face-off

High Sticking

Above the normal height of the shoulders

Above 4 feet

Last play face-off unless committed by a team of great strength in which case end zone face-off

End zone face-off of offending team

Position of Fouled Player to Award a Penalty Shot on a Breakaway

Beyond center red line

In his attacking zone

Icing

Originates from behind center red line	Originates from offending team's defending zone
Completed when touched by defending player other than goalkeeper	Completed when the puck crosses the goal line
Nullified if the puck passes through the goal crease before it goes over the goal line	No such rule

Player in Goal Crease

If an attacking player precedes the puck into the goal crease, any goal scored will be disallowed.	Unless the goalkeeper is out of the crease, no attacking player shall be allowed to enter the crease. For a violation—neutral zone faceoff.

Fouling the Goalkeeper

Major penalty only for charging goalkeeper in the goal crease. All other fouls are minor penalty.	Major penalty for any foul if the goalkeeper is in his crease.

Leaving the Players' or Penalty Bench During an Altercation

Double minor and a game misconduct to the first player and misconducts to all others up to a maximum of five per team.	Major or disqualification penalty to all players up to a maximum of five per team
Any player who comes off the bench and receives a penalty for his action shall also receive a game misconduct.	No such rule
A player coming off the penalty bench shall be assessed a minor penalty and a game misconduct unless he was penalized as the first man off either bench.	No such rule

Throwing a Stick (or any Object) at the Puck

By defending player in his defending zone—penalty shot not in defending zone—major penalty.	To prevent a goal—penalty shot, otherwise—minor penalty.

Throwing a Stick out of the Rink

Misconduct or game misconduct. If in protest of an official's decision, a minor penalty plus a game misconduct.

Misconduct

Coincident Major Penalties

No such rule

The teams shall be permitted immediate substitution.

PLAYING RULES
Major Differences—IIHF—NHL

	IIHF	NHL
CAPTAIN	May come off the players' bench to get an interpretation of a ruling.	May not come off the players' bench unless invited by the referee
*COINCIDENT MAJOR PENALTIES	No rule	Teams do not serve shorthanded
MEASUREMENT OF EQUIPMENT	Referee may measure at any time.	Referee may measure only upon a request of opposing team
*ATTEMPT TO INJURE A TEAM OFFICIAL	Gross misconduct	Game misconduct
REPLACEMENT FOR BROKEN STICK THROWN FROM THE PLAYERS' BENCH	Bench minor plus minor to receiving player only if he picks it up	Bench minor and minor to receiving player whether he picks it up or not
CHARGING GOALIE IN THE GOAL CREASE	Major	Minor or major
*DELIBERATE INJURY TO OPPONENT PLAYER	Match—team Shorthanded 5 minutes	Match—team Shorthanded 10 minutes
*TO TEAM OFFICIAL	Gross misconduct	Game misconduct
BUTTING ENDING (incl. Attempt)	Minor or major plus automatic misconduct	Major

DELIBERATELY DIS-PLACING GOAL AND ILLEGAL SUB-STITUTION	Penalty shot if in the last 2 minutes of the game	Penalty shot if insufficient time to serve penalty
*OFFSIDE ON FACE-OFF	Play to continue if non-offending team gains possession of the puck	Immediate stoppage of play
*FIGHTING	Match penalty to player starting fight	Major or major and game misconduct to player starting fight
	Minor, double minor, major, or match penalty to retaliator	Minor, double minor, major, or game misconduct to retaliator
PLAYERS NOT INVOLVED IN ALTERCATION	No rule	Misconduct for not going to the designated area upon the signal of the referee.
GOALKEEPER THROWING PUCK FORWARD	No penalty if first recovered by an opponent	No penalty if first recovered by an opponent and he scored a goal
*BATTING THE PUCK WITH THE HAND INTO THE GOAL	No goal	Valid goal, if it deflects off of an opposing player other than the goalkeeper
*PLAYING THE PUCK WITH A HIGH STICK TO A TEAMMATE BY A TEAM OF GREATER NUMERICAL STRENGTH	Last play face-off except for attacking player in attacking zone	End zone face-off of offending team
*ATTACKING PLAYER STANDING IN THE GOAL CREASE	No goal if scored	Minor penalty—no goal if scored

PLAYING RULES

PLAYERS, OTHER THAN THE FIRST ONE OFF, LEAVING PLAYERS' BENCH DURING AN ALTERCATION	Misconduct up to a maximum of five	A fine—no penalty
A TEAM OFFICIAL GOING ONTO THE ICE DURING A PERIOD	Game misconduct	Bench minor
*A TEAM OFFICIAL GUILTY OF ANY TYPE OF MISCONDUCT	Game misconduct	Bench minor
*INTENTIONAL OFFSIDE BY A SHORT-HANDED TEAM	End zone face-off of offending team	Neutral zone face-off of offending team
ATTACKING PLAYER OVER THE CENTER RED LINE WHEN PUCK CROSSES LINE ON A PASS FROM A TEAMMATE IN HIS DEFENSIVE ZONE	Can make himself eligible to play the puck by touching center red line with either skate	Cannot make himself eligible to play the puck
TEAM ON THE ICE REFUSING TO PLAY	Minor penalty 30 seconds after warning by referee	Minor penalty after 15 seconds
TEAM OFF THE ICE REFUSING TO PLAY	Forfeited after 2 minutes	Forfeited after 5 minutes
SWING STICK AT AN OPPONENT DURING AN ALTERCATION	Major or match penalty	Fine
SPEARING (incl. Attempt)	Minor or major penalty plus automatic misconduct	Major
TIMEOUT	None	One 30-second timeout per game

12

THE CHAMPIONS

THE STANLEY CUP WINNERS

STANLEY CUP WINNERS

Season	Champions	Manager	Coach
1984–85	Edmonton Oilers	Glen Sather	Glen Sather
1983–84	Edmonton Oilers	Glen Sather	Glen Sather
1982–83	New York Islanders	Bill Torrey	Al Arbour
1981–82	New York Islanders	Bill Torrey	Al Arbour
1980–81	New York Islanders	Bill Torrey	Al Arbour
1979–80	New York Islanders	Bill Torrey	Al Arbour
1978–79	Montreal Canadiens	Irving Grundman	Scotty Bowman
1977–78	Montreal Canadiens	Sam Pollock	Scotty Bowman
1976–77	Montreal Canadiens	Sam Pollock	Scotty Bowman
1975–76	Montreal Canadiens	Sam Pollock	Scotty Bowman
1974–75	Philadelphia Flyers	Keith Allen	Fred Shero
1973–74	Philadelphia Flyers	Keith Allen	Fred Shero
1972–73	Montreal Canadiens	Sam Pollock	Scotty Bowman
1971–72	Boston Bruins	Milt Schmidt	Tom Johnson
1970–71	Montreal Canadiens	Sam Pollock	Al MacNeil
1969–70	Boston Bruins	Milt Schmidt	Harry Sinden
1968–69	Montreal Canadiens	Sam Pollock	Claude Ruel
1967–68	Montreal Canadiens	Sam Pollock	Toe Blake
1966–67	Toronto Maple Leafs	Punch Imlach	Punch Imlach
1965–66	Montreal Canadiens	Sam Pollock	Toe Blake
1964–65	Montreal Canadiens	Sam Pollock	Toe Blake
1963–64	Toronto Maple Leafs	Punch Imlach	Punch Imlach
1962–63	Toronto Maple Leafs	Punch Imlach	Punch Imlach
1961–62	Toronto Maple Leafs	Punch Imlach	Punch Imlach
1960–61	Chicago Black Hawks	Tommy Ivan	Rudy Pilous
1959–60	Montreal Canadiens	Frank Selke	Toe Blake

STANLEY CUP WINNERS

Season	Champions	Manager	Coach
1958–59	Montreal Canadiens	Frank Selke	Toe Blake
1957–58	Montreal Canadiens	Frank Selke	Toe Blake
1956–57	Montreal Canadiens	Frank Selke	Toe Blake
1955–56	Montreal Canadiens	Frank Selke	Toe Blake
1954–55	Detroit Red Wings	Jack Adams	Jimmy Skinner
1953–54	Detroit Red Wings	Jack Adams	Tommy Ivan
1952–53	Montreal Canadiens	Frank Selke	Dick Irvin
1951–52	Detroit Red Wings	Jack Adams	Tommy Ivan
1950–51	Toronto Maple Leafs	Conn Smythe	Joe Primeau
1949–50	Detroit Red Wings	Jack Adams	Tommy Ivan
1948–49	Toronto Maple Leafs	Conn Smythe	Hap Day
1947–48	Toronto Maple Leafs	Conn Smythe	Hap Day
1946–47	Toronto Maple Leafs	Conn Smythe	Hap Day
1945–46	Montreal Canadiens	Tommy Gorman	Dick Ivan
1944–45	Toronto Maple Leafs	Conn Smythe	Hap Day
1943–44	Montreal Canadiens	Tommy Gorman	Dick Irvin
1942–43	Detroit Red Wings	Jack Adams	Jack Adams
1941–42	Toronto Maple Leafs	Conn Smythe	Hap Day
1940–41	Boston Bruins	Art Ross	Cooney Weiland
1939–40	New York Rangers	Lester Patrick	Frank Boucher
1938–39	Boston Bruins	Art Ross	Art Ross
1937–38	Chicago Black Hawks	Bill Stewart	Bill Stewart
1936–37	Detroit Red Wings	Jack Adams	Jack Adams
1935–36	Detroit Red Wings	Jack Adams	Jack Adams
1934–35	Montreal Maroons	Tommy Gorman	Tommy Gorman
1933–34	Chicago Black Hawks	Tommy Gorman	Tommy Gorman
1932–33	New York Rangers	Lester Patrick	Lester Patrick
1931–32	Toronto Maple Leafs	Conn Smythe	Dick Irvin
1930–31	Montreal Canadiens	Cecil Hart	Cecil Hart
1929–30	Montreal Canadiens	Cecil Hart	Cecil Hart
1928–29	Boston Bruins	Art Ross	Cy Denney
1927–28	New York Rangers	Lester Patrick	Lester Patrick
1926–27	Ottawa Senators	Dave Gill	Dave Gill
1925–26	Montreal Maroons	Eddie Gerard	Eddie Gerard
1924–25	Victoria Cougars	Lester Patrick	Lester Patrick
1923–24	Montreal Canadiens	Leo Dandurand	Leo Dandurand
1922–23	Ottawa Senators	Tommy Gorman	Pete Green
1921–22	Toronto St. Pats	Charlie Querrie	Eddie Powers
1920–21	Ottawa Senators	Tommy Gorman	Pete Green
1919–20	Ottawa Senators	Tommy Gorman	Pete Green
1918–19	a — No decision		
1917–18	Toronto Arenas	Charlie Querrie	Dick Carroll

a — In the spring of 1919 the Montreal Canadiens travelled to Seattle to meet Seattle, PCHL champions. After five games had been played—teams were tied at 2 wins and 1 tie—the series was called off by the local Department of Health because of the influenza epidemic and the death from influenza of Joe Hall.

STANLEY CUP WINNERS PRIOR TO FORMATION OF NHL IN 1917

Season	Champions	Manager	Coach
1916–17	Seattle Metropolitans	Pete Muldoon	Pete Muldoon
1915–16	Montreal Canadiens	George Kennedy	George Kennedy
1914–15	Vancouver Millionaires	Frank Patrick	Frank Patrick
1913–14	Toronto Blueshirts	Jack Marshall	Scotty Davidson*
1912–13**	Quebec Bulldogs	M.J. Quinn	Joe Malone*
1911–12	Quebec Bulldogs	M.J. Quinn	C. Nolan
1910–11	Ottawa Senators		Bruce Stuart*
1909–10	Montreal Wanderers	R. R. Boon	Pud Glass*
1908–09	Ottawa Senators		Bruce Stuart*
1907–08	Montreal Wanderers	R. R. Boon	Cecil Blachford
1906–07	Montreal Wanderers (March)	R. R. Boon	Cecil Blachford
1906–07	Kenora Thistles (January)	F.A. Hudson	Tommy Phillips*
1905–06	Montreal Wanderers		Cecil Blachford*
1904–05	Ottawa Silver Seven		A. T. Smith
1903–04	Ottawa Silver Seven		A. T. Smith
1902–03	Ottawa Silver Seven		A. T. Smith
1901–02	Montreal A.A.A.		C. McKerrow
1900–01	Winnipeg Victoria		D. H. Bain
1899–1900	Montreal Shamrocks		H. J. Trihey*
1898–99	Montreal Shamrocks		H. J. Trihey*
1897–98	Montreal Victorias		F. Richardson
1896–97	Montreal Victorias		Mike Grant*
1895–96	Montreal Victorias (December 1896)		Mike Grant*
1895–96	Winnipeg Victorias (February)		J. C. G. Armytage
1894–95	Montreal Victorias		Mike Grant*
1893–94	Montreal A.A.A.		
1892–93	Montreal A.A.A.		

*In the early years the teams were frequently run by the Captain. *Indicates Captain.
**Victoria defeated Quebec in challenge series. No official recognition.

NHL REGULAR SEASON CHAMPIONS

1917–18   Montreal Canadiens won the first half
          Toronto Maple Leafs won the second half
1918–19   Ottawa overall point leaders
          Canadiens won first half
          Ottawa won second half
1919–20   Ottawa overall point leaders
          Ottawa won both halves

1920–21	St. Patricks overall point leaders	
	Ottawa won first half	
	St. Patricks won second half	
1921–22	Ottawa	
1922–23	Ottawa	
1923–24	Ottawa	
1924–25	Hamilton	
1925–26	Ottawa	
1926–27	Canadian Division	Ottawa
	American Division	Rangers
1927–28	Canadian Division	Canadiens
	American Division	Bruins
1928–29	Canadian Division	Canadiens
	American Division	Bruins
1929–30	Canadian Division	Canadiens
	American Division	Bruins
1930–31	Canadian Division	Canadiens
	American Division	Bruins
1931–32	Canadian Division	Canadiens
	American Division	Rangers
1932–33	Canadian Division	Maple Leafs
	American Division	Bruins
1933–34	Canadian Division	Maple Leafs
	American Division	Red Wings
1934–35	Canadian Division	Maple Leafs
	American Division	Bruins
1935–36	Canadian Division	Canadiens
	American Division	Red Wings
1936–37	Canadian Division	Canadiens
	American Division	Red Wings
1937–38	Canadian Division	Maple Leafs
	American Division	Bruins
1938–39*	Bruins	
1939–40	Bruins	
1940–41	Bruins	
1941–42	Rangers	
1942–43	Red Wings	
1943–44	Canadiens	
1944–45	Canadiens	
1945–46	Canadiens	
1946–47	Canadiens	
1947–48	Maple Leafs	
1948–49	Red Wings	

360

1949–50	Red Wings
1950–51	Red Wings
1951–52	Red Wings
1952–53	Red Wings
1953–54	Red Wings
1954–55	Red Wings
1955–56	Canadiens
1956–57	Red Wings
1957–58	Canadiens
1958–59	Canadiens
1959–60	Canadiens
1960–61	Canadiens
1961–62	Canadiens
1962–63	Maple Leafs
1963–64	Canadiens
1964–65	Red Wings
1965–66	Canadiens
1966–67	Black Hawks

1967–68 Canadiens—Eastern Division
Flyers—Western Division
Canadiens most points overall

1968–69 Canadiens—Eastern Division
Blues—Western Division
Canadiens most points overall

1969–70 Black Hawks—Eastern Division
Blues—Western Division
Black Hawks most points overall

1970–71 Bruins—Eastern Division
Black Hawks—Western Division
Bruins most points overall

1971–72 Bruins—Eastern Division
Black Hawks—Western Division
Bruins most points overall

1972–73 Canadiens—Eastern Division
Black Hawks—Western Division
Canadiens most points overall

1973–74 Bruins—Eastern Division
Flyers—Western Division
Bruins most points overall

1974–75 Canadiens—Norris Division
Flyers—Patrick Division
Sabres—Adams Division
Canucks—Smythe Division

1974–75 (continued)
    Canadiens, Flyers and Sabres tie for overall point title with 113
1975–76   Canadiens—Norris Division
    Flyers—Patrick Division
    Bruins—Adams Division
    Black Hawks—Smythe Division
    Canadiens overall point champions
1976–77   Canadiens—Norris Division
    Flyers—Patrick Division
    Bruins—Adams Division
    Blues—Smythe Division
    Canadiens overall point champions
1977–78   Canadiens—Norris Division
    Islanders—Patrick Division
    Bruins—Adams Division
    Black Hawks—Smythe Division
    Canadiens overall point champions
1978–79   Canadiens—Norris Division
    Islanders—Patrick Division
    Bruins—Adams Division
    Black Hawks—Smythe Division
    Islanders overall point champions
1979–80   Canadiens—Norris Division
    Flyers—Patrick Division
    Sabres—Adams Division
    Black Hawks—Smythe Division
    Flyers overall point champions
1980–81   Canadiens—Norris Division
    Islanders—Patrick Division
    Sabres—Adams Division
    Blues—Smythe Division
    Islanders overall point champions
1981–82   Canadiens—Norris Division
    Islanders—Patrick Division
    North Stars—Adams Division
    Edmonton—Smythe Division
    Islanders overall point champions
1982–83   Chicago—Norris Division
    Boston—Adams Division
    Philadelphia—Patrick Division
    Edmonton—Symthe Division
    Boston—overall point champions

1983–84   Minnesota—Norris Division
           Edmonton—Smythe Division
           Boston—Adams Division
           Islanders—Patrick Division
           Edmonton overall point champions
1984–85   St. Louis—Norris Division
           Edmonton—Smythe Division
           Montreal—Adams Division
           Philadelphia—Patrick Division
           Philadelphia overall point champions
*End of American and Canadian Division and single division winner.

GLOSSARY

Assist

The pass or passes that lead to a goal. No more than two assists may be awarded on a goal. The record for assists in a season is held by Wayne Gretzky: 125. The record for assists in an NHL career is held by Gordie Howe: 1,049.

Back-Check

Covering an opponent, usually a player's opposite—left wing on right wing, for example—in the defensive zone. Good back-checkers are referred to as "two-way players." Two of the sport's best ever were Bob Davidson of the 1940s Maple Leafs and Milt Schmidt of the 1940s Bruins.

Backhand

A shot or pass using the closed end (heel) of the stick from a player's "other" side. A right-handed shot would *take* a pass on the *back* of his stickblade, with the stick to his right. To *make* the pass or shot his stick would move across his body from right to left, in the direction intended by the shooter. Maurice "Rocket" Richard and Red Berenson had good backhand shots.

Back-Pass

A pass pushed backwards by the puck carrier.

Blocker

The glove worn on the stickhand of the goaltender. It is used to deflect pucks shot high, to the goaltender's stick side. Emile Francis is credited with the creation of the blocker.

Blue Line

There are two blue lines. Together with the center red line, they break up the ice surface into three sixty-foot sections. The blue lines are located sixty feet from the end goal lines. Lester and Frank Patrick are credited with the introduction of the blue lines in 1918.

Boards

Together with the glass, the boards enclose the playing surface. Boards are constructed of wood or fiberglass and are a standard forty-eight inches high. The Minnesota Fighting Saints of the WHA had transparent boards so spectators could see the puck at all times.

Boarding

A minor penalty: causing an opponent to be thrown violently into the boards.

Bodycheck

Hitting an opponent cleanly with a shoulder or hip is referred to as a bodycheck. Ching Johnson, Eddie Shore, Bill Ezinicki, Bob Plager, and Brad Park are examples of great bodycheckers.

Breakaway

A player skating in alone on the goaltender in an attempt to score.

Butt-Ending

A major penalty: jabbing an opponent with the butt-end of the stick.

Charging

A minor penalty: taking more than two strides before hitting an opponent.

Clearing the puck

Getting the puck away from in front of the net or sending the puck out of the defensive zone while killing a penalty.

Covering up

When a player stops play by keeping the puck motionless, he is covering up. This term usually referes to goaltenders who stop play after making a save.

Crease

An area four feet long and eight feet wide, marked by a red line, in front of the goal cage. No opposing player may enter the crease subject to a two-minute penalty for interference. Goaltenders Gerry Cheevers and Bill Smith believed that too many opponents invaded their territory, so they kept the crease clear by force.

Crossbar

The horizontal pipe across the top of the goal cage: four feet above the ice and six feet long.

Defenseman

A team puts two defensemen on the ice at a time. The defenseman follows the play up-ice and is primarily responsible for protecting his end of the ice and breaking up an opposing attack. Usually defensemen run the power play. There are two types of defensemen: offensive and defensive. Offensive defensemen, typified by Bobby Orr—who led the league in scoring for two years — and Doug Wilson, take more of a part in scoring goals. Defensive defensemen, typified by Mike Milbury and Ken Morrow, are concerned only with keeping their end of the ice free from opposing forwards.

Deflection

A puck is shot toward the goal and changes direction after striking a skate or stick. Many players practice deflecting the puck past the goaltender.

Deke

A fake executed by moving the puck from the forehand part of the stick to the backhand.

Delay of game

A minor penalty assessed for deliberately stopping play by throwing the puck out of the rink or for refusing to obey a referee's call.

Delayed penalty

A referee signals a delayed penalty by raising his arm and not stopping play. This is done because the nonoffending team has possession of the puck and the delay allows them a chance to create a play. The second the offending team touches the puck, the referee whistles a stoppage of play and assesses the penalty.

Diggers

Those forwards who work the boards and the corners in order to gain possession of the puck. They are best exemplified by Ted Kennedy of the 1940s Maple Leafs and John Tonelli of the New York Islanders.

Drop-Pass

A "pass" that leaves the puck where it is. The man with the puck leaves the puck behind him for a trailing member of his team to pick up. This differs from a back pass in that the puck is not moved backwards but is left where it is.

Elbowing

A minor penalty: it is illegal to hit an opponent with the elbow.

Face-Off

A face-off occurs at the beginning of a game, after a goal, and after every stoppage of play. The two teams line up opposite each other and parallel to the goal lines. The puck is then dropped between the opposing centers. On important face-offs coaches often put two centermen on the ice in case one gets thrown out of the face-off by the linesmen. Face-offs are also known as "draws." Two of the best face-off men of recent years are Bobby Clarke and Bryan Trottier.

Fighting

A major penalty: anyone who fights receives a penalty. A minor penalty, which is what usually causes the fight, is generally assessed with the fighting penalty.

Forechecking

Checking by the offense in the offensive zone in order to gain possession of the puck is known as forechecking. Coaches develop elaborate systems for forechecking. Conservative forechecking systems send one forward into the zone to press for the puck. Less conservative systems call for two or three forwards to check for the puck. Wayne Babych, Bernie Federko, and Brian Sutter of the St. Louis Blues are excellent forecheckers.

Forwards

The players who attack in the offensive zone are known as forwards. Their primary responsibility is to score goals. There are three types of forwards: the left wing, who skates up the left side, the center, who is responsible for the middle of the ice, and the right wing, who covers the right side. Records for forwards are held by Gordie Howe, who scored 1,850 NHL points in his career, and Wayne Gretzky, who scored the most points ever in a season: 212. Those forwards who also concentrate on defense are called "defensive forwards." Some of the best players in this category have included Bob Gainey, Walt Tkaczuk, and Steve Kasper.

Freezing the puck

This is the same as covering up.

Glass

The glass, along with the boards, encloses the playing surface. The glass is either Plexiglas, Herculite, unbreakable plastic, or real glass.

Goal

When the puck crosses completely over the goal line and into the goal cage, a goal has been scored. A goal is one point. The record for most goals in a career was set by Gordie Howe: 801 goals in 1,767 NHL games. The record for goals in a season is held by Wayne Gretzky: 92. The record for goals in a game is held by Joe Malone: 7.

Goal Cage

The goal cage is four feet high, six feet wide, and two feet deep. The crossbar and goal posts are painted red, and the posts are anchored in place by pipes that extend at least eight inches into the hollow posts. Mark Howe almost lost his life when he was impaled on the base of the net.

Goaltender

The player who protects the goal and attempts to prevent goals from being scored is the goaltender. When he stops the puck he is said to have made a save. Glenn Hall holds the goaltenders record for consecutive, complete games: 502. Terry Sawchuck holds the record for career shut-outs: 103.

Green Light

Behind the glass at each end of the arena, red and green lights are suspended. The green light is lit to signify that time has expired. No goals may be scored after the green light has been lit.

Hat Trick

Scoring three goals in a game is called a hat trick. The record for most hat tricks in a career is held by Phil Esposito: 32. The record for hat tricks in a season is held by Wayne Gretzky: 10.

Head-Manning

Passing the puck to a teammate up-ice is called head-manning.

High sticking

There are two types of high sticking. The first involves playing the puck with the stick above the shoulders. This is illegal and results in a face-off. The second type of high sticking involves injuring an opponent with the stick while it is carried above the shoulders. This results in a minor penalty.

Holding

A minor penalty: grabbing, clutching and holding an opponent so as to impede his progress is known as holding, and is illegal.

Hooking

A minor penalty: impeding the progress of an opponent by using the stick.

Icing

Shooting the puck from behind the center red line across the opponent's goal line is icing. Play is stopped and a face-off occurs back in the defensive zone. If a team is shorthanded there is no icing. A linesman can "wave off," not call, the icing if he feels that the other team could have played the puck.

Interference

A minor penalty: preventing the opponent from reaching and playing the puck.

Linesmen

The officials charged with calling off-sides, icing, too many men on the ice. They drop the puck for all face-offs excluding the ones that occur after a goal has been scored.

Neutral zone

The area between the two blue lines is called the neutral zone.

Offside

There are two types of offsides. Both involve a player being ahead of the puck. First: a player is offside when he crosses the opposing blue line ahead of the puck.

Second: a player is offside if the puck crosses two lines on a pass. For example: Player A is behind his own blue line. Player B is across the center red line. A passes to B. B is offside because the puck crossed two lines—the blue line and the center red line—before B received the pass.

Playmaker

A forward, usually a center, who is able to create scoring opportunities by setting up plays with his skating and passing. Bobby Clarke and Stan Mikita are examples of playmakers.

Penalty

There are three kinds of penalties in hockey.

(1) The minor penalty: any penalty calling for two minutes in the penalty box.

(2) The major penalty: any penalty that requires five minutes in the penalty box.

(3) The misconduct penalty: misconducts are "awarded" for abuse of officials, obscene language, or refusing to obey the referee's instructions. A misconduct penalty is ten minutes long and is served by the offending player. His team is not shorthanded for the time he spends in the penalty box. Game misconducts serve to remove a player from the rest of the game, regardless of time remaining to play.

Penalty Box

Where all penalties are served.

Penalty killers

The players assigned by the shorthanded team to defend against the power play. This is also known as "killing off a penalty." Two of the finest penalty killers were Nick Metz, of the 1940s Maple Leafs, and Derek Sanderson, of the 1970s Bruins.

Penalty shot

The referee awards a penalty shot to a player who is breaking in alone on the goaltender and is fouled from behind in such a way as to eliminate his chance of scoring. Penalty shots are very rarely seen and could be called much more often than they are.

Period

Hockey is divided into three twenty-minute segments known as periods.

Point

A spot just inside the opposing team's blue line, normally near the right or left boards, rather than center ice. Usually a defenseman is stationed there to feed passes to forwards or to take a shot on goal. On the power play, a coach often designates a forward to play one of the points, or the team's most offense-minded defenseman.

Poke-Check

Using the stick to knock the puck off the puck carrier's stick by suddenly poking the puck away. The move was supposedly invented by Dickie Moore of the 1902 Montreal AAA club. Jacques Laperriere and Ken Morrow also excelled at this technique.

Power play

When a team has a one-man or two-man-advantage because of penalties assessed on its opponents, that team is on a power play. The Montreal power play of the 1955–60 Stanley Cup years was so formidable that their success forced the NHL to change the rules governing penalties. At that time, a player served the duration of his penalty in the box, regardless of how many goals the other team scored. The Canadiens would often score two, three, or four times and effectively end the game within the two minutes. Subsequently the NHL rearranged the rule so that the penalized player returns to the ice after one goal is scored against his team, returning the teams to equal strength. The team that has scored the most power-play goals in a season is the Pittsburgh Penguins. During the 1981–82 season, the Penguins scored ninety-nine power-play goals.

Puck

The three-inch wide, one-inch thick rubber disc used in hockey. Art Ross is the man who "created" the NHL puck. He beveled the puck's edges to keep it from rolling. Because many people claimed that the puck was difficult to see on television, the WHA experimented with a red puck. They discarded it, however, because the chemical used in the red paint allowed the puck to bounce too much.

Pulling the goalie

Removing the goalie for an extra skater. This is done by teams losing in the final minutes of the game. They then attempt to overpower the opposing defense and goaltender. This maneuver is also used during a delayed penalty.

Ragging the puck

A player—or sometimes several—who holds onto the puck through fine stick-handling or passing. This is a defensive or penalty-killing technique used when defending against the power play.

Rebound

A puck that bounces off the goaltender or the boards. Good goaltenders control their rebounds.

Red light

The red light is suspended behind the glass in back of the net and is lit by the goal judge when a goal is scored.

Red line

The center line that divides the ice. It is used for offsides and icing calls. It was introduced by Frank Boucher and signaled the beginning of hockey's modern era.

Referees

The men in charge of the game. They alone administer the rules and dole out the penalties. There is a single referee per game.

Rink

Where hockey games are played. Most NHL rinks are a standard 200 feet long and 85 feet wide. However, certain rinks, such as Boston Garden, are older and don't meet modern standards. The difference in size is made up for by shortening the neutral zone. This keeps both areas inside the blue line at 60 feet.

Roughing

A minor penalty assessed when the referee decides that unnecessary force has been used in checking an opponent.

Save

Stopping a shot from going into the goal. Usually only goaltenders make saves, but occasionally, when the goaltender is trapped out of position, an alert defenseman keeps the puck out of the net. Goaltender Sam LoPresti of the 1941 Chicago Black Hawks made the most saves in one game, 80, against the Boston Bruins. The Bruins won the game, 3–2.

Screen shot

A shot on goal that comes to the net through a maze of players. Goaltenders say that screen shots and deflections are the most difficult to stop.

Shorthanded

A team is shorthanded when they are killing a penalty. The Boston Bruins of 1970–71 hold the record for the most goals by a shorthanded team, and Marcel Dionne holds the season record for a player: 10.

Slapshot

A shot on goal taken by raising the stick to shoulder height, slapping the puck, and following through almost like a golf drive. Bun Cook is given credit for first using the slapshot consistently, but there are many other players who used it just as well. Included in that group would be Bernie "Boom-Boom" Geoffrion, Reed Larson, Doug Wilson, and Bobby Hull. Hull's slapshot was once timed at 118 m.p.h.

INDEX

Abel, Clarence (Taffy), 52, 53, 155
Abel, Sid, 74
Abrahamsson, Christer, 141
Abrahamsson, Thommy, 141
Adam Cup, 125
Adams, Charles F., 32, 52
Adams, Jack, 39, 64
Adams, Weston, Jr., 32, 33, 84
Aitkenhead, Andy, 56
Alberta Oilers, 95
all-star games, 104–9
Amateur Hockey Association of the United
    States (AHAUS), 9, 123, 159
American Hockey League, 121, 122, 124
Anderson, Osborne, 156
Anderson, Wendell, 162
Apps, Syl, 108
Arbour, Amos, 34
Archer, Alexander, 158
Arnold, Steve, 89, 90
Atlanta Flames, 83
Avco World Cup, 97

Backstrom, Ralph, 136
Bailey, Ace, 104, 105
Baker, Bill, 166
Baker, Francis F., 158
Baker, Hobey, 25–26
Baldwin, Howard, 90, 97

Ball, Gary, 190, 205, 207
Ball, Rudi, 158
Baltimore Blades, 97
Bathgate, Andy, 123
Bauer, Bobby, 61, 65, 107, 161
Bawlf, Nick, 34
Beddoes, Dick, 135, 136
Beliveau, Jean, 78, 103, 106
Bell, David, 227
Benedict, Clint, 33, 34, 42
Bent, John P., 156
Bentley, Doug, 107, 108
Bentley, Max, 107, 108
Berenson, Red, 117, 119
Bergman, Thommie, 141
Berry, Bob, 143
Bertini, Ben, 162
Birmingham Bulls, 97
Bjorkman, Ruben, 161
black players, 98–104
Blackman, Marty, 89, 90
Blake, Hector (Toe), 73
Bossy, Mike, 124
Boston Bruins, 33, 46–47, 58, 84, 87
Boston Pere Marquettes, 32
Boston Westminsters, 32
Bouchard, Emile (Butch), 107, 108
Boucher, Billy, 41, 42
Boucher, Bobby, 42